Succeeding with Difficult Clients

Applications of Cognitive Appraisal Therapy

Succeeding with Difficult Clients

Applications of Cognitive Appraisal Therapy

Richard Wessler
Sheenah Hankin
Jonathan Stern

Academic Press

San Diego   London   Boston   New York   Sydney   Tokyo   Toronto

Academic Press
A Harcourt Science and Technology Company
525 B Street, Suite 1900, San Diego, California 92101-4495, USA
http://www.academicpress.com

Academic Press
Harcourt Place, 32 Jamestown Road, London NW1 7BY, UK
http://www.academicpress.com

Library of Congress Catalog Card Number: 0-12-744470-X

International Standard Book Number: 2001088744

PRINTED IN THE UNITED STATES OF AMERICA
01 02 03 04 05 06 SB 9 8 7 6 5 4 3 2 1

To our children, our students, and all of our clients.

CONTENTS

PART **III**
Applications of CAT

ACKNOWLEDGMENTS

First, we would like to acknowledge the presence in our professional and personal lives of some wonderful colleagues and collaborators: Jesse Rosenthal, Mildred Borrás, Vincent Minetti, and Windy Dryden. We would like to thank our editor, George Zimmar, for his good natured intelligence and encouragement in helping to bring this book to fruition and our spirited secretary, Maureen Coveney, for putting up with us during the writing of this book.

We also would like to tip our hats to colleagues whose theoretical and clinical writings have been invaluable influences on our therapy and catalysts to our thinking: Theodore Millon, John Bowlby, Mary Ainsworth, Mary Main and her colleagues, Robert Plutchik, Jeremy Safran, Drew Westen, Donald Nathanson, and Stanley Greenspan.

Finally, Jonathan would like to thank his wife, Sandra Waugh, for tirelessly transcribing tape recordings of our peer supervision sessions and for sweeping the kids away to give him time to write.

PART I

Cognitive Appraisal Theory

CHAPTER 1

What Makes Difficult Clients Difficult

AN INTRODUCTION TO COGNITIVE APPRAISAL THERAPY

The origins of Cognitive Appraisal Therapy (CAT) are primarily cognitive–behavioral in nature. While CAT has developed into an integrated approach to psychotherapy for personality disorders, it can be applied to working with all clients. CAT assumes that affect, behavior, and cognition are interdependent, mutually influential psychological components, and that a significant source of motivation is a person's seeking psychological security by repeating certain familiar experiences. Our approach contains elements of several cognitive–behavioral therapies as well as elements of other approaches to psychotherapy. Its theory draws upon attachment theory, social learning theory, and interpersonal theory, and its procedures include elements of person-centered counseling, experiential therapy, and Rational–Emotive Therapy (RET). Millon's (1996) theory of personality also heavily influenced CAT's conceptualization of the personality disorders.

CAT can be the approach of choice when therapy stalls. Though practitioners hold to the familiarity of a favored set of theoretical concepts and clients to familiar affective habits, it is helpful for clinicians to experience the unfamiliar and experiment with CAT's approach, especially for personality disturbances and the more recalcitrant clients for whom this approach was created. CAT is not a set of specific procedures laid out in cookbook form. Rather, it is a unique theoretical understanding of affect that a client can comprehend and then use to change.

CAT began as an alternative version of RET (Wessler, 1984, 1987). RET theory assumes that there are two parallel processes of emotion—one mediated by rational beliefs and another separate process mediated by irrational beliefs (Ellis, 1977)—and that rational beliefs result in "healthy" emotions and irrational beliefs in "unhealthy" ones. The parallel process theory of emotions and the RET theory that "musts" are causative factors in psychopathology lack supporting evidence (Wessler, 1996). Having omitted the theoretical cornerstones that distinguish RET from other forms of cognitive–behavior therapy, our approach to therapy could no longer be called RET. The phrase Cognitive Appraisal Therapy was adopted to emphasize the fact that the evaluative cognition (a synonym for appraisal) continued to be a target for therapeutic intervention.

It became increasingly apparent to us that people are seldom aware of some of their most significant appraisals. These appraisals function as nonconscious algorithms—stored routines for the processing of social information (Wessler & Hankin-Wessler, 1989). (Algorithms are specific and separate rules for evaluating experiences, and they are not assumed to cluster together as schemas. The concept of schema is seldom used in CAT.) This discovery also signaled a shift in emphasis from consciously held cognitions to nonconscious cognitions that must be inferred from what people say and do.

Like most forms of psychotherapy in the early 1980s, CAT was used mainly to treat such Axis I conditions as anxiety and depression. Some clients did not improve, did not maintain their improvement, or continued in therapy after they improved (Wessler & Hankin-Wessler, 1991). Why? The answer was found in their *predisposing personality characteristics.* As Millon (1996) expresses it, clinical conditions are the result of psychosocial stressors interacting with personality variables. CAT quickly responded by focusing almost exclusively on the treatment of personality variables and vulnerabilities (Wessler, 1993a,b). We have found that by using this focus and coupling it with integrative, attachment-based interventions, we are able to work easily and powerfully with clients whom many consider to be "difficult."

DIFFICULT CLIENTS OR DIFFICULT THERAPISTS?

After the third session of outpatient therapy, Kiesler and Watkins (1989) asked 36 pairs of clients and therapists to record their perceptions of the therapeutic alliance and to rate each others' behaviors during therapy using an interpersonal circumplex inventory. They found that angry, hostile clients and clients exhibiting "extreme" behaviors are correlated with therapists' feeling uncomfortable about the therapeutic alliance. Should we therefore call these clients "difficult" for therapists to work with, or should we instead call into question the therapists' skills at dealing with such clients?

Perhaps there is no such thing as a difficult client; there are only difficult therapists. When we call a client difficult, what we really mean is that we, the therapists, are having difficulty working with him/her. When we decide that a client is difficult, the use of this term means one of two things. "Difficult" may suggest that something about the client's personality is different enough from the norm of the client population with whom we have worked to date so as to present novel challenges to us. This term also can mean that a client triggers some of the therapist's own negative (or difficult) feelings and issues (Cashdan, 1988; Kiesler, 1996; Safran & Segal, 1990).

Thus, when a therapist uses the word "difficult" to describe a client, what he/she really means is: "I am having difficulty working with this person due to either my own emotional issues or a lack of experience working with clients like this." In essence, using the word difficult to describe a client should be a signal to the therapist that he/she needs to grow in some way personally (and interpersonally).

It is our hope that the reader will not become defensive when reading that difficulty with clients may indicate that the therapist might have to do some soul-searching as well as possibly making some technical improvements. Similarly, it is our hope that when a therapist is faced with a difficult client, he or she will not stop working with that client to avoid having to learn, grow, and adjust to this challenging situation. Many people in many careers who take their jobs seriously and want to be the best they can be assess themselves critically from time to time and feel badly about themselves. It is only the truly dedicated therapist or counselor who is willing to acknowledge and assess his or her weaknesses honestly, agonize over them (up to a point), and work to improve them.

Certainly, theories of competence (e.g., White, 1960) and research on self-efficacy (e.g., Bandura, 1977) and response expectancy (e.g., Kirsch, 1985, 1990; Ohlwein, Stevens, & Catanzaro, 1996) teach us that we will improve and succeed as professionals as long as we expect that setbacks and struggles are part of positive change—that the road to success is and should be paved with failure (as long as we are willing to keep on walking).

WHAT CREATES "DIFFICULTY" FOR A THERAPIST

In general, difficult clients can leave the therapist feeling either confused and stymied or feeling a variety of negative emotions. The first of these possibilities, confusion, occurs when a client says something that the therapist has never heard before or says something in a way that the therapist has not previously heard. Confusion also ensues when the client plays out an interpersonal pattern of interaction that may be alien to the therapist or that is so "out of sync" with what the therapist is trying to say or do that the result is confusion on the therapist's part (and often on the client's part as well). My (Jonathan's) initial experience with this category of difficulty often felt like somebody pushed me into a revolving door, spun me around in it, and spit me out again, leaving me dizzy and directionless.

While confusion is often the predominant in-the-moment experience for the therapist, negative feelings may subsequently arise. A therapist who has felt stuck, confused, or helpless during a session may subsequently, depending on his/her own personality, feel ashamed, embarrassed, angry at him/herself or at the client and self-critical or judgmental toward the client. Depending on the therapist's personality, he/she may feel these emotions only in relation to working with this particular client ("This is one of the most daunting, frustrating people I've ever worked with. I'm no good as a therapist with him/her.") or may generalize these emotions ("You see. I don't know what to do with clients. I'll never be an effective therapist. I'm just fooling people that I'm any good."). Some therapists, however, may simply experience confusion with these clients without negative feelings and use this confusion as a signpost that they are working with a challenging client and perhaps need to take a somewhat different approach.

The second category of difficult clients, those who stir up negative feelings in the therapist immediately and powerfully, has two subsets. The first involves negative feelings elicited in the therapist by the client and the second occurs when feelings stemming from the therapist's own issues emerge during the session. This is basically the important distinction made by contemporary psychoanalysts between objective and subjective countertransference (Epstein & Feiner, 1979; Kiesler, 1996). These two subcategories can co-occur during a session, but it is possible to tease them apart. For example, the following interaction between a client and a therapist occurs during the early portion of a third session:

> *Therapist: What would you like to talk about today?*
> *Client: I don't know. You're the shrink. You tell me.*
> *Th: Whatever you'd like.*
> *Cl: I don't think this therapy is helping me. You're too wishy-washy. You're not giving me helpful suggestions or a sense of direction.*
> *Th: Well, I'm sorry you feel that way.*
> *Cl: That's all you're going to say? I'm paying a lot of money for this and you're not delivering. You went to graduate school to learn how to sit there and just listen to me? A chimpanzee could do the same thing and would be a hell of a lot more entertaining.*

The client here is clearly being challenging in a disrespectful way toward the therapist, and many therapists might feel justifiably angered and insulted by this interaction, not so much by the fact that the client has concerns about the therapy but by the demeaning put-downs and challenging, confrontative style of the client. And chances are that this client elicits similar angry, potentially rejecting reactions in others in his life.

The therapist's angry reaction, however, may be amplified further in a therapist who, for instance, has little self-confidence. The initial internal response of "This client is putting me down" might give way in this therapist to "Damn it, the client's right. I don't know what the hell I'm doing. I hate the client for finding me out and I hate myself for being a failure." The therapist may then find a way to punish the client, react defensively and/or, after the session, wallow in self-criticism and self-pity. Thus, difficult clients can elicit feelings in the therapist which they evoke in many others in their lives and the therapist can also react with the feelings that he/she brings to difficult situations in his/her own life.

Additionally, therapists can experience certain clients as difficult when they are not eliciting negative feelings in the therapist but incidentally trigger issues for the therapist which are laden with negative affect. A client who is histrionic might frighten or subdue a therapist who came from a buttoned-down family, or a client who is passive–aggressive may frustrate a therapist who derives his/her self-confidence from quickly and efficiently fixing problems.

In chapter 3 we will discuss in detail what the predominant negative feelings are in difficult clients (and, in essence, in all clients). However, at this point, it is worth noting that similar negative feelings may arise in the therapist during a session with a difficult client: shame, rage, and self-pity. These feelings arise because the client speaks the language of these emotions and is therefore adept at evoking them in the therapist and/or the therapist him-herself has longstanding issues which are intertwined with these affects. It is therefore a central part of the therapist's job to notice when he/she is experiencing shame, rage, and/or self-pity during or after a session and to pinpoint whether these feelings are elicited by the client or come from within. We will discuss throughout this book not only how therapists can teach clients to manage their longstanding negative affect more effectively, but also how they can identify and manage these feelings in themselves during and between sessions.

A WHO'S WHO OF DIFFICULT CLIENTS

If you were to ask a large sample of therapists who they consider to be the most difficult client to work with, probably most would respond the borderline personality disorder. However, we have not found this to be true, given our approach to therapy. For us, clients with various personality styles (which we will distinguish in chapter 4 from personality disorders) bring certain predictable challenges to the therapist. Depending on what the therapist feels, how the therapist manages these feelings, and the therapeutic stance that he/she adopts, either an ongoing therapeutic alliance rupture (Safran & Muran, 1998) can prevail or the client's view of him/herself and others can be powerfully disconfirmed (Safran & Segal, 1990) and the therapy can proceed without its being considered difficult by the therapist. Hard work, yes, but difficult, no.

At this point, without resorting to diagnostic categories, it may be helpful to introduce the reader to common difficult clients. We're sure that you have already met many of them professionally as well as socially. Please note two basic assumptions that we make about clients, which will be presented in Part I of this book: (1) that people are nonconsciously motivated to recreate familiar interpersonal patterns and feelings, and certainly do so in therapy; and (2) that among the negative feelings which people seek to recreate (in various combinations, depending on the individual) are shame, rage, and self-pity.

Also keep in mind that the client–therapist dialogues in this chapter are composites of typical "difficult" interactions in therapy. More importantly, the therapists' statements are *not* necessarily what we recommend from a CAT perspective but are simply our approximation of what typical responses by a therapist to such clients might be.

INTIMIDATING CLIENTS

These are clients who (often nonconsciously) attempt to avoid feeling ashamed of themselves when the therapist really gets to know them by bullying the therapist or putting him/her on the defensive. The client hopes that if he/she can make the therapist feel scared and ashamed, then the client will not have to experience similar feelings. This client perceives the world as dog-eat-dog: "Either I am being blamed or shamed or I'm doing it to someone else. Better that I'm on the giving than the receiving end." Consequently, the client often succeeds in eliciting anger and rejection from the therapist, which resonates with how the client has been treated by others numerous times throughout his/her life. The therapist's reaction confirms the client's world view that he/she is unworthy and unlovable and that the world is a cold, cruel, rejecting place. From an attachment theory perspective, which we will discuss in chapters 2 and 4, these clients are bonded to others vis-á-vis blame and shame, parry and thrust.

Here follow various subtypes of the Intimidating Client.

THE CRITICAL CLIENT

This interaction occurs during a first session:

> *Client: I think that a knowledge of child development is essential to helping me, since I was emotionally abused as a child. Do you have extensive knowledge in this area?*
> *Therapist: Well, I've studied what I believe to be most helpful to clients. Why don't you see how I work with you to give you an idea of what I do?*
> *Cl: That's not good enough. I want some assurance that you really know your stuff. I mean, why should I go to you just because you have a diploma on the wall? Convince me that you have what it takes to work with somebody like me. If you won't discuss your training in child development theory with me, then perhaps you can tell me if you integrate behavioral interventions into your work and, if so, how?*

This client's strategy, often nonconscious, to pull rejection from the therapist involves deeming many things the therapist does as "not good enough." This not-good-enough judgment is something that the client has undoubtedly heard from others about him-herself, and he/she now keeps the world angrily at bay by judging others as deficient. These clients also judge themselves as not competent in various ways, which some will readily admit and others deny.

Therapists invested in feeling not good enough will react internally with an "Oh no, the client has found me out!" and concomitant feelings of shame. Those who often feel mistreated and unjustly criticized, victimized, or unappreciated by others will react with self-pity and rage at the client. Even if the therapist is adept at not converting such thoughts and feelings into behaviors, we believe that the client (who is primed to perceive such reactions) will nevertheless pick up on them.

THE RAGEFUL CLIENT

Here, shame is avoided by finding reasons to explode at the therapist.

> *Therapist: What would you like to work on today?*
> *Client: Maybe I don't want to work at all today. Maybe I just want to talk.*
> *Th: How come you feel that way today?*
> *Cl: I don't have to answer that question.*
> *Th: Well, that's true. You sound extremely angry as you say that to me.*
> *Cl: I don't have to discuss my feelings with you. That's a controlling thing to say, and you can't control me.*
> *Th: It wasn't my intention to control you. I'm sorry if you felt that way. I was just trying to understand what I did that led to your feeling angry with me.*

> Cl: I don't have to respond to that. In fact, I'm going to call it quits for today's session and maybe for the therapy as a whole. [Voice getting louder, standing up] I'm very agitated today in here, as you can see, and you're only making it worse. [Shouting] I'm sick of your trying to control me and your insensitivity to my needs. Of course, I'll leave you your check for this session—since that's all you really care about anyway. [Storms out of the office.]

This interpersonal style is perhaps most prevalent with borderline clients, who are fluent in the language of inappropriate rage and feeling "abandoned." Again, the interpersonal cycle is clear and predictable: "I'm feeling threatened by you, uncared for, and afraid of feeling ashamed, which makes me enraged, and I'll hold you at bay and punish you by exploding ragefully. Then, you'll reject me, which will confirm my perception that no one really cares about me."

THE THREATENING CLIENT

Male client to female therapist early in the therapy:

> Client: I have relationship problems. Most women are scared of me because I'm a big guy, and I let people know I'm tough. The girls I've dated know of my reputation as a guy who might slap around a girl if I don't like her attitude or how she's behaving. I guess I can be pretty hot-headed and frightening at times, and I don't know how to control it often, especially with girls I feel close to.
> Therapist: Is your violence something I should be concerned about in here?
> Cl: Nah. No. I doubt it, but life's full of surprises.

The message to the therapist is clear: "Keep your distance from me. If you threaten my extremely low and vulnerable self-respect, I'll punish you. You better let me run the show here, so I can feel safe and respected." This is a more macho, primitive version of the two previous interpersonal stances (Mosher & Tomkins, 1988), but it is also motivated by an avoidance of the potential to feel ashamed of oneself in the session and criticized, judged, or blamed by the therapist. Clearly, clients with this style come from homes where the threat of danger and violence was frequently in the air.

THE UNCOOPERATIVE CLIENT

Uncooperative clients are those who either overtly or covertly do not do the work of therapy. Ultimately, this often pulls anger from the therapist, who may feel that therapy with such a client is fruitless and a waste of time ("I could be giving this hour to someone who really wants to work to change his/her life."), who may feel disrespected and taken for granted by the client, or who may feel frustrated and impotent when his/her numerous suggestions and hard work have no noticeable impact or effect on the client. It is common to hear therapists who are not aware of their anger at an uncooperative client describe themselves as feeling bored during sessions.

Here is an example of such a client in therapy:

> *Client: Nobody cares about me, so I don't even bother trying to make friends anymore.*
>
> *Therapist: Sounds like you're feeling sorry for yourself and hopeless.*
>
> *Cl: Not really. I just don't like people. There's nothing I can do about it.*
>
> *Th: Well, it looks like you've decided not to change.*
>
> *Cl: I haven't decided anything. I can't change.*
>
> *Th: So where does that leave us and our work together?*
>
> *Cl: I don't know. Maybe you could give me some advice here.*
>
> *Th: Well, you could try making friends even though you don't think it's going to work.*
>
> *Cl: No, that wouldn't work.*
>
> *Th: How about entertaining the idea that people might actually respond positively to you if they got to know you?*
>
> *Cl: No way.*

THE AUTONOMOUS CLIENT

This client is similar to the uncooperative client in that he/she disagrees with most of what the therapist says and suggests, as well as with the therapist's approach to doing therapy. However, unlike the more passive uncooperative client, this client makes more of a point of actively disagreeing with the therapist's approach, often from a fairly intellectual standpoint.

> *Therapist: It might be important here to try calming down your feelings when you are getting so enraged.*
>
> *Client: I don't believe that calming down my feelings would work. I believe more in expressing my feelings, letting them all out, in order to get on with my day.*
>
> *Th: How do you think others might feel if you did this around them?*
>
> *Cl: You often ask questions like that and I don't really think they're helpful to my working through my problems. It's not about how I affect other people— they can take care of themselves. It's about the changes inside me that I make. Your approach is too other-focused for me.*

As you may have surmised, many of these clients tend to be other therapists! What is notable here is that the client's way of relating and attaching to
the therapist involves his/her constantly establishing his/her independence
from the therapist. While the client's intention may be simply to proclaim
his/her autonomy, the effect this has on some therapists is one of repeated
rejection and devaluation, and it often ends up pulling anger and, ultimately,
resignation from these therapists.

The Passive–Aggressive Client

These clients seem receptive to a therapist's suggestions and homework assignments, often receiving them overenthusiastically and with a tight smile. They
frequently praise the therapist for his/her ingenuity and proclaim that these
suggestions will most probably alter their lives. Next session, they will return
and either say that they don't remember what was said during the previous session nor that they had received a homework assignment, or they sheepishly
confess that they did not do the agreed-upon assignment. In the latter situation, the client often expects the therapist to be highly critical and blaming of
his/her noncompliance, and he/she may anticipate this by heaping criticism on
him/herself or apologizing profusely.

Therapists often react in two ways, sometimes concurrently. First, the
client's self-critical behavior may pull sympathy from the therapist, who may
end up soothing and taking care of the client's apparent "pain": "It's OK. Don't
worry about the homework assignment. I wouldn't want to make you feel so
uncomfortable and down on yourself in therapy." The therapist may then take
a supportive stance and, in the language of some 12-step programs, "enable"
the client's sympathy-seeking and noncompliance.

Second, the therapist may feel angry and perhaps even sorry for him-herself ("unappreciated"), as though he/she has offered numerous pearls of wisdom to a client who has rejected them all. A sense of betrayal may also be
felt by the therapist, who initially perceived the client as so receptive and
adoring, and who subsequently feels unheeded and rejected by him/her. If
the therapist him-herself is also passive–aggressive, an angry response to the
client's noncompliance may be turned into a tit-for-tat stance: "Well, if the
client's not going to work in therapy, neither will I. I'll just sit here and listen, but that's it."

Passive–aggressive clients are uncooperative for two basic reasons. First,
they resent having to work. A therapeutic homework assignment, and sometimes even just doing the in-session work of therapy, makes them feel put-
upon and burdened. Invested in being people-pleasers, passive–aggressive
clients will not dare to say to the therapist "I don't want to do this assignment."

Instead, they act out by not doing it. Second, passive–aggressives are, in the language of attachment theory (Ainsworth, Blehar, Waters, & Wall, 1978), ambivalently attached to significant others. They maintain bonds where they are often being told what to do, resenting it, and then rejecting others' suggestions. This then pulls anger from others, some of whom consequently try even harder to guide and take care of the passive–aggressive.

Therapists who want to take charge of sessions and quickly fix problems will be the most daunted, frustrated, and enraged by these clients. Fixers usually avoid feeling ashamed of themselves via their competence at solving problems. Thus, the passive–aggressive's challenge to the fixer's ability to fix threatens to unearth the fixer's sense of incompetence. Fixers often find themselves angrily blaming passive–aggressive clients in a way which feels very familiar (and untherapeutic) to the client.

A variation of this client is one whom Yalom (1985) terms the help-rejecting complainer. This client does not comply with any of the therapist's suggestions, makes little attempt to use therapy to change, and incessantly whines and complains about how horrible and immutable his/her life is. The therapist may be left feeling impotent to help the client and extremely annoyed, if not enraged, that he/she must listen to the client droning on week after week with niggling complaints. The client's stance ultimately pulls anger and rejection, in the form of either blame and impatience or withdrawal from the therapist. This enables this self-pitying client to then conclude: "Just as I thought: no one really cares about me and no one can help me. My situation's hopeless."

THE MISTRUSTFUL CLIENT

The beginning of a session:

> *Therapist: What do you want to work on today?*
> *Client: I don't know. [Long silence.]*
> *Th: Well, how was your week?*
> *Cl: About the same as usual. Pretty average, I guess. [Long silence.] How was your week?*
> *Th: Oh, pretty good, thanks. [Long silence.] I notice that your foot is shaking back and forth very forcefully. Are you anxious about something, or maybe even angry, perhaps?*
> *Cl: Not really. It's just a habit. [Long silence.]*
> *Th: I would imagine that I might shake my foot nervously if I were having difficulty deciding what to say in therapy or whether I should share something with my therapist, who I really don't know that well at all.*
> *Cl: Not really. [Long silence.] I'm just shaking my foot. I do it a lot. It's a habit. I could stop it if you'd prefer.*

Th: No, it's perfectly fine. I was just making a comment to try to get to know you better.
Cl: [Long silence.] *Oh, I see.* [Long silence.]
Th: What are you feeling right now as we have this discussion?
Cl: Nothing, really. Fine, I guess. Good. [Long silence. Looks at the floor, then out the window.]

Clients who are reticent to talk very much, but who keep returning to therapy of their own free will (as opposed to teenagers, partners, or court-ordered clients who are often being influenced by someone else to attend) may do so for several reasons. First, some of these clients may have extreme difficulty trusting the therapist and may have great fear of being judged, criticized, or humiliated by him/her. These clients may have only known attachments where the other person was either someone who could not be trusted to be consistently receptive and empathic or where the other was consistently withdrawn and stand-offish. The former scenario more likely involved inconsistency and some sort of abuse on the other's part, which led to an extremely avoidant interpersonal stance on the client's part, while the latter may have prevented the client from knowing what an intimate relationship can offer, let alone being motivated to seek out closeness with another.

A second, and perhaps milder, form of the latter scenario, is the client who is intensely insecure, who has never before been in therapy, and who has led a life filled with little insight into what makes him or her tick. He/she simply does not speak the language of intimacy, and more than superficial conversation becomes highly confusing and perhaps threatening to him/her.

This category of challenging client differs from the passive–dependent and passive–aggressive clients in that the latter are more apt to have the following variation of the above interaction with the therapist:

Therapist: What do you want to work on today?
Client: I don't know. [Long silence.] *What do you think I should work on?*
Th: Well, how was your week?
Cl: About the same as usual. Pretty average, I guess. I'm still having problems standing up to my boss and my wife when they're angry at me. Do you think this would be a good topic to discuss again?
Th: Well, possibly. Do you think it would be helpful to you to begin here?
Cl: I really don't know. We've discussed this topic before, and nothing's changed.
Th: You sound somewhat hopeless that this will change. I wonder if you're angry at me for not having helped you to change this aspect of your life as quickly as you had hoped.

Here, the client looks to therapist for guidance as to where to begin, but he can be engaged by the therapist in discussing an issue, focusing on a feeling (here, anger), and talking about the therapeutic relationship. The client's response to the therapist's last question is irrelevant. He may agree that he is angry at the therapist or deny experiencing this feeling. The important point is that the client will respond at least somewhat self-disclosively to the question. The mistrustful client would never allow an opening for the therapist to engage in such a conversation, and therapists who move too quickly with such a client, most probably out of their own anger, frustration, or insecurity with silences and lack of quick progress, will damage the alliance or lose the client.

THE ACTING-OUT CLIENT

This 41-year-old female client has just finished telling how lonely she feels, how unlovable she is, and how the rest of her life will be a meaningless failure. She then begins to cry, which rapidly escalates from a gentle sobbing into series of extremely loud wails, resembling the loud cries of a small child in pain. This crying goes on for 15 minutes. The therapist gives the client tissues and leans forward in his chair, looking empathically at the client as she sobs loudly. After she quiets down, the following interaction occurs:

> Therapist: *You have so much sadness in you.*
> Client: [In hurt, pouting little girl's voice] *I do.*
> Th: *How are you feeling now, having shared this sadness with me?*
> Cl: *Embarrassed.*
> Th: *What is making you feel embarrassed?*
> Cl: *What do you think is making me feel embarrassed? I just cried for 15 minutes in front of someone who doesn't care about me.*
> Th: *What makes you think I don't care about you and your sadness?*
> Cl: *Oh, shut up. Just shut up. How can you care about me? You just sit there asking me those fucking questions.* [Voice getting loud and enraged in tone] *I pay you to care. You say you care to everyone who comes through that door.* [Imitating the therapist in a patronizing, "know-it-all" tone of voice] *'What makes you think I don't care about you and your sadness?' Shit! You care about your fucking wife and family. Why should you care about me?* [Still shouting] *Do you care about my sadness like you care about her sadness? You're full of crap, Herr Doctor. This session is over!*

The feelings expressed by this client are different from those expressed by the intimidating client. The rageful and critical clients' often nonconscious goal is to push away the therapist, eliciting a familiar angry and rejecting response from him/her while also preventing the therapist from exploring the client's shameful feelings. The acting-out client's goal is more self-indulgent: to act like a child and reinvoke childish feelings, no matter what the consequences. Of course, here, too, the client's behavior may pull anger and/or rejection from the therapist, thus repeating familiar interpersonal scenarios. However, the underlying logic behind this emotional self-indulgence stems from a feeling of self-pity and deprivation: "My life has been so disappointing and filled with failure that at least I can have a little pleasure indulging myself emotionally." The bulimic compensates for a feeling of deprivation and unworthiness with food; the kleptomaniac with stealing; and the acting-out client with childish tantrums and tears—and some therapists are left not knowing how to respond to these emotional tempests or, in fact, attempting to soothe them in a way which reinforces their usefulness to the client (i.e., pulling sympathy from another).

Many couples therapists write of the husband and wife who are so entrenched in their patterns of conflict that they would rather play them out during sessions than learn to interact differently or pay attention to the therapist (e.g., Lederer & Jackson, 1968). Similarly, family therapists have described families who move from one "crisis" to the next in a way which often sweeps the therapist up into the crisis du jour rather than having the therapist focus on longer-standing systemic patterns and core family issues (e.g., Kantor & Lehr, 1975). These couples and families nonconsciously kick up emotional sandstorms in order to divert the therapist from attempting to change the couple's interactions and to maintain the longstanding emotional and interpersonal climate.

THE UNEMPATHIC CLIENT

Some clients are so driven by and wrapped up in their own feelings and thoughts that they fail to see how what they say and do affects others. This can make clients difficult to work with in two ways. The first has been frequently identified and described (Millon, 1996; Yalom, 1985) and needs only brief mention here. This client, usually quite narcissistic, makes comments during sessions which are offensive to the therapist, and this may continue after the therapist has objected to these comments repeatedly. Certainly, this type of interaction can overlap with the extremely insulting or callously critical remarks made by the intimidating client; however, it can consist of a different sort of communication as well. For instance, the client who makes derogatory comments about race or gender preference or highly judgmental remarks about any type of person may offend or enrage the therapist. These comments may be made to pull such anger from the therapist or simply because the client does not see or care about the therapist's reaction ("Hey, you're a therapist. You should be able to handle anything I say without getting your feathers ruffled.")

Similarly, client behaviors can also be unempathic and self-centered: the client who always shows up late for sessions and then wants to stay overtime finishing his/her train of thought; the client who frequently fails to attend sessions without calling to notify the therapist; the client who often interrupts what the therapist says or responds to the therapist's comments by changing the subject; the client who changes his/her appointment numerous times during the week in an entitled tone of voice.

The other subtype of unempathic client does not do or say anything untoward to the therapist. Instead, he/she describes acting toward others in a highly self-centered, perhaps exploitative fashion. This, then, may highlight a clash of values and ethics between therapist and client, which can certainly jeopardize the therapeutic relationship. (In chapter 7, we will discuss making the therapist's implicit values explicit.) For example, one such client would be an individual who talks of cheating customers or colleagues out of money at work, believes that everybody does this so he/she should too, says that he/she does not understand what the therapist is so upset about, does not want to understand the effects of his/her actions on others, and continues to do this in spite of the therapist's recommendations that he/she stop. The therapist is then left managing his or her own feelings of anger, disapproval, and perhaps disgust, as well as frustration that the client is doing harm to others and the therapist cannot alter this situation.

THE WEALTHY, INFLUENTIAL CLIENT

Younger and less experienced therapists are often intimidated by wealthy and influential clients. While it is rare that therapists-in-training or recently graduated therapists have the opportunity to do therapy with the rich and famous, as their careers progress, they often encounter clients who have experienced some degree of success. Such clients may, at this point in their lives, have high expectations of others and appear quite demanding, entitled, and inflexible in social interactions. Moreover, they may make it more apparent than some other clients that they are purchasing a service from the therapist and that what they say goes. For example, one recent client repeatedly mentioned to me (Jonathan) that he was the CEO of a business that grossed more than $160 million per year, and his son frequently spoke of taking the family Lear Jet to visit friends all over the United States during summer vacation.

Up to a point, such demanding behavior in successful clients is quite healthy, as it has contributed to their many achievements in society and is the norm in their social and work environments (and an assertive, strong, self-promoting, hardworking, go-getter stance is certainly reinforced in some subsets of American culture currently). It is not to be confused with narcissism, although it certainly does not rule out the additional presence of narcissistic traits. However, here the responsibility lies with the therapist: can he/she remain collaboratively in charge of the therapy and focused on the client's emotional and behavioral difficulties without becoming envious of and resentful toward the client, without being intimidated by the client's larger-than-life presentation, or without being seduced by the thrill of working with someone who might lead a lifestyle that is valued and envied by many? (While I was certainly interested that this boy traveled regularly on a Lear Jet, I was not interested in how fast the plane could fly, how many stewardesses it had, or the color of its upholstery. I wanted to know why it was important for this boy to impress me with stories of his jet and why he was so angry at his father.)

Here, some therapists who feel sorry for themselves, angry, and deprived in life might react by thinking: "I wish I had this person's lifestyle and money. I'm working really hard here to help him and I'm getting paid one-millionth of what he does per hour. It's not fair." Others who experience much shame might assume that they, humble therapists that they be, will not be able to help such a successful person. These therapists, feeling unworthy, then tend to allow the client to run the show in therapy.

There are many variations of this dynamic. The young therapist with an older client may be told or may feel that he/she has not lived long enough and experienced enough to help the client. Parents may tell the childless therapist, "You can't work with us since you haven't experienced what we have" or the therapist might feel this way him-herself while working with parents. Some clients may not actually be rich, successful or famous, but present themselves with the same take-charge, I'm-in-the-driver's seat demeanor. And then the most difficult client of all: another therapist, who may be wed to his/her approach, highly critical of and competitive with the therapist, and unable to take advice from another. All of these situations can also evoke strong feelings in therapists who are unsure of their abilities, inexperienced, and/or nonconsciously motivated by self-pity and anger.

THE ANGRY VICTIM WITH CULTURAL OR GENDER DIFFERENCES

In our politically correct climate, much has been written about taking the client's cultural background and differences into account while doing therapy (e.g., McGoldrick, 1998; McGoldrick, Pearce, & Giordano, 1982). Similar articles have been written about working with clients of different gender identities (e.g., Brooks, 1981; Clark & Serovich, 1997) and different age groups (e.g., Kiernat, 1984; Steuer & Hammen, 1983) as well. We certainly believe that it is important for all therapists to be knowledgeable about the values, perceptions, and beliefs of different cultures, as well as to know how people from different backgrounds express and manage their emotions and perceive the world. Certainly, interpersonal perception research (e.g., Scheiner, 1969) suggests that areas of interpersonal behavior that are culturally determined (such as status for Japanese, and generosity, hospitality, and nurturance for Muslims) influence person-perception independently of affective reaction to an individual.

However, we also believe that "cultural differences" can be used by a therapist or client as an excuse either to manage (defend against, as some would say) feelings of inadequacy or to elicit self-pity and anger. For example, a therapist who may be having difficulty working with any of the aforementioned clients may use the explanation, "Maybe I don't understand enough about this client's culture to be effective" when, in fact, other issues may be afoot.

A gay client may say that a therapist cannot possibly understand or empathize with him/her because he/she is not also gay. Is this client's belief legitimate, given who the therapist is, or does this explanation do nothing more than fuel the client's self-pitying belief that, "Nobody will ever understand, and therefore care about, me"? A minority client angrily accuses a non-minority therapist, "You don't understand what it's like to be a victim of oppression." Is this client accurately highlighting a miscommunication due to cultural differences, sensing a lack of empathy on the therapist's part, or is the client generating familiar, longstanding feelings of rage and self-pity in himself—and enraging and alienating the therapist in the process?

CONCLUSION

To summarize the main points of this chapter:

1. "Difficult" clients are really angry, hostile clients who exhibit "extreme" behaviors and trigger either confusion or some combination of shame, self-pity, and anger in the therapist. These feelings can either be elicited by a client or generated apart from a client's behavior by a therapist who is dominated by one or more of these feelings.

2. An angry, hostile client can exhibit these emotions either actively (e.g., aggressively) or passively (e.g., by withholding or avoiding).

3. Clients who typically elicit confusion or a combination of shame, anger, and self-pity in the therapist are loosely categorized as Intimidating (with the subcategories Critical, Rageful, and Threatening), Uncooperative, Autonomous, Passive–Aggressive, Mistrustful, Acting-out, Unempathic, Wealthy and Influential, and the Angry Victim with Cultural or Gender Differences.

This book will not only give therapists an approach to working effectively with these "difficult" clients, it will also reframe the concept of personality in a way that makes these clients' challenging behaviors seem not that different from those of clients considered to be less difficult. After we have presented our CAT conceptualizations of motivation, affect, cognition, behavior, and personality in chapters 2, 3, and 4 we will then in chapter 5 reframe the difficult clients presented in this introduction in terms of personality styles and we will explain the universal motivation behind their apparently difficult interpersonal stances.

Part II of this book will outline a general CAT approach to working with clients which renders difficult behaviors and interpersonal interactions basically the same as nonproblematic ones. Part III will then apply our approach to working with client populations who are often considered to be difficult. It is hoped that, by book's end, the reader will see that more flexibility, persistence, a wider array of interventions based on a theory that understands what "difficult" really means, emotional self-care on the therapist's part, and a strong understanding of clients' personality styles are needed to work with difficult clients. Ultimately, it is hoped that these clients will not be more threatening, daunting, or puzzling to the therapist than any others.

CHAPTER 2

Motivation and Attachment

We have found that three commonly held assumptions about therapeutic change do not help clients – and not just difficult ones – to improve as much as they might. The first assumption, held mostly by cognitive and cognitive–behavioral therapists, is that changes in cognitions lead to changes in affect but not usually vice versa. The second assumption, held by psychoanalysts and behaviorists alike, is that human beings are motivated to avoid pain (or unpleasure) and to seek pleasure. The third assumption, most often espoused by experiential therapists, is that change stems from the experiencing and awareness of emotions.

We will discuss the limitations of the first two assumptions in this chapter, as they both involve models of motivation, and the third in the next chapter, which discusses emotion. This chapter visits those developmental and attachment theories which are the bedrock of CAT's motivational assumptions and which contradict the basis of many cognitive and cognitive–behavioral approaches to therapy.

A LIMITATION OF COGNITIVE–BEHAVIORAL
APPROACHES TO THERAPY

Cognitive Appraisal Therapy (CAT) takes from general systems theory (Bateson, 1972) the assumption of interdependence among components. In CAT, the components are the psychological processes affect, behavior, and cognition. The term *affect,* as we use it, refers to subjective emotional feelings and bodily sensations. (The term *emotion* refers to physiological changes as well as overt actions and facial and postural displays.) *Behavior* refers to patterns rather than to isolated events, especially those that occur between people— interpersonal behaviors are more significant in understanding personality than are an individual's tics. Cognition refers to the content of mental activity and can consist of logical and illogical sentences, factual and fantastic information, images or pictures in the mind, and, most importantly, evaluative cognitions or appraisals.

Cognitive dissonance theory (Brehm & Cohen, 1962; Festinger, 1957) supports the idea of the interdependence of affect, behavior, and cognition. The research it inspired shows that changes in overt behavior result in internal changes in affect and cognition, contrary to the commonsensical assumption: If you change your mind, you will act differently.

Many forms of cognitive and cognitive–behavior therapy acknowledge the interdependence of these three components but do not employ them extensively in practice. This may be due to their adopting a mediated stimulus–response model in which emotion is seen as a result of the cognitive processing of certain internal and external stimuli (see Wessler, 1996). In Rational–Emotive Therapy (Ellis, 1977), for example, beliefs are said to mediate between a stimulus and an emotional response, and beneficial results are achieved by changing beliefs in order to have new emotional responses. This is what might be called the "frightened animal" model of emotion—an animal reacts with fear and flight to a stimulus it first perceives and evaluates as dangerous. This we term the "emotional episode."

The emotional episode (Wessler and Hankin-Wessler, 1990) consists of the following steps: (1) stimulus; (2) detection of stimulus; (3) covert description of observed stimulus; (4) inferences about the perceived stimulus, including attributions, forecasts, and other elaborations; (5) appraisals; (6) emotional response determined by appraisals; (7) behavioral response and decisions about how to react; (8) feedback (reinforcement) about behavioral response. In addition to external stimuli, human beings react to the internal stimuli of their own thoughts and feelings.

In using this model of therapy—a model which is the backbone of both Beck's and Ellis's cognitive–behavioral approaches—we have found four basic common scenarios wherein clients were not helped to change. And these clients were not necessarily those whom a therapist would consider to be difficult. First, we found that some of our pre-CAT clients did not improve even when we did what we were supposed to and in the right way. For example, in originally doing parent training with a primarily cognitive–behavioral approach (the approach that many therapists argue is the most effective to improve parenting skills; see Clark, 1985; Forehand & McMahon, 1981; Mash, Homerlynk, & Handy, 1976), I (Jonathan) found that parents fell into two basic groups: those who said they wanted to use behavioral and cognitive tools and did so effectively, and those who said they wanted to use these tools and then instead employed a variety of strategies to undermine the effectiveness of these tools (Stern, 1996).

The latter group kept returning to therapy even though they repeatedly did not implement any of the techniques they had learned. Instead, they chose to complain, get angry, feel incompetent, and/or feel sorry for themselves—but they continued to come back for more.

Second, in our pre-CAT days, we (Richard and Sheenah) found that some clients improved, presumably as a result of what we did in therapy, but they did not stay better. Their symptoms reemerged, in spite of their clearly wanting to maintain the gains they had made and their understanding what they could do to continue progressing. Altered beliefs about themselves and the world did not lead to permanent change in behavior and affect.

Third, some clients improved and maintained these positive changes, but they continued to want to be our clients in spite of ostensibly getting what they wanted from therapy! The therapeutic relationship became more compelling to them than behavioral and cognitive change itself.

Fourth, clients' irrational beliefs (Beck, Rush, Shaw, & Emery, 1979; Ellis, 1977) about themselves and others could often be successfully debated and refuted to the point that clients no longer believed them to be true. However, many still *felt* them to be true. For example, a smart, successful man who believed for years that he was "a moron" could be faced with the facts that he graduated at the top of his class in college and was running his own successful company. He could even then acknowledge that these were concrete evidence of his gifted intellectual capacity and that his belief that he is a moron was totally unfounded and irrational. Nevertheless, he would still describe himself as *feeling* like an idiot in many situations and then acting based on the feeling rather than on his belief that he is, in fact, intelligent. What we term "felt logic" took precedence over cognitive logic for this and many other clients.

The reason for these anomalies in therapy, we came to discover, had not to do with our technique nor, for that matter, with our model of psychology. It had to do with what we were focusing on in therapy: on behaviors and cognitions but not on the person and the person's affect. Therefore, CAT treats affect as first among equals in relation to cognitions and behaviors. Furthermore, it assumes that people have *emotional habits*—that they are accustomed to, drawn to, and seek out certain emotional feelings. In order to sustain their emotional habits, they must bring their thoughts and actions into harmony with their feelings. (Note here the difference from traditional cognitive dissonance theory: behaviors and cognitions shift to conform with affect as opposed to beliefs changing to be congruent with behaviors. Perhaps we could call this phenomenon "cognitive–behavioral dissonance.")

This emphasis on affect intuitively makes sense when we think of how clients often present their problems to us in therapy. They never say, "I want to change the way I think" but instead "I want to feel better" or "I want to start (or stop) doing such-and-such a behavior."

THE PRIMACY OF AFFECT

> The infant, the child, and the adult act on the world, regulate emotional states, and communicate affectively. And for all of them the working of the communicative process—its degree of interactive coordination and affective reparation—is what is critical to their outcome. (Tronick, 1989, p. 118)

Psychologists would be wise to derive their models of the mind and motivation from human development and Darwinian notions. Studying what is fundamental to all life must have implications for what is central to human life, and studying the origins of human life must have major significance for the course of that life. We do so here with affect, as it is at the core of our understanding of personality, psychopathology, and our approach to treatment.

Daniel Stern's (1985) work on infant development was some of the first to emphasize the centrality of affect to the infant's developing sense of self and interrelatedness. This work, which has found much empirical support (see Tronick, 1989, for a partial review of these studies) is a benchmark in defining behavior and cognition, as well as a sense of self and others, as springing from affect. Additionally, he highlights how affect is the first language of the infant–parent relationship and, in essence, how affect, this relationship, and the world are one and the same for the infant.

It becomes clear from reading Stern and his developmental colleagues (e.g., Emde, Klingman, Reich, & Wade, 1978; Rovee-Collier, Sullivan, Enright, Lucas, & Fagan, 1980) how the focus of cognitive and cognitive–behavioral therapists on the centrality of thoughts and beliefs flies in the face of developmental theory and research. It also becomes clear that, when a client does not respond, or responds only temporarily, to a cognitive intervention, the primacy of the client's affect is not being taken into account in the therapy.

ATTACHMENT THEORY: MEANINGFULLY INTEGRATING AFFECT WITH COGNITION AND BEHAVIOR

CAT is not only based on the primacy of affect but also on the belief that we are driven to seek out and recreate longstanding familiar affect. We do so in part via repeated patterns of interaction. Therefore, an understanding of attachment theory and its relation to affect is fundamental to an understanding of CAT.

Tronick (1989) highlights how emotions serve both as evaluative feedback to the infant about whether a goal is being attained and, more importantly for our purposes, as behavioral motivators. If a goal is being met, the infant experiences joy or interest, thus motivating further involvement. If a goal is not being met but there is a chance that it might be, the infant experiences anger (an active emotion), which further motivates him/her to try to remove an obstacle to the goal. If a goal is not being met and there is no chance that it will be, the infant experiences sadness (a passive emotion), which motivates a shutting down and disengagement.

Furthermore, Tronick observes that infants do not come into this world fully equipped to attain goals on their own: "the infant is part of an affective communication system in which the infant's goal-directed strivings are aided and supplemented by the capacities of the caretaker. An infant's affective displays function as messages that specify the infant's evaluation of whether he or she is succeeding in achieving a goal. The caretaker 'reads' this message and uses it to guide his or her actions for facilitating the infant's strivings." (p. 113)

It can therefore be seen that change must not only be based on the primacy of affect but also on the centrality of the interpersonal. And no theory has described the interpersonal more richly, and with more empirical support, than Bowlby's (1969, 1973, 1980) work on attachment.

Basing his theory on the animal research of Harlow (1958) and Tinbergen (1951) among others, Bowlby equated attachment with survival and the seeking out and attainment of proximity to the caregiver with a sense of security in the infant. Attachment brings security via the knowledge (felt logic) that survival is ensured. And, conversely, the seeking out of security reinforces and strengthens attachment, which ensures survival.

Bowlby's profound ideas gave birth to an entire generation of research on attachment, spearheaded initially by Mary Ainsworth and then by Mary Main and her colleagues. Scores of studies have shown that infants adopt a basic style of attachment to their mother which persists well into childhood (Goldberg, Muir, & Kerr, 1995) and that the relationship with the father can also play a significant role in defining the quality of attachment (Chibucos & Kail, 1981; Cox, Owen, Henderson, & Margand, 1992; Belsky, Rosenberger, & Cernic, 1995). Recent studies have further indicated that one's attachment style may well persist throughout the life span with only moderate variation and elaboration. (See, for example, Cicirelli, 1991; Feeney & Noller, 1990; Hazan & Shaver, 1987, 1990; Parkes, 1972; Simpson, 1990). Therefore, *the drive toward attachment may well be our primary motivation in life and emotions are the primary source of feedback as to whether we are successfully maintaining an attachment or not.*

ATTACHMENT-BASED THERAPIES

Two schools of psychotherapy have attempted to expand the limited boundaries of cognitive therapy by integrating affect and cognition via attachment theory and by redefining behavior as predominantly interpersonal in nature. In their 1983 book, *Cognitive Processes and Emotional Disorders,* Guidano and Liotti stated: "The 'medium' through which developmental processes (cognitive and emotional) advance is the relationships with those people who make up the child's early environment. On the basis of the possibilities offered by the gradual cognitive and emotional growth, this medium supplies a great deal of material that the child will progressively process into self-knowledge and knowledge of the world" (p. 17).

Guidano and Liotti (1983; see also Liotti, 1986) define psychopathology in terms of pathological attachment. Following from attachment research (e.g., Ainsworth et al., 1978), they describe how attachment and exploration (which leads to a sense of self) can be hampered by (1) the relative absence of reliable attachment figures, (2) the general expectation of losing an attachment figure, (3) an attachment figure who actively prohibits autonomous exploration, or (4) contradictory and misleading behavior on the part of the attachment figure(s). They use these attachment patterns to explain the etiology of depression, eating disorders, agoraphobia and other simple phobias, and obsessive–compulsive disorder.

However, as Guidano and Liotti's initial attachment-based formulations predated Daniel Stern's work on the importance of emotion to the infant–parent bond, their treatment method mainly combines taking an individual's developmental history in light of attachment theory with very traditional cognitive–behavioral strategies, such as assertiveness training, cognitive modeling, coping imagery, self-instructional training, and stress inoculation training (Mahoney & Mahoney, 1976; Meichenbaum, 1977; Novaco, 1975, 1977). The authors further rely on Beck's (Bedrosian & Beck, 1980; Beck, 1976) and Ellis's (1962) cognitive interventions to debate what they term "patients' deeper theories," that is, those beliefs which spring from a client's early attachment style. Therefore, the therapist is left with the same cognitive interventions he or she might use without knowledge of attachment theory, and the centrality of affect to attachment is left unaddressed.

In *Interpersonal Process in Cognitive Therapy*, Safran and Segal (1990) see early attachment to parents as the nexus for (1) the development of the self and an understanding of others, (2) emotional development, and (3) the development of cognitions and expectations which are erected around self-knowledge and emotions. In this work and others, Safran (Safran, 1998; Greenberg & Safran, 1987; Muran & Safran, 1993; Safran & Muran, 1998) draws on and beautifully integrates Bowlby, Stern, and other infant–parent researchers with Sullivan (1953, 1956), the ecological psychologists (Gibson, Shaw, and Turvey), and affect theorists (Tomkins and Izard) to create a therapy that is both experiential (i.e., affect-oriented, present-centered) and interpersonal in nature—a therapy that more directly addresses longstanding attachment-based interpersonal and emotional patterns.

Safran and Segal (1990) identify the cognitive–interpersonal cycle: "People develop interpersonal schemas that are adaptive in a developmental context because the schemas permit the prediction of interactions with attachment figures. Unfortunately, these interpersonal schemas often fail to adapt to new circumstances because they continue to shape interactions" (p. 73). For example, a person's early attachment experiences may lead him to believe that others are aggressive. As an adult, he therefore may act in a self-protective, aggressive way, thus pulling angry responses from others that confirm his beliefs about others.

The interpersonal–experiential therapist therefore first determines the client's cognitive–interpersonal cycle. Working empathically in the here-and-now, the therapist looks for interpersonal markers of the cycle, whereby the client is playing out the cycle in the therapy session. Ruptures in the therapeutic alliance provide the therapist with opportunities to explore the cycle, and the client's difficulty accessing feelings and automatic thoughts also provides the therapist with such an opportunity (Muran & Safran, 1993; Safran & Muran, 1998). The therapist does not offer interpretations and does not debate the client's illogical thoughts, etc. Instead, recurrent feelings, and how the client blocks such feelings, are explored by heightening emotional expression and exploration in sessions.

Change also occurs via the disconfirmation of the cognitive–interpersonal cycle using both out-of-session material and material generated during sessions themselves. Safran and Segal argue that it is this experiential, felt disconfirmation of longstanding attachment-based patterns that most effectively leads to change in clients.

CAT sometimes employs similar attachment-based, interpersonal and affect-oriented interventions to those of Safran's interpersonal–experiential therapy (IET). However, as will be discussed in future chapters, CAT more than IET (1) overtly presents to clients a more explicit belief system about negative feelings and their relation to thoughts and behaviors; (2) is more explicit in presenting a set of health-promoting values and philosophy to clients; and (3) takes the individual's personality style into account in determining appropriate interventions and the most impactful stance taken by the therapist during sessions.

THE FALLACY OF HEDONISM AS A MOTIVATIONAL EXPLANATION

Why do clients who improve their behaviors and belief systems sometimes return to old, more negative, and unhelpful ways of acting, feeling, and thinking? Why do some children who have been severely abused and/or neglected and who are subsequently removed to a safe, loving environment prefer to return to their abusive parents rather than stay with affectionate, attentive caregivers? (In working with young children in an excellent residential treatment facility, Jonathan saw this scenario time after time.) Why do battered women remain married to their abusers?

Psychologists who embrace hedonism—the idea that people seek pleasure and avoid pain—may explain these behaviors by concluding that individuals who engage in them are masochists; that is, they derive pleasure or positive reinforcement from physical pain, psychological humiliation, or repeated disappointments (see Freud, 1924, for example). Millon (1996) accounts for this phenomenon by determining that pain and pleasure got reversed as the individual developed: a reversal of the pain–pleasure polarity.

In *Beyond the Pleasure Principle,* Freud (1920) himself moved away from explaining human beings as motivated by the pleasure principle, which maintained that people derive pleasure from discharging any perceived build-up of internal pressure. Stemming from his attempts to explain psychological phenomena in terms of neurology, Freud's (1895/1954) original model was a quantitative one; that is, it held that unpleasure occurs when internal, psychical pressure accrues. Realizing that motivation may be qualitative rather than quantitative in nature, Freud replaced the pleasure principle with the death instinct, which eventually permitted human motivation to be explained in terms of the interpersonal rather than an immutable drive toward pleasure and gave birth to object relations theory (Greenberg & Mitchell, 1983).

Nevertheless, Freud's early embracing of hedonism as a motivational force stuck in our culture. It is still intertwined with Freud's public image, and many psychology textbooks currently dedicate more space to explaining the id, the libido, and the pleasure principle than to describing object relations theories. This may be due, in part, to the popularity of behaviorism's assumption that human beings, like the pigeons in Skinner's experiments, seek out positive reinforcement and avoid punishment. Again, most basic psychology textbooks devote much more space to the work of Watson and Skinner than they do to Bowlby's theory and Harlow's findings, which clearly demonstrate that attachment can override hedonism as a motivational force.

Therefore, in psychology, hedonism is a principle that supposedly *describes* what makes organisms act as they do (although it is really more of an assumption than a description). For its definition of hedonism, psychology has relied on popular usage, which equates "pleasure" with *bodily* pleasure. Thus, to describe someone as a hedonist is to imply that he or she is dedicated to sensual gratification—the pleasures of the id or the basic drives needed for survival. (Interestingly, the pleasure sought by philosophers throughout history who embraced hedonism has typically involved the pursuit of mental and moral pleasures over physical ones, with the greatest pleasure being doing what is ethically right.)

The popular "philosophy" of the 1960s in the United States, with some psychological theories such as humanism following suit, was: "If it feels good, do it!" The whole notion of "feeling good" is so entrenched in American culture that Burns (1980) wrote a book about the cognitive therapy of depression entitled *Feeling Good: The New Mood Therapy,* which continues to sell vigorously even today. The difficulty is that cognitive therapy is not about "feeling good"; it is really about not feeling depressed (Beck et al., 1979). Cognitive therapy combats depression, as well as other psychological problems, but it does not advocate any means by which you can "feel good."

EMOTIONAL SECURITY AND ATTACHMENT AS MOTIVATORS

If we abandon the notion of bodily pleasure as defining "pleasure" and see instead the maintenance and reestablishment of attachment as a primary positive reinforcer, then we have a ready explanation for why an abused child or wife prefers to seek out more abuse, why a person continues to engage in self-defeating behaviors even though he/she "knows better," and why someone who achieves gains in therapy returns to previous maladaptive patterns. *It is the familiarity and security of the primary attachment that is reinforcing, not whether such an attachment is pleasurable or painful.* The pleasure *is* the primary attachment itself, in essence, not what we psychologists traditionally have defined as pleasure.

In loosely behavioral terms, if maintenance of the attachment is the primary reinforcer and motivator, then a sense of security, the emotions that are linked to the attachment and all subsequent similar relationships can be viewed as secondary reinforcers. In this way, a person can repeatedly evoke *aversive* feelings if they were central to his/her primary attachments. Izard, Haynes, Chisholm, and Baak (1991), for instance, have shown that insecurely attached infants may "react to stressful events with excessive negative emotion or behavior in order to obtain attention and nurturance from relatively unsociable and emotionally unresponsive mothers" (p. 914). Lee and Gotlib (1991) found that adjustment difficulties persisted in 7- to 13-year-old children after their mothers' depressive symptoms had abated. It may be possible, therefore, that a person who, for example, frequently experienced feelings of anger and anxiety in the primary attachment as a child might, as an adult, actively (though nonsconsciously) behave in ways which elicit reactions from others that provoke anger and anxiety in him/her.

One who was abused by the primary caregiver equates this abuse with attachment and therefore later seeks it out to obtain the familiarity and sense of security that go along with such an attachment. One who, as the result of therapy, forsakes old ways of relating and feeling then experiences a fear of the unknown and the unfamiliar, and therefore returns to the security blanket of longstanding, though maladaptive, actions, thoughts, and emotions. Therefore, our clients sometimes rekindled old problems after having experienced marked (but threatening) changes in therapy, and others were more invested in maintaining their secure and familiar relationship with the therapist than in leaving treatment and being on their own. Still others were nonconsciously motivated to hold onto familiar attachment-based feelings about themselves ("I'm a moron") rather than accepting what they knew to be true ("I'm intelligent"). And while the parents with whom I (Jonathan) worked in therapy consciously wanted to change, they were nonconsciously invested in maintaining a familiar attachment to their children, to the therapist, and to the world in general. They were therefore nonconsciously invested in *not* changing.

We propose to understand what some term masochism with the need to have a sense of security based on reexperiencing familiar feelings. If pain (a sensation) is familiar to a person, then it can be said to bring pleasure (an emotional experience); and if pleasure (a sensation) is foreign to one's accustomed way of feeling, it will be painful and aversive (an emotional experience).

The reason for a person's repeatedly seeking disappointment, failure, humiliation, etc. is that these are familiar feelings. He/she does not "like" these feelings, but "needs" them in order to regain a sense of security. He/she may consciously like conventional pleasurable feelings, but derives a needed sense of security from unpleasant ones. Thus, there is no reversal of the pain–pleasure polarity, as Millon (1996) would have it, but painful sensation provides pleasurable emotional experiences, namely, the satisfying sense of security.

Families have their own value systems and personal rules of living, expectations, modeling of thoughts, emotions, and behaviors, and perceptions of what role each individual should play in the family system. All of these combine to define and reinforce the individual's attachment to the world around him/her. A family's personal rules of living, or family mythology, is the collective belief network that is passed down from parents to children. One client, for example, grew up in a family that believed that you could only succeed by failing. To actually succeed would be a betrayal to the family, and to the father in particular, who almost reveled in all of the missed opportunities and rejections in his life. Feeling successful caused an enormous amount of anxiety and cognitive dissonance in the client, and he inevitably did something to sabotage his own success, or he interpreted a success as a failure to maintain the family belief system, his loyalty to the family, and the quality of his attachment.

Expectations and other messages from the family become absorbed over time. Like other forms of propaganda, they may contain little truth. Their mere repetition over time does the job of planting them in the mind, where they form part of an automatic response system. And perhaps much as, in social learning theory, expectancies become generalized and applied to similar and novel situations (Rotter, 1966, 1978), repeated family expectations gradually form the template for attachment and general expectations concerning oneself and the world. It is not necessary for one to be aware of them for these internalized rules to be powerful in shaping behavior. People simply follow them automatically and without reflection, and feel strangely uncomfortable when they do not act consistently with them.

While some recent literature (Harris, 1998) purports that peer relationships are more important to the child's development than parental ones, much evidence from the attachment research world exists in support of the longstanding power of attachment. Ainsworth's three basic infant attachment styles (Ainsworth et al., 1978)—secure, ambivalent, and avoidant—can be replicated in about the same proportions for an adult population and are repeated in the quality of adult bereavement (Parkes, 1972), adult romantic relationships (Feeney & Noller, 1990; Hazan & Shaver, 1987, 1990; Simpson, 1990), and attachment to one's elderly parent in adulthood (Cicirelli, 1991).

THE MOTIVATIONAL ASSUMPTIONS OF COGNITIVE APPRAISAL THERAPY

Given the above discussion, therefore, CAT is predicated on the following motivational assumptions:

1. the primary attachment(s), most typically with mother and/or father, are equated for the infant with survival, and in subsequent years, with security;

2. the "language" of the primary attachment(s) is emotion for the infant, and therefore those emotions which are predominant in the infant–parent attachment become equated with security in the child and later in the adult;

3. as we are motivated to seek out situations which ensure our basic survival and its derivative, a sense of security, so too are we (often nonconsciously) motivated to act, think, and relate to others in ways which elicit the subset of emotions which stems from our primary attachment(s);

4. familiar, attachment-based emotions can be positive (e.g., joy, excitement) *or* negative (e.g., shame, anxiety). The link with the primary attachment(s) is what makes these emotions reinforcing, *not* whether they attain pleasure or avoid pain;

5. the CAT therapist defines psychopathology as resulting from (a) longstanding attachment-based emotions, thoughts, and behaviors which are experienced consciously as negative, painful, unhelpful and/or unsatisfying, but are nonconsciously reinforcing; (b) the drive to repeat attachment-based patterns of interaction, beliefs, and emotions that are mismatched with the demands of one's current life situation; (c) not having differentiated sufficiently from one's primary attachment(s) to give one the flexibility to, at times, seek out the unfamiliar, risky, and new rather than rigidly recreate the familiar, secure, and attachment-based.

CHAPTER 3

Basic CAT Concepts

Personotypic Affect, Justifying Cognitions, and Security-seeking Behaviors

Although people are motivated to maintain their primary attachment(s), this, of course, is not always possible—parents die, we move apart geographically, adult children decide to involve their parents less in their lives. Therefore, we can maintain these attachments psychologically by repeating characteristics of the primary attachment(s) in subsequent relationships and/or by feeling about our adult relationships the same as we felt about our original attachment(s).

Ainsworth, Main, and their colleagues (e.g., Ainsworth et al., 1978; Main, 1995) have shown that attachment behaviors are, more or less, predictable, repetitive, and probably longstanding in nature. We argue that the "pitch" and the subset of emotions that are linked to one's attachment behaviors are also predictable, repetitive, and longstanding.

Plutchik (1997), among others (e.g., Tronick, 1989), has argued that, "Emotions may be conceptualized as homeostatic devices designed to maintain a relatively steady (or 'normal') state in the face of interpersonal challenges. Emotions represent transitory adjustment reactions that function to return the organism to a stable, effective relationship with its immediate interpersonal environment when that relationship is disrupted" (pp. 20–21).

For Plutchik, emotions are signals which allow us to maintain important social relationships and social cohesion. Greenberg and Safran (1987) have argued elegantly that the distinction between affect, behavior, and cognition breaks down to such a degree that the three are often indistinguishable and intertwined. (Since emotions are messages to us about behavior and relationships, they therefore can become cognitive in function.) It appears, then, that not only can emotions signal to us when an important relationship is threatened and has been reestablished, but also these relationships may serve to reactivate familiar, attachment-based emotions. Emotions often may be an end in and of themselves.

Think of a person who, while driving home from work, thinks to himself, "I was so stupid at that meeting today. People were looking at me like I was a moron while I was speaking." Assuming that this thought is a misconception and that this person generates similar unjustified cognitions frequently, this cognition might serve two purposes. First, it reinforces his predominant belief system (what we call his personal rules of living) and this may ensure that he continues to relate to the world in a familiar manner. He may arrive home, complain mournfully to his wife about his performance at work, and receive the sympathy from her to which he is accustomed. His perceived role as somebody who needs to be reassured and cared for due to his incompetence is reinforced. Or, in a variation of this scenario, he complains to his wife for the millionth time, and she responds with anger, impatience, and frustration. In this variation, his role as somebody who is typically met with anger and rejection from others is secured, and he can complain to himself (once again), "Nobody cares about my pain."

Second, this thought may simply revivify the feelings of shame and self-pity that he often experiences. Perhaps he won't complain to his wife or perhaps he lives alone. The repetition of this thought may have no direct impact and only little indirect influence on others. Instead, the "revving up" of longstanding, attachment-based emotions is the goal, as these feelings bring an internal sense of familiarity and security with them.

THE EMOTIONAL SETPOINT

If the revivifying of longstanding, attachment-linked emotions is one of our nonconscious goals in life, then not only a particular subset of emotions may be most familiar (and central) to us, but also the "pitch" or degree of the emotions may serve to define who we are and how we relate to others. It is clear that different families have different degrees of emotional expressiveness (Brown, Bone, Dalison, & Wing, 1966). One family's rage is another family's tranquility, and sadness and guilt may be the currency of one family while these feelings may never be expressed in another family.

For example, I (Jonathan) come from a passive–aggressive family where anger was hardly ever expressed openly and directly. I remember the shock I felt when, as a 10-year-old boy, I went to my friend Justin's house for a sleep-over and he and his mother got into a loud shouting match in front of me, and then his older brother joined in. The yelling must have lasted for only a few minutes, but it seemed like an eternity to me. And then I was equally amazed that, a few minutes later, my friend and his family were speaking calmly to one another, as if they had never been shouting. Growing up in my family, I came to believe that, if the pitch of anger ever reached that level, something catastrophic might occur: an unmendable rift between family members, divorce, world destruction. Over the years, as I continued to visit Justin's house and observe more fights like this, I came to realize that this was just the status quo for his family, as not fighting openly was for mine.

According to CAT, each person naturally assumes the emotional pitch of his/her family. Therefore, he/she has a nonconscious personal rule of living that prescribes how he/she should feel. This is known as the *emotional setpoint*. When one's subjective emotional feelings fail to match his/her emotional setpoint, automatic processes are activated to return the person's feelings to the prescribed range around that setpoint (or pitch). Deviations below the setpoint—i.e., when one feels worse than the setpoint prescribes—are corrected by certain mood-lifting thoughts and actions. These are commonly known as defenses.

Psychological defenses, according to CAT, are simply automatic processes that return a person's emotional state to a familiar setpoint. By screening out certain emotionally painful thoughts and perceptions from awareness, by distorting perceptions to lessen their emotional impact or by anticipating emotionally painful situations, we can preserve our emotional setpoint. In anticipation that a situation may cause feelings to fall below the setpoint, we may knowingly or unknowingly avoid that and similar situations. Phobic avoidance is an example, one that is usually consciously selected. Anticipating that a certain situation may make one deathly afraid, the person chooses to avoid it and, in so doing, avoid deviating from the emotional setpoint that prescribes how much unpleasant fear one should experience.

Conversely, when one's feelings exceed that setpoint—i.e., when one feels too good—automatic processes (also defenses) go to work to return the individual to his/her accustomed (and therefore secure) state. We seek to have negative experiences whenever we feel too good. Again, this is not because we are masochistic or "need" to have negative feelings. It is the familiarity of the emotional setpoint (as well as the feelings associated with it) that is reinforcing, not the pleasure or pain that the setpoint brings.

This explains the struggles we so often see in therapy when clients achieve desired change and then return to their old ways of feeling, thinking, and/or behaving. Even when desperately desired consciously, change poses a dire threat to our drive to maintain the familiar. To one whose emotional setpoint has always involved feeling ashamed and anxious, for example, feeling self-confident and relaxed for a sustained period of time threatens the very core of his/her personality. It is common to see clients revert back to thinking shame- and anxiety-inducing thoughts to return them to their emotional setpoint at this point during change. In fact, we often say to clients who have changed in a desired direction that now we are concerned, as they will now most probably try to bring themselves back to old ways of thinking, feeling, and behaving. We then predict how clients might do this and work with them not to be self-critical when this reversion occurs, as it is a natural part of the process of change.

> *Jonathan heard a poignant example of this recently from the parents of a 10-year-old boy. This boy clearly loved and was attached to his parents, but for years he had been locked in an interaction wherein he sought his parents' anger by acting out. A developmental history revealed that, even as an infant, this boy expressed a variety of emotions (sadness, frustration) as anger, and over the years, his parents reacted to him with increasing rage, frustration and intolerance. Their childhoods revealed a tendency toward anger as well. During one session, his parents said that evening interactions tended to be less imbued with anger than previously, but almost every night, as he was going to bed, this boy would pick a fight with his parents and end up being enraged with them, even if they responded lovingly to him. They believed that their son needed to expend energy so that he could sleep soundly, and they thought he did so through his anger. Jonathan believed, however, that after experiencing a new loving, calm relationship with his parents, he needed to return to his emotional setpoint of extreme anger, and he used his parents to do so. His parents also needed to return their setpoints to high anger, although they were unaware of this nonconscious process as they angrily tried to calm down their son. It was clear that this boy's anger brought him security: as some children need a security blanket or teddy bear (parent surrogates) to lull them to sleep, this boy's security blanket was his high pitch of anger. Only then, when security was attained, could he calmly fall asleep.*

The opponent-process theory of emotion (Solomon & Corbitt, 1974) proposes a theory of motivation that assumes that many emotional states are automatically opposed by mechanisms that reduce the intensity of the activated feelings, both pleasant and aversive; opponent processes are, in general, strengthened by use and weakened by disuse. Thus, the feelings of an emotionally aroused person do not return directly to neutral but instead are followed by an opposite state before reaching neutral.

Schwartz (1986) postulates a cognitive–affective setpoint that, like the emotional setpoint, when not matched by experience motivates the individual to have compensatory experiences.

The work of Maturana (1975) has shown that neural systems create meaning out of opponent processes, and it has been discovered that all biological systems involve dynamic and complementary opponent processes (Mahoney, 1985, 1991). Therefore, there exists support for the natural fluctuation between positive and negative emotions apart from reactions to varying external events. It is possible, we hypothesize, that the opponent-process theory may, in part, be capturing the dynamic between our nonconscious drive towards emotional familiarity (and security) and our conscious desire to improve our emotional state.

The emotional setpoint may be not only an important component of motivation and our emotional selves, but also may be integral to learning and changing. It is, therefore, not surprising that change has often been described as oscillating in nature, involving "conflicts, tensions, and (in one form or another) resistance" (Mahoney, 1991, p. 332). The change process we observe in our clients highlights the struggle between moving toward something new emotionally and reverting to a familiar, longstanding "pitch" of emotion. However, what is termed "resistance" by psychoanalysts may, in fact, be part of the learning process of therapy, with a return to the setpoint preparing the client to change subsequently.

PERSONOTYPIC AFFECT

In addition to a familiar setpoint for one's longstanding, attachment-based emotions, a certain subset of emotions is linked with the familiarity, comfort, and security of the primary attachment. Familiarity comes from repeated exposure not only to certain events, usually within the family, but also to certain models of emoting and interacting. (Do remember that the word "familiar" itself derives from "family.") In CAT, familiar emotional experiences that provide a sense of security are called *personotypic affects*. When they are positive, no one pays them much attention, because there is a cultural value (at least in the United States) that feeling good is good. We consciously strive to experience positive feelings and are motivated to engage in pleasurable activities and satisfying interpersonal relationships.

However, when one's personotypic affects are negative (e.g., anxiety, anger, sadness), they (mostly nonconsciously) motivate people to seek experiences that produce negative feelings. The person is "starved" for negative but familiar affects and seeks them out. At the same time, the person consciously subscribes to the cultural norm that feeling good is good. Such a discrepancy between what one consciously wants and, at times, nonconsciously seeks can be confusing and dissonant for the person and prompt him/her to seek help. Treatment, however, will be limited by the client's need to feel contrary to what he/she deems desirable. The conservative (i.e., attachment-based) tendencies of personotypic affects impede progress toward the goals of therapy, and lead to the retaining of symptoms. And in clients whom we consider to be difficult, the pull of the primary attachment(s) and the hold of negative personotypic affects are more rigid and powerful than in other clients.

> Stephanie managed to persuade Sheenah's strong secretary Maureen to give her an initial appointment much earlier than people can normally get one. Stephanie could, in fact, persuade anyone to give her anything, as she was very attractive, outgoing, and intelligent. Stephanie was extremely persistent, and Maureen finally gave her an early appointment just to get rid of her.
>
> Stephanie began her first sesion with Sheenah by describing how "unhappy and depressed" she was feeling since she could never keep a job, a partner, or a friend, and she couldn't understand why since she reported that she was a terrific, people-oriented person—very giving, very loving, and warm. But she was also very demanding. For example, Stephanie had just gotten a great new job, and she immediately demanded of her boss that he give her a five weeks' vacation instead of the normal three after six months since she had a child to take care of. She persisted in this demand and her boss fired her. Stephanie would constantly get people to become angry at her like this.
>
> When Stephanie spoke of her parents, she described her father, in brief, as highly critical and nasty and her mother as very passive, self-centered, and uncaring. Thus, Stephanie was used to getting everything that she wanted by herself—no one, she believed, would give her anything unless she fought for it. This fighting often angered others, who would then criticize and reject her, and Stephanie would ultimately be left feeling very hurt, misunderstood, and puzzled.
>
> Early in the therapy, therefore, Stephanie rejected any cognitive interventions aimed at her acting less aggressively toward others, as being less aggressive would cause her to feel passive and removed like her mother. Instead, she was helped by coming to understand how, while she consciously wanted to be successful professionally and personally and also believed that she had to fight aggressively to achieve these goals, she nonconsciously was motivated to reactivate her childhood feelings of shame and self-pity at the hands of angry and rejecting others: "No one will love me and give me what I want. Instead, they hate me and are enraged by me even though I treat them so well. There must be something dreadfully wrong and flawed with me for people to treat me this way."

We now turn to a description of shame, anger, and self-pity as the basic personotypic affects, why they are so fundamental to people's unhappiness, and how they relate to one another.

SHAME

> In the 20 years I have stayed awake at case conferences, attended lectures, professional meeting, and symposia, I have never heard a single case in which embarrassment, ridicule, humiliation, mortification, or any other of the shame family of emotions, was discussed (Nathanson, 1987).

While this statement holds true in our experience for clinical conferences even 10 years after Nathanson's statement was penned, a small literature has arisen, some theoretical and clinical (e.g., Nathanson, 1992) and some empirical, which addresses the centrality of shame to emotional and interpersonal dysfunction. These will be discussed in the following text.

Richard and Sheenah came upon shame as a central personotypic affect not by reviewing the studies that will be mentioned, for they did not yet exist, but instead through years of clinical experience. Time and time again, clients spoke of feeling worthless, dumb, inadequate, embarrassed, and ashamed of themselves, in spite of all evidence to the contrary. It became clear to us that most of our client's unfulfillment in life as people and interpersonally stemmed from this emotion.

Shame is a feeling of personal deficiency, of personal flaws and defects that are so bad that they must be kept secret. Unlike guilt, which pertains to acts that violate a group's rules, society's norms, or a religion's commandments, shame pertains to a feeling of personal inadequacy or unworthiness. It is a form of self-criticism and self-damnation so pervasive that one feels like an outcast from the company of friends and family. These feelings may be accompanied by self-imposed alienation and isolation to avoid exposure and further criticism. Anxiety occurs when one fears that one's secret weaknesses will be discovered by others. Lewis (1992) has said that experiencing shame may be the most painful emotional experience a human being can have.

Shame underlies the self-evaluation "I am a bad person." Clients often do not use the words "shame" or "ashamed" when describing how they feel, but it underlies such statements as "I feel inadequate," "I feel worthless," "I feel unloved," "I feel like a wimp," and "I'm a freak." The most commonly heard expressions of shame center around the following five concerns: "I'm stupid, fat, ugly, a loser, and/or old."

Feelings such as "embarrassment," "hopelessness," and "powerlessness" are facets of or synonyms for shame as well (Tangney, Wagner, Fletcher, & Gramzow, 1992). If the therapist probes certain other feelings, such as fear, worry, sadness, depression, and, sometimes, guilt, shame issues almost always emerge. For example, a mother with whom Jonathan recently worked who said she feels guilty while thinking, "What did I do wrong with my child?" was then asked, "What would it mean to have done something wrong while parenting?" She responded, "That I am a bad parent," thus exposing a shame-related belief. A mother who said she feels afraid that "something is very wrong with my son" as she parents him then revealed that this would mean she is a failure as a parent, again indicating that her fear is ultimately about feeling ashamed of herself. Finally, a mother who feels powerless, thinking, "I can't change anything," said that she feels inadequate to change anything in her life, again suggesting shame with the use of the word "inadequate."

While shame leads to the conclusion "I am a bad person," guilt leads to the conclusion "I did something wrong." As Klass (1990, p. 386) has put it, "*Guilt* involves self-reproach and remorse for one's behavior (thoughts, feelings, and actions), as if one has violated a moral principle (Klass, 1987). *Shame* involves a humiliating sense of exposure of central personal inadequacies ... while *embarrassment* involves discomfort with how one appears to others, an upsetting sense that the presented self is receiving negative evaluation."

Guilt is actually a helpful emotion in that it signals to the individual that he/she did something wrong that can be corrected in the future: "If I don't spit at people in public anymore, I might be received more favorably by others." Shame, on the other hand, serves no self-corrective function: "Whether I spit at people or not, I'm still a miserable, washed-up cretin." The belief that one is a bad person no matter what one does can only lead to a state of learned helplessness (Seligman, 1975) and, ultimately, hopelessness (Beck et al., 1979).

As Tangney (1996) has pointed out, guilt can sometimes be fused with shame. The thought "What a horrible thing I have done" can be followed by "And aren't I a horrible person." For this reason, many clinicians have thought that shame-based issues are really guilt-related, and have underestimated the profound pain that the ashamed person can be experiencing. And various measures purporting to measure shame are really measuring guilt or a mixture of guilt and shame (e.g., Mosher, 1966). It is therefore essential that the clinician probe to differentiate guilt from shame in the client, as they have very different implications for treatment. (Many clients actually need to experience more guilt to be more effective interpersonally and as parents, while hardly anyone should be shame-driven.)

The work of June Price Tangney and her colleagues over the past 10 years has provided much-needed empirical support for the relationship of shame to various negative styles of thinking and psychopathologies, and it has served to experimentally differentiate shame from guilt and embarrassment as emotions. (See Tangney & Fischer, 1995, for an overview.)

Most relevant to CAT's work with shame, Tangney and colleagues have found that shame correlates consistently significantly with negative aspects of the self and psychopathology while shame-free guilt does not (Tangney, Miller, Flicker, & Barlow, 1996). Tangney, Burggraf, and Wagner (1996) report that shame-proneness was consistently negatively correlated with measures of self-esteem and stability of the self and positively correlated with self-consciousness, fear of negative evaluation, social anxiety, and use of splitting as a defense. Conversely, shame-free guilt was positively or negligibly correlated with self-esteem, stability of the self, and social anxiety, and unrelated to self-consciousness, fear of negative evaluation, and splitting.

In the interpersonal realm, shame (1) is likely to short-circuit feelings of other-oriented empathy, (2) motivates active avoidance or a tendency to blame others involved in the shame-provoking situation, and (3) causes people to be angrier and manage their anger unconstructively, often making the situation worse. Conversely, guilt was found to strengthen and enhance interpersonal relationships. It (1) fosters an other-oriented focus which promotes empathy and interpersonal reparation; (2) causes people to own the offending behavior, take responsibility for changing it, and experience remorse and regret for their actions; and (3) make constructive use of everyday episodes of anger (Tangney, 1996). Furthermore, while both shame and guilt were found to arise from concerns of one's effects on others, only shame was related to concern with others' evaluations (Tangney, 1992).

It is therefore not surprising that Tangney has found shame, but not guilt, to correlate with a slew of psychopathologies, such as depression (Tangney et al., 1992), all of the SCL-90 symptoms—somatization, obsessive–compulsive, psychoticism, paranoid ideation, hostility–anger, interpersonal sensitivity, anxiety, phobic anxiety, and depression—(Tangney, 1994), and narcissism and splitting (Gramzow & Tangney, 1992).

The message is clear: help clients to become guiltier for their actions but less ashamed of themselves. And this is what CAT aims to do: *to decrease the pull toward the personotypic affect of shame while holding people personally responsible for their actions and behaviors toward others.*

> *Deborah, an unemployed 25-year-old woman who lived with her mother, complained in a whiny voice of all the parking tickets she was receiving recently and how "overwhelmed" she was having to buy holiday presents for her parents and sibling. When the therapist asked Deborah why she was telling this to him, as he could not help her with the shopping or the tickets, she replied that she had hoped the therapist would feel sorry for her and, yes, that her previous therapist had tried (unsuccessfully) to get her excused from paying her parking tickets. To this, and after exploring what she had done to receive the tickets, the therapist responded that Deborah indeed deserved the tickets and should work to improve her driving. He would not infantilize her by trying to get her off the hook (as her parents had often done). She then burst into tears saying that she is "worthless" and "hopeless" and feels "humiliated at having to ask for people's help getting out of these jams." The therapist could then focus on the shame-based feelings and thoughts (e.g., her worthlessness) while not giving in to the client's sympathy-seeking behaviors by making her feel less responsible for her actions.*

SELF-PITY AND RAGEFUL ANGER

As we have seen, shame can be an extremely painful and humiliating emotion to experience. As such, some people may try to diminish the pain of shame by converting it into other feelings and, as a result, by constructing a new cognitive scaffolding (perceptions of oneself and others) to justify these new feelings. Similarly, they may then behave in ways which elicit responses from others that also justify these feelings.

> *Bob is a 30-year-old man who comes from a very tight-knit family where the parents bind their children to them by suggesting that they are incompetent (the father explicitly by berating them and rushing in to take care of their lives financially, the mother implicitly by always "being there" as the eternal nurturer and dispenser of advice to tell them what to do). Bob likes to stay at home most of the time when he is not working in the family business. Whenever he has to go to a movie, a restaurant, or a social event (mostly dragged there by his girlfriend), he experiences stomach cramps and believes that either something bad will happen to ruin his evening or that he will not be able to handle it. A trip to the movies is preceded by ruminative thinking about whether the theater will be too crowded, whether people will bump into him or be rude to him, whether he will get his preferred seat on the aisle or not, whether the movie will be bad and therefore a waste of his time.*
>
> *Sometimes Bob's anger elicits angry responses from others, which then justify his perception of the world as uncaring and hostile. For instance, Bob, already angrily ruminating about the world, entered a revolving door in a store at the same time as another man. Bob's angry reaction elicited anger in the man, and a fight almost ensued. Bob's girlfriend felt embarrassed by all this and told Bob to calm down. Bob then exploded at her, saying she should take his side more often. His angry behavior therefore elicited a response from the world which then reinforced his belief that those around him are uncaring and angry.*
>
> *These thoughts are accompanied by what Bob experiences as "anxiety," but probing in therapy reveals much anger ("People and situations can be rude, uncomfortable, and obnoxious."), self-pity ("Why do I have to put up with this? People take advantage of me. My girlfriend always drags me to these uncomfortable places.") and fear ("I won't be able to handle an uncomfortable situation."). Upon further exploration, the latter feeling, fear, leads to the realization that underlying all of Bob's feelings is the shame-based belief that he is incompetent to take care of himself in a world filled with adversity—that he is a weak, helpless person. It becomes clear how the anxiety, anger, and self-pity that he is aware of feeling intensely on a daily basis really are constructed*

around the core feeling of shame and the core belief that he is weak, dependent, and incompetent in a dangerous, demanding world.

It was less painful for Bob to go around feeling angry and victimized by the world than feeling ashamed of himself. We learn from Tomkins (1982) and Nathanson (1992) that anger is an active, activating emotion while shame, like sadness, "shuts down" the emotional and physiological systems and can be quite debilitating. It's easier, therefore, to live with anger than shame on a daily basis.

We have found from our clinical experience that people in therapy tend either to wallow in their shame or to diminish its pain by instead feeling anger and/or self-pity. Anger and self-pity take away self-blame from one's experience. They enable one to blame others and/or to feel sadness for oneself at the hands of supposedly uncaring, sometimes cruel others. In this way, the pain of self-blame is diminished.

The anger we are talking about here is what Greenberg and Safran (1987, p. 176) have called a secondary emotion: "They are dysfunctional emotional responses—often defensive coping strategies or responses to some underlying process. Usually, they are of relatively high intensity and function as expressions of distress in response to something ... These negative emotional reactions are indicators that more primary underlying factors need to be addressed to achieve therapeutic change." The anger we refer to here is not the anger one feels when a parent is dying, when one is punched in the eye or spat on by a stranger on the street, or the annoyance a parent may experience when his or her child has demanded a piece of candy for the 400th time that day.

This rageful anger is usually out of proportion to what is occurring in one's life and, like all personotypic affects, is almost constantly being experienced by the client ("If I'm not pissed off at my wife's stupidities, then my boss's idiocy gets to me. And if that doesn't do it, then I'm always angry at those losers on my favorite sports team, who could always be playing better.") In other words, this is a rageful anger generated from within in response to many situations which would not be anger-provoking to other people; it is not the justified anger that almost everyone would feel at having a serious misfortune or threat occur to oneself (e.g., a death, rape, or natural disaster).

One way the therapist can distinguish the rageful anger we focus on in CAT from anger and annoyance which are more logic-based or situationally based is to look at how the client expresses the anger. If anger is expressed behaviorally in an adult fashion, through assertiveness and clear verbal expression, then it most probably is not personotypic affect. If the anger is expressed as explosive tantruming, as sulking, or in other childish ways, then it most probably involves rageful personotypic affect.

Self-pity often goes hand in hand with the anger we have described, although some people focus more on the self-pity side of the coin while others become more engulfed in the anger. Self-pity is sadness that one feels for one's state in life and/or for how one is being treated by others. It is the feeling that one is weak and disadvantaged through no fault of one's own—a victim. The perpetual victim always feels sorry for him-herself: "How can they treat me this way? People are nasty, abusive and self-centered. No one cares about me." Some people who experience shame also focus on the self-pity: "I'm a poor incompetent fool. Why was I born this way? Why did this have to happen to me? My life is so miserable and hopeless. Poor me..."

Self-pity is ubiquitous in the United States today and perhaps elsewhere as well. A society strongly influenced by the "do-your-own-thing" and "turn-on and drop-out" philosophy of the 1960s, coupled with the self-centered materialism of the 1980s, now finds itself entrenched in raising generations who are spoiled and feel entitled. An increasing number of parents defer to their children or treat them like mini-adults, to be reasoned and negotiated with. Consequently, these children become selfish, entitled, antisocial, and prone to addiction.

So too has the predominant philosophy in the United States reared legions who, when they don't get their way quickly and without having to work too hard or at all, feel victimized, enraged and sorry for themselves. Moreover, these individuals not only expect that life should be easy for them, but feel intensely angry and sorry for themselves if unlimited wealth and opportunity do not just fall at their doorstep. Complaining and whining have become the national pastime, replacing baseball, a game now replete with players who whine and go on strike over their multimillion dollar contracts.

The pity people typically feel for the less fortunate may motivate them to help, and a technique used to elicit help from others is to portray oneself as a poor, deserving victim of injustice or indifference. Pity for oneself, however, does not lead to self-help initiatives because the feeling confirms that one is powerless. When self-pity is a personotypic affect, people often engage in behaviors that result in others taking advantage of them, and they justify self-pity by thinking of themselves as victims. Because they imagine themselves as weak but deserving of help, they appear passive, dependent, and reluctant to take responsibility or initiative to satisfy their own wants and desires. Depressed people commonly see themselves as victims, and as we will discuss later, self-pity must be addressed in treating depression.

Self-pity and shame are often implicated in rageful anger. When prompted by shame or self-pity, the target of anger is usually those who shamed or victimized the enraged person or who refused to help. Because one feels weak whenever one experiences shame or self-pity, the rage is impotent and seldom expressed directly toward the appropriate target due to fear of retaliation. In treating anger problems, it is advisable to look for shame and/or self-pity and self-perceptions that one is inferior and/or a disadvantaged victim. More on this later.

Clients do not often use the words "angry" or "feeling sorry for myself" when expressing anger and self-pity in therapy. The therapist must listen for the synonyms and variations of these feelings. "Resentful," "annoyed," and even sometimes "panic attack" can be grouped under anger. With regard to the latter, Wessler and Hankin-Wessler (1997) have found that if feelings coinciding with reported panic attacks are probed, anger is often predominant. A typical CAT discussion of this might be:

> Client: I began to have a panic attack.
> Therapist: What do you mean by panic attack? What were you feeling?
> Cl: I was breathing rapidly and felt like I was going to faint. I was feeling really, really anxious.
> Th: What were you feeling anxious about?
> Cl: That I wasn't going to get my way.
> Th: And how would you feel if you didn't get your way?
> Cl: Well, anxious.
> Th: Would you feel anything else in addition to anxious if you didn't get your way?
> Cl: Well, upset that, again, I didn't get what I wanted.
> Th: What thought might you have as you felt upset?
> Cl: "Damn it, give me what I want for once in my life!"
> Th: What tone of voice were you using there?
> Cl: Anger. It was an angry tone. I guess I'd be feeling angry as I thought that.
> Th: So maybe you were having an anger attack rather than a panic attack.

Feelings such as "pain," "protective," and "resentful" may lead to a discussion of self-pity. A father recently said in therapy that he felt "protective" while disciplining his daughter, as he thought "The world is hard enough on her as it is." He then revealed that he assumed this since he believes that the world has treated him unfairly. This response is often heard from clients who are extremely attached to and identified with their pets and starving children in other countries: "the world is a cold, cruel place and I must protect all weak creatures, as I wish some would protect me, but no one will." We call this the Mother Teresa Syndrome—a sure indication of self-pity and anger. A mother who said she felt "resentful" and thought, "Ay, another problem to deal with" while parenting revealed the additional thought, "I always have to deal with everybody's crap. Why don't they solve their own problems and leave me alone?" While there is certainly some anger in this statement, exploration of this belief led to a "poor me" feeling in the mother.

Nathanson (1992) theorizes that people manage (or defend against) the extreme painfulness and humiliation of shame in four basic ways: withdrawal, avoidance, attack self, and attack other. The withdrawer isolates him-herself and privately wallows in shame; the avoider uses addictive behaviors to side-track him-herself from shame; the self-attacker makes self-deprecating comments in anticipation of presumably being shamed by others; and the other-attacker shames others before they can shame him/her. In terms of personotypic affect, people who withdraw and attack themselves tend to acknowledge their shame but more likely wallow in self-pity (and perhaps some anger at themselves), the first group privately and the second publicly. The shame avoider and the person who attacks others basically deny the existence of their shame, and the latter tends to be the person most consumed by rageful anger at the world.

Therefore, people coming to terms with powerful shameful feelings tend to vary along the dimensions of denying versus experiencing shame, turning it into anger and/or self-pity, and finding the locus of these emotions internally versus externally. Again, where one falls along these dimensions most probably results from how one's parents experienced, managed, and expressed shame, anger, and self-pity, and how they responded to such feelings in their children.

While anger and self-pity are often used as secondary emotions to defend against the devastating painfulness of shame, we do not believe that, developmentally, these emotions arise subsequent to shame. All three emotions develop when the world does not respond to the infant or toddler in a health-promoting or validating way. Shame (or, really, the emotional precursor to shame) is the infant's most passive reaction to not getting what he/she wants or needs from others: the infant shuts down and gives no signal to the world that he/she wants something. Anger is the most active signal the infant can give that he/she is not getting what he/she wants or needs. And self-pity (really again, the emotional precursor to this feeling, which may be represented by crying, whimpering, whining, or sulking) is a signal of moderate intensity also signifying that the infant is not getting what he/she wants or needs.

THE DIFFICULT CLIENT AND
PERSONOTYPIC AFFECT

Naturally, everybody has personotypic affect and an emotional setpoint. Some of us are fortunate enough to have had parents who instilled in us positive personotypic affect, a realistically positive emotional setpoint, and a healthy attachment style. However, others of us are less fortunate, in that our parents bequeathed to us negative personotypic affect, a negative emotional setpoint, and a maladaptive attachment style. Is the latter a formula for becoming one whom we call a difficult client in therapy? Not really.

Probably every person who attends therapy does so due to at least some negative personotypic affect and an emotional setpoint which is experienced consciously as painful or unpleasant. What, then, differentiates the difficult client from other unhappy clients? Kiesler (1996) summarizes the contributors to maladjusted behavior from interpersonal research: (1) extreme interpersonal behaviors; (2) misperceptions concerning one's impact on others or the impact of others on oneself; (3) the communication of discrepant, mixed, and inconsistent information to others which, in turn, pulls forth similar reactions from others; (4) rigid and extreme interpersonal behaviors which elicit similar reactions from others, resulting in the individual's feeling rejected or abandoned; (5) escalating their rigid patterns under stress; and (6) a higher level of interpersonal distress than that found in others.

Recast in CAT thinking, the interpersonal variables described by Kiesler suggest that difficult clients bring their personotypic affect into sessions more often and more powerfully than do other clients. Moreover, they most probably have more negative and dramatic emotional setpoints than do other clients, so the reactivating of personotypic affect during sessions also becomes quite dramatic and "out of sync" with the nature of the interaction or with the therapist's communication. As Kiesler might agree (see also Westen, 1991), the difficult client also experiences a greater number of interactions with the therapist as "stressful," "overwhelming," and/or threatening and he/she furthermore has a limited repertoire of responses, ultimately always displaying the same negative personotypic affect and emotional setpoint in his/her reactions to the therapist. And, with a rigid emotional and interpersonal repertoire and a greater need to reactivate personotypic affect, the difficult client more often uses the therapist to reexperience personotypic affect and bring himself or herself back to the familiar emotional setpoint.

> *Almost every second or third session, especially when a positive therapeutic alliance was being deepened, 36-year-old Judy would hear a communication from her therapist as "controlling," "patronizing," or "hostile." The comments made by the therapist ranged from fairly neutral (e.g., "What would you like to work on today?"; "What are you feeling now?") to more directive and problem-solving in nature. She would then get angry and insulting toward the therapist and occasionally leave the session. During the next session, the therapist would explore with Judy what she was feeling at those moments. She could say "scared and helpless" and link these feelings to how she felt during childhood around both her parents (her mother was physically abusive and highly critical and her father, now deceased, had been a nonmedicated bipolar); however,*

Judy initially would not come up with or follow through with another way of interacting with the therapist when feeling scared and helpless. She maintained that the only way she could cope with these feelings was by fighting and then fleeing, although she acknowledged that perhaps this was not the most helpful or productive interpersonal response for her to make.

COGNITION AND AFFECT

Although both Ellis (1977) and Beck (1976) conceive of affect and cognition as interdependent, their therapies are primarily unidirectional; that is, they focus on how cognition controls affect. In CAT, the assumption that affects prompt certain cognitions is taken seriously in that it informs many of our interventions. Cognition and affect are dealt with in a bidirectional fashion. The therapist examines and corrects negative thinking (here called personal rules of living) in the manner long associated with classic cognitive therapy. However, when it becomes apparent that thoughts are being *generated* by feelings and not by misinterpretations of events (here called justifying cognitions), these are dealt with in a way which diverges from traditional cognitive therapy.

For convenience, cognition can be divided into three categories: observations, elaborations, and appraisals. Observations are mental representations of events as they are happening. If you have the thought, "I am reading this page," you have given yourself an example of an observation. Elaborations occur when our words depart from merely trying to describe what we observe and add what we think about what we observe. The elaborations we make are based on the reality we have learned to construct for ourselves from the bits and pieces furnished by other people in our lives (e.g., Minuchin & Fishman, 1981) and by our past experiences (as with social learning theory's generalized expectancies for reinforcement; see Rotter, 1954; Rotter, Chance, & Phares, 1972).

When our words about events past, present, and future, real or hypothetical, depart from neutral, they are no longer observations or even elaborations. They are appraisals. Appraisals color our experience with *values*. They convey a judgment of what is right or wrong, good or bad. Our appraisal of an individual event derives from a mental guidebook that sets forth what we value. The guidebook need not be consistent nor conscious (see, for example, Leventhal, 1984). It is active, nonetheless, every time we assign a degree of worth or desirability to an actual or hypothetical event or to ourselves or other people. These appraisals are based on individual versions of moral principles and social values. We refer to them as prescriptive *personal rules of living.*

PERSONAL RULES OF LIVING

Richard initially coined the phrase "personal rules of living" as an alternative to Ellis's (1977) concept of irrational beliefs and as an extension of Beck's (1976) statement that each person has an explicit guidebook for deciding and evaluating his or her own conduct and that of other people (Wessler, 1987). Personal rules may be classified as either descriptive or prescriptive—that is, propositions about the nature of things or about the way things ought to be (Wessler, 1986).

Descriptive rules have also been called natural or inferential rules (Wessler & Hankin-Wessler, 1989). They are statements of one's understanding about how events in the natural and social world are ordered. They may be correlational or cause-and-effect propositions, and may be tacit or explicit, such as when they are expressed as aphorisms ("Hard work leads to success" or "Strike while the iron is hot"). These personal rules are individual versions of natural law—statements about how and why events occur. Such rules allow people to predict events in their lives, to make events happen, and, when necessary, to take adaptive action.

Prescriptive rules (elsewhere termed moral rules) specify how one *should* act and how others *should* act. They are beliefs about proper conduct and appropriate behaviors—personal versions of moral principles and social values. They form the basis for evaluating oneself and others, and include rules such as "I must work hard in order to consider myself to be a good person" or "I must protect myself from the dangerous world out there." Prescriptive rules are implicated in affective processes. Shame, guilt, anger, remorse, and jealousy are some emotions involving appraisals of oneself or others, appraisals that are based on one's values.

The learning of personal rules continues throughout life, although for most people, the truly significant rules are learned early in life (Wessler, 1988). Rules are stored as nonconscious algorithms for processing social stimuli and may once have been conscious but eventually become automatic. In some instances, they were never learned at the level of conscious awareness. Lewicki (1986) presents extensive experimental data to support this contention about algorithms.

Personal rules may also be thought of as schemas or generalized cognitive structures (Wessler & Hankin-Wessler, 1989). Self-schemas are rules about the self and standards for one's own conduct, or what Horowitz (1988) identifies as role schemas and value schemas. Safran and Segal (1990) maintain that an interpersonal schema is a self–other relationship that allows the person to maintain interactions with attachment figures (see also Muran & Safran, 1993). A similar assertion appears in object relations therapy (Cashdan, 1988) and in interpersonal therapy (Andrews, 1991). Personal rules, then, include nonconscious descriptions and prescriptions about how to behave in ways that promote feelings of security derived from overt and symbolic actions and interactions with other people.

Rules have three functions: (1) as conscious cognitions that mediate (that is, cause or contribute to) emotional experiences; (2) as components in an interactive system of cognitions, affects, and interpersonal behaviors; and (3) as nonconscious algorithms that operate as stored programs for value-based responses. Rules pertain to more than just the nonconscious schemas that spawn specific appraisals. They pertain to an important aspect of personality itself; they form cognitive maps that account for consistency of behavior and affect over time and place. Personal rules are fundamental defining structures of the person and of his or her integrity as an individual.

People's rules of living are usually more adaptive than maladaptive, and they aid people by reducing decision making and choice to more or less automatic, and therefore efficient, processes. They therefore are survival-promoting. However, rules may also promote negative emotional experiences by requiring the person to act in ways that are nearly impossible. For example, one client had a rule that she should please everyone in order to sustain interpersonal relations. Such a rule is nearly impossible to live by, unless the person exists within narrowly defined social limits, and a result of this rule is unhappiness, anxiety, and despair.

People cannot be asked to recite their rules or to write them on blank paper or printed forms. Rules are a matter of inference, and the raw data for inferring rules are what the person says and does over a period of time. Rules can be inferred from opinions one expresses and from attending to the patterns of one's actions in similar and diverse situations.

When used in a fairly conventional cognitive therapy manner, rules, like automatic thoughts (Beck et al., 1979; Ellis, 1977), can be reviewed for empirical support, disputed like irrational ideas, and examined for their utility; that is, the client can be asked whether a rule promotes the affective and interpersonal outcomes he or she desires (Wessler, 1984, 1987). And a person can know that his or her cognitive rules, like his or her automatic thoughts and irrational beliefs, are misconceptions, but he or she still can continue to be guided by them.

> *Carol was a young woman who became "nervous" in public whenever she could not see who else was in her presence. When riding a bus, Carol could not read a book without glancing up at each stop and checking who was getting on and off. Hers was more than a normal concern for safety. After all, no one wants to be caught reading if a mugger gets on the bus or if the bus is about to be commandeered by a terrorist. She was concerned about how she looked—would other passengers find her well-groomed and attractive? She did not want to meet anyone and have them comment on her appearance. She simply wanted to know that they were not thinking critically of her.*

*Her fear can be summarized as: "It is very bad if they find me unattractive."
She was barely aware of thinking this thought, but came to realize in therapy
that she had worried about people's criticisms of her looks for so long that the
thought was no longer an explicit sentence but had become an appraisal habit.
Carol's appraisal prompted her to feel anxious about the possibility that she
would be found unattractive, even though she never asked the passengers what
they thought of her and would have rebuffed their attempts to tell her. Instead,
she drew conclusions from how she thought they looked at her.*

*Her appraisal in this specific situation was based on a more general per-
sonal rule of living. She valued people's admiration, as many of us do.
However, Carol, used people's admiration (or what she took to be their admiration) to validate her sense of self. Her rule was, "I must consider myself a
'special' person. In order to consider myself a 'special' person, I must get people's admiration." In other words, Carol's rule governing her self-appraisals
correlated with another rule about what has to happen in order to make
highly positive self-appraisals. Self-judgment about being special depended on
others' opinions. Therefore, every passenger who got on the bus presented
another opportunity for confirmation or rejection of being special. Each person
was a new test. Little wonder that she was nervous and couldn't read and ride
at the same time.*

Just as specific appraisals are governed by personal rules of living, so too are
the decisions we make. We have general rules about the way things are and the
way things work. Carol held the belief that people notice each other and form
judgments about their appearance. We don't quibble with her conclusion but
merely point out that it was based on what *she* did and would do, not on extensive knowledge of human nature. This rule is not based on values but on presumed regularities about the way things are. Thus, her belief that "specialness
is good" is a prescriptive rule based on her personal sense of values. Her belief
that one can win approval by conforming to certain ideals of beauty and
grooming is not prescriptive of what to do; rather, it is descriptive of how to
effect outcomes. Not surprisingly, when Carol felt anxious in the presence of
others, she made extra effort to appear "right," a decision based on her rules
about how things work and what she must do to get the reactions she needed
to validate her sense of specialness.

WHEN PERSONAL RULES OF LIVING ARE NOT
ENOUGH TO EXPLAIN COGNITION AND AFFECT

Because they seldom exist in neat, consistent sets, rules may clash and produce
negative affective experiences. For example, a person may hold a rule about
pleasing others but also try to believe and live by a rule that says that one must
please oneself. When they clash, which rule will prevail? The rational answer

is that the more adaptive rule will replace the less adaptive one and that the person will then lead a more satisfying life. A typical procedure in traditional cognitive therapy is to replace a maladaptive cognition with a new, more adaptive one. But our hypothesis is that the rule that is associated with the person's usual familiar affective experiences will prevail, regardless of how adaptive it might be. Affects "eat" cognitions; we nonconsciously demote rules that are inconsistent with familiar affects.

Cognitive psychotherapists are especially challenged by clients who know that certain of their beliefs and thoughts are irrational and negative but continue to hold them. Explaining to one such client that his thoughts are irrational and negative would be both wasteful and ineffectual, for he most probably already knows this. Worse, it would further convince him that he was either stupid for still believing invalid ideas or wicked or lazy for not changing what he knew should be changed. Using conventional interventions can prove nontherapeutic and even antitherapeutic (and potentially shaming or humiliating), just as assigning behavioral homework to a person who cannot do it further enhances a sense of failure and thus increases anxiety and depression. One can well imagine a client who suffers from great shame and self-doubt participating in a traditional cognitive therapy, acknowledging irrational beliefs that he or she then cannot change, perhaps then frustrating the therapist (who has limited tools to deal with such a situation), and ultimately feeling even more shame, incompetence, and self-doubt now that he or she has further experiential support for such feelings.

> During several sessions with Carol, Richard began to piece together a portion of her rule book and to learn the conditions she had to fulfill in order to declare herself to be a good person. Among the salient rules that emerged in working with Carol was one about having fun. In effect, Carol's descriptive rule was: "If you have fun, you are an idiot; intelligent people are serious, solemn, and sober, not frivolous and fun-loving." The prescriptive counterpart said, "I should not be an idiot; I should be a good person and that means not having fun." Carol's depressed feelings provided ample evidence that she had little fun and was, therefore, a good person.
>
> Consciously, however, she did not want to experience depression and, for this reason, sought treatment. Insight into her personal rule book was one component of her improvement because this insight was followed by an invitation to modify these rules. Using self-disclosure and modeling, I (Richard) showed her my own sense of fun and humor, hoping to provide further confirming evidence that fun and intelligence are compatible. But the modification of her rule, and the behaviors and affects associated with it, awaited two further interventions: insight into the origins of her rules and the influence of her personotypic affect on these rules.
>
> Like all of us, Carol learned most of her rules during childhood. The one about fun and idiocy we traced to her mother, who frequently criticized her

father for his fun-loving, irresponsible ways. Carol's mother had made love and approval contingent on Carol's adopting her mother's values. Carol emerged into adulthood with well-learned but nonconscious rules about fun and badness. She also became a depressed person because of self-condemnation if she had fun or feelings of deprivation if she did not have fun: a clear lose–lose situation.

JUSTIFYING COGNITIONS

One way to produce and/or justify familiar emotional states (personotypic affect) is to link them with congruent thoughts. Stated more simply, we find that some of our thinking is motivated by our affect. At times, we think what we do because it is consistent with feelings we seek, and we are often unaware of this process.

For example, if anxiety is a familiar feeling that promotes a sense of security, we tend to think thoughts that stimulate and "rev up" anxiety. We begin to think fearful thoughts, dwelling on possible dangers, such as those social dangers called failure and rejection. The dangers need not be real or even probable. It is enough that they *might* exist in our lives or that they *could* exist. The endless "what if's" of worry produce anxiety with usually reliable results.

It is somewhat misleading and mechanistically linear to speak of the need to reexperience personotypic affect as prompting the thinking of certain thoughts, which is then followed by the experiencing of these familiar, sought-after feelings. Strong arguments have been made for how affect and cognition are intertwined in a complex, interdependent way (Lewis, Sullivan, & Michalson, 1984; Safran, 1998). This cognition-to-personotypic affect pattern is only one possible sequence. Another is that the need to reexperience personotypic affect is fulfilled by having a familiar longstanding feeling, which is then followed by thoughts that are "recruited" in the service of this feeling (Westen, 1985). Stated differently, we must justify our feelings by having certain thoughts that are appropriate to those feelings. We can't just feel anxious; we must feel anxious *about* something, so our minds search for something to think of as fearful. Similarly, we can't just feel enraged; we need to be enraged *by* or *at* something or someone for a particular reason. Since we are not endlessly inventive, our minds usually return to the same themes time and again. It may be one reason why we don't easily learn from experience where strong emotions are concerned. We are loath to give up tried and true methods of generating personotypic affect.

These beliefs are seldom based on reality, and the person seldom attempts to validate them. It makes little difference. These beliefs, called *justifying cognitions,* are not based on reality; *they are based on feelings.* The person actually knows and admits that what he/she believes is not factual, but continues to hold to the belief anyway. Thus, these cognitions cannot be disputed in the usual fashion of cognitive therapy because the person believes them but knows they are not true. More accurately stated, the person logically *knows* that these cognitions are false but *feels* them to be true. We call this type of felt (but irrational) truth *felt logic*, as opposed to rational logic.

An important implication of the robustness of beliefs and their resistance to change is that it is hard to change someone's mind, and even harder to change one's own. *We are more highly motivated by a sense of security than by a need to have correct information.* When our thoughts are prompted by feelings— indeed, recruited by those very feelings in order to justify them—no marshaling of facts or persuasive arguments is likely to budge them. Another approach is needed, which we will discuss at length in Part II of this book.

> *A young man became very "nervous and upset" when he accepted the offer of a new job which offered significant advancement in his career. He had been working in his field for about 5 years following graduation from college and had experienced some success and no real failures. Still, his opinion, and that of those who knew his work, was that he had not come close to fulfilling his potential. At least, that is what he thought when he stayed within the routine of his present job. When given a truly good opportunity, he began to doubt his ability and worry that he would fail.*
>
> *So far, his story may seem unremarkable. Many of us have apprehensions about starting a new job or responding to a challenging assignment. This young man, however, did not reassure himself about his ability, even though in therapy he could and did cite ample evidence to conclude that he was able. He would not face the worse-case scenario, but instead focused on his not deserving advancement. At the same time, paradoxically, he acknowledged that he was capable, that he had a good employment history, that his work was praised by his boss and others, and that to think of himself as "undeserving" was nonsense.*

Why did he continue to speak as though he were convinced of the truth of his allegations? How could he say he was hopelessly incompetent in one breath and point to his record of success in the next? Was he merely trying to gain sympathy and support by describing himself to the therapist and others in such unflattering terms?

He had created a myth about himself (with the unwitting help of his parents, as it turned out). The myth had no factual basis. He could and would admit that the facts of his life contradicted his personal myth. Yet, with a zealot's faith, and following his felt logic, he clung to his mythical view of himself.

He did not create his personal myth upon the occasion of a new job offer. He simply revived it. The myth had been created a long time ago, constructed out of parental messages about how difficult it is to succeed, how hard work was to be avoided as too taxing, and that the right thing to do was to take it easy and avoid upsetting challenges.

When clients say that they believe their feelings to be a guide to truth, that feelings as evidence outweigh what can be consensually validated, and that feelings are to be trusted as bases for decisions, they provide clues to their justifying cognitions. The justifying thought is not prompted by external events but by internal processes. External events may simply be used as the medium for such internal processes (that is, to "rev up" personotypic affect). We base our explanation on the motivating power of affect rather than on fact. The myth remained for our young man because it was a reliable way to create (or, more accurately, reexperience) anxiety.

As counterintuitive as it might seem, CAT maintains that the young man needed to feel secure when faced with a career move that commonly provokes apprehension in most people. Instead of soothing his feelings with self-assurance, he sought security by reviving his personal myth and by experiencing the anxious feelings that evoked it. His personotypic affect, though negative and consciously dreaded, provided an uncanny sense of security. In addition, his personal myth (composed of justifying cognitions) and his anxiety provided a connection with his family, which, in turn, supported his self-view and reinforced his idea that he was not up to the task. The way to remain attached to his family emotionally was to present himself as inadequate and undeserving and as "overwhelmed" by a world too difficult to cope with.

His beliefs about himself furnished justification for the feelings he had. This is important since we cannot simply experience familiar feelings; we must justify their presence. As studies on cognitive dissonance (Brehm & Cohen, 1962) and attribution theory (Heider, 1958; Kelly, 1955) have repeatedly shown, human beings abhor an explanation vacuum. Thus, to feel anxious for no apparently logical reason is not acceptable. We must justify it to ourselves. Therefore, while we "need" to have familiar emotional experiences in order to feel secure, we also "need" certain cognitions in order to justify having those emotional experiences (not to mention that these thoughts also intensify such experiences). The emotions capture correlated thoughts, and we come to rely on certain recurring thoughts whenever we "need" to have a certain personotypic emotional experience.

SECURITY-SEEKING BEHAVIORS

At the apogee of his popularity and success as President of the United States, Bill Clinton had an affair with Monica Lewinsky and then lied about it publicly and under oath. How could he have acted in such an irresponsible,

risky, and potentially self-destructive way? A woman finally divorced an abu-
sive, alcoholic husband. Soon she was involved with another man who was
also alcoholic and who abused her. They married. She wondered why. A stu-
dent complained that he always waited until the last minute to write papers
that had been assigned. Each time, he swore he would not do it again, but
instead would finish well before the deadline. Of course, he never did, despite
the agony brought on by his repeated procrastination.

The simple way to explain these actions is to label them. They are "self-defeating behaviors" caused by the fact that people who engage in them have "self-defeating personalities." Another pseudo-explanation is to label both the behaviors and the persons as "neurotic." And, indeed, they are, if you take neurotic to mean that a person acted stupidly when he or she did not have to. But name-calling neither enlightens anyone nor points out how matters can change. Instead, CAT conceptualizes the actions of these three individuals as security-seeking behaviors.

Security-seeking behaviors are actions that influence a person's social environment so that its responses prompt personotypic affects, restore the emotional setpoint, confirm one's personal rules, and thus evoke a sense of security. Andrews (1991) reviewed a great deal of literature concerning the self-confirmation hypothesis and found general support for the proposition that the individual typically interacts in ways that "pull" responses from others that confirm the person's self-concept and produce typical affective experiences.

Our concept of security-seeking behaviors overlaps with constructs from various interpersonal therapies. See, for example, Sullivan's (1953) notion of "security operations"; Kiesler's (1986, 1996) Maladaptive Transaction Cycle; and Safran's (1998; Safran & Segal, 1990) cognitive–interpersonal cycle. More so than these other approaches, CAT explains *one's motivation to repeat maladaptive interpersonal cycles as actively driven by the search to reexperience attachment-based personotypic affect.* When a person acts in ways that thwart the attainment of consciously desired goals, he or she is typically said to act defensively in order to avoid the arousal of anxiety (Sullivan, 1953; Safran, 1998). For example, Carol avoided social contacts with men even though her consciously held goal was to have a good romantic relationship. Her avoidance was due less to anxiety and more to the familiar feelings it promoted; she could feel ashamed of herself for not trying and for lack of success and could confirm her self-image as weak and ineffectual.

When anxiety-reducing efforts fail, there is reason to suspect that the maneuver is not defensive but security-seeking, and a different approach to treatment is warranted. A person may seek treatment for dysfunctional aspects of his/her affect and action patterns without realizing that these very patterns satisfy tacit needs. These same tacit needs may result in resistance to change and in setbacks following therapeutic change. This is the very "dilemma of change" highlighted by Peggy Papp (1983) in her strategic family therapy: the therapist presents to the family the obvious benefits of change but also the threat to the family—the loss of each family member's longstanding role and identity—inherent in this very change. Therefore, the strategic therapist may say to a family, "Perhaps it's important that Billy continue to fail in school in order to distract his parents from their own marital tensions. If Billy were to do better in school, his mom and dad might get a divorce."

> Alvin is a 42-year-old man who presents in therapy with panic attacks and a high level of anxiety almost all of the time. He says that he wants to learn "stress management techniques" and relaxation techniques to calm himself down when on the verge of panicking. He lives with his wife and son in an apartment next to his parents. Alvin spends much time at home crying and complaining to his wife and parents that he fears getting laid off from his job and feels that no other company would hire him. He claims this in spite of having no idea whether other companies would hire him and in spite of 20 years of seniority at his current job, which strongly mitigates against his getting laid off. Alvin spends much time getting soothed by his family and having them make suggestions as to how to better his life ("Don't worry so much—things will turn out just fine"; "You should start looking for a better job."). Alvin says he will follow others' suggestions and then does not, continuing instead to cry and complain. Family members, especially his wife, are quickly becoming annoyed and impatient with Alvin's fruitless help-seeking and complaining, to which Alvin then criticizes himself even more for being such an unproductive burden on his family.
>
> In therapy, it quickly became apparent that Alvin was looking to the therapist to repeat this familiar pattern: he would complain to the therapist, seek out the therapist's problem-solving and caretaking, and then ignore it, feeling ultimately helpless and unhelped by the therapist. During sessions, when the therapist would begin to make solution-oriented suggestions, Alvin would respond with more anxious and negative concerns, as if he had not even heard what the therapist was suggesting to him—clear evidence that Alvin was using the relationship to reexperience familiar longstanding feelings and beliefs about himself and others. Alvin's use of therapy was more security-seeking in nature than change-oriented. It was only after this was pointed out to him repeatedly—that he was nonconsciously engaging in security-seeking behaviors to maintain personotypic affect and that his "panic attacks" were nothing more than security-seeking behaviors (which he could control) pulling unhelpful caretaking from others—that the real work of therapy could begin.

And so we can now return to Bill Clinton. Clinton's actions with Monica Lewinsky can be understood as security-seeking behavior. And it is pretty clear at this point that many other political successes on Clinton's part have been undone or almost undone by similar dalliances, suggesting a repeated, long-standing drive to return to the emotional setpoint. When Clinton begins to feel successful, competent, and adultlike in his behavior, then he must humiliate himself to bring his setpoint back down to the embarrassment and shame felt by a bad little boy caught with his pants down. It can be seen that Clinton therefore engaged in security-seeking behavior to enable him to return to long-standing personotypic affect—that of a son raised by an alcoholic, narcissistic, abused mother and a physically abusive, emotionally unavailable stepfather. One can clearly see that Clinton's decidedly unpresidential behaviors periodi-cally elicit the feelings in him of this boy rather than those befitting the President. Unfortunately, he is motivated to access the former affects from time to time rather than the latter.

The woman who divorced one abusive, alcoholic husband only to marry another can be understood in terms of her feelings of familiarity. The actions she took in order to reestablish the familiar overcame her conscious desires to be rid of such a life. And the student who waited until the last minute to write papers was likewise motivated by a need to feel secure. He dealt with the stress of a class assignment by leaving things until the last minute. In addition to whatever benefits resulted from his avoidance, he also had the opportunity to experience (and reexperience) intense anxiety. Did this motivate his procrasti-nation? We answer yes if we can find a pattern of procrastination and evidence from his testimony that anxiety (and perhaps other associated affects such as shame) is a personotypic affect.

ANXIETY AS A SECURITY-SEEKING EMOTION

Recently, we have come to reevaluate the function of anxiety. So many clients describe themselves as feeling "anxious," but this emotion is experienced dif-ferently by different clients, and often clients resort to using other feelings to describe the anxiety they are experiencing. For example:

> *Client: I was feeling anxious*
> *Therapist: What did your anxiety feel like?*
> *Cl: Well, I was feeling anxious because I was afraid that I would get yelled at by my boss when I arrived at work*
> *Th: So you were feeling afraid of your boss's anger at you. Any other feel-ings you were having?*
> *Cl: Yes. I was feeling badly that I have such a mean boss and such a lousy job, and that I have done nothing to improve my work situation.*

Th: *What do you mean by feeling badly?*

Cl: *Well, I guess I was feeling sorry for myself that I get treated so horribly by my boss, but really also angry at myself for not doing anything about it.*

Traditionally, anxiety has been seen as a signal that warns of danger. Following in Darwin's footsteps, both Freud (1926) and Bowlby (1973) maintained that anxiety serves an adaptive function, as it warns one ahead of time that danger or, in some cases, an excess of stimulation is about to occur. Both men describe the function of anxiety in almost behavioral terms (e.g., Stampfl & Levis, 1967): that it gets linked to an actual danger and precedes it, allowing the individual to take action to diminish the anxiety and thus avoid dealing with the actual danger. For example, both a particular street and anxiety become associated with being mugged there. The next time the victim walks near that street, he feels anxiety, which signals him to avoid the street and the possibility of being accosted there again.

For Safran (1998), the client's (and, for that matter, the therapist's) anxiety becomes an opportunity to explore the client's cognitive–interpersonal cycle. Anxiety occurs as warning that the client's typical way of relating to the therapist is threatened, and the client then redoubles his/her efforts to maintain his/her characteristic ways of relating to the therapist.

We have come to view anxiety less as a signal than as the emotional equivalent of a security-seeking behavior. Thus, we call anxiety a *security-seeking emotion*. In listening to our clients describe what makes them anxious, we have come to realize that anxious feelings anticipate situations in which clients may feel ashamed or sorry for themselves, and sometimes also enraged. In a sense, then, anxiety does signal danger— the danger that an individual may feel ashamed, humiliated, or sorry for him-herself in the near future.

However, anxiety appears to do something else as well: it actually *activates* feelings of shame, self-pity, and sometimes anger as the individual begins to experience these emotions in anticipating the problematic situation. In this sense, then, anxiety may actually stir up the negative personotypic affect that it supposedly seeks to avoid or prevent.

Lucy is a quite dependent 24-year-old young woman living with her over-protective parents. She has been procrastinating at looking for a job, not due to the fear that she might be turned down but due to the fear that she might actually be hired. (Not looking for her job also maintains her dependence, but that is not our focus here.) The very thought of being hired makes Lucy "highly anxious," as she describes it. When asked what her anxiety consists of, Lucy can describe numerous scenarios in which she is given instructions or asked to perform a task at work, cannot understand what she has to do, fails to do the assignment, is fired and then derided by family and friends. She ends up feeling humiliated and like "a total failure." Lucy was not able, at the ther-

apist's request, to generate a possible job scenario with a positive outcome, but she had no difficulty generating dozens of negative ones.

Lucy has never had such a failure experience in her life. She was an excellent student at school and did very well on internships to train her for her current profession. Her parents were not critical of her, although her mother is an extremely histrionic, anxious worrier. When she would worry as Lucy was growing up, Lucy would take this to mean that she could not be competent at the task about which her mother was worrying.

As Lucy would become anxious, the scenarios would become vivid in Lucy's mind, and a feeling of anxiety would give way to a sense of shame ("I'm an incompetent failure.") and self-pity ("I'll never be able to succeed at a job. Why didn't my parents teach me how to succeed in life?").

For Lucy, anxiety not only warned of potentially humiliating situations, but it actually "revved up" feelings of shame and self-pity.

It should be noted that anxiety can serve a positive adaptive function, much as Freud and Bowlby described. If you are in a taxicab driven by a maniac driver, your anxiety may alert you to be on guard and to protect yourself (e.g., to say "Hey, buddy, please slow down" or simply to brace yourself in case of a crash). However, when the scenarios which accompany the anxiety are less reality-based and rational, as in Lucy's case, since she had only experienced work success previously, then the anxiety may serve the security-seeking function of stimulating personotypic affect.

"RESISTANCE" IN THERAPY AS SECURITY-SEEKING BEHAVIOR

We hope that it is clear to the reader by this point that we CAT therapists do not believe in "resistance" in therapy, nor do we understand a client's "noncompliance" in the way that some cognitive–behavioral therapists do. We see the client, especially the "difficult" client, as using his or her relationship with the therapist as security-seeking behavior. In other words, the client nonconsciously positions himself or herself to pull reactions from the therapist that elicit familiar feelings (personotypic affects) and thoughts (justifying cognitions) in the client, thus helping the client to achieve familiarity (and therefore security) in the therapy relationship. Alternatively, the client may not actually elicit certain security-seeking behaviors in the therapist but may misperceive what the therapist is saying and doing in order to stir up his or her personotypic affect and justifying cognitions. Clients may also behave in ways which either "heat up" or "cool off" the emotional climate of the sessions in order to use the therapy to reestablish their emotional setpoint.

Like interpersonal (e.g., Kiesler, 1982, 1986; Safran & Muran, 1995; Safran & Segal, 1990), family systems (e.g., Papp, 1983) and object relations therapies (e.g., Cashdan, 1988; Ehrenberg, 1992), we do not see difficult behavior as something to be gotten around, conquered, or blamed. Rather, it provides key information concerning the client's maladaptive behaviors, beliefs, and emotions. As will be illustrated in Parts II and III of this book, the CAT therapist spends much time helping the client to understand his or her maladaptive security-seeking behaviors, justifying cognitions, personotypic affect, and emotional setpoint. Unlike other approaches, the therapist highlights the non-conscious motivational component of these maladaptive phenomena (familiarity) to the client. This explanation serves to reduce the shame the client feels when examining maladaptive thoughts, behaviors, and feelings. Furthermore, unlike many of the previously mentioned approaches, the CAT therapist becomes quite active in working with clients to design and implement strategies for soothing or diminishing unhelpful personotypic affect, as well as identifying and stopping irrational justifying cognitions and changing security-based behaviors.

SUMMARY

This chapter has highlighted the following points concerning CAT:

1. Our families pass on to us an emotional setpoint, or a certain emotional "pitch" or degree, which we are motivated to reexperience, as it is linked to the drive to reexperience the primary attachment(s). When we feel substantially different from this setpoint (e.g., too happy or too sad), we are motivated to think or act in ways which bring our emotions back to this familiar, attachment-based setpoint (e.g., just sad or happy enough).

2. Personotypic affect are the longstanding feelings which were intertwined with and therefore defining of the primary attachment(s). We seek to reexperience the primary attachment(s) by reinvoking the personotypic affect linked with these attachment(s).

3. Personotypic affect can be positive or negative in nature, depending on what the predominant emotions were that were associated with the primary attachment(s).

4. The basic negative personotypic affects which lead to dissatisfaction and maladaptive interpersonal stances are shame, rageful anger, and self-pity. Shame is predominant, as it is central to difficulties in the parent–child interaction.

5. Different families cope with the extreme painfulness of shame in different ways, by denying its existence, wallowing in it, or converting it into anger and/or self-pity. The latter scenario absolves the individual of blame and proj-

ects it onto others. Different families and different individuals experience different degrees of anger versus self-pity.

6. Difficult clients have more extreme emotional setpoints for their negative personotypic affect, as well as more rigid coping styles, and they are therefore motivated to recreate interpersonal interactions in therapy which enable them to reexperience dramatic negative personotypic affect, as well as associated interactions and thoughts.

7. The interaction between affect, behavior, and cognition is seen as bidirectional. When the direction of influence is from cognition to affect and behavior, we say that personal rules of living are involved. Personal rules may be classified as either descriptive or prescriptive—that is, propositions about the nature of things or about the way things ought to be.

8. When the direction of influence is from affect to cognition and behavior, we say that justifying cognitions are involved. More specifically, in order to reexperience personotypic affects that create a sense of security, a person will produce certain characteristic cognitions (justifying cognitions) and behaviors (security-seeking behaviors) and will seek out and elicit familiar interpersonal situations.

9. Justifying cognitions both elicit and explain personotypic affect. Certain cognitions reliably produce certain affects. For example, thinking, "I always get used by others" may elicit anger and self-pity. Cognitions can also explain affects that may not always make rational sense. For instance, a successful person who still feels like a failure may think, "Obviously all this success is pure luck. It won't last and people will find out what a failure I really am."

10. Security-seeking behaviors, especially interpersonal ones, elicit personotypic affect. For example, a person may nonconsciously seek out a series of humiliating experiences when humiliation, or shame, is a personotypic affect. While the person consciously wants to avoid humiliation, nonconsciously he/she acts in ways that elicit it.

11. Anxiety is a security-seeking emotion, as it serves to stir up shame, self-pity, and/or rage as a person anticipates a situation in the future (often totally imagined or unrealistic on the person's part) in which he or she may experience these emotions.

12. "Resistance" is not viewed as the client's noncompliance with therapy. Instead, it is seen as a security-seeking behavior and therefore as something to be explored and understood in light of how the client uses the therapy relationship to rekindle personotypic affect, justifying cognitions, etc.

CHAPTER 4

Patterns of Personality

THERAPISTS WITH AXIS I MINDS IN AN AXIS II WORLD

Clients with anxiety, depression, and maladaptive patterns of interpersonal behavior may not respond to cognitive and behavioral interventions developed to treat these disorders. (See, for example, Bandura's, 1977, and Barlow's, 1988, discussions of how emotional change cannot be accomplished by cognitive interventions alone.) Very often, clients do not respond because of the therapist's failure to diagnose and treat the underlying personality difficulties or disorders associated with these symptoms. In my (Richard's) own development as a psychotherapist, at some point I cannot exactly identify, I stopped treating symptoms and started to treat personality as well. I was forced by experience to conclude that personality variables are of more than passing importance in treating depression and other DSM–IV Axis I disorders. Disordered aspects of personality had to become the focus of treatment in order to effect change in clinical symptoms.

We believe that many different pathways can lead to the formation of any Axis I symptom. Certainly, biochemistry can predispose a person toward experiencing depression, for example, and a person can become depressed as the result of a life tragedy (e.g., the death of a loved one) or a traumatic event. Clearly, in these instances, depression remains an Axis I phenomenon. However, one's personality style—"a *pattern* of deeply embedded and broadly exhibited cognitive, affective, and overt behavioral traits that persist over extended periods of time" (Millon & Everly, 1985, p. 4)—can also account for depression. A life dominated by shame and self-pity, coupled with intensely negative, judgmental thinking and an interpersonal stance which alienates friends and gets one fired from jobs repeatedly, will undoubtedly lead one to feel depressed, if not suicidal, at times. A life filled with fear of not being able to handle life's challenges, or anger at having to deal with such challenges, may well result in panic attacks, phobias, or other anxiety disorders. And a life defined by intense shame and anger at one's parents for pushing one to be perfect can result in an eating disorder or substance abuse, which serve both to soothe and to perpetuate one's personotypic affect.

The therapist who has an Axis I mind in a predominantly Axis II world may help clients to alleviate some symptoms temporarily, but these symptoms will reappear in one form or another and the underlying psychogenesis of the symptoms—inherent in one's personality style— will remain untouched. The therapist who sees "resistance" or "noncompliance" in therapy as merely the client's being defensive or stubborn misses the fact that they are part of the client's drive to maintain the security of his/her emotional setpoint, personotypic affect, etc. When clients' lack of progress or failure to maintain changes is due to certain features of personality, no new selection of techniques or increased activity of therapists will overcome it. Instead, a new focus is needed.

Almost all therapists, whether they realize it or not, treat personality-disordered clients. The most obvious of these clients have had many therapists, have had a series of Axis I symptoms, and/or have been in psychological treatment for a long time *but not specifically for personality disorders.*

The classic example of this is a client who has been treated for panic attacks, depression, "anger management," and perhaps agoraphobia as well as weight problems over the years. She has seen a series of therapists who have attempted to treat her symptoms by placing her on a weight management program, by teaching her relaxation techniques to decrease her anxiety and anger, by teaching her self-statements to use when she experiences "low self-esteem" and when she is angry, by using systematic desensitization for her agoraphobia, and by sending her to a psychiatrist for antidepressant and antianxiety medication. She has been diagnosed over the years as having a recurrent major depression, various anxiety disorders, and bulimia nervosa, nonpurging type (all Axis I diagnoses). One psychiatrist, noting her fluctuations between angry, energized outbursts and depression diagnosed her as a rapid cycling bipolar, and another therapist considered a diagnosis of post traumatic stress disorder related to his suspicions that her being overweight and having panic attacks might stem from unresolved sexual abuse during childhood.

Naturally, and we're sure that you are way ahead of us here, this client's symptoms result from an undiagnosed borderline personality disorder. All of the Axis I symptoms here result from the client's dealing with longstanding difficulty managing her shame, self-pity, and rage, and a tendency to place herself in situations where she ends up feeling these affects strongly. A history might uncover a very passive, subservient, long-suffering mother and a highly critical, overinvolved, emotionally abusive, perhaps sexually inappropriate father in a family who modeled difficulty modulating anger and fostered the client's dependence on her parents. Unless her therapists were able to frame her Axis I symptoms in terms of her personality disorder, treatment will be ineffective in the long run and she will be left feeling more ashamed of herself and enraged at a world that, as she might perceive it, does not care and cannot help her.

Despite the prevalence of personality disorders, the literature of cognitive–behavioral therapy overwhelmingly deals with treatment of anxiety and affective disorders and provides few guidelines for working with personality disorders (Pretzer & Fleming, 1989). Beck's cognitive therapy (1976) was devised for the treatment of anxiety, phobia, and panic disorders. Meichenbaum's (1977) cognitive–behavior modification was developed to control impulsive behaviors. Ellis's (1977) rational–emotive therapy was designed for neurotic symptoms associated with a person's thoughts about what absolutely must occur or exist. A. A. Lazarus's (1976) multimodal therapy is mainly a framework for psychological assessment.

Personality itself does not receive much attention in the literature of cognitive–behavior therapy. Ellis (1977) claimed that his ideas about disturbance constitute a theory of personality, but, given their lack of attention to affect, motivation, and individual differences in personality formation and style, clearly they do not. Others, such as Beck, deal not with personality but with cognitive structures, which are organized representations of prior experience that allow a person to decide on a course of action. Cognitive structures may be tacit or nonconscious and influence people without their awareness (Meichenbaum & Gilmore, 1984); however, cognitions are not enough for a comprehensive theory of personality or of its disorders. Affect, motivation, and interpersonal behavior must be considered as well.

Recently, Beck (Alford & Beck, 1997; Pretzer & Beck, 1996) and Ellis (1994), among others, have addressed working with personality disorders, but their theories and interventions are based on an Axis I view of the person, and they are being grafted onto problems stemming from Axis II disorders.

PERSONALITY IN THREE DIMENSIONS

While we have presented how the motivation to reexperience shame, rageful anger, and self-pity are the common elements of what causes longstanding unhappiness and dissatisfaction for our clients, this alone does not explain how these affects are experienced and used differently by different clients. If all the therapist had to do were to address these three affects in therapy, then our approach could be cookbook in nature and change in therapy could be quick and easy with all clients.

Instead, CAT draws on three approaches to describing personality which are compatible with what we have thus far outlined as our theoretical bedrock and which have never before been integrated with one another: Millon's (1996) "evolutionary" or biosocial learning model, interpersonal (circumplex) theory, and attachment theory. These three approaches can be boiled down to three intersecting personality dimensions—basic dimensions which have been replicated time and again both empirically and in many different theoretical approaches. And it is these dimensions upon which we draw when we are formulating our goals and our therapeutic stances as CAT therapists.

MILLON'S BIOSOCIAL LEARNING MODEL

Millon's approach (1996) looks at how basic biological factors (e.g., heredity, prenatal maternal factors), bioenvironmental (i.e., neuropsychological) factors, and environmental factors (e.g., contiguous learning, instrumental learning, and vicarious learning) combine developmentally to form what he terms "personality patterns." These patterns are most immediately molded by reinforcement strategies involving three polarities: the *nature* of the reinforcement one is seeking (positive versus negative), the *source* of the reinforcement (self versus other), and one's *instrumental behavior* in obtaining the reinforcement (active versus passive).

Millon's instrumental polarity is extremely helpful in defining the style by which a person relates to the world of other people. A person with an *active* style will try to make his or her experiences turn out satisfactorily. At the other extreme, a person with a *passive* style lets the world come to him or her and looks for satisfactory experiences but does nothing to make them happen. We hasten to note that the question to answer about a person concerns the *extent* to which any individual is active or passive in his/her approach to life. Further, few people are either active or passive all the time. They may be active or passive in general, but, at times, may act in the opposite manner. And they might be quite different in stressful situations from how they are under ordinary circumstances.

Whether their style is active or passive, what is it that people want to experience? Millon, taking a biosocial learning perspective, says they want to obtain positive reinforcers or avoid negative ones (the nature of the reinforcement polarity). Thus, some people want to have their personal wishes and desires fulfilled, and this would be so regardless of how trivial or sublime those desires are. Other people are more concerned with avoiding negative experiences, such as criticism. Their actions can be seen as more self-protective than self-gratifying. Of course, it is possible to want both and to be ambivalent about which is preferable, the pleasure of gratification or the discomfort of criticism. Such ambivalence leads to vacillations in approach, and if such vacillations are customary for a person, then that is his or her style.

With his reinforcement source polarity, Millon also distinguishes between the independent style of the person who relies on self for obtaining satisfying experiences (even though the style used to obtain satisfaction may be passive) and the dependent style in which the person looks to others as the source of satisfying experiences. Millon then combines these three polarities to generate various categories of personality, which he then relates to the DSM–IV personality disorders classifications.

CAT is interested in two out of three of Millon's polarities. As we have already discussed in chapter 2, we believe that people are motivated to reexperience personotypic affect which stems from the primary attachment(s) rather than to hedonistically seek pleasure and avoid pain. Therefore, we reject Millon's reinforcement nature polarity in favor of one's seeking to recreate personotypic affect and returning to the emotional setpoint. In fact, Millon himself generates most of the personality disorders with which we typically deal in therapy by combining the reinforcement source and instrumental behavior polarities.

We will focus on the combination of these two polarities and the six personality styles that Millon derives from them (see Fig. 4–1), and, for simplicity's sake, we will not review the other nine personality types he derives from adding the pain–pleasure dimension and an ambivalent variation of this dimension. (See Millon, 1996, for a description of these.) By combining the instrumental and source polarities, we can then see that a dependent personality is focused mainly on others and relates to them in a passive (take-care-of-me) manner and the histrionic personality is also focused mainly on others but relates to them in an active (dramatic, highly attention-seeking) fashion. The narcissistic personality is mostly focused on him-herself and takes a passive stance toward the world in that he or she simply expects to get what he or she wants without having to work for it. The antisocial personality, like the narcissist, is self-focused but attempts to get what he or she wants in an active manner. In a mild form, this can look like productive, appropriate assertiveness with others; at the extreme, it can take the form of interpersonal exploitation and callousness toward others' feelings.

Therefore, there is a dependent–histrionic personality axis, where one is focused on (dependent on) others, either passively or actively, and a narcissistic–antisocial axis, where one is self-focused, either passively or actively. Millon then defines a more dysfunctional variation of these two axes. Borderline personality disorder, he says, is a more dysfunctional variation on the dependent–histrionic axis. It is characterized by dramatic swings along this polarity from an active to a passive interpersonal stance and, of course, intense emotional dysregulation and lability. He differentiates three borderline subtypes—borderline–dependent, borderline–passive–aggressive and borderline–histrionic—to highlight that "borderline" itself can fall along all points of this axis. What remains constant is a highly emotional, dysfunctional focus on other people. He places paranoid personality disorder on the narcissistic–antisocial axis, as self-focus is maintained by a vigilant mistrust of others and extreme defensiveness against the anticipation of the slightest criticism.

For our purposes, it is also important to note that Millon sees these personality patterns (with the exception of the dysfunctional variants of borderline and paranoid) as each existing along a continuum which moves from a healthy to a dysfunctional pattern. As such, then, the healthy variant of the antisocial personality disorder is what Millon terms the forceful personality: an adventurous, assertive risk-taker. That of the narcissistic personality disorder is the confident personality: an imaginative, poised, confident person. That of the histrionic personality disorder is the sociable personality: an animated, charismatic, and charming person. And that of the dependent personality disorder is the cooperative personality: an open, tender, and sensitive person.

THE INTERPERSONAL CIRCUMPLEX

The circumplex has a 50-plus year history of attempting to measure personality and emotions (LaForge, Freedman, & Wiggins, 1985; Wiggins, 1985). As Plutchik (1997) states, "the underlying assumption of this approach is that a relatively seamless circular ordering or circumplex is a parsimonious description of the relations among traits and among emotions" (p. 1). The basic circumplex is formed by intersecting two fundamental dimensions or polarities of personality. Four endpoints are generated by this interaction, with various combinations of the interaction lying on a circle which bisects the four endpoints. This model therefore represents continuous characteristics of the interaction of these dimensions. Other dimensions can be added to the basic two, generating more circles of interactions within the primary circle.

When the circumplex has been applied to interpersonal behavior (Freedman, Leary, Ossorio, & Coffey, 1951; Leary, 1957), the two most common dimensions have been power (also known as status and the need for control) and affect (also known as attachment and the need for affiliation). These dimensions are represented by the polarities dominant–submissive and friendly–hostile (Carson, 1969). From these two dimensions, the interpersonal approach can create from 4 to 16 categories of interpersonal behavior along a continuum, depending on the degree of detail desired. The basic four categories created by the two dimensions are: friendly–dominant, friendly–submissive, hostile–dominant, and hostile–submissive.

For example, these dimensions have been drawn on extensively in the Impact Message Inventory (IMI) circumplex (Kiesler, 1987; Kiesler, Anchin, Perkins, Chirico, Kyle, & Federman, 1976, 1985; Kiesler & Schmidt, 1993; Perkins, Kiesler, Anchin, Chirico, Kyle, & Federman, 1979), which "was designed to measure the distinctive covert behaviors between individuals as they reciprocally interact during a particular interpersonal transaction." (Kiesler, Schmidt, & Wagner, 1997, p. 221). The circumplex maps out a person's characteristic pattern of interpersonal behavior. In other words, this circumplex attempts to build a bridge between interpersonal interaction and emotion by showing that many emotions are transactional–interpersonal in nature. As Kiesler et al. (1997) review, numerous studies on the IMI have supported the validity of parsing one's interpersonal stance in terms of the friendly–hostile and dominant–submissive dimensions, and there is about a half-century of research on small group behavior to verify the two dimensions on the interpersonal circumplex. (See Kiesler, 1996, and Plutchik & Conte, 1997, for a partial review of these studies.) While the IMI generates 16 basic interpersonal categories, CAT mostly uses the 4 basic combinations of the friendly–hostile and dominant–submissive dimensions.

There are three basic propositions about these interpersonal categories (Kiesler, 1996). First, affect pulls similar affect. For example, friendly behaviors pull friendly responses, and hostile behaviors pull hostile responses. Second, dominant behaviors pull submissive responses and vice versa. Third, a person whose interactions consistently fall within one circumplex category may be said to have that personality style (e.g., a friendly–dominant personality style, etc.).

Kiesler describes two important conclusions from the circumplex model for psychotherapy. First, when a client is chained to an unhelpful interpersonal stance, the therapist can use therapy to move the client toward a complementary interpersonal style: "The goal of therapy is to facilitate an increased frequency and intensity of interpersonal actions with significant others from segments *opposite* on the circle to the segments that define the patient's pattern of maladaptive interpersonal behavior" (Kiesler, 1996, p. 245). Second, the

therapist must disengage from repeatedly playing out a complementary interpersonal position to the client's maladaptive one, which simply serves to reinforce the client's maladaptive stance. Disengagement becomes more difficult
when the therapist him-herself has an interpersonal style which is already
complementary to the client's.

A COMBINED INTERPERSONAL–EVOLUTIONARY MODEL

Both the Millon and the interpersonal approaches are useful models for
describing a person and identifying targets of change. Persons at the extremes
of any of the dimensions do not function optimally and would benefit from
moving farther along the continuum, away from the extreme. Flexibility, not
rigidity, is the goal.

In CAT, we combine the Millon and the interpersonal dimensions of personality, as they overlap, to derive the most parsimonious description of predominant personality patterns. Empirical evidence supports our use of
combined Millon–interpersonal dimensions to delineate personality patterns,
and this evidence comes from an area of research which receives scant attention these days: the semantic differential (Osgood, May, & Miron, 1975).
Semantic differential refers to measuring the connotative meaning of concepts—meanings of concepts beyond their dictionary definitions. For example, a psychotherapist can be labeled with the neutral term "therapist,"
positively represented by the term "helper," humorously cited by the term
"shrink," or negatively connotated by the words "money-grubber" or "quack."

Many extensive factor analyses (see Osgood et al., 1975) of semantic differential data obtained in many different languages to ascertain the emotional
connotation of all language have yielded three connotative components of concepts: evaluative connotation (good–bad, positive–negative, warm–cold),
potency connotation (weak–strong, vulnerable–powerful, large–small), and
activity connotation (fast–slow, active–passive). Now, notice how these three
components of language correspond to Millon's three polarities and the interpersonal circumplex's two dimensions:

> Evaluative: pleasure–pain (Millon); friendly–hostile (interpersonal)
> Potency: independent–dependent (Millon); dominant–submissive
> (interpersonal)
> Activity: active–passive (Millon); no interpersonal equivalent

Starting from the clinical observation that passivity can be powerful, upon
which we will elaborate in chapter 11, it can now be seen that this seeming
contradiction—passive power—is possible because potency and activity are not

the same. This explains the client who enters many situations withholding his opinion, able to get others around him (and especially the therapist) to work very hard to "draw him out of his shell," and making others extremely uneasy by not expressing what he wants and likes. Therefore, descriptions of interpersonal behavior can be enhanced by adding Millon's active–passive dimension. A three-dimensional model is therefore more useful to us than a two-dimensional one, although the latter cannot easily be drawn on paper!

Only one empirical study to date has related Millon's model of personality disorders to interpersonal theory (DeJong, van den Brink, Jansen, & Schippers, 1989). These researchers obtained a result they did not expect. Correlating the Structured Interview for DSM–III Personality Disorders (Pfohl, Stangl, & Zimmerman, 1983) with the Interpersonal Check List (LaForge & Suczek, 1955), a measure of Leary's (1957) interpersonal categories, they found that all of the personality disorders clustered together in hostile territory. This finding is not surprising, as all personality-disordered individuals have disrupted interpersonal relations characterized by hostile attachments rather than friendly ones (with friendly interactions being the cultural norm). If atypical, abnormal personality styles fall in the hostile quadrants, then it follows that typical, "normal" personality styles should fall in the friendly quadrants.

Recall Millon's four "normal" variations of personality styles that we discussed earlier (the forceful, the confident, the dramatic, and the cooperative personality). These might well explain DeJong et al.'s findings in that the more normal variants of the personality disorders were not being measured. A theory of personality, therefore, must take into account not only the disordered variants in the hostile quadrants, but also the more functional personality style variants in the friendly quadrants.

CHANGING PERSONALITY PATTERNS IN THERAPY

Although no research confirms the continuity between the "normal" personality and the disordered personality, these descriptors provide a useful clinical heuristic. Instead of seeking improvement in terms of moving away from the extremes of active or passive, independent or dependent, interventions instead can be aimed at making the person more normal. This is what Kiesler's (1982) interpersonal approach attempts to do by moving clients toward an interpersonal stance complementary to the dysfunctional one that they maintain. Persons will continue to be characterized as active–independent and so on, but as they become more "normal," they will be less hostile and more friendly. To state it another way, normality is defined by maintaining culturally normative

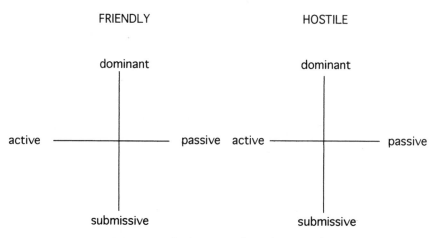

FIGURE 4–1   The CAT Personality Style Circumplex

interactions, that is, friendly or affectively positive ones. One's personality style can remain the same but it must be functional within society's normative standards. More specifically, one can remain a narcissist or a dependent, but one must be helped to be a friendly, attuned, prosocial narcissist or dependent rather than a hostile, misattuned, self-centered one.

Having previously rejected Millon's pleasure–pain dimension, as it contradicts the backbone of CAT (the drive to reexperience personotypic affect and reestablish the emotional setpoint), we are now left with the following three personality dimensions: *friendly–hostile, active–passive, and dominant–submissive.* Figure 4–1 presents the combinations of these dimensions in circumplex format. The active–passive and dominant–submissive dimensions combine to define various personality styles, and the friendly–hostile dimension represents the continuum between functional and dysfunctional variations of these styles.

ATTACHMENT THEORY

As the thinking behind CAT has been influenced profoundly by Bowlby's attachment theory, as already described in chapter 2, it is important to note that the findings of attachment research provide strong empirical support for the significance of the friendly–hostile dimension of personality. First, one must understand that the friendly–hostile dimension is defined as an *interpersonal* stance along a continuum of behaviors which are meant to be welcoming or rejecting to others. "Friendly" can be redefined in attachment terms as

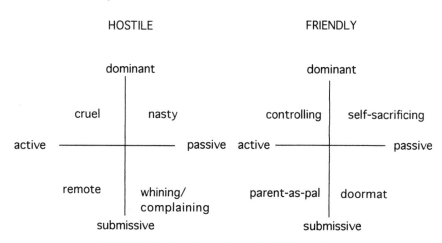

FIGURE 4–2   Parenting styles on the CAT circumplex

attuned (and therefore experienced as welcoming and validating) and "hostile" as *misattuned* (and therefore as rejecting). This dimension finds its equivalent in the four attachment styles which have been copiously researched and replicated by attachment researchers (see Goldberg, 1995, and Main, 1995, for a summary of many of these studies).

Numerous studies have used the classic Strange Situation (Ainsworth et al., 1978) with infants (Ainsworth et al., 1971; Crittenden, 1985, Main & Solomon, 1986), preschoolers (Cassidy & Marvin, 1987/1992; Crittenden, 1992; Shouldice & Stevenson-Hinde, 1992), and 5- to 7-year-olds (Main & Cassidy, 1987). This situation involves infants' and parents' behaviors, proximity-seeking and facial gestures being observed and coded as the parent briefly leaves the infant alone in a room with toys and then returns. Adolescent attachment styles have been measured using observation of reunions with a parent (Cobb, 1993), and adult attachment has been measured using the Adult Attachment Interview, a measurement based on discourse analysis of interviews with adults (Main, Kaplan, & Cassidy, 1985). A longitudinal study has yet to be completed which follows attachment style throughout the life span. Nevertheless, the same four basic attachment styles have been replicated in about the same percentages for each of the aforementioned age groups.

For the infants, about 55–65% are classified as *securely attached,* which consists of using the caregiver as a "secure base" from which the infant explores his/her environment. The infant may or may not show distress upon separation from the caregiver, but greets the caregiver positively upon reunion and uses the caregiver if distressed, following this with another period of exploration. About 20–25% of the infant population are *avoidantly attached* to the caregiver. This consists of showing minimal interest in and involvement with the caretaker. Minimal distress is shown at separation, and the parent is primarily ignored at reunion. About 10–15% of the infants are *ambivalently attached,* as demonstrated by their showing minimal exploration, being preoccupied with the caregiver, having difficulty settling down, and both seeking and resisting contact with the caregiver during reunion. These infants either display anger or are very passive. Finally, *disorganized* infants compose about 15–20% of the population. These show disorganized and/or disoriented behavior when the parent is present, as indicated by trancelike freezing, anomalous postures, and approach to caregivers with their heads averted. In contrast to the other attachment types, disorganized infants showed sequences of behavior that appeared to lack a clear goal, intention, or explanation (Main, 1995). This category has been targeted as a possible developmental precursor to borderline personality disorder (Fonagy, 1996; Fonagy, M. Steele, H. Steele, Leigh, Kennedy, Mattoon, & Target, 1995; Main, 1995).

These styles have been replicated in quality and in approximately the same proportions for the 5- to 7-year-old, adolescent, and adult populations. Interestingly, the caregivers of the children and adolescents have been found to show similar attachment styles to their offspring (Ainsworth & Eichberg, 1991; Fonagy, Steele, & Steele, 1991; Benoit & Parker, 1994).

It appears therefore that there is a continuum of attachment which runs from unattached (or highly avoidant) to securely attached. Technically, this continuum would run from unattached to enmeshed (overly or highly attached). However, the mothers of ambivalently attached infants, those that are highly involved with their infants *but* noncontingent in their interactions, most resemble overprotective, enmeshed parents (Main, 1995). If attunement is the core of the friendly–hostile interpersonal dimension, then the enmeshed mothers do not fall at the endpoint of the dimension; rather, the securely attached mothers do. The continuum looks like:

unattached - - - - disorganized - - - - avoidant - - - - ambivalent - - - - secure

Thus, if the friendly–hostile dimension is both continuous and interpersonal in nature, it can be seen as similar to attachment styles, running from actively alienating to highly attuned and welcoming. Ainsworth et al. (1978) enumerated subtypes in each of the three original attachment categories. Avoidant infants were split into highly avoidant and mixed-response infants; ambivalent infants were divided into angry and passive infants; and secure infants into relatively independent infants, relatively clingy infants, and a category lying in between the other two subtypes. Later, when the disorganized category was discovered (Main & Solomon, 1986, 1990), infants in this category were also given a secondary classification from one of the three other attachment styles. We mention these subtypes simply to highlight the continuous nature of attachment styles along the friendly-hostile dimension.

One study to date has attempted to integrate attachment theory with the interpersonal circumplex. Bartholomew and Horowitz (1991) formed a 2×2 matrix, crossing subjects' views of themselves (positive versus negative) with their views of others (also positive versus negative) as culled from semi-structured interviews. Interestingly, this interaction yields, in essence, the four adult attachment styles: secure (positive self-image and positive model of others), preoccupied (negative self-image and positive view of others), fearful (negative model of self and others), and dismissing (positive self-view and negative model of others).

CAT'S THREE-DIMENSIONAL MODEL OF PERSONALITY AND THERAPEUTIC CHANGE

Therefore, the dimensions which CAT uses to assess and then treat an individual are: active–passive, dominant–submissive, and friendly–hostile. The first two dimensions can be combined to yield four basic personality styles, and the latter indicates how functional versus maladaptive that particular style is (i.e., whether the style simply describes one's personality or a personality disorder). The four personality styles, with their functional to dysfunctional variants, are as follows:

Active–independent: the forceful/the antisocial personality
Passive–independent: the confident/the narcissistic personality
Active–dependent: the dramatic/the histrionic personality
Passive–dependent: the cooperative/the dependent personality

In terms of treatment, an assessment of the friendly–hostile dimension yields how dysfunctional one's personality style is. The combination of the other two dimensions defines not only how the individual relates to the world, but also how the therapist can move the individual from a less to a more functional expression of his/her personality style. In other words, knowing that a client is dependent versus narcissistic, for example, has significant implications not only for the goals of the therapy but also for the stance the CAT therapist takes with the client and the types of interventions the therapist makes. We will discuss this in detail in Part II.

Like Millon, we believe that the borderline personality style is a more dysfunctional variant of the dependent personality styles. As such, borderline clients tend to fall either in the dependent (or passive–aggressive) borderline category or the histrionic borderline category. We will address this definition and these borderline subgroups further in chapter 12.

SUMMARY

We will discuss how we assess and work with the different personality styles in Parts II and III of this book. To summarize the basic points in this chapter:

1. The CAT therapist often (but not always) views presenting problems as part of a longstanding personality style, and the therapist frequently works more with that underlying style than with the presenting problems (while certainly not ignoring the latter).

2. Personality styles can be obtained by assessing individuals along three dimensions of personality, which are derived from attachment theory, Millon's evolutionary theory, and the interpersonal circumplex. They are friendly–hostile, dominant–submissive, and active–passive.

3. The goal of the CAT therapist is not to help clients change their particular personality style, it is instead to move clients from a hostile, misattuned expression of that personality style to a more friendly, attuned, and therefore adaptive version of their style. While the CAT therapist can make some shifts in how active–passive and dominant–submissive a client is, the main focus of change is on the friendly–hostile axis.

CHAPTER 5

The Difficult Client Revisited

Having covered the theory behind CAT, let us now return to the *Who's Who* of difficult clients that we outlined in the Introduction. We identified nine basic types of difficult clients, with some of these types having subcategories. If we plot these nine types using the three dimensions of personality described in chapter 4, various commonalities appear across the types. (See Fig. 5–1 for the CAT personality circumplex of these types.) The first and most obvious finding is that all of these types appear on the hostile circumplex as opposed to the friendly one. This makes good sense, as difficult clients tend to kick quite a lot of interpersonal and emotional sand in the therapist's face. This also resembles DeJong et al.'s (1989) findings that we described in chapter 4, that all of the personality disorders measured by the interpersonal circumplex fell in the hostile quadrants.

It can also, therefore, be assumed that, first, there exist friendly variants of the nine difficult types of clients and, second, these variants are not experienced by the therapist as difficult. For example, certain clients describe problematic interpersonal and emotional patterns but do not bring these patterns into the therapy relationship to any great extent. The client who describes

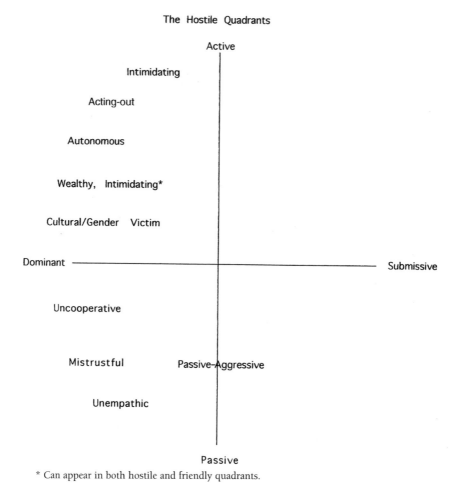

FIGURE 5–1   "Difficult" clients plotted on the CAT Personality Style Circumplex

being extremely intractable and angry in his relationship with his wife but who does not show these qualities in the therapy relationship or in his ability to change might serve as a friendly variant of the client who is angry and rigid in as well as out of therapy.

Other clients may present themselves in the same way both in and out of therapy but possess a relatively friendly stance toward all. For example, a client may be initially resistant to the suggestions of others, a procrastinator, and also mildly dependent on the directions of others, but may still possess a solid relationship and a good job, as well as a sense of humor and perspective on the problems she has. She may be coming to therapy to "fine tune" these problems but not, as might the full-blown passive–aggressive client, to alter extremely self-defeating lifelong patterns which have led to few friendships, no relationships, and a series of failed employment experiences. In turn, she may hem and haw initially when the therapist makes a remark and may experience mild annoyance, but no major ruptures in the therapeutic alliance (Safran, 1998) occur, and she will ultimately act on what she has gained from therapy. This stands in marked contrast to the whiny, covertly enraged noncompliance of some "difficult" passive–aggressive clients—those whom Yalom (1985) has termed "help-rejecting complainers"—who fall in the hostile domain of the personality circumplex.

The second finding of note when we look at Fig. 5–1 is that eight (actually, eight and a half) of the nine types of difficult clients fall in the *dominant* quadrants of the hostile circumplex. This finding makes great sense when we keep in mind interpersonal research on therapist–client matching (see Kiesler, 1996, Chapter 10). These studies have found that (1) therapists experience dependent clients as warmer and more sociable (Stuart, Pilkonis, Heape, Smith, & Fisher, 1992); (2) self-effacing clients with managerial therapists tend to become more dominant and friendly, more flexible interpersonally, and less anxious than do those with docile or ambiguous-role therapists (Rice, 1970); and (3) friendly–submissive interpersonal problems are positively correlated with a positive therapeutic alliance while hostile–dominant problems are negatively correlated with such an alliance (Muran, Segal, Wallner Samstag, & Crawford, 1994). Berzins (1977) concluded that, "Favorable pairings generally conjoined submissive, inhibited, passive patients with dominant, expressive, active, cue- and structure-emitting therapists, and sometimes vice versa" (p. 243).

In other words, the therapeutic alliance is perceived as most positive, with less premature client dropout and the greatest likelihood of change in therapy, when a dependent (submissive) client is paired with a nondependent (dominant) therapist. This starkly contrasts with our nine types of difficult clients, all of whom fall in the dominant–hostile interpersonal quadrants. The question for the therapist, therefore, becomes: How does a therapist position himself or herself to work with dominant–hostile clients? How does he or she react to clients who potentially challenge his or her sense of power, confidence, and effectiveness as a therapist?

Third, Fig. 5–1 highlights that difficult clients fall in either the active or passive quadrants of the dominant–hostile domain. It should be remembered that one can be dominant either actively *or* passively, since dominance is most often equated only with being active. Passive power, in fact, is often more powerful (by dint of its not seeming to be what it is) than active power. The tortoise has a greater chance of defeating the hare than does another hare. In forming two superordinate categories of what causes ruptures in the therapeutic alliance, Safran, Crocker, McMain, and Murray (1990) also emphasize the existence of both active and passive power on the client's part in the therapeutic relationship. As Safran (1998, p. 218) summarizes, these two overarching categories are "(1) confrontation ruptures (in which the client directly expresses negative sentiments toward the therapist), and (2) avoidance of confrontation ruptures (in which the client deals with the breach through withdrawal, distancing, or avoidance)."

"Difficult" clients, therefore, are those who challenge the therapist's sense of efficacy, knowledge, self-confidence, and power, with personality styles falling in the active–dominant–hostile and the passive–dominant–hostile quadrants. By way of setting the stage for Part II of this book, we now will briefly revisit our Who's Who to highlight where each difficult client falls on our personality circumplex, and how his or her personality style can be reframed using CAT concepts. We present Table 5–1 to summarize the predominant personotypic affect, typical justifying cognitions, and security-seeking behaviors of each difficult client.

ACTIVE–DOMINANT–HOSTILE CLIENTS

Intimidating clients attempt to avoid shame or being shamed by others by attacking first: "I'll shame, embarrass, and humiliate you before you have a chance to do it to me." This is the interpersonal stance of the bully. These clients are clearly active in that they avoid shame aggressively; dominant in that they actively force others into the submissive, defensive role; and hostile in that they see others as threatening and, therefore, choose to threaten them. Shame is continually avoided via rage toward others (and some self-pity, which serves to intensify the rage). This style clearly falls in the antisocial domain, as these clients tend to put their own needs (here, shame–avoidance and recreating a hostile, threatening, mutually rejecting environment) before the feelings of others.

These clients typically had one or two controlling parents who bullied, dominated and disciplined them into submission, teaching them in the process to expect the world to be angry and hostile and to respond in kind to this treatment. Moreover, the parents of these clients were usually so domineering that clients learned to avoid potential difficulties by always being on the aggressive, even in situations where no such behavior is elicited by others. The degree and overtness of aggression modeled by the parent(s) and other family members of these clients determine whether their active–dominant–hostile stance will take the form of rage, threats, or criticism (i.e., the most to the least hostile).

TABLE 5–1 Predominant Characteristics for Each Type of "Difficult" Client

Client Type	Predominant PA	Typical JC's & SSB's
Intimidating	Rage & shame-avoidance	"I'll get you before you get me." Aggression
Acting-out	Self-pity & rage covering shame	"Nobody cares about me." "I can do whatever I want." High emotion & disregard of others
Autonomous	Shame-avoidant	"I only like to do things my way." Noncritical rejection/disregard of others
Cultural/Gender Victim	Rage & self-pity to avoid shame	"No one understands me. I am a victim." Angry confrontation
Wealthy, Intimidating	Shame-avoidance, some anger	"Use others to get what you want." Callous & bullying
Uncooperative	Self-pity	"It's hopeless. I can't change & nobody can help me." Help-rejecting complaining
Mistrustful	High shame-avoidance, some self-pity	"People will take advantage of me if I open up to them." Suspicious & avoidant
Unempathic	Shame-avoidance, dissatisfaction & annoyance	"I am right in my actions & don't care about others." Superior & demeaning toward others
Passive–aggressive	Shame & anger	"I can't do things on my own but resent you for telling me what to do." Passive resistence

The Acting-Out Client experiences more deprivation and self-pity than the Intimidating Client, who is more often wracked with rage. As such, the Acting-Out Client still falls in the active–dominant–hostile quadrant but takes a less consistently hostile stance toward the therapist. If left unchallenged by the therapist, this client's histrionics frequently dominate the interpersonal process; however, while the Intimidating Client takes a consciously aggressive stance ("I'm pissed off at this therapist and won't let him get away with treating me this way"), the Acting-Out Client is often quite oblivious to the therapist's feelings and intentions, and indirectly, nonconsciously dominates the session via his/her dramatic and overpowering emotional intensity. While anger, shame and self-pity all bleed into the session for these clients, self-pity is often predominant, leading to prolonged crying jags.

These clients typically describe parents who were a combination of criiti-cal and nasty and weak. The criticizing/rejecting portion of this parenting combination led these clients to feel an overriding sense of being unlovable and self-pity and anger at having been unloved by their parents. These clients then play out this dynamic with the therapist, whom they perceive as uncaring, critical, and unavailable. The weak component of their parents engendered an emotional self-indulgence in these clients, who believe that they can express their feelings as often and as powerfully as they want, whenever they want. This belief can eventually push away the exasperated and drained therapist, thus confirming the client's belief that he/she is unlov-able and unloved.

Autonomous Clients can have the same effect on the therapist as Critical Clients in that they frequently reject what the therapist says and suggests. However, these clients tend to be less hostile and somewhat less active in their interpersonal stance, as their goal is not to intimidate the therapist with criti-cism but instead to keep a safe distance from the therapist (reaffirm independ-ence) by rejecting his or her comments. This rejection ("I disagree with you") is typically less hostile than that of the Critical Client ("You don't know what you're talking about") but more overt than that of the Passive–Aggressive Client ("That's a great idea but I probably won't do it").

These clients are accustomed to distance from another person and, there-fore, maneuver themselves interpersonally to maintain that distance and inde-pendence by rejecting what others have to offer. And so it is with the therapist as well. These clients tend to be less angry and aggressive than Intimidating and Passive–Aggressive Clients. While it is difficult for the therapist to get the Autonomous Client to experience and express emotions, such clients often feel ashamed of themselves since they have been unattended to by significant oth-ers; and they also feel sorry for themselves in that they did not receive the love and attention they would have liked.

Naturally, clients from different cultures and religions or with different gen-der identifications are not difficult per se and can fall anywhere along the friendly–hostile, dominant–submissive, and active–passive dimensions. How-ever, those clients in this category who are difficult use their difference from the therapist to feel enraged at him/her for ostensibly not understanding and accepting who they are, and consequently feel self-pity at supposedly being misunderstood or even "victimized." Here, too, appears the dynamic of cover-ing over one's shame by blaming another and feeling sorry for oneself. As with the Intimidating Client, this stance takes an active, dominant and hostile form, as these clients often actively and aggressively accuse the therapist of wrong-ing them. Shame and humiliation are avoided by trying to put the therapist on the defensive, so to speak. Many of these clients, like Intimidating Clients, had at least one, if not two, parents with a cruel, overly critical parenting style, engendering in these clients a great sense of shame and an interpersonal style that involves attacking before supposedly being attacked.

Finally, the only potentially difficult client who does not necessarily fall in the dominant–hostile quadrant is the Wealthy, Intimidating Client. These clients are active and dominant, but they are not necessarily hostile. As Millon's nonpathological variant of the antisocial personality is the forceful personality, so too can successful, strong clients be either aggressive to the point of hostility or strong, charismatic, and forceful but welcoming and attuned to others.

A therapist's negative reaction to the friendly variant of this client has more to do with who the therapist is than with the client. Therapists who are passive and submissive but hostile themselves may resent clients with a complementary personality pattern, and therapists who themselves are dominant and active may resent the competition. (Recall Berzins' [1977] conclusion that dominant–submissive pairings of clients and therapists are optimal.)

However, those Wealthy, Intimidating Clients who are hostile as well as active and dominant may present themselves in the antisocial mold as callous toward the therapist's feelings and as bullying—two-thirds the Intimidating Client mixed with one-third the Autonomous Client. Such clients themselves often had extremely critical, nasty parents, engendering an aggressive, sometimes suspicious, stance with others and a drive toward perfection and success at any price. Shame is avoided at all costs with a mixture of perfectionism and of anger and demandingness toward others. And the therapist, therefore, is turned into someone to be dominated and intimidated, as well as someone who must also be perfect in how he or she performs.

PASSIVE–DOMINANT–HOSTILE CLIENTS

All difficult clients in this quadrant of our circumplex use *passive power* in interpersonal situations. By not aggressively nor overtly challenging the therapist while also not complying with him or her and with the process of change, these clients try to hold the power in the session. While growing up, all of these clients learned that they could avoid shame and blame, as well as avoiding responsibility, by *not* doing something. Not responding to one's parent might lead to anger in the parent but also avoids exposing oneself to possible condemnation by the parent. Passive–dominant–hostile clients see the world as either shaming them or enraged at them, and they choose to avoid feeling shame via passivity while incurring the flustered, frustrated rage of others. In fact, this rage signals to the client with passive power that he or she has "won" and therefore does not risk being exposed to the other as incompetent or flawed.

Uncooperative Clients are driven primarily by self-pity and hopelessness. They truly believe that they cannot change, and there is nothing the therapist can say or do to alter this paralysis. Unlike Passive–Aggressive Clients, Uncooperative Clients are more overt in professing their hopelessness to the therapist. ("It's no use. I'll never change. Woe is me.")

Why do these clients seek out and continue in therapy? They seek it for the same reason that most people do: they are in emotional pain and often quite alone and lonely. They remain in therapy because their relationship with the therapist feels familiar to them (i.e., it is a security-seeking behavior). Most probably, Uncooperative Clients had whiny and complaining parents who were depressed and hopeless themselves and/or who made these clients feel stuck, powerless, and helpless themselves. Moreover, these parents probably expressed anger and resentment at having to care for their child when they were so wrapped up in their own feelings of despair and ineffectiveness.

Parents of these clients therefore also have a predominantly dominant–passive tendency themselves. They give two messages to their children repeatedly: "I cannot take care of you" and "I resent the fact that you may have needs too." As such, children of these parents are left believing that others cannot help them, longing for others to care for them as they never have, expecting anger and resentment if they were to ask for the attention and caretaking that they crave, and whining and complaining about their state in life.

And so it is, too, with the therapist. The Uncooperative Client expects to remain unfixed and unchanged but hopes beyond all hope that the therapist will fix or cure him/her. The client expresses hopelessness in the hope that the therapist will dispute this but knowing full well that the therapist will ultimately be unable to convince the client that change is possible. The therapist becomes the inadequate caretaker of the inadequate client. Some therapists who encounter this dynamic feel incompetent and/or enraged by the client's noncompliance and implicit dismissal of the therapist's abilities. This rage and frustration on the therapist's part, if directly or indirectly expressed, further serves to confirm the client's world-view: that seeking help and reassurance only leads to resentment and frustration on the other's part.

Mistrustful Clients (those who are low trusters rather than merely new to the word of therapy and self-exploration) also use passive power to avoid what they see as a potentially shaming interaction. These clients are more passive than Uncooperative ones; however, they avoid the therapist by not disclosing rather than by quite actively professing hopelessness. These clients typically had one of two types of parents. Some had a parent or parents who were domineering and inconsistent. (Not all cruel parents are inconsistent.) These parents would noncontingently lash out at the child, making him or her not only highly avoidant but also highly suspicious of interactions with the parent. As a result, in therapy, these individuals remain guarded, withdrawn and in some cases almost paranoid, as they are just waiting for the therapist to lash out in some way. They have been trained to be supremely shame- and anger-avoidant.

Behavioral psychology tells us that intermittent reinforcement is the slowest to be extinguished. Therefore, these clients remain guarded and suspicious for quite a long time, as the therapist's failure to lash out does not readily disconfirm these clients' expectations of being aggressed upon and shamed.

Other mistrustful clients might have had suspiciousness and withdrawal modeled to them by remote parents on a regular basis, as well as resentment by the parent(s) when the child tried to attain closeness. As such, these mistrustful clients work hard to repeat this dynamic with their therapist. Eventually, these clients' withdrawn stance may pull similar withdrawal from the therapist, as well as mild resentment and frustration, thus repeating the parent(s)' stance toward the mistrustful child.

Unempathic Clients fall into two subcategories, one of which actually falls in the active–dominant–hostile quadrant and the other in the passive–dominant–hostile quadrant. The former consists of the narcissistic client who is so unconcerned with the therapist's feelings that he or she will voice criticisms and cutting remarks toward the therapist and make unthinking demands of him or her. This often elicits anger from the therapist, much as would the comments of the critical Intimidating Client.

These Unempathic Clients most likely had parents with a nasty parenting style who frequently modeled taking a narcissistic position toward others. Made to feel demeaned and uncared for by these parents, the Unempathic Client learned to avoid his/her shame by turning it into superiority. The fear of being shamed by others is replaced with obliviousness to their needs and experiences. This stance often pulls disapproval and anger from others, and often mirrors the stance the nasty parent took toward the unempathic client as a child.

The second subtype of Unempathic Client, the passive–dominant–hostile version, is not necessarily passive in interacting with others (in fact, he or she can be quite actively exploitative), but his or her "difficultness" is not usually expressed actively and directly toward the therapist. This is the client who might describe cheating on an exam or lying to a partner or friend without understanding that these actions are morally wrong and without taking into account the impact of these actions on others.

While this client's out-of-session behaviors are certainly active, as well as dominant and hostile, the in-session negative impact on the therapist is indirect (i.e., an assault to the therapist's morality) and therefore passive. These clients typically have parents who are both similarly exploitative of others (who modeled cheating on one's partner without regret or embezzling money, for example) and anxious, victimized, and critical. Usually, one parent is the exploiter and the other the exploited (or passively unhappy with the former's exploitation of others). The client then may be playing out a familiar interpersonal scenario when he or she mentions a manipulation in passing and elicits disapproval, anxiety, and perhaps anger in the therapist. When the client then does not understand or agree with the therapist's reaction to his or her behavior, this interaction escalates.

Finally, Passive–Aggressive Clients technically oscillate between the passive–dominant and the passive–submissive quadrants, as they vacillate between feeling ashamed of themselves (as incompetent and inadequate) and dependent on others and enraged at this dependence and the supposed power of others. When the Passive–Aggressive Client is being passive–submissive (agreeing with the therapist, asking the therapist for advice, etc.), the therapist does not experience this client as difficult. However, when this client flexes his or her passive power and does not comply with the therapist nor attempt to change in any way—that is, when the client is passive–dominant—then the therapist may experience him/her as difficult and disagreeable. Naturally, the therapist only experiences this client positively when he/she is behaving passive–submissively at the outset of therapy. Once the therapist catches on to the passive–active vacillation, then he/she knows better than to feel complacent when the client is behaving passive–submissively.

These clients describe having self-sacrificing parent(s) (most commonly an overprotective parent with or without the need to be taken care of by the child) who frequently whined and complained. As such, the Passive–Aggressive as a child comes to doubt his/her ability to be self-sufficient and successful in life (shame) but also develops rage at the parent who kept him/her from doing what he/she wanted while growing up. Similar feelings are experienced toward the therapist, with anger expressed mostly through not doing something (missing sessions, showing up late, not following through with suggestions, etc.) rather than actively.

A DIFFICULT THERAPIST NO MORE

In the Introduction, we stated that clients are not difficult; therapists are. In light of our discussion in this and previous chapters, it can be seen that therapists can be difficult either because they are inexperienced in dealing effectively with hostile–dominant clients and/or because, due to their own personality styles and emotional setpoints, they are dominated by some combination of shame, rageful anger, and self-pity. These therapists may be hostile–dominant themselves, or perhaps they are submissive, which would certainly predispose them to being overpowered by more dominant clients.

Muran, Samstag, Jilton, Batchelder, and Winston (1992a,b) found that the dominant–submissive dimension, rather than the friendly–hostile dimension, of the circumplex was most predictive of therapeutic outcome. Moreover, Muran et al. (1994) concluded that clients' hostile–dominant behaviors predicted a poor alliance and that friendly–submissive client behaviors predicted a positive alliance. These findings offer empirical support for the common theme running throughout our types of "difficult" clients.

Therapists who were raised in families with a primarily submissive and/or friendly stance may be particularly inexperienced at interacting with hostile–dominant clients. They may react to the sometimes aggressive confrontation of these clients by becoming confused or scared, or with an anger that they have not learned to understand, channel, or express effectively. The "emotional vocabulary" of these therapists' families simply did not prepare them for hostile–dominant interactions, and the foibles of their own personality styles may surface in an unhelpful manner when confronted with what for them is a novel and difficult situation.

Therapists who were raised in primarily hostile–dominant families themselves may turn many clients, even relatively therapist-friendly ones, into difficult clients by dint of the therapists' unwelcoming interpersonal stance. Active–hostile–dominant therapists may be overcontrolling, verbally aggressive (as opposed to challenging), and highly critical of clients, while passive–hostile–dominant therapists may be so nondirective and withdrawn as to be unhelpful to clients. Additionally, the latter may be passive–aggressive, internally critical of clients, and resenting all the "hard work" they have to do when it is the clients themselves "who should know better and work harder." These therapists, whether more active or passive, tend to personalize the therapy (i.e., view a client's reenacting his/her usual interpersonal stance as a personal attack or as an interference to the therapy) and are ruled by shame, rage, and self-pity in their perceptions of the client–therapist relationship.

Moreover, therapists with an emotional setpoint that is highly discrepant from that of a client may also not know how to respond to the client's attempts to use the therapeutic relationship to reestablish his or her familiar setpoint. Therapists who come from emotionally muted family backgrounds, for example, may feel scared, confused, and paralyzed when faced with a client's extreme rage, self-pity, shame, sadness, anxiety, etc. Unintentional attempts by the client to engage the therapist in this level of emotionality may be experienced by the therapist as threatening, off-putting, or highly unfamiliar.

Conversely, therapists who come from relatively emotional families of origin may be thrown off by a client with a significantly muted setpoint. The therapist may end up coming across like an emotional "bull in a china shop" and may scare away, inhibit, or covertly anger the reserved client.

We believe, therefore, that the training of therapists should explicitly address how to understand and interact therapeutically with hostile–dominant clients and with clients with emotional setpoints different from one's own. This training would not only necessitate an understanding of these challenging clients, but would also help therapists to understand how their own personality styles and emotional setpoints interface with those of their clients—that is, what feelings and reactions get stirred up in the therapist by a clients' hostile–dominant stance. Additionally, therapists would need to learn how to manage their affect and its influence on their behavior in therapy, much as we teach clients how to manage unhelpful personotypic affect and justifying cognitions and alter longstanding maladaptive interpersonal patterns. (Refer to chapter 8 for a discussion of this.) In learning how to understand and manage personotypic affect and associated cognitions and behaviors, the therapist will be able to teach this to his or her clients as well.

All therapists who practice CAT must understand their own personotypic affects and emotional setpoints, especially as they influence interactions with difficult clients. Therapists should ask themselves the following questions to determine dominant personotypic affect and their own emotional setpoints:

1. What was the emotional climate of my family when I was growing up? What do I remember about my father's and my mother's predominant emotions?

2. What was the emotional "pitch" or intensity level in my household? Quiet, loud, highly emotional, or unemotional? Which feelings usually were expressed (and felt) loudly and which usually were expressed (and felt) quietly? How did my family maintain its typical emotional pitch or intensity level?

3. In what ways do I emotionally resemble my father? My mother? How did I learn to be like each of them?

4. What familiar feelings do I remember as a child growing up? What was my own emotional pitch or intensity level like?

5. Was there something that I routinely did not get from my mother and/or father that I wanted, and how did that typically make me feel? Was there something that I routinely did get from my mother and/or father that I did not want, and how did that typically make me feel?

6. What feelings do I seem to return to when I feel stressed? What is their typical level of intensity?

7. Conversely, what feelings do I seem to return to after I feel really good, and what is their typical level of intensity?

Once the therapist has a feel for his or her own personotypic affect and emotional setpoint, he or she should then identify typical justifying cognitions and security-seeking behaviors, since they may well be played out in the therapy relationship by the therapist. Questions the therapist can ask of him/herself include:

1. What do I typically think of myself, of what I do, and who I am? What are my typical thoughts about my role in life?

2. What do I typically think of others and the world in general? What do I think of how others treat me and of how I treat them?

3. Is there something that I always want from others but do not get? Is there something that I always get from others but do not want? What is my role in this?

4. What do I think of hard work and responsibility? Do I honestly enjoy working hard, resent it, or vacillate between the two?

5. What is my characteristic way of relating to others? Am I usually the dominant or submissive one; the friendly or withdrawn or angry one; the active or passive one? Is this consistent in relationships, in friendships, at work? If not, how much does this vary and how?

Additionally, the therapist may find it helpful to identify how he or she was parented. This may give him or her insight into his or her personality style, as well as into how he or she might relate to the client. More specifically, does a client with a personality style similar to one's parent(s) more strongly activate the therapist's personotypic affect, justifying cognitions, and security-seeking behaviors? How does the therapist's own personality style, molded in part by how he or she was parented, affect the client?

Finally, given all of the above, the therapist should ask him/herself the following additional questions:

1. What type of people in general do I find difficult or disagreeable, and why?

2. How do I typically react to and deal with such people? How do they react to me as a result?

3. How do I typically react to and deal with hostile–dominant people? How do they react to me as a result?

Once the therapist has answered these questions, then he or she is ready to work with difficult clients, to see these clients as not particularly difficult to work with, after all, and to do CAT without overpersonalizing what clients say and do, without being ruled by shame, self-pity, and anger, and without being judgmental or blaming toward who clients are and what they do in therapy.

SUMMARY

The following points were discussed in this chapter:

1. "Difficult" clients fall almost exclusively in the hostile–dominant quadrants of our personality style circumplex. These clients can, therefore, be

either active–dominant–hostile or passive–dominant–hostile (with "passive power").

2. Active–dominant–hostile clients include:

(a) Intimidating Clients, who bully the therapist to avoid feeling shame;

(b) Acting-Out Clients, who openly and self-indulgently express shame, rageful anger, and self-pity, which often pulls rejection or annoyance from the therapist;

(c) Autonomous Clients, who distance themselves from the therapist and from feeling shame by rejecting the therapist;

(d) Angry "Victims", who use anger and self-pity to avoid underlying shame;

(e) Unempathic Clients (first subtype), who are narcissistically critical, demanding, and unthoughtful toward the therapist;

(f) Some Wealthy, Intimidating Clients, who are oblivious of the feelings of the therapist, bullying, and overly demanding. The friendly variant of this client is only difficult for therapists who feel sorry for themselves and not-good-enough (ashamed) and who therefore envy and make themselves feel intimidated by this client;

3. Passive–dominant–hostile clients include:

(a) Uncooperative Clients, who cling to self-pity, resentment, and hopelessness, much as their parents did;

(b) Mistrustful Clients, who avoid being shamed by the therapist by withdrawing;

(c) Unempathic Clients (second subtype), who pull disapproval from the therapist by unempathically exploiting others;

(d) Passive–Aggressive Clients, who fluctuate between compliance and noncompliance with the therapist, the former's passivity pulling some therapists to be overly directive and the latter's rebelliousness pulling the therapist to become annoyed and/or distancing;

4. Therapists must therefore learn how to interact therapeutically with hostile–dominant clients by addressing the facets of their own personality styles which may be poor matches for such clients. Therapists who are submissive–friendly, dominant–hostile themselves, or who have emotional setpoints that are markedly discrepant from the client's, may have particular difficulty working with dominant–hostile clients;

5. Therapists must understand their own personotypic affect, emotional setpoint, justifying cognitions, and security-seeking behaviors, and they must understand how these characteristics interplay with all clients and especially with dominant–hostile ones.

PART II

Cognitive Appraisal Therapy

CHAPTER 6

The CAT Assessment

This chapter describes how we typically assess and formulate a treatment approach for clients from a CAT perspective. We use a very basic model for representing the various components of personality with which we work in therapy. This ABCDE model (see Fig. 6–1) is similar to some others (e.g., Lazarus, 1976) in that it ties together the affective (A), behavioral/interpersonal (B), cognitive (C), developmental (D), and environmental (E) contributors to the client's personality. It is also therefore compatible with models from other orientations, as these models either are composed of all the aforementioned personality contributors or emphasize some of these variables. What is unique to our model is not the personality contributors themselves, but the content of the contributors (refer to Fig. 6–2). Certainly, this content can be integrated with or added to that of other approaches as well.

All of the variables represented in Fig. 6–2 need to be assessed by the therapist. When integrated with one another, they yield the client's particular personality style, its content and expression, and they have implications for treatment goals, potential interpersonal difficulties/challenges for the therapist, and the most helpful therapeutic stance that the clinician should take. Before turning to the ABCDE assessment, we will address a few related diagnostic issues.

Affect
Behavior
Development
Cognition
Environment

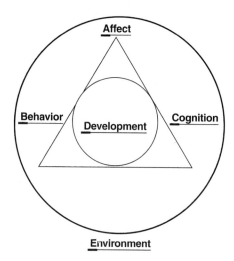

FIGURE 6–1 Basic components of the CAT assessment.

AFFECT
• personotypic affect
• emotional setpoint
• anxiety (either as security-seeking emotion or as rage)
• situational/reactive feelings
• defense against shame
BEHAVIOR
• security-seeking behavior
• defense against shame
• interpersonal stance:
(1) friendly–hostile
(2) active–passive
(3) dominant–submissive
DEVELOPMENT
• parents' styles
• biochemistry & temperament
COGNITION
• justifying cognitions
• personal rules of living
ENVIRONMENT
• stressors
• events reinforcing ABC

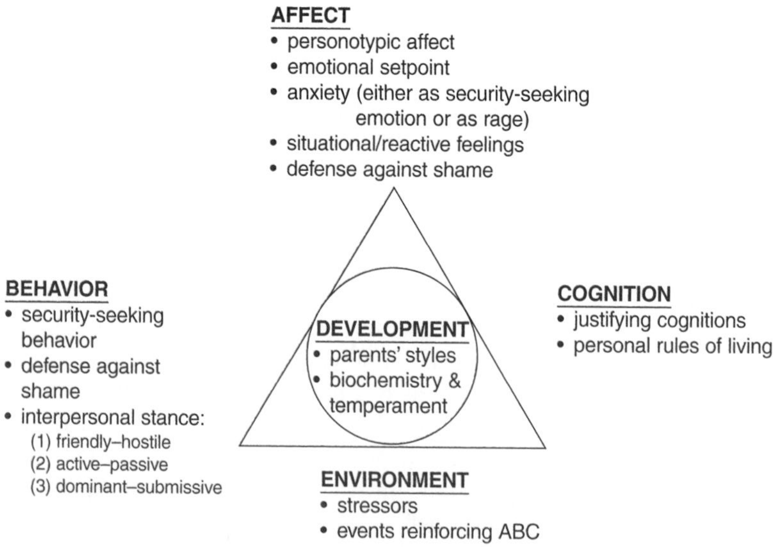

FIGURE 6–2 Detailed components of the CAT assessment

DIAGNOSING ON AXIS I AND/OR AXIS II

Each criterion in DSM–IV describes a set of behaviors that can serve as the target for intervention (assuming the client displays behaviors consistent with the criterion). All diagnoses in DSM–IV are described as more or less overt behaviors without psychodynamic or other vocabulary, theory, and assumptions (except in a few categories). Further, in addition to the current clinical condition, the longstanding patterns of behavior, thinking, and emoting that both precede and follow an acute episode are classified using criteria that are, with some exceptions, theoretically neutral (on Axis II of the multiaxial diagnostic system, these are personality disorders). Even with revisions, the classifications are not perfect. However, they call attention to personality traits as predisposing factors in psychiatric disorders and to dealing with the person and not just the person's symptoms.

A "disordered" personality consists of relatively enduring traits that subvert one's adjustment to life's circumstances. The criteria emphasize interference with the pursuit of social relationships and work-related activities. If a person encounters conflict on the job or has difficulty keeping one, this evidence points to a possible disorder of personality. If a person does not get along with others, or is indiscriminately angry or fearful, or avoids social and family interactions, this too is evidence of a personality disorder.

To make a diagnosis of personality disorder, it is necessary to eliminate certain other possible causes of interference in love and work. As in so much of medicine, the procedure is to rule out other causes, especially acute or transient ones. For example, if depression or anxiety temporarily interferes with work or family relationships, these symptoms rather than personality traits suggest a diagnosis on Axis I (current clinical condition). The key to diagnosis on Axis II is how long the person has displayed a certain psychological pattern.

At times, it is not easy to make such discriminations, but the same statement can be made of other symptoms. For example, paranoid ideas may indicate schizophrenia, bipolar disorder, organic brain syndrome, or a central feature of personality. Which is it? The diagnosis depends on additional information. If there are indications of thought disorder in addition to paranoid features, schizophrenia is indicated; if there is evidence of mood disorder, major depression or bipolar disorder is likely; signs of cognitive impairment point to organicity as the likely diagnosis. If none of these is present, and delusional disorder can be ruled out, and if the suspiciousness and guardedness is a longstanding pattern, paranoid personality disorder is the likely diagnosis.

In practice, diagnosing a patient on Axis I or Axis II is not an either–or choice. We believe that, *when there is an Axis I disorder, there is probably a diagnosable personality disorder as well. The reverse is not necessarily true—there can be evidence of personality disturbance without an Axis I disorder.* There are at least two reasons for this.

First, the person may not show any symptoms that can be classified on Axis I. Second, when the client recovers, he or she may continue to exhibit thoughts and behaviors that are consistent with Axis II criteria. Indeed, this is exactly what is expected in, say, a successfully treated schizophrenic episode; the client very likely will continue to exhibit traits consistent with schizoid or schizotypal personality disorder. These diagnostic categories were created, after all, to describe people who no longer actively hallucinate or speak of delusions, but who continue to appear odd or eccentric and live isolated from others.

THE AXIS I MISTAKE

We place many Axis I-type presenting problems in the context of an Axis II-type personality style. We don't consider all clients to have an Axis II personality disorder, but we do believe that all clients have a personality, and so we describe them in terms of the personality styles outlined in chapter 4. It is our wish that, to be helpful to clinicians, DSM–V will not only have an optional Axis II diagnosis if criteria are met for a personality *disorder,* but also a mandatory Axis IIa diagnosis for one's personality *style* even when criteria are not met for an Axis II diagnosis.

We believe that presenting problems such as depression, anxiety disorders, obsessive–compulsive disorder, chronic fatigue syndrome, attention deficit disorder, post-traumatic stress disorder and, in some cases, even abuse are merely symptoms that do not explain what causes and maintains these symptoms. This is not to say that we do not believe in understanding Axis I symptoms or in exploring the client's experience of such symptoms, but we almost always place these symptoms in the broader epigenetic context of personality style. For example, we clearly acknowledge distinct causes of depression: one person's depressive episode may have a heavy biochemical component; another's may be reactive to the death of a parent; and yet another's may result from longstanding interpersonal and emotional maladaptive patterns.

Superficially, it would seem that only the third person's depression is influenced by his or personality style. However, the way in which persons one and two react to and cope with their depression—how they *use* that depression— is also influenced by their particular personality styles. Person one might say that fighting her depressive symptoms has only made her a stronger person; or she may go around moaning to others that it is unfair that she must bear the burden of depression while everyone else is running around happy and care-free. Similarly, person two may acknowledge that he will have to go through the process of grieving for some time and then get on with his life; or he may hold on to a self-pitying rage for the rest of his life that his deceased parent deserted him. Thus, one's personality style plays a significant role in causing, shaping, maintaining, and/or making sense out of Axis I-type symptoms, and it is, therefore, critical that every client's personality style be assessed as soon as possible by the therapist. (Using the CAT method, it should only take a clinician at most a few sessions to do this.)

Additionally, what is termed "depression" really denotes an absence of feeling (an emotional "numbness"), an absence of energy and of positive, encouraging thoughts. Depression, therefore, may be a protective shutting down of one's body and emotional system when the individual is faced with extremely painful, powerful negative feelings and situations. In terms of the fight-or-flight reaction to aversive stimuli, depression may be a hardwired, internal flight from painful, overpowering stimuli. As such, depression is not a cause of—but a reaction to—other fundamental difficulties. It is those difficulties that must be understood by the client and therapist if change is to occur. Working with the depression per se will not yield much useful, long-term change.

We have already mentioned that we reframe anxiety either as misunderstood rage or as a security-seeking emotion, anticipating and actually reinvoking shame, self-pity, and, in fewer instances, anger. We will discuss this further in the Assessing Affect section of this chapter. Suffice it to say that, while we acknowledge that anxiety disorders and panic attacks certainly exist and can be diminished with medication and symptom-focused interventions such as relaxation training, they will not go away permanently and without medication unless they are understood by the client in a new way related to his or her particular personality style, emotional setpoint, and personotypic affect.

While the thoughts and behaviors of obsessive–compulsive disorder certainly exist, we have found that compulsive behaviors almost always serve two functions: (1) they help to soothe the negative personotypic affect (usually shame) associated with obsessive thoughts (which are very strong justifying cognitions); and (2) they are security-seeking in that the client usually feels quite embarrassed or ashamed of his or her compulsions. An example highlights this:

> Whenever 35-year-old Dina felt that she was an incompetent mother, she would ruminate self-critically for hours, lock herself in her room, and sink into a depression. This happened at least a few times per week, and Dina acknowledged that, before she became a mother, she would do the same thing with other aspects of her life ("I am a bad wife, a bad daughter," etc.).
>
> After one of these "depressed" episodes, Dina would then clean her entire apartment two or three times. This would distract her from these thoughts of incompetence and soothe the associated painful shame she felt. However, Dina would then criticize herself for using valuable time that she could have been spending with her children in order to clean, and this started the cycle of shameful thoughts all over again.

It is clear in this example that the obsessions are really shame-evoking justifying cognitions and that Dina's compulsive cleaning not only calms her down temporarily but ultimately stirs up her shame even more. For Dina to truly understand why she acts to shame herself, and then for her to begin breaking this habit, she must relate this pattern to aspects of her personality style and how she herself was raised.

It has been our experience that people with obsessive–compulsive tendencies tend to experience the shame that comes from being overly dependent on parents and spouses, and they have not learned how to soothe their negative feelings adequately. They, therefore, experience shame frequently and use compulsive means to diminish this affect since they did not learn to do so noncompulsively in their families of origin. Clients with this picture usually fall in the dependent or dependent–borderline spectrum.

We also believe that attention-deficit disorder (ADD), such a popular diagnosis at present, is often not a useful diagnosis. Interestingly, the most common treatment for ADD in children consists of a concentration-enhancing drug such as Ritalin and behavior therapy employed by the parents (Barkley, 1990). However, these medications have been noted to enhance attention and concentration in a non-ADD population as well, and an identical behavioral approach is also often the treatment of choice for non-ADD oppositional–defiant children. If there is really no specific treatment protocol for ADD above and beyond medication, then does it actually exist? Some therapists, such as Armstrong (1995), believe that it does not, and he suggests reframing attentional difficulties in terms of other variables, such as poor parenting and the child's having acquired poor self-confidence, poor impulse control, an impaired ability to organize him-herself and his/her surroundings, and/or poor emotional and behavioral self-control. Armstrong's 50 therapeutic interventions are more pointedly targeted toward these characteristics than those of many therapists who just treat an entity termed "ADD."

Jonathan has also noted in his psychological evaluations of children and teenagers with a potential diagnosis of ADD (the majority of his testing referrals) that almost all of these examinees' problems stem from an often fairly subtle learning difficulty or a combination of learning difficulties in conjunction with the emotional turmoil that has arisen from these undiagnosed difficulties throughout the years. Years of being called lazy or fearing that one is stupid, in addition to the frustration of repeatedly failing in spite of making great efforts to achieve, coalesce to make the child or teenager anxious and avoidant in the classroom and while doing homework—and this understandable tendency most often surfaces as attention and concentration difficulties. Who wouldn't have difficulty attending and concentrating on tasks that make him or her feel inferior to peers, stupid, and intensely frustrated and helpless? Again, ADD may often be nothing more than symptoms of a more complex and subtle interaction between cognitive deficits and their impact upon one's self-image and self-confidence.

Therefore, *how* the child and his/her parents understand and cope with problems that are labeled as ADD become quite significant. Does one feel sorry for him-herself and helpless to concentrate unless taking Ritalin, or does one believe that he/she can improve his/her concentration through effort? Some clients cling to diagnoses such as ADD as an excuse not to do the work of therapy or take responsibility for change, while others see it simply as a problem to be solved. Again, the client's personality style often becomes more significant in treating such difficulties as ADD than the existence of the ADD itself.

Chronic fatigue syndrome (CFS) is another supposed diagnosis used by many self-pitying dependent clients to justify not being responsible for their lives and instead being cared for by others. Showalter's (1997) review of the research on CFS finds no clear support for an organic cause of the syndrome. She cites a review (MacLean & Wessley, 1994) of all articles published on CFS between 1980 and 1994. This review found that while only 31% of articles in medical journals favored organic over psychological explanations for CFS, 69% of the articles in newspapers and women's magazines supported organic explanations. Showalter concludes that "the majority of doctors and researchers maintain that CFS is a psychological syndrome, *and* that its symptoms and effects are real" (p. 130). She goes on to hypothesize that CFS is a modern version of hysteria.

We have mostly had reports of CFS, as well as of Epstein–Barr Virus, Lyme disease, and connective tissue disorder, from self-pitying, responsibility-avoidant, dependent, sometimes passive–aggressive clients; that is, from clients falling in the passive–submissive personality domain. We are, therefore, more convinced that having CFS and its sibling diseases helps one to avoid responsibility, avoid the potential of failing, and therefore avoid the possibility of feeling ashamed and embarrassed. Or, similarly, it allows one to work hard and then, feeling "burned-out," "overwhelmed," and sorry for oneself, it provides an excuse for dropping out and avoiding work. It also allows one to be taken care of and repeat the dependent interpersonal pattern of one's childhood. CFS is, in essence, a security-seeking behavior. However, if the therapist stops at the CFS diagnosis and fails to reframe CFS in terms of its security-seeking function and the client's passive–submissive personality style, the CFS will not disappear and the individual will continue to be passive, somaticizing, and dependent.

It appears that abuse and personality style may be intertwined. Herman, Perry, and van der Kolk (1989), for example, found that severe trauma was reported significantly more by borderline subjects than by subjects with other diagnoses. Sixty-eight percent of their borderline sample reported having been sexually abused and 71% physically abused. Herman and van der Kolk (1987) and others (e.g., McCann and Pearlman, 1990; Westen, 1991) have concluded that early severe traumatization may significantly influence personality development and may be instrumental in the formation of borderline personality disorder.

However, the question must be asked: When the onset, frequency, and severity of the abuse are held constant, why do some abused or traumatized individuals *not* experience crippling long-term symptoms while others do?

After all, a recent meta-analysis performed by Rind, Tromovitch, and Bauserman (1998) has found no significant difference in long-term distress and disturbance between college students who recalled being sexually abused as children and those who did not.

The answer to this question is in the personality style of the individual. McCann and Pearlman (1990) cite these four "self capacities" as being instrumental to how one reacts to a traumatic experience: the ability to tolerate and regulate strong affects without fragmentation or acting-out; the ability to be alone without feeling lonely or empty; the ability to calm oneself through processes of self-soothing; and the ability to moderate self-loathing in the face of criticism or guilt. The more of these abilities one has, therefore, the more one can rebound from abusive experiences.

Certain personality styles may, by their very nature, cause individuals to be lacking in McCann and Pearlman's self capacities. A submissive–passive person, for instance, may thrive on having others calm him down and, therefore, may be poor at soothing himself and moderating self-loathing. An active–submissive person, like the histrionic, may thrive on acting-out and not modulating her affect in order to attract others' attention. As such, certain clients may have experienced abuse but this becomes only a small part of the therapy for them, while others focus on the abuse as central to all of their difficulties in life. It is their personality style (how they perceive the abuse and to what ends they consequently use that experience) that determines the effects of the abuse.

This is similar for those with post-traumatic stress disorder (PTSD) as well. It is well documented that, among other variables (see van der Kolk, 1987, for a review of these), there is a strong relationship between preexisting personality characteristics which affect one's coping abilities and chronic PTSD symptoms (Brill, 1967; Burgess & Holstrom, 1974; Horowitz, 1976). Again, it is not the symptoms per se that need to be treated, but the personality that gives rise to the symptom formation and the inability to cope with life's adversities.

THE AXIS I EXCUSE

We now want to highlight another major pitfall of the therapist's focusing solely on Axis I symptomatology: *reinforcing the client's use of his or her symptoms as an excuse to avoid responsibility and to avoid addressing shame-based issues.* Many clients *reify* their symptoms. All emotional and interpersonal difficulties are framed by them as an "illness" that seems to be out of the client's control. It is almost as if the symptom were a separate entity with a life of its own. We often hear statements by these clients such as: "I can't possibly work so hard because I have chronic fatigue syndrome," "The OCD makes me unable to socialize as often as I'd like to," "The depression makes me fall asleep all the time," or "I'm an adult with ADD. I can't possibly pay attention at work. My job requirements will have to be simplified and I'm basically not responsible for any mistakes I make."

Not only do such clients use symptoms to avoid taking responsibility for their thoughts, feelings, and actions, as well as for changing them, but they also use their symptoms to pull sympathy from others and to get taken care of by them. "I have [fill in the blank with any of the above Axis I diagnoses]. I'm not responsible for my actions. Therefore, you must take care of me." Therapists who adhere solely to an Axis I model of diagnosis and then place all of their emphasis on one set of symptoms often reinforce their clients' self-image as helpless and dependent. Additionally, some therapists tend to view *everything* in terms of the disorder they specialize in treating and fail to place the "entity" they are treating in the larger context of personality style and the interpersonal message of the symptoms (e.g., "You must take care of me"; "I'm not responsible for my actions").

Additionally, reifying one's Axis I symptoms avoids having to acknowledge, confront, and resolve painful shame-based issues. The biochemical model for Axis I symptomatology has become increasingly popular over the past decade or so as more medications have been developed that address more specific symptoms (e.g., Zoloft reportedly alleviates not only depressive symptoms but also anxiety). As such, OCD, ADD, etc. are seen as biochemically based and, therefore, out of the control of the client (see Borden & Brown, 1989).

Thus, clients can cling to their diagnostic labels as a way of ceasing to intro-spect and work to change: "I am compulsive because I was born with OCD," instead of "I deal with painful, shameful feelings about myself, which come from how my parents treated me, by using compulsive behaviors to calm down my shame and the related rage and self-pity." The former belief uses circular reasoning and renders the client helpless and passive. The second offers a causal explanation which gives the client an understanding of what he or she can change and how to do it. However, there is risk in owning one's behaviors: one must explore and work to alleviate one's painful shame.

Therapists who share in the reification of the clients' Axis I symptoms help clients to become shame-avoidant, passive, and dependent, as well as narrow-minded in the way they understand their problems. In this way, a form of ther-apeutic co-dependence occurs. As CAT is dedicated to working with clients' personality styles, we now return to our ABCDE model of personality to show how we assess the whole person and not just an isolated set of relatively mean-ingless symptoms.

ASSESSING AFFECT

As can be seen in Fig. 6-2, the A in our ABCDE personality model stands for affect, and it is composed of the various emotional characteristics that we described in Part I of this book. Two basic types of emotions are typically described by clients during sessions, those related to personotypic affect and those that are genuine in-the-moment reactions to current events. Witness the following conversation between a client receiving help with his parenting skills and his therapist:

> Client: So I told my 4-year-old son Brian that we could not buy any candy in the store because it was right before lunchtime and we have a rule in our family: no sweets before a meal. I told this to Brian before we went into the store to buy cat food, so he knew what the deal was. But when I was at the cash register, he repeatedly asked me for candy and, getting annoyed, I repeatedly told him no. So far so good. Then, he kicked me really hard in the knee, and I tell you it really hurt, so I got angry and told him he would have a time-out outside the store after we paid for the cat food. Brian then yelled, "You're a bad daddy; I hate you," in front of everybody in the store.
>
> Therapist: How did you feel when he said that?
>
> Cl: I felt mortified and enraged. Humiliated, too, like now everybody in the store was thinking that my kid hates me; I'm a terrible father; and my kid's rotten behavior in the store was proof of what a lousy father I am. I admit that, when we left the store, not only did I give Brian a time-out, but I didn't talk to him for practically the rest of the day.
>
> Th: So you felt humiliated and ashamed of yourself as a father in front of the people in the store, and angry at your son for causing you to feel that way.
>
> Cl: Yeah, I guess so, and I took it out on poor Brian by giving him the silent treatment for the rest of the day, just like my mother used to do to my pop when she was upset. I'm glad I gave Brian the time-out. It was definitely appropriate, but I guess the silent treatment was not necessary.

The client's annoyance at his son's repeatedly asking him for candy and his anger at his son for kicking him in the knee are normal in-the-moment emotional reactions to the situation (i.e., inflicted physical pain leads to anger). However, the client becomes aware of the fact that his son's reaction—quite appropriate for a 4-year-old, even if not desirable or acceptable—caused him to feel more humiliated, ashamed, and then enraged than was called for in the situation. And the client's behavioral reaction, his silent treatment of his son, was out of proportion to the situation. The client also becomes aware that this reaction is rooted in how his parents behaved. This overreaction, the family history of this reaction, and feelings of humiliation, shame, and rage are all signals to the therapist that personotypic affect (and the emotional setpoint, security-seeking behaviors, justifying cognitions, etc.) are all afoot here. Therefore, the therapist must become adept not only at sniffing out personotypic affect but also at differentiating personotypic affect from normal, in-the-moment, usually adaptive emotional reactions.

Greenberg and Safran (1987) differentiate primary from secondary emotions. The former are genuine, powerful, longstanding feelings which, often out of the client's awareness, nevertheless dictate his or her longstanding interpersonal patterns. The latter are defensive coping strategies or responses to primary emotions; that is, they arise to obscure or diminish the pain that awareness of primary emotions might bring. For example, anger at someone else (a secondary emotion) might be less painful and threatening to experience than would be the underlying sadness and despair (primary emotions).

CAT does not quite make the primary–secondary emotion distinction, but it does assume that most negative emotions that are not simple, in-the-moment reactions to an aversive stimulus are expressions of personotypic affect. That is, shame, rageful anger, and self-pity are the personotypic affects underlying all longstanding negative feelings. Other feelings are either variations of these personotypic affects (e.g., humiliation or embarrassment for shame; annoyance or resentment for rageful anger; deprivation for self-pity) or they are actually these personotypic affects described with other labels. Not only is it difficult for clients to fully understand longstanding affect, but they also often use words other than shame, anger, or self-pity to describe what they are feeling (e.g., "anxious" or "upset" for anger; "victimized" for self-pity; "like a bad person" for shame). This can result either from not having the emotional vocabulary to describe their feelings with specificity; that certain words were used in their families of origin to describe feelings (e.g., "bothered" for enraged or even "angry" for ashamed); or from not having read our work(!). As such, it is the therapist's job during the assessment to listen for underlying shame, anger, and self-pity, to elicit its description from the client when possible, and/or to translate in his or her mind certain emotional descriptors used by the client into shame, anger, and self-pity.

Table 6–1 lists questions that the therapist should answer during the first few sessions to determine both the client's predominant personotypic affect and the emotional setpoint. The therapist can answer these questions either by asking them directly during sessions when appropriate (and, hopefully, not in a formulaic or cookbook fashion) or by deriving many of them from the client's own narrative.

CAT rejects various Axis I diagnoses since they are not clinically useful and reframes them in terms of personotypic affect. When a client presents as depressed, the CAT therapist certainly assesses the nature, history, and extent of the depression and checks to see if there is a family history of depression, etc. The CAT therapist also assesses the impact of the depression on the client's past and current functioning. However, while there are clear physiological manifestations of depression, such as low energy, abnormal sleeping and eating habits, and predominantly negative, sometimes hopeless thoughts (Beck et al., 1979), depression is also characterized by a numbness of positive feelings,

TABLE 6–1

Areas to Assess in Determining a Client's Predominant Personotypic Affect and Emotional Setpoint

(1) What was the emotional climate of the client's family of origin? What does the client recall about his/her father's and mother's predominant emotions?

(2) What was the emotional "pitch" or intensity level in the client's household? Quiet, loud, highly emotional, or unemotional? Which feelings usually were expressed (and felt) loudly and which usually were expressed (and felt) quietly? How did the client's family of origin maintain its typical emotional "pitch" or intensity level?

(3) In what ways does the client emotionally resemble his/her father? His/her mother? How did the client learn to be like each of them?

(4) What familiar feelings does the client remember having as a child growing up? What was the client's own emotional "pitch" or intensity level like?

(5) Was there something that the client routinely did not get from his/her mother and/or father that he/she wanted, and how did that typically make the client feel? Was there something that the client routinely did get from his/her mother and/or father that he/she did not want, and how did that typically make the client feel?

(6) What are the emotional climates of the client's current family environment (e.g., partner, children) and work setting? Are they similar to that of his/her family of origin, and how so?

(7) What feelings does the client return to when he/she feels stressed? What is their typical level of intensity?

(8) Conversely, what feelings does the client return to after he/she feels really good, and what is their typical level of intensity?

(9) What feelings does the client typically show during therapy, either directly or indirectly? What is the emotional climate of the therapy relationship? What feelings and reactions to the client does the therapist have that he/she may not typically experience with people in general?

---

or anhedonia (Joiner, 1996; Joiner, Catanzaro, & Laurent, 1996). As such, to not explore *beyond* this apparent lack of emotions—to not understand that depression is a defense against and/or a result of other negative emotions and interpersonal patterns—will leave the therapist without the key to helping the client diminish his/her depression and related symptoms.

As we have previously discussed, a client's experience of anxiety can either signify that the client is really feeling anger that he or she does not understand or is not willing to accept, or that the client's anxiety is a security-seeking emotion. In families where it is unacceptable to express or even experience anger, clients may instead label this feeling as anxiety and even experience it as such. By exploring the thoughts associated with a client's panic attacks, we have frequently found that these panic attacks are really rage attacks. We have noted that panic attacks often occur in clients who are dependent and/or passive–aggressive, suggesting that, for them, the overt expression of anger would threaten the closeness of their attachments to others. Conversely, then, these clients feel that it is less risky to their dependence to express anger as anxiety.

Alternatively, anxiety can be the emotion associated with thoughts predicting scenarios which will lead to situations where the client might experience shame (or humiliation or embarrassment), self-pity, and, to a lesser extent, anger. Here, anxiety not only serves as a signal that such an event may occur, but it actually evokes negative personotypic affect and can therefore be seen as security-seeking in nature. We do not argue with findings that there are physiological shifts specific to anxiety, such as physiological hyperarousal (see Joiner, Steer, Beck, Schmidt, Rudd, & Catanzaro, 1999). We simply believe that anxiety serves to rekindle negative personotypic affect.

The CAT therapist must not, therefore, accept a client's anxiety, depression (or many other Axis I symptoms) at face value. The therapist must elicit other associated feelings that lead up to or coexist with anxiety or depression. In this way, the therapist can determine the relationship between the client's anxiety and his or her personotypic affect, which sets the stage for reframing anxiety or depression in terms of personotypic affect for the client during the CAT therapy.

Finally, in assessing the client's particular affective characteristics, the CAT therapist must examine how the client copes with his or her shame. Does the client deny his or her shame versus experiencing it? Does the client maintain an internal (that is, self-critical) locus of blame for his or her shame versus an external locus of blame (i.e., the belief that others caused the client to be "a bad, unlovable person"). What combination of self-pity and rageful anger has developed to detract from the painfulness of experiencing shame? With regard to the latter, does the client wallow in self-pity, angrily accuse others of not caring and being abusive, or both of these, to diminish the greater pain of experiencing shameful thoughts and feelings?

We do not imply that rage and self-pity are merely defenses against shame. They can exist without much shame being experienced by the client, and developmentally, the emotional precursors of self-pity and shame probably evolved around the same time as the precursor of shame. However, each client usually comes to therapy with a distinct interrelationship among two or three of these personotypic affects, and this must be assessed accurately by the therapist.

ASSESSING BEHAVIOR

In assessing the client's behavioral patterns from a CAT perspective, the therapist's main objective is to determine (1) how the client's behaviors help to maintain personotypic affect and the emotional setpoint and (2) what is the client's interpersonal stance (which we equate with one's personality style). Secondarily, the therapist should identify what the client does to manage (or defend against) the pain of shame, as this also can contribute to the client's behavioral patterns and interpersonal stance. These three domains of behavior are not necessarily discrete. A hostile–active–dominant person, for example, may defend against shameful feelings by angrily attacking others, which also may further rekindle longstanding rage and self-pity. Nevertheless, it is helpful to the clinician to think of the client's behavioral patterns as containing security-seeking, interpersonal, and defensive characteristics.

To target security-seeking behaviors, the therapist must identify ongoing behavioral patterns that result in the client's feeling longstanding, familiar negative feelings (shame, rageful anger, self-pity) at a familiar emotional pitch (the setpoint). An example illustrates this:

> During a first session, 40-year-old Simon has difficulty staying focused on one topic and identifying clear goals for his therapy. He looks at the therapist and says, "I don't know. What do you think my goals in therapy should be, given what you've heard so far?" He maintains that he is coming to therapy mainly because his psychopharmacologist insisted on it if he were to continue medicating Simon. Simon says that he definitely needs therapy, but he probably would not be motivated to follow through with it if not forced to do so by his psychopharmacologist.
>
> Simon, currently unemployed and living with his mother, has a history of being initially enthusiastic about a project but then losing interest rapidly and dropping out before completion. He did this with college, with subsequent entrepreneurial projects, with relationships, and with previous therapies. Every time he has done this, Simon's mother harshly criticizes him and tries to offer him numerous suggestions for how to improve his life, all of which he angrily rejects. Simon says that he repeatedly feels angry and resentful at the progressive boredom of having to attend to and complete the details of projects, angry at himself and like a "wash-up" (i.e., ashamed of himself) after such failures to follow through with commitments, and enraged at his mother for "meddling" in his life.
>
> When the therapist asks Simon how he could see this pattern playing out in therapy, Simon responds that he could either stop attending sessions or not respond to the therapist's suggestions and feel increasingly angry at the therapist's comments.

The security-seeking behaviors are clear here. Simon's prematurely terminating commitments causes him to reinvoke the shame and anger toward himself that he has felt his whole life, presumably initially due to his mother's critical stance towards him as child. (Simon's father died when he was a toddler.) After each failure, Simon then seeks out contact with his mother, nonconsciously to elicit the same criticism and overprotectiveness from her that he has always received, so he can then feel enraged at her and sorry for himself: "She's smothering me." Finally, Simon's exaggerated enthusiasm and idealization of each new project sets him up to then be disenchanted with it when he has to deal with the boring details and setbacks that any major project or commitment inevitably involves. And, as Simon is well aware, this security-seeking pattern may well play itself out in therapy, with Simon unintentionally casting the therapist in the role of his mother.

Therefore, the therapist can quickly obtain descriptions of a client's security-seeking behaviors (1) by looking for behaviors, often interpersonal, that are repeated across situations; (2) by seeing whether they also were present consistently in the client's childhood, with the client now pulling responses from others similar to the stance his or her parent(s) typically took toward him or her; (3) by identifying behavior that repeatedly leads to the experiencing of some combination of shame, rageful anger, and/or self-pity by the client; and (4) by noting that such behaviors are already beginning, within the first three or four sessions, to repeat themselves between client and therapist. Another example follows:

> Twenty-six-year-old Betty began her first session by complaining that nobody cared about her, that her parents favored her older brother over her and were extremely narcissistic, and that she had been rejected numerous times by friends. She consequently felt angered and sorry for herself: "Why can't people treat me with just a little understanding and sympathy? Everybody else gets taken care of but me. What the hell's wrong with people? What's wrong with me?"
>
> During the next three sessions, a pattern emerged in the type of relationship that Betty was beginning to form with the therapist. She began crying at the end of each session. (The therapist actually noticed that Betty would glance at her watch toward the end of sessions and then begin to cry.) Betty would then beg the therapist for more time since she was in such "pain" and, when no extra time was given, she would storm out of the therapist's office, accusing him of only caring about his payment and not about her. Betty also began calling the therapist every few days, with no pressing issue or problem to discuss. She would talk nonstop in a "chatty" manner and when the therapist ended the conversation after about ten minutes (his normal limit on phone conversations that were nonemergencies), she would again become enraged, saying, "My last therapist would speak to me on the phone for as long as I wanted," angrily accuse the therapist of not caring about her, and hang up on him.

Betty's security-seeking behaviors are clear. She would push the boundaries and rules of the therapy in various ways, overtly seeking the therapist's sympathy and caring while nonconsciously seeking his rejection of her, and then she would feel her personotypic affects of rage at her supposedly uncaring therapist ("If you really cared about me, you'd break the rules and do exactly what I want.") and self-pity ("Why can't you give me what I want? Nobody does.").

The client's interpersonal stance/personality style can also be culled from similar information. For example, Betty was frequently and increasingly hostile, rather than friendly, toward the therapist. She took a passive stance both in the therapy and out, as she hoped that by being helpless and "in pain," others might take care of and care about her. However, Betty was not submissive and passive, as many dependent clients are. Instead, her stance with the therapist and others was dominant: "You must do things my way or I will be disapproving of you and enraged." Therefore, Betty's personality style is hostile–dominant–passive.

Simon's personality style is similar, with a few significant differences. Like Betty, Simon takes a passive stance in life. While he starts out active ("This time, I'll throw myself into this great project"), he quickly bottoms out into passivity. While he appears to be more friendly to others and his therapist than Betty, he too gets increasingly angry toward others and therefore ultimately falls in the hostile personality quadrant. Unlike Betty, however, Simon is truly dependent, taking a submissive stance toward others (albeit the angry–submissive stance of the passive–aggressive), as evidenced by his looking to the therapist to set the therapeutic agenda, by being taken care of by his mother, and by pulling advice from her. His personality style, therefore, is hostile–submissive–passive.

Nathanson's (1992) four ways of defending against shame (which he terms the "compass of shame"; see our review of them in chapter 3), serve as a good model for identifying defensive behaviors the client repeatedly uses to cope with the painfulness of experienced shame. Does the client tend to *withdraw* from the world and wallow in his or her shame? Does the client typically *avoid* shameful affect by abusing substances, developing an eating disorder, becoming perfectionistic and compulsive, or engaging in fast and furious behaviors (e.g., thrill-seeking, workaholism) to distract him or her from this predominant feeling? To determine this, the therapist must first assess that shame is a predominant personotypic affect and must link certain extreme behaviors to it. After all, some people are workaholics simply because they enjoy their jobs while others might be so to avoid painful feelings. Does the client frequently *attack others* ragefully and/or critically, as it is actually less painful to blame others and be enraged than to blame oneself and feel humiliated and worthless? Or does the client typically beat others to the punch by frequently *attacking him-herself*—by putting him-herself down in front of others, either in a joking or dead serious manner?

Betty clearly avoided the intense shame she often felt about herself ("People don't care about me because I am a worthless, disgusting person.") by angrily criticizing others for not caring about her and by being disappointed in them. Her stance toward others, including her therapist, was filled with sarcastic put-downs, annoyed, whiny criticism, and a general irritability. Simon, on the other hand, would often put himself down with his soft, hesitant voice: "I'm such a schmuck. I keep making the same mistakes over and over again. I don't know why I don't see them coming the next time. You're probably thinking, 'My God, what a pathetic loser.' Well, you're in good company with that thought, let me tell you." While Betty uses Nathanson's "attack other" defensive style, consistent with her hostile–dominant qualities; Simon employs an "attack self" defensive stance, consonant with his hostile–submissive style.

ASSESSING COGNITION

The two types of cognitions that the CAT therapist addresses are justifying cognitions and personal rules of living. Justifying cognitions are unique to CAT among the cognitive therapies in that their goal is to reinvoke personotypic affect. The therapist can identify such cognitions by assessing their impact upon the client's affective state: does a particular thought stir up personotypic affect or not? For example, if anxiety is a personotypic affect, a person might believe that something dreadful will happen. When there is no evidence that anything dreadful might happen and the person *continues* to think that it will, this then is a justifying cognition—the thought justifies and further rekindles the feeling.

Justifying cognitions can often be identified when they fly in the face of what is rational and logical and when they serve to reinstate the emotional set-point. They are often quite dramatic in tone, as well they should be, since they often represent the internal opera the client creates to rev up his or her melodramatic personotypic affects: "Nobody cares about me!"; "I'm a total failure"; "Everybody's out to use me." These thoughts most typically are the mouthpieces for shame, rage, and self-pity, and so they talk of the self as unloved and unlovable, the world of others as cold, cruel, and overwhelming, and how one is treated as pitiful and unjust. They also voice irrational fears about one's future and one's ability to perform, as these fears are the partial fuel of shame and self-pity.

> *Every time 30-year-old Jane would make a commitment to a relationship or a job, she would think: "I feel boring and empty. Is this all there is to life—going home to the same person day after day and doing the same job year after year? I feel like I'm shriveling up and dying; like I'm invisible."*
> *Consequently, Jane would feel intensely sorry for herself and resentful of the apparent tedium that commitment brings. As a result, Jane would cheat on her boyfriend or quit one line of work and move to another. Then she would feel like a failure, since none of the things she began ever came to full fruition.*

Here, Jane's justifying cognitions are her thoughts concerning being boring and feeling empty that accompany a commitment she makes. These cognitions stir up her feelings of resentment and self-pity at being responsible and committed—thoughts and feelings modeled to her in a variety of ways by her divorced parents as she was growing up.

The therapist can key into the client's personal rules of living by listening to the implicit rules and belief systems the client has about how the world is and should be. They are subjective rules that are often nonconsciously experienced by the client as objective truths. In Jane's case, she holds the following personal rules: (1) if my life is routine, then I will be boring to others; (2) I can never be boring to others or else they will reject me; and (3) I can never be rejected by others. Consequently, Jane was quite histrionic in her presentation to others: always entertaining them, the "life of the party." If she ever failed to be the charming center of attention, Jane had justifying cognitions that would make her feel rejected by others and worthless, which repeated how she felt growing up when she was not being witty and entertaining to her self-involved parents.

A more involved excerpt from one of Richard's therapy sessions with a 35-year-old female client may be helpful at this point to elucidate how we identify personal rules of living and justifying cognitions in therapy.

> *Richard: What would you like to work on?*
>
> *Client: My mother is in the hospital. She's having her leg amputated, and I'm dealing with feelings of—I guess I'm tormented by guilt because I'm not running up to see her. And two years ago, she had her other leg amputated, and I went to see her every day. Today, I'm not doing that.*
>
> *R: Why the difference?*
>
> *Cl: Well, for one thing, my mother is very self-destructive, so this is a continuous pattern. And, for another thing, I realize now that I have a life of my own and I will go up and see her when time permits. I'm not driven to see her because she's in the hospital and is ill. But, it really doesn't make me feel very good.*
>
> *R: I'm picking up that you don't want to see her that often.*
>
> *Cl: Right!*
>
> *R: So, you're happy enough to see her when you want to see her.*
>
> *Cl: Right, but I'm not comfortable with the fact that I don't feel very good about myself because I'm not running up to see her.*
>
> *R: Yeah, you feel guilty because you think you're doing something wrong. That's the only time people feel guilty. People don't feel guilty when they are doing something right.*
>
> *Cl: That's true.*
>
> *R: So, what are you doing wrong?*
>
> *Cl: I feel that, as a daughter, I should run up to see her. I feel compelled to see her every day.*
>
> *R: Because that's the right thing to do?*
>
> *Cl: That's what a daughter would do.*
>
> *R: So, you have suddenly decided not to be a daughter?*

Cl: Ah, I've suddenly decided to grow up and say I have responsibilities.

R: So, you're a daughter, but you're something else, too. Is that what I'm hearing?

Cl: Yes! I'm finally beginning to recognize that I am also an adult.

R: You're a daughter and an adult, and there are two very different sets of rules. The rule for a daughter is you go to see your mother every day in the hospital, and the rule for an adult is what?

Cl: Go and see my mother when time permits.

R: So, you're struggling hard to follow that adult rule, as you understand it, but what is interfering is the older rule—the daughter rule—and there is here a clash between the two rules. And sometimes the daughter rule wins out. And that's when you feel guilty.

Cl: Right. Unfortunately, the feeling of the daughter rule, the guilt feeling, is overwhelming, but the adult rule on this particular day is, I guess you say, is winning out, because I haven't, I'm not running up to see her —

R: So, if you went with your feelings, you'd do what? You'd...

Cl: I'd go every day. And if I didn't, I would be, I would be a bad daughter and I should be ashamed of myself.

R: Sure. You're going against your feelings. Is that OK with you?

Cl: Ah, well, it's OK, but it doesn't feel like it.

R: That's right. It's hard to do, isn't it?

Cl: [laughs] That's right.

R: Because you're trying to make a transition from one rule to another, and the old message keeps coming back: Go to see your mother like a good daughter should. If you don't, then you're a bad daughter and should be ashamed of yourself.

Cl: Right.

R: Where's that old message coming from? Does it sound familiar hearing it?

Cl: That was my life. I was always expected to do what my mother wanted or needed, or I was called a bad daughter, among other things.

R: Now, let me stop you there. You just said "I was expected." In grammar or something, that's the passive voice. Now, somebody expected you to do that? Who was it? It wasn't just that you were expected. Somebody expected you to do it.

Cl: That's how I was conditioned. My mother conditioned me to take care of her.

R: Your mother was Ivan Pavlov? [Cl laughs] Or B.F. Skinner maybe? Your mother taught you this rule, didn't she? She said, "You're supposed to do what I want you to do. That's what a good daughter does. A good daughter obeys her mother." Which means that the mother is the absolute master, and the daughter is the absolute what? What is the opposite of master?

Cl: Servant.

In this excerpt, Richard clearly identifies the two conflicting personal rules of living in the client. The old rule which the client grew up with is: "If I do not obey my mother at all times and take care of her, then I am a bad daughter." The new personal rule, gained through the client's therapy and maturation, is: "I can see my mother when it is convenient, as I am an adult with my own responsibilities."

While much of this excerpt is spent identifying and discussing the client's personal rules of living, later in the session it emerged that, on a day when she does not visit her mother, the client ends up not only feeling guilty about being a bad daughter, but also turning her guilt into shame. After all, the client recalls that her mother said that she should "be ashamed" of herself if she acts like a bad daughter. The very use of the phrase "bad daughter" implies that more than guilt is at stake here—failure to go to the hospital may generate a slew of justifying cognitions ("You're a bad daughter"; "You should be ashamed of yourself") that stir up the personotypic affect of shame.

ASSESSING DEVELOPMENT AND CURRENT ENVIRONMENTAL STRESSORS

CAT initially assesses developmental and environmental contributors to a client's difficulties as would many other therapeutic approaches. Developmental factors that can affect one's current difficulties include biochemical and temperamental variables, and we refer the reader to others who have written extensively on these topics (e.g., Greenspan, 1992; Kagan, 1989).

After assessing whether, in fact, a client's condition is heavily biochemical in nature, as in the case of someone with schizophrenia or bipolar disorder, we then determine whether medication may be a helpful adjunctive component to someone presenting with Axis I symptoms that may get in the way of the client's making optimal use of therapy. We then refer the client, accordingly, to a psychopharmacologist.

It is our belief that for nonpsychotic and nonbipolar Axis I-type disorders, a brief (3- to 6-month) period of medication may help the client make better use of psychotherapy. However, we suspect that prolonged use of many current medications may actually contribute to the client's emotional difficulties or add new one's to the client's roster of problems. Prolonged medicating may also give the client the message that he or she is not and never will be responsible for effecting change. (See Brickman et al., 1980, for a discussion of how use of the medical model in psychotherapy squelches personal responsibility.)

We use the model presented in Table 6–2 to determine how the client was parented by each parent, and what the effects of the combination of the two parents' parenting styles are on the client's personality style and current func-

TABLE 6–2   CAT's Grid of Parenting Styles and their Impact on (Adult) Children

Parenting style (Personality dimensions) Characteristics	Children's feelings	Children's responses	Kids become as adults
Cruel (hostile–active–dominant) yelling & abuse	Intimidation, resentment	Obey due to fear	Passive, dependent enraged
Controlling (friendly–active–dominant) kind but domineering	Incompetent, ashamed	Obey without question	Dependent, immature, fearful
Nasty (hostile–passive–dominant) highly critical	Ashamed, criticized	Perfectionism	Perfectionistic & depressed
Self-sacrificing (friendly–passive–dominant) passive power	Guilty	Obliged & obedient	Compliant, people-pleasing
Remote (hostile–active–submissive) dismissive	Unwanted, unloved	Isolates	Avoidant
Parent-as-pal (friendly–active–submissive)	Unprotected	Timidity	Self-effacing, withdrawn
Whining & Complaining (hostile–passive–submissive)	Pity for parent	Obey due to guilt	Whiny, complains, resentful, caretaker
Doormat (friendly–passive–submissive) defers to kids	Entitled	Kid has power	Selfish, antisocial, addiction-prone
Respectful, encouraging (Ideal)	Secure	Cooperative	Autonomous yet loyal

tioning. It is beyond the scope of this book to describe each parenting style in great detail, but suffice it to say that they have been derived both from hearing hundreds of clients describe their parents and from the three-dimensional model of personality that we outlined in chapter 4.

We generally listen to the client's narrative concerning his or her parents and then ask pointed questions to further ascertain the parents' specific parenting styles. In the excerpt from the therapy conducted by Richard presented in the previous section of this chapter, Richard already ascertained that the client's mother treated her like a "servant" and made her feel like a "bad daughter" if she was not caring for her. This exploration of parenting style then continues:

Richard: You grew up as a servant?

Client: I was a servant.

R: Found guilty when you didn't do what the master said to do.

Cl: Right. I was also made to feel guilty.

R: Of course, how did this expert make you feel guilty?

Cl: By speaking to me in a very angry, demeaning way, and I also paid a very severe price for not doing what was expected of me. I was punished and...

R: Physically punished, but more importantly, psychologically punished, emotionally punished.

Cl: Right, because the physical punishment only lasted momentarily.

R: Right, you get over that.

Cl: And the psychological punishment just went on for days.

R: Right. The blows to self continued. How did she punish you psychologically?

Cl: By constantly making me feel that —

R: No, that was the result. How did she do it? How did she make you feel bad?

Cl: She would say, "Because you didn't do this yesterday, this is what we have to do today. It's all because you didn't do what I asked you to do yesterday."

R: So there you were, creating problems and complications and more work and more work!

Cl: Right.

R: And that was pretty effective. That made you feel bad. Does that still work today?

Cl: Ah, well...

R: If I said to you, "I've got more work for you to do today because you didn't do something yesterday," would you feel guilty or ashamed?

Cl: No.

R: You mean I'm not as powerful as your mother?

Cl: [laughs] No, actually you're not. You're not as powerful as my mother.

R: [laughs] I'm not as powerful as most people's mothers.

Cl: Because I don't see you as my mother.

R: Good, I'm glad. I'd hate to be seen as anybody's mother. I have a hard enough time being seen as somebody's father. OK. So, what does make you feel guilty today?

Cl: Just the emotions of being someone's daughter.

R: You mean all you have to do is think about the fact that you are still this lady's daughter and you feel guilty?

Cl: Not to the same degree. Because I'm still—that's why I'm very torn—because I'm still—well, I'm trying to conduct my life in an adult manner, which is very difficult. It's a struggle, because I'm still tinged with guilt.

R: The old feelings keep coming back. And the old message she kept giving you about you; and, how wonderful you were when you did the wrong thing? No. How what were you when you did the wrong thing?

Cl: How terrible I was. And she still sends that message. She says that her health is failing because she doesn't have me to come up and visit her. I'm making her depressed.

R: You'll probably kill this woman, don't you think?

Cl: Well, I used to think I actually would kill her.

R: *I thought so.*

Cl: *But I don't anymore. And she's very self-destructive, and she will eventually kill herself.*

R: *You mean she'll do all this herself without your help?*

Cl: *Yes. And it really hurts me to say that she will kill herself. I mean, her health will just continue to fail and she'll eventually die.*

R: *Why is she doing that? Is she unhealthy because she is still trying to control you?*

Cl: *She just believes that if she stays ill she will receive attention.*

R: *Wow! What a big price to pay!*

Cl: *Yeah.*

R: *And it's not working. You're not giving her the attention. You know what's going to happen? She's going to try harder.*

Cl: *She has.*

From this client's description, it appears that her mother acts primarily in a whiny and complaining (hostile–submissive–passive) manner as she attempts to get the client to take care of her and to feel intensely guilty (and perhaps ashamed) if she does not. As a result, we can see that the client has become, until recently, the dutiful caretaker of her mother, with concomitant rage and self-pity resulting from her situation. The mother appears also to be quite nasty and demeaning (hostile–dominant–passive) at times, which only serves to intensify the shame the client feels about herself when not being the perfect caretaker.

To gain a complete assessment of how this client was parented and its effects on her personality style, Richard will also assess the client's father's predominant parenting style. For some people, both parents have equal effects on their personality style—that is, both parents had about the same emotional presence and valence for the client when he or she was growing up. For other people, one parent was the emotionally dominant one and that parent's parenting style might have had a more lasting imprint upon the child's personality style (although the emotional absence or weakness of the other parent can be in and of itself a significant determinant of the child's personality style).

THE MCMI

We give each client the Millon Clinical Multiaxial Inventory (Millon, 1987, 1992) at the end of the first session and ask him or her to return it at the second session. We give the MCMI for various reasons. First, since our approach to personality was influenced by and is, in many respects, compatible with Millon's theory, the MCMI provides a rapid confirmation of our clinical assessment of the client's personality style. Second, the MCMI assesses many facets of personality, such as one's clinical personality pattern (schizoid, avoidant, depressive, dependent, histrionic, narcissistic, antisocial, aggressive/sadistic, compulsive, passive–aggressive, self-defeating), severe personality pathology (schizotypal, borderline, paranoid), clinical syndromes (anxiety disorder, somatoform disorder, bipolar disorder, manic disorder, dysthymic disorder, alcohol dependence, drug dependence, post-traumatic stress), and severe syndromes (thought disorder, major depression, delusional disorder). While the first two categories address Axis II pathology, the latter two categories assess current Axis I symptomatology. This allows us not only to compare our impression of the client's personality style with that of the MCMI, but it helps us to place Axis I symptoms in the context of personality style. The MCMI also evaluates response style (disclosure, desirability, and debasement), which often gives us an assessment of how the client may be presenting him-herself to the therapist.

Third, the MCMI has been carefully constructed and validated, and has excellent test–retest reliability (see Choca, Shanley, & Van Denburg, 1992, for a review of this). As such, it is not sensitive to how a client is feeling during the first session (a state measure), but instead represents the client's ongoing emotional and personality characteristics (a trait measure). Fourth, most clients can complete the MCMI in about half an hour and, given its short administration time, it yields very rich personality data.

The MCMI is computer-scored and, while one can receive a computer-generated report for each individual, we only request and use results in bar graph form (see Millon, 1987, for examples of these results; see also Choca et al., 1992, for a manual on how to interpret various combinations of the clinical personality pattern dimensions). The bar graph is informative not only for those dimensions a client scores high on (over 75 out of 100), but also for those dimensions on which he or she scores quite low (below 35). The graphed results yield a rich topography of one's predominant personality characteristics as well as those facets of personality in which one is lacking.

For example, a typical pattern of results might yield significantly high scores in the clinical personality pattern domain for avoidant and dependent and significantly low scores for histrionic and narcissistic. One can hypothesize from this that this individual not only is highly ashamed of him-herself, doubtful of his/her own capabilities, and, therefore, avoids social and work situations where his/her supposed flaws may be discovered by others, but also that this person might benefit from becoming more confident (the healthy variant of narcissistic) and sociable (the healthy variant of histrionic).

We interpret the results of the MCMI and compare them to our own clinical impressions. When the MCMI does not correspond to our perceptions of a client, this provides us with an opportunity to explore these areas of discrepancy with the client to determine whether we missed some element in our assessment or whether the MCMI has misrepresented one element of a client's personality as something else, which it sometimes does. (For example, in our experience, anger is often represented by a high anxiety-disorder score but may not necessarily appear on the aggressive/sadistic or passive–aggressive score.)

When we receive the MCMI results, we generally share them verbally with the client. This is done, first, to avoid keeping secrets from the client (see our discussion of creating a shame-free environment in chapter 7) and, second, as a valuable opportunity to discuss the client's personality style with him or her early in the therapy. It should be noted that we make sure the client understands that high or low scores on the MCMI are not "good" or "bad," nor do they represent that one is "crazy" or "healthy." We emphasize that they simply represent, in a nonjudgmental way, the characteristics that are most and least prevalent in one's personality, which may explain why the person is experiencing some of his or her presenting problems.

Discussing the MCMI results with a client is often helpful in setting a mutually agreed-upon agenda for the therapy. For example, in the case of the person high on avoidant and dependent and low on narcissistic and antisocial, the therapist and client could agree to help the client become more self-confident and less embarrassed in social situations.

GIVING THE CLIENT FEEDBACK DURING THE ASSESSMENT

Psychotherapy is a business. As such, clients come to us (consciously) wanting to change and to change as quickly and efficiently as possible. They are paying us a lot of money to work with them and often investing much emotional effort, sometimes quite painful, to better their lives. In short, and especially in this age of managed care and fast food, clients want to know that they are getting "bang for their buck." Therefore, we find it extremely helpful to the therapeutic alliance and the course of therapy to give clients feedback concerning how we conceptualize their problems and how we plan to work with them by the end of the first or, at the latest, second session.

We find it insulting to clients' intelligence and self-respect when they return to therapy week after week and are met with silence from the therapist. If your car were not working, would you return week after week to your mechanic, only to be met mostly with his silence and the words, "Let's continue to work on fixing your car. You'll slowly come to understand what the problem is as you tell me how your car is not functioning properly"? You would probably consider your mechanic to be a charlatan after one such visit and leave him immediately. Why should this be any different with a therapist? The answer is that many clients still do not know that therapists can accurately assess them and formulate a treatment approach in one or two sessions, coupled with the lingering belief from the early days of psychoanalysis that therapy should be a somewhat mysterious, oblique experience for the client until, one day, three or four years into the therapy, he or she has a powerful "aha" experience. And many therapists believe that the therapy should be slow and unfolding because they are not competent at diagnosing their clients rapidly and accurately.

Using our ABCDE assessment model, we typically formulate a client's personality style and concomitant personal rules of living, personotypic affect, emotional setpoint, justifying cognitions, and security-seeking behaviors in the first session or two. This enables us, often at the end of the first session, to give some feedback to the client concerning what we believe is the underlying cause of the client's presenting problems, and to discuss how we will work to change it. We also elicit in the first session the client's goals for his or her therapy. Our feedback concerning what might be causing the client's difficulties has as its end the attainment of at least some of the client's own goals. In this way, we are never working at cross-purposes with a client in a way that will make the client feel overridden by what we want. Instead, we hope to give the client a new way of looking at his or her problems and, therefore, a new means of addressing them.

For example, a client might present with the problem that he is feeling depressed because he cannot get ahead in life, in terms of both maintaining a relationship and gaining respect from his coworkers and boss. He might say that he feels anxious and self-doubting both at work and while dating. He describes a mother who dotes on him and to whom he still goes to solve his problems and a father who has always been extremely critical of him, angry, self-pitying, and self-involved. From this, and the client's pleasant, people-pleasing presentation in therapy, the therapist can quickly determine that the client is friendly–submissive–passive and that he harbors much pent-up anger toward others for not treating him fairly enough, much as his father often feels.

The therapist can then say at the end of the first session: "I think you've been having trouble gaining the respect of others because you've been trained by your parents—unintentionally by them, of course—to feel ashamed of yourself, unable to do your job well enough, and not desirable enough to a date. You don't believe you have a lot to offer. I think you're also very angry. Pleasing others all the time never allows you to get what you want in life, and that must leave you feeling used by others and resentful toward them. And that rage seems to guide many of the decisions you're making in your life now. I'd love to help you work to improve your self-respect, to learn to stand up for yourself appropriately, and especially to handle your anger differently. I think then you'd get a lot of respect from others at work and admiration from women. What do you think?"

We now present several case examples to give the reader a feel for how we assess new clients.

FRANK

Thirty-one-year-old Frank sits forward in his chair during the first session and speaks throughout in a rapid, pressed tone of voice. His fiancée recently broke off their engagement and moved out on him, and Frank is also in the throes of deciding whether he should remain in his secure job with a corporation or become an entrepreneur. He comes from a business family; his father is an entrepreneur, as is his older brother, and his sister works for a large corporation. He said the following:

> I have to get out of my job at [a major corporation]. I can't stand it anymore. I've been there 10 years and I'm a real mover and shaker, but it's not offering me anything. You know, I want to be an entrepreneur, but I just—you know, I have like a million ideas a day but I just—when it's time to come up with a business plan for myself, I just can't do it. I can't do it. My mind goes blank. And I know lots of people; I'm very well connected, but when it's time to sit down and come up with a plan... You know, I'm too tired. I've been working 15 hours a day; nothing comes to mind. I get all confused and I go nowhere with it. So I'm here to figure out why I can't move ahead with things and, you know, I want to be able to move ahead and pick something in particular for my work. [pause]
>
> Therapist: You also just broke up with your girlfriend?
>
> Client: She broke up with me. But I've got to say that I contributed to it because I withdrew from her for 3 or 4 months. I was so wrapped up in being unhappy at my job and in what am I going to do that I withdrew. She would ask me, "What are you thinking? What are you thinking?" I told her some but, after a while, I felt like I didn't want to burden her; I didn't want to bore her. And I guess I just kind of withdrew. She wasn't going to give me what I wanted in the relationship either. I talked to her about it. It's not like I withdrew from her to that extent, but her parents were very in there, controlling what she was thinking, feeling, and doing in terms of the relationship, and I felt I was more marrying the family than her. I felt, so I wasn't happy. I tried to address it with her a bunch of times, but she just said, "No. That's not going on. You're making it up," so I started thinking that I was making it up, but I don't think so. Lots of evidence. I think back over my memories and I realize that the father was always saying, "Why don't you make more money? I can set you up with this person and that person who can help you. You know, my daughter wants this; my daughter wants that."
>
> Later in the session, after discussing how he has been ambivalent not only about making the break from his job but also ambivalent for a long while about his relationship, the therapist asks Frank how he usually makes major decisions in his life. He responds:

"I usually obsess about it for the longest time. I always do that. I chew everybody's ear off about my decision, especially my father's. He's been—it's like he's been very supportive. He listens, and sometimes gives his opinion, but mostly just provides a sounding board for me. My brother is a little fed up with my indecision and just tells me to make a choice and, really, in essence to stop bothering him. My sister's more of a listener, more supportive, like my father.

"Growing up, my father wasn't around so much. Usually on the road work-ing. My mother was extremely warm and supportive but I didn't really ask her opinion about major decisions. My brother's quite a bit older, so he felt like— so I treated him like a second father and went to him often for advice, which he usually was good at giving. But I was fairly shy until college, 50 pounds heavier than I am now, and I relied on my brother and now on my father to listen to me and give me input."

Frank's personality style is friendly–submissive–passive. He has no history of overt hostility or anger toward others, has many friends, and has little conflict in his family of origin, and he presented in the session as friendly toward the thera-pist. His current and past history of confusion and reliance on others to make decisions for him highlights Frank's basic dependence on others and, therefore, his primarily submissive stance. While he is a responsible, effective worker, he nevertheless sits around and allows others to make decisions for him, and he is, therefore, more passive than active. During another part of this session, Frank noted that perhaps his unwillingness to open up and share what he was going through with his fiancée may have actually been a passive way of shutting her out and doing the inevitable—breaking off the engagement. He also admitted that he really wished for someone to offer him the opportunity to start a business for them rather than his having to initiate a company from scratch and on his own.

Given Frank's submissive–passive position in the world, he is quite fright-ened of standing on his own as an entrepreneur (or, for that matter, as a hus-band). Like most dependent people, Frank is rebellious against authority fig-ures: his current job, his father-in-law, his fiancée. He also appears to be rebel-lious against another "authority": the reality that drawing up a business plan in one's spare time requires much work, self-discipline, and motivation. Some of his personal rules of living may well be: "Authority figures only take advan-tage of you. Resist them."; "Getting ahead in life should not be so hard."; and "I cannot make correct decisions on my own. I must get the input of others."

As such, it appears that Frank's primary personotypic affects are self-pity and resentment (mild anger). He feels sorry for himself in his current job and spent much of this session complaining about how he is treated unfairly by his new boss (another authority figure) and, formerly, by his father-in-law-to-be. He also voiced resentment toward this treatment. Self-pity and resentment also surfaced when he discussed how many of his friends are earning more than he and work less, and some have inherited money through trust funds. Also, these feelings predominate when he discusses how he feels about having to sit down and develop a business plan after a long work day: it's not fair, he's too tired, etc. He, like many Americans these days, was indulged as a child: someone will solve your problems, so don't work too hard. Frank's having been 50 pounds overweight as a child and young man also speak to his indulgence and lack of self-discipline.

Frank's rapid, pressed tone of voice and his numerous worries concerning becoming an entrepreneur also highlight how anxious he is. Here, it seems that his anxiety is really a security-seeking emotion for self-pity. It is probable that Frank is not only afraid of making a poor business plan and failing at entrepreneurship, but also that he will feel like a victim of all the work and self-motivation that it will take to be a successful entrepreneur. While the former fear speaks to some underlying shame on Frank's part, the latter fear highlights how Frank equates hard work on his own with self-pity.

Consequently, Frank is more accustomed to being a self-pitying, resentful rebel against authority than being an authority figure himself. Whenever he comes close to becoming an authority himself—an entrepreneur or a married man—he manages to undo this. This, as well as his frequent confusion and reliance on others when making decisions, is his security-seeking behavior.

While Frank only touched during the first session on how he was parented, we do know that his family as a whole (his mother and brother while he grew up and, now, his father and sister) has tended to overprotect and perhaps overindulge him. Their friendly–active–dominant (overprotective) parenting style provides a perfect complement to Frank's friendly–submissive–passive personality style. As a result, Frank has also developed a somewhat passive–aggressive stance toward those he deems authority figures. This may well have been played out with his parent(s) while he was growing up, although he provided little evidence for this during the first session.

SILVIA[1]

We present the background information on Silvia in greater detail here, as we will use this case illustration again in the following chapter.

Silvia is a 27-year-old woman who lives with her husband, Daniel, in Valencia, Spain. Her case was presented to Richard by Dr. Isabel Caro at the 1998 World Congress on Cognitive and Behavioral Therapies. Dr. Caro was looking for a consultation from a therapist with a different cognitive orientation from her own, which focuses on the use of language in therapy (Caro, 1996).

---

[1]This section is based on Wessler (2001).

According to Dr. Caro, before her recent psychotherapy, Silvia received psychiatric treatment for depression for one year. This was precipitated, according to Silvia, by her feeling tired and "fed up" with others and with herself, as well as her occasionally fainting. Prior to this psychotherapy, Silvia was hospitalized for one month as the result of a suicide attempt. She was placed on antidepressant medication at that time. Objective assessment measures administered prior to medication and psychotherapy indicated that Silvia scored in the symptomatic ranges for depression and anxiety.

During her first session with Dr. Caro, Silvia was asked to describe her problems. She again said that she was "fed up" with everything and with herself. According to Dr. Caro, Silvia rejected her current life; did not want to be around others or do anything; she only wanted to do what she wanted. She said that she had married to get out of her parents' home and "to have freedom," and she got pregnant prior to her marriage as a way of pushing away her parents. Nevertheless, Silvia continues to be quite involved with her parents.

Silvia has three young children, aged 6^1/$_2$, 4, and 2 years of age. She said that she now realizes that marriage and children have not given her more freedom at all. Instead, she feels saddled with a new family and even more responsibilities, and her mother-in-law and sister-in-law frequently criticize her and interfere with her marriage. Silvia describes a turning point in her marriage as a discussion she had with her mother-in-law, wherein her mother-in-law said that she had doubts concerning who the father of Silvia's first child was. Silvia was infuriated at her mother-in-law, but even more so at Daniel, who said and did nothing. Since that time, according to Silvia, there have been constant marital arguments, and she frequently expresses her dissatisfaction to her husband.

Silvia is very concerned about how her depression is affecting her children. When she and Daniel have fought or she reports feeling particularly "tense," she can overpunish, unfairly yell at, or hit her children. Daniel has a similar parenting style, according to Silvia. The youngest child exhibits frequent prolonged temper tantrums, and the middle child has been seen in therapy at the local psychotherapy clinic for the past year. The oldest child often expresses worries about his parents getting divorced and frequently asks Silvia about this possibility. She is able to reassure him that this will not happen and says that all couples have their difficulties, but this apparently does not mollify him.

Concerning how she feels about herself, Silvia reportedly feels guilty about her difficulties coping with her role as wife and mother. She considers herself a worthless person, with little self-respect and self-confidence, since she is a failure as a wife and mother. However, she also blames others, primarily her hus-

band and mother-in-law. She also stated that she has little sense of who she is or where she is going in her life.

She maintained that she always dreamed of and anticipated a happy life for herself: full of joy and with no obligations at all. Thus, she assumed that her marriage would free her from responsibility. Instead, she feels trapped by her life and ruled by others.

Relevant history includes Silvia's description of her father as a very strict person who did not love or care about her. She reported feeling quite afraid of him while growing up. She described her mother as very weak, but also as one who was effective in forcing Silvia to do what she wanted. Silvia described her family's atmosphere as positive while she was young, but as progressively deteriorating due to frequent quarreling between her parents. They also often blamed Silvia for the family's problems and held her failures up to her.

She never held a steady job. During her adolescence, Silvia worked in her parents' store. She discontinued school after high school. She then worked for 3 months at a low-paying job in a hospital, but she was fired for arguing with co-workers. Similarly, she was fired from a housecleaning job when she argued with her employer. She is currently overweight.

Silvia has received the diagnosis of major depression, and there is little doubt that she has experienced episodes of major depression. However, anti-depressant medication does not appear to have helped very much, having done little more than stabilize her condition. In terms of personality style, Silvia fits in the hostile–submissive–passive category, as she (1) can be quite argumentative and hostile toward others, and clearly sees others as being unsupportive and victimizing of her; (2) in spite of her argumentativeness, she mostly withdraws from interpersonal contact rather than attacking others (and her anger is often passive–aggressive rather than straightforwardly aggressive); and (3) she is very dependent, as she wishes for others to take care of her and relieve her of responsibilities.

Moreover, there is evidence in support of a DSM–IV diagnosis of borderline personality disorder with passive–aggressive features. Silvia's interpersonal relationships have been fairly unstable consistently; she has a poor sense of herself and an ongoing sense of emptiness; she often feels intensely angry, although she often, but not always, keeps this feeling to herself; and she is quite dependent on others and afraid of not being cared for. These features, rather than biological diathesis, make Silvia prone to episodes of depression, and they should figure prominently in a treatment plan.

Silvia is a woman whose attachment to others is based on feelings of victimization and aversive emotional experiences, namely, enraged anger and feelings of self-pity. These are her personotypic affects. She has replicated in marriage (security-seeking behavior) the relationships within her family of origin, and the emotional pitch of her marriage with its frequent arguments and anger (the emotional setpoint) mirrors that of her parents. We hypothesize a need to maintain a sense of security by replicating familiar emotional patterns: self-pity, shame, and rage.

Silvia habitually thinks of herself as a victim of others whom she both depends on and resents. Victims are powerless and, therefore, prone to depression. In addition to this self-handicapping misconception, she has immature, unrealistic expectations about other people and about role-relationships and responsibilities within a family. Her way of dealing with what she perceives as others' demands on her is to rebel or withdraw. Rebellion led to pregnancy and an inappropriate marriage; withdrawal from others allows her to avoid direct conflict and criticism but results in an unrewarding life and symptoms of depression.

Rebellion and withdrawal are active and passive modes, respectively, of resisting the expectations, wishes, and demands of other people. They are ways of telling others, "I will not conform; I will do what I want." Such independence is possible if one is willing to take its consequences, but this young woman also sought the protection of others without giving them her cooperation in exchange. She expresses this pseudo-independence/covert dependence in passive–aggressive behaviors, as she *appears* to comply but actually follows her *own* wishes.

The main subjective emotional feeling that emerges in this case is *anger.* Anger can be mistaken for anxiety because they both involve psychic tension; in this case, displeasure about other people's actions and attitudes is prevalent, rather than fear, which is associated with anxiety. Depression is a shutting-down of affect, not an emotion in and of itself and, in this case, it relates to themes of powerlessness and impaired interpersonal relations due to hostility toward others. CAT looks for longstanding patterns of affect, and the one that recurs as a theme in this woman's life is *rage*—at her parents, especially her father, at her mother-in-law and sister-in-law, at her husband, and at her children (she reports being "fed up" with all of them and with herself).

This woman's enraged anger is related to two highly negative appraisals. *Shame* results from the negative appraisal of self (she describes herself as a bad wife and mother), and *self-pity* results from negative appraisals of others (she describes others as unloving and critical and as causing difficulties over which she has no control—that is, she is powerless). Silvia blames others for either shaming her with criticism or victimizing her, thus prompting self-pity. Reducing shame and self-pity can modulate anger.

Silvia sees her husband and mother-in-law as impossible to please, and she may have given up trying. If she has a personal rule of living that says she should please them, her failure to do so or even to try will produce guilt. Wrongdoing associated with guilt (i.e., genuine moral transgressions) should be identified, criticized, and corrected. However, attempts to please others are associated with immaturity—the individual does not know what is right and, therefore, takes a cue from others. If they are pleased, then she must have done what is right. If she cannot please them, then it must be impossible for her to do what is right and she should feel guilty. Both guilt and shame in this instance are defended by anger.

This client's cognitions or beliefs about human relationships are inconsistent with reality on several points, and she needs to be correctly informed in order to function better in the world. For example, she needs to learn about the nature of marriage. Like many young persons, she seems to think that marriage is an extension of dating—that it is a hedonistic institution created for personal enjoyment and satisfaction. While this version of marriage may hold true for some childless couples, it is inaccurate for a family that includes three children. The client criticizes herself for being a "bad" wife and mother, but seems to have little information about the responsibilities and obligations of these roles. Further, she resents adult responsibilities and wants to be the child who is taken care of.

SUMMARY

1. CAT almost always places Axis I symptoms (e.g., depression, anxiety disorders, OCD, ADD, chronic fatigue syndrome, and even, sometimes, abuse and PTSD) in the context of personality style, as we believe that personality style evokes and maintains such symptoms. An Axis I focus also can collude with clients, especially those who are self-pitying and enraged, in not taking responsibility for their behavior and changing it.

2. CAT assesses affect by (a) identifying the client's predominant personotypic affects; (b) reformulating Axis I symptoms in terms of personality style and personotypic affect; and (c) examining how clients cope with underlying shame.

3. CAT assesses behavior by (a) examining how behavior maintains and evokes personotypic affect; (b) determining clients' personality styles (we initially use the MCMI to help us do so); and (c) exploring how behaviors defend against the pain of shame.

4. CAT assesses cognition by determining clients' predominant personal rules of living and justifying cognitions.

5. CAT assesses developmental influences by determining the degree of influence of biochemical factors (and referring clients for medication evaluations, if necessary) and by exploring how clients' parenting molded their personality styles.

   6. We give feedback to clients at the end of the first or second session that highlights how the client's personality style is leading to his or her symptoms. Taking the client's own goals for therapy into account, we then offer how we can help alleviate difficulties by modifying certain aspects of the client's personality style.

CHAPTER 7

Interventions Based on the CAT Model

We want to emphasize at the outset of this chapter that CAT is, first and foremost, a *philosophy* that can be incorporated into almost any therapeutic approach (any approach that is potentially philosophically compatible with CAT, that is). While we will present in this chapter various therapeutic strategies and interventions that grow out of our beliefs about personality and change, we do not present here a "cookbook" of techniques to be followed rigidly or overly systematically. To be an effective CAT therapist, one has to believe in and, hopefully, live the philosophy of CAT.

CAT can be conceptualized in terms of a foreground and a background. The *background* is composed of the philosophy and set of values that underlie CAT. The background is expressed both directly, in terms of specific interventions which promote CAT's beliefs and values, and indirectly, implicit in interventions which more directly address other facets of the therapy. An example of the former might be a statement that the CAT therapist makes to the client concerning personal responsibility: "You say that you cannot overcome your passivity. In fact, you *can* overcome it; you are choosing not to. And this choice serves some familiar purpose. Let's take a look at what this familiar purpose is."

An example of the latter occurs when the therapist is helping the client to develop ways of soothing and diminishing personotypic affect. A client, for instance, complains that he felt enraged at work when his boss asked him to do tasks that he believed were beneath his level of expertise. As a result, he played sick, and took two days off from work. The therapist then links this reaction to the client's personal rule of living that he should only do what he enjoys, prompted by his parents' never setting appropriate limits for him as he was growing up. The therapist then helps the client to calm his rage toward responsibility in such situations and do the right thing to promote his career (e.g., sometimes doing boring or aversive tasks). Implicit in this strategy is the CAT tenet: "One should not always engage in hedonistic pursuits. Sometimes, success and satisfaction come from sacrificing short-term pleasure for long-term gain. Learn to calm down personotypic affect that promotes inappropriate hedonistic ends."

The *foreground* of CAT involves interventions that focus on more specific therapeutic goals such as understanding one's personotypic affect, security-seeking behavior, etc., learning emotional self-care, diminishing shame through promoting self-respect and self-confidence, and breaking unhealthy ties to one's family of origin.

Certainly, the foreground and the background of CAT are interdependent and often intertwined during therapy, but it may be useful to think of categories of CAT interventions in these two ways. The first part of this chapter will show how the central beliefs of CAT are manifested in CAT therapy. The subsequent sections of this and the next chapter will present some central CAT interventions, many of which are affect-based, work with the client's particular personality style, focus on strengthening the client's self-respect, and help the client to actively break away from unhealthy ties to his or her family of origin.

As CAT is an integrative treatment approach, the interventions we make often combine various elements of the ABCDE assessment model presented in chapter 6. Our therapeutic goals, such as "emotional self-care," combine working with affects, cognitions, and behaviors. We will, therefore, present CAT interventions not under discrete conceptual categories such as "Working with Affect" or "Working with Cognition," but instead under the therapeutic goals we are addressing, such as "Differentiating the Past from the Present" and "Fostering Self-Respect and Self-Confidence."

INTERVENTIONS STEMMING FROM CAT VALUES

Every form of psychotherapy has a set of values, either explicit or implicit, and any therapy that professes to be value-free is not being honest with itself, let alone with its clients. Therapists who believe that they are keeping their values and beliefs from clients are usually experienced as withholding or one-up by clients, and their values are almost always conveyed to the client anyway, if not directly, then indirectly.

Some therapists may withhold their own value systems and beliefs out of shame, as they may be insecure about how others will react. However, this then is an issue for the shame-based therapist to resolve: if he or she has such little faith in what he or she fundamentally believes, then how can he or she help others to feel more self-confident and respectful of themselves?

There is an old joke told to me (Jonathan) by Julian Rotter, the creator of social learning theory. A man enters his Rogerian therapist's office and says, "Doctor, I'm feeling really hopeless and desperate." The therapist, trained to empathically reflect and unconditionally accept his client's responses, replies, "So, I hear that you're feeling at the end of your rope." The man continues, "Yes, Doctor, that's it. I feel like killing myself." "So, right now you're thinking of ending it all," the Rogerian responds, calmly and warmly. "Yes," says the client, "I think I might do it right now. I think I might actually jump out of that window over there." The therapist then comments, "So, I hear that you're thinking of jumping out of that window over there right now or in the very near future." The client goes over to the window, opens it, and jumps up onto the windowsill. The therapist acceptingly reflects, "Right now, you are going over to the window, opening it, and standing on the sill. It sure looks like you're thinking of jumping." The client shouts, "I've had it with this stinking world! I'm better off dead than alive!" The therapist calmly responds "So, right now you're basically feeling that you would be happier dead than alive." With that, the client jumps out of the window. The therapist walks over to the window, looks out of it for a short while, and warmly says "Splat."

This Rogerian clearly believes that, by not taking a philosophical stance and imposing it on his client, he is fostering his client's personal growth. (Of course, humanists believe that unconditional acceptance usually leads to positive human growth rather than suicide.) However, by not taking a stance, the therapist is actually taking one, just as an active–submissive person (a passive–aggressive, for example) expresses his/her anger by not expressing it. For a therapist, there is no escaping the expression of values and beliefs, nor should there be. There is only the choice to express these beliefs openly (and own them as one's own rather than presenting them to the client as "Truth") or to express them indirectly and run the risk of being perceived by the client as "manipulative" or "controlling."

CAT's values, which become an explicit part of the therapy, are as follows: (1) we must take responsibility for our actions; (2) self-respect and self-confidence are gained through personal responsibility and doing what is right at any given moment; (3) people should do what they deem right (within moral and ethical bounds) rather than pursuing hedonistic ends; (4) the client has the choice to change; (5) the therapist should share his or her personal values with the client when necessary; and (6) just as people should not be self-critical unless they have unjustly hurt others, people should not be critical toward others but respect them when they do what is right.

In addition to these values, the CAT therapist adheres to the core belief that people are motivated to reexperience personotypic affect and the emotional setpoint, and that they use justifying cognitions and security-seeking behaviors to do so. Likewise, the therapist must believe that change and therapy are threatening to this motivation, and that many clients are driven to rekindle personotypic affect vis-à-vis the therapy relationship.

FOSTERING SELF-RESPECT AND SELF-CONFIDENCE IN CLIENTS

Shame is the result of negative self-evaluation, of finding fault or defects within oneself. It is based on feelings, not on facts. Shame prompts undeserved self-criticism. One can become aware of such self-bias and make a conscious effort to disregard it and work against it—in other words, to minimize the effects of shame in everyday life. Guilt, on the other hand, is about actual wrongdoing (Baumeister, Stillwell, & Heatherton, 1994; Klass, 1990; Lewis, 1992; Tangney, 1994).

No emotional state is inherently negative. Guilt and shame, though unpleasant to experience, contribute to the regulation of behavior. Humans can avoid guilt by acting correctly or they can escape self-criticism and shame by making amends when they do not act correctly. Such self-regulation of behaviors is necessary when one's actions cannot be regulated by others. Group membership depends upon a large measure of conformity, but it is inefficient to devote time and energy to the monitoring of group members. It is more efficient when a person acts as self-monitor and engages in self-criticism.

Merely noting that behavior is deviant is not sufficient for self-regulation. Affect rather than cognition motivates behavior (Lazarus, 1991); therefore, the person must anticipate or experience unpleasant affect as a condition for altering behavior. The recognition that "I did not act as I should have" is more likely to lead to corrections when it prompts guilty feelings. When one acts improperly, one *should* feel guilty. (See chapter 3.) Do what is correct, and you will not feel guilty. If you feel guilty and you are doing what is not correct, stop doing it. Feeling bad as a result of self-criticism is productive in this situation.

There are some exceptions. One is when a person feels guilty but has done no wrong. Another is when the guilt is disproportionate to the wrongdoing. These are examples of what Tangney (1996, p. 2) has termed "feelings of guilt fused with feelings of shame." Also, when a person feels bad not for wrongdoing but for who he or she is, shame rather than guilt is the feeling the person experiences. These are all instances of self-criticism gone wrong in the service of shame. The result is emotional debilitation rather than self-regulation. These instances must be dealt with in psychotherapy.

The psychotherapy of self-criticism involves working with a person's moral principles and social values—with his or her personal rules of living. Self-appraisals of worth should be based on facts that answer the question, "Do I act according to my personal rules?" Worth is a moral issue. There is an inescapable religious or philosophical dimension in the psychotherapy of self-appraisals. It is possible to tell clients how to act without imposing our rules on them. We can say, "Do what is right as you understand it at this moment. Later, you might define what is right differently, but that doesn't matter. *Self-respect depends on your doing what is right now,* even if you think differently in the future." This is the only way to secure self-respect without uncritically and grandiosely declaring oneself to be good no matter what—without singing undeserved songs of self-praise.

The humanistic movement, combined with the effects of the 1960s, often fosters narcissistic self-love: "Whatever I do is always right and I should love myself for it." For this reason, we do not use the word "self-esteem" (which really translates into self-love); instead, we use the terms self-respect and self-confidence in therapy. We also forbid clients from using "self-esteem," because it can foster an arrogant narcissism and self-indulgence.

No other criterion for judging self-worth allows the person to take responsibility for his or her actions and only for his or her actions. Criteria such as success or achievement depend on extraneous factors beyond the person's control. *It is how you play the game that counts, not whether you win or lose.* Since our best efforts may not get good results, it is wise to base self-worth on effort rather than outcome.

The message in therapy, therefore, is that *self-respect should be based on how well the client conforms to his or her consciously held personal rules of living.* One goal of CAT is to make these often implicit rules more apparent, in order to enable a client to live up to them, as well as to replace unhelpful, maladaptive rules with more helpful, mature ones. Groundless self-accusations merely make one feel bad without offering hope for improvement or relief from bad feelings. They are aimed at promoting personotypic affect, not at bringing about changes. Clients should become aware, as a result of therapy, that they often act to rekindle personotypic affect and the emotional setpoint rather than doing what they currently see is right by working against their feelings.

This notion of self-respect based on moral actions is a departure from certain other formulations. Ellis's RET dispenses with the concept of self-respect and substitutes the concept of self-acceptance. Self-acceptance is the neutral range between high and low self-respect, since it represents neither positive nor negative appraisals of the self. The self is seen as so complex as to defy simplistic ratings of good or bad (R. A. Wessler & Wessler, 1980). Unconditional self-acceptance, without any form of self-rating, is a good idea but seems too ideal for humans to sustain. It is fine to say, "I am neither good nor bad; I am just myself," but humans seem to be inherent evaluators of everything, including self and others. Perhaps this is the reason that some clients, for all their knowledge of RET, cannot apply its message to themselves. The client who thinks he is an idiot feels like even more of an idiot for being too stupid to stop rating himself!

Ellis's view is, however, an improvement on what can be termed the notion of inherent self-worth. Proof of one's worth cannot exist; it is an assumption about human existence. The assumption can be justified on religious grounds through the belief that inherent goodness is due to our likeness to God or that humans are born evil but can be redeemed by God's goodness. A secular version of this doctrine that is used in psychotherapy is often linked with the humanistic school. It states that humans are naturally good but can be misled into thinking they are not good by criticisms and conditions of worth placed on them by parents and other agents of socialization.

In CAT, *self-respect is seen as something to be earned, not inherited. It should* be based on morality and, in turn, it promotes morality. Individuals should suffer for breaking rules; but the avoidance of such suffering is also an incentive for living by the rules. CAT helps clarify the rules and, more importantly, it helps people to break away from criticisms learned from others, especially parents, and to begin to appraise themselves in an independent and responsible manner. A hallmark of adult responsibility is to base self-appraisal on one's actions rather than on events that one cannot control.

Here is an example of how the CAT therapist can address the difference between following one's personotypic affect and being true to one's current personal rules of living, the former affecting shameful feelings while the latter fostering self-respect and personal growth. This example is part of the session presented in chapter 6, where Richard was doing therapy with the woman whose demanding mother was in the hospital. Recall that, previously, one of the client's personal rules of living was: "I am a bad daughter if I do not always obey my mother." This rule has recently been replaced with: "I have responsibilities to my family and myself. I should pay attention to my mother only when it is acceptable to me."

> Client: *Every day my mother calls and every day I arrive home and my answering machine is blinking, and I know she's on the answering machine. She always says, "Call your mother before 10." And I didn't do it yesterday. I didn't call her before 10.*
> Richard: *And how did you feel? Guilty?*

Cl: No! Well, actually, I felt annoyed and just a little bit guilty. But I said, "I'm not calling her before 10. I'm not calling her today."

R: So, you were listening to your own voice that time, weren't you? *[Richard differentiates her old, childhood personal rules from her new, adult ones.]*

Cl: Right. But it's still not comfortable. I can't listen to myself and be comfortable with it.

R: Because you are still listening to her, too, aren't you?

Cl: Yes.

R: Would you like to say something back to that voice? Her voice?

Cl: Yes.

R: What would you like to say? This is your chance.

Cl: "You don't have to call me every day. I know you're sick. I will get up to see you when I have a moment." *[This helps the client to solidify her new personal rules by breaking old interactions with her mother that were rooted in childhood security-seeking behaviors.]*

R: How does it feel when you say that?

Cl: Well, saying it to you is easy.

R: OK. But I want you to say it to the voice.

Cl: Well, it's uncomfortable, because I don't say it to my mother.

R: Why would you ever want to say it to your mother?

Cl: Because it would hurt her feelings.

R: Yeah, but why would you want to say it to her?

Cl: Because it would be—she would—it would be a way of her—it would be a way of my stopping the control.

R: How? By her changing her mind and not saying it to you anymore? *[Many clients have the fantasy that they can get their parents to change quickly and significantly, which does not often occur. Their frustrations when parents do not change can lead to further self-pity, rage, and hopelessness. Richard is making sure that the client is not setting herself up with false hopes here, which it subsequently seems that she is not.]*

Cl: No. By just me having the courage to stand up to the message and say, "Don't call me today."

R: Look, you can stand up to the message without standing up to the messenger.

Cl: Maybe that's what I'm doing.

R: I think you are.

Cl: I'm trying anyway.

R: I think the fact that you're feeling guilty is an indication that that's what you are doing. And, in fact, you are doing very well. Every time you feel guilty, you should feel good. "I must be doing something right. Look how guilty I feel."

Cl: Well, you know, that's really astounding, because I never associated guilt with good feelings. I always had guilt associated with pain and shame. [Richard highlights that guilt and shame are not the same feeling, and that guilt here is positive, as it is a signal that childhood personal rules are not being obeyed by the client.]

R: Guilt can be painful and shameful, there's no doubt about it. But, look what's happening: you're feeling guilt because you are breaking the old rule—her rule—and you're following your own rule. So, you're doing the right thing by following your rule; the right thing, as you understand it, and the way you want to live your life. But unfortunately, that means you've got to go against the old rule—the old message—and you're going to feel guilty. But I'm going to predict that you're not going to feel guilty if you keep doing what you think is right.

SELF-RESPECT-ORIENTED INTERVENTIONS

TAKING PRIDE IN EFFORT OVER ACHIEVEMENT

As previously mentioned, we encourage our clients to feel satisfied at their efforts (working hard to do the right thing) rather than only at the attainment of success, since the latter is often affected by factors outside the individual's control. A person who works hard to prepare an excellent presentation for a conference, only to discover that her presentation was canceled since only three people signed up, should not put herself down for the poor enrollment. She should instead feel pride at the excellent presentation she created and all the hard work she did in preparing it, although, naturally, she will feel disappointed at not being able to share it with others.

Similarly, we challenge clients' notions that satisfaction and happiness should be handed to us on a silver platter. This is simply not how life works for most of us. Some clients who nonconsciously want to find fuel for their self-pity look at others to whom success has been handed (e.g., the independently wealthy, a movie star or a supermodel who was "discovered," someone who won the lottery) and use these rare instances as a means to feel sorry for themselves or angry that "life is so unfair." We stop clients from thinking this way, point out how rare these cases are, and show clients how they use such thoughts as justifying cognitions for longstanding self-pity and resentment.

ACCEPTING THAT CHANGE CAN BE UNCOMFORTABLE

How do we help clients try out new behaviors that might be scary, painful, or simply unfamiliar? We suggest to them that the self-respect that results from attempting to do difficult things comes from making choices that involve (1) working against indulgence and familiarity; and (2) therefore, doing things that make one feel uncomfortable. In the preceding excerpt from Richard's session, Richard suggests to the client that her guilt at standing up to her mother is a positive feeling (unlike guilt at doing something wrong), since it signals that she is taking a risk and doing something new: "no pain, no gain," as the truthful adage goes. We constantly challenge clients' beliefs that life should only be filled with happiness and that all effort should be pain-free. To the contrary, all change involves some discomfort, and nobody ever said that life is consistently filled with enjoyment—this is what we wish for but it is unrealistic.

Therefore, we often express our satisfaction to clients who say how difficult and painful their changing is. Rather than fostering our clients' proneness to self-pity by "supporting" their pain, we use this as an opportunity to reframe this brand of pain as a celebration of positive change and hard work. We also help clients to deal with the painfulness of doing new, uncomfortable things by helping them to soothe and manage the negative feelings associated with these changes, which we will describe further in the "Emotional Self-Care" section in chapter 8.

> Brenda is a 39-year-old woman who has never been married but says that she wants to be. She is currently dating a long-term friend and they seem to be genuinely in love with each other. However, Brenda often complains that she doesn't like his eating and spending habits, is scared to share an apartment with him because she will have to live with some of his furniture, which she dislikes, and is hesitant generally to share the same space with him. She does not appear to be afraid of getting close to him and feeling embarrassed or ashamed of herself, as some clients do. Rather, Brenda simply wants things her way—she has lived by herself for many years and admits to being very inflexible when it comes to compromise or giving up what she describes as "goodies." She feels this way about change in therapy as well.
>
> The following dialogue ensues in her therapy with Jonathan:
> Client: I love him but all of his habits really bother me. Maybe I'm not cut out to be with him or with anybody, for that matter.
> Jonathan: Maybe you're not.
> Cl: Jonathan, don't say that.
> J: Well, you can't go into a long-term relationship expecting him to change a lifestyle that he's had for 45 years. If he changes a little, great—that's a bonus, but you can't expect to change him. That's a set-up for disappointment on your part and resentment of you on his.
> Cl: But I hate the way he eats and the way he lives—no, some things about his lifestyle.
> J: Well, you can either accept them or not go out with him. That's your choice, but if you stay with him, bug him constantly, and resent him, then that

doesn't sound too great unless you both enjoy your being the nag and his being the henpecked husband. Some couples like playing those roles.

Cl: Ugh, that's not for me. But I just have so much trouble giving up certain things that I want in my life.

J: That's important, what you're saying. It's really difficult for you to compromise, to give up some things to get others. How does it feel to have to make sacrifices?

Cl: Terrible. It makes me feel angry and, well, I guess ... trapped, in a way. I hate the way that sounds.

J: How come?

Cl: It sounds—I sound so spoiled, like a little girl who wants her friends to play her way or she's gong to take all of her marbles and go home.

J: Yeah, it sounds spoiled to me too. I don't believe that you or anybody can get 100% of what they want in life. We have to give up some stuff to get other stuff that we want. If we don't accept this, then we turn—then we become bitter and resentful. Brenda, you're not going to have change in your life, any type of change, unless you're willing to sacrifice some of what you want.

Cl: I know that, but I hate it.

J: Well, you can either let that hate run the show and then you won't change, which is fine, if that's what you want. Or you can get over the hate—calm it down—in order to change. The choice is yours.

Cl: I know.

J: But, if you choose to make some sacrifices, you must do so cheerfully.

Cl: What do you mean?

J: Many people go into relationships saying that they'll compromise with their partner on this or that, but then they use that compromise to resent their partner—sometimes to feel victimized by him or like a martyr. If you willingly agree to give up something, you must take responsibility for your choice and never use it against your partner.

Cl: Being in a relationship is so hard. I hate it.

J: It's very hard. It takes a lot of work. That's my experience in my marriage. You have to think—you have to decide whether you want to do a lot of hard work to get the good stuff with your boyfriend or not.

ASSUMING RESPONSIBILITY ENHANCES SELF-RESPECT AND SELF-CONFIDENCE

In using attribution theory to identify different models of helping and coping, Brickman, Rabinowitz, Karuza, Coates, Cohn, & Kidder (1980) identified four basic types. They varied responsibility for having caused the problem (self versus other) and responsibility for solving the problem (self versus other) to derive these four basic models. The first, the *moral model,* holds the individual responsible for both causing and solving the problem. The second, the *compensatory model,* maintains that one is not responsible for having caused, but is responsible for solving, the problem. In the third, the *enlightenment model,* the individual is seen as responsible for the problem but unable or unwilling to provide solutions, and must, therefore, need discipline and guidance to solve it. The fourth, the *medical model,* views the individual as helpless in causing and solving the problem, and he or she must give over total control for understanding and remedying problems to a more knowledgeable professional. Brickman et al. maintain that, "Unfortunately, choice of models is determined not only by their effectiveness but by their familiarity, their apparent fairness, and their congruence with existing power relationships" (p. 1).

CAT's model of helping is a combination of the compensatory and moral models. We believe that a sense of personal efficacy, self-respect, and an internal locus of control can be fostered by the individual's taking responsibility for his or her actions. Clearly, we do not believe that the individual is the cause for many of his or her problems. First and foremost, one's family of origin—most notably one's parents—greatly shaped one's personality style. If one were born with a particular temperament or genetic constellation that predisposes one to certain difficulties, again, it is the parents who can reinforce or work against that predisposition.

However, we do not blame parents for engendering problems in our clients. In fact, we are not in the business of blaming or judging anybody, nor do we encourage our clients to do so. Instead, we sometimes use parents as explanations for the personotypic affects, emotional setpoints, etc. that our clients struggle to modify. However, our clients' parents had parents too, and, in most cases, they were trying the best they could to rear their children, given the cards that they were dealt in their families of origin.

We do expect clients to be responsible for changing their lives, since no one else will realistically do this for them. And we also hold clients responsible for maintaining and continuing their problems (not the moral model, in the strictest sense, but veering in this direction)—that is, for indulging in security-seeking behaviors, especially after they are aware of their existence.

As such, we challenge our clients' shirking of responsibility in various ways. Self-pity and rageful anger are often predicated on not being treated well by others. At their extremes, they foster a sense of angry victimization in clients. Clients then repeatedly blame their parents for having handed them a miserable personality or a miserable life; or they blame their boss or society for oppressing them ("We live in such a materialistic society. My creativity is squelched in such an environment"; "Nobody gives you the time of day anymore unless you're a Donald Trump or a Rupert Murdoch"); or they continually gripe about their spouse ("He never listens to me"; "She never tells me she loves me") or their children ("They don't appreciate all I do for them"; "I'd be happy if my kid would do what I want just once").

In CAT, we disallow blame for one's behavior and always give the responsibility back to the client. Not only does this combat personotypic self-pity and rage, but it also gives the client credit when he or she changes. We might empathize with a client whose spouse constantly is angry at or critical of them, but we then ask, "So what are you doing to pull such anger/criticism from your partner?" To the parent who whines the refrain, "My children disrespect me," we might empathize with how difficult it is to live under such conditions but we always query, "What have you done to lose your kids' respect?"

If the client with the angry spouse counters that she is doing nothing to pull anger from her partner, then we might suggest that she either married an angry individual, which may serve to rekindle personotypic affect, security-seeking behaviors, etc. from her family of origin, or that she must be doing something because people don't go around being angry without provocation. We do the same with a parent: either his children are going through a normal development phase where they should be bridling against his authority and he should be countering with firm, effective limits and consequences (which, clearly, he is not), or he is doing something since children are normally programmed to listen to and learn from their parents. We then forbid such blaming of others and explore where this tendency to blame came from in the client's family of origin.

To the client who complains and feels "powerless" in his or her life, we ask, "Are you an actual victim or a psychological one?" This helps to differentiate actually having been traumatized (e.g., a rape or some sort of significant abuse) from repeatedly feeling like a victim. In the latter case, then we can ask, "Who taught you to feel like a victim?" and invariably one or both of the client's parents frequently felt like a victim in their lives.

> Andrew, a 40-year-old physician, frequently expressed uncalled-for rage at his son Ronald. He said that he dreaded coming home from work, and often felt like he was "trapped," being "taken advantage of," or "victimized" by his son. Andrew often used the refrains, "He doesn't appreciate me" and "He does things just to spite me." After much exploration, it was determined that Ronald's behavior fell in the range of normal 6-year-old behavior, although, naturally, Ronald was beginning to display anxious, fearful, and angry behavior as the result of Andrew's outbursts.
>
> The therapist had a session with Andrew alone, and he discovered that Andrew felt victimized (his word) by his neighbors, who often complained of the noisiness in Andrew's apartment, various co-workers, his wife's family, and his wife. (Andrew blamed his wife for "forcing" him to buy their current apartment and have a child, although Andrew admitted that basically he just

"gave in" to what she wanted rather than standing his ground.) Andrew said that, growing up and to the present day, his mother also always felt like a victim, was a highly suspicious person, and bitterly complained and whined about being taken advantage of. Andrew's father died when he was an adolescent, and he had very fond memories of his being a kind and wise parent, although somewhat passive in the face of his wife's complaining. Andrew also said that, personality-wise, he resembled his mother, although he longed to live up to his father's example.

The CAT therapist basically helped Andrew to see that, in fact, he was not a victim in his life but that he often set the stage, either behaviorally by ceding the power to another or in how he misperceived situations, to feel like an enraged victim. The therapy then involved Andrew and/or the therapist catching Andrew playing the role of the victim, most pointedly with his son, and then helping Andrew to attribute his angry victim feelings to his childhood and not to the present, and giving him a variety of strategies to calm down these feelings.

Just as we disallow blaming others for one's problems, we also prohibit clients from blaming themselves. It is health-promoting to acknowledge that one needs to correct a maladaptive thought or behavior; it is unhealthy (that is, shame-promoting) to berate oneself repeatedly for engaging in such thoughts and behaviors. If a client, for example, repeatedly puts himself down for not changing quickly enough or for repeating longstanding maladaptive patterns anew, we stop him from doing this, we also remind him of the power of the emotional setpoint—that change is difficult and nonlinear in nature and, if he insists on putting himself down for not changing in a perfect, unrealistic way, then he is doing so to rekindle his personotypic shame and self-pity.

We also point out the minutiae of self-pity in order to discourage clients from shirking personal responsibility. It is common to have certain clients begin sessions with a litany of complaints about trivia: the weather has been horrible, they couldn't find a decent parking space, nothing has been going right for them today, etc. We jokingly label this attitude Ripped-Off Disorder (ROD) to such clients, and point out how automatic their thoughts eliciting self-pity are. Clients with chronic ROD view themselves as beleaguered by the world, as basically having an external locus of control, and, therefore, as not responsible for much that happens in their lives. We challenge this vigorously (and often with humor).

We also disallow clients' use of certain phrases and perceptions in therapy that imply that the client has no control over and responsibility for his or her actions. We make clients change phrases that place them in the passive position or that imply that they are not in control of their destiny with those denoting active involvement and control. Thus, "I can't change" is substituted with

"I will not change." Statements by clients such as, "He made me do it" or "She's controlling me" are challenged by the CAT therapist: "Unless he/she had a gun to your head, he/she did not make you do it. You allowed him/her to have his/her way."

Active is substituted for passive language. Phrases such as, "When I am less depressed" are replaced with, "When I am able to address my feelings effectively." In a similar vein, we do not allow clients to reify their diagnoses or supposed conditions to let them off the hook for change. Reifying ADD, depression, chronic fatigue, obsessive–compulsive disorder, etc. (see chapter 6) in order to negate personal responsibility is not accepted by the CAT therapist. We show clients, when they are ready to accept hearing it, that they use these "illnesses" to fuel self-pity and anger, and to avoid feeling uncomfortable as they do something new and different to change.

We also challenge clients' use of words such as "abandoned" ("When my boyfriend broke up with me, I felt abandoned by him") and "support" ("I need your support during this rough time") since these are the requirements of a child who needs to be cared for but not those of a self-sufficient adult. To the client who feels abandoned, we might say, "Only children are abandoned by neglectful parents. You are a self-sufficient adult who may feel annoyed, disappointed, or sad when your boyfriend broke up with you, but you will not shrivel up and die as a result of this." To the client who wants support or, worse, "unconditional love," we might say, "Only underwear provides support to adults; and parents provide support to their children. You must find a way to reassure *yourself*, rather than depending on others do this for you." To the person seeking unconditional love, we may respond, "Only parents give unconditional love to their children. Love between adults *should* be conditional—based on how respectfully one adult treats another. If you abuse me in some way, I most certainly will not love you unconditionally. I'll leave you. Harmful, negative behaviors should have negative consequences."

TO CHANGE OR NOT TO CHANGE: THAT IS THE CLIENT'S CHOICE

One facet of giving clients responsibility for their actions is helping them to see that it is their choice to change or not to change. During the first session, we usually do a functional analysis with the client by asking two basic (but often overlooked) questions: (1) What do you want (to change)? (2) What are you willing to do to get it? Clients often have no difficulty listing the changes they want to have in their lives, but they often stumble over the second question. The second question not only implies that it is the client's responsibility to effect change, but that such change involves work and, often, sacrifice. As clients (especially passive ones who expect change to occur just by their attending therapy) struggle with taking responsibility for change, we return to the second question of the functional analysis throughout the therapy.

Therapist: So what is it that you'd like to change?

Client: I don't want to live at home anymore. I'm an adult being treated like a child by my parents.

Th: What then are you willing to do to move out?

Cl: Well, I'm really pissed at my parents because they won't pay for the rent for an apartment for me.

Th: Well, since that's not a possibility, what do you need to do to move out?

Cl: If only I could convince my parents…

Th: Have you tried?

Cl: Yes, I've tried everything. Nothing will work.

Th: Then it looks like you'll have to rely on yourself. What do you need to do to move out?

Cl: Get a job, but I just don't have the stamina or the confidence to get and keep a job. You don't understand. I can't do it.

Th: You can do it but you won't. You don't believe that you can handle it.

Cl: Yes.

Th: Then you're stuck living at home.

Cl: No way! [angrily] I thought you're supposed to help me!

Th: I am, but your only available choices are to live with your parents or work with me to develop the strength and the skills that it takes to get a job and live independently. That's how I can help you. What do you think?

Cl: I'd rather that my parents paid the rent, but if that's a done deal, then I guess I'll have to learn to do it on my own. I just don't think I can. I don't know what it takes.

Th: I know, and it must be scary to think of doing all of this on your own. But let's start by defining what you must learn to do in order to become self-sufficient. OK?

Cl: Yes.

Moreover, we never superimpose any change-oriented goals on our clients. We often help clients to define what they need to do to get the changes they desire, and to consider the positive and negative consequences of both changing and not changing. If a client realizes in the course of therapy that he or she does not want to do the work required to change, then the therapy has been valuable to that client. We are not in the business of forcing clients to change; it is our job to help clients to make informed decisions. In doing so, we help clients improve their sense of responsibility and self-respect.

Lance is a 45-year-old man who has always lived with his mother. During the course of therapy, he came to realize that he really enjoyed how his mother *cared for him and considered the changes necessary to getting married, one of his initial goals for therapy, to be too aversive for him to take on. He decided that he would remain with his mother and stop feeling "like a loser" and "left out" by doing so. Lance and his therapist then worked on ways to calm down and challenge his shame and self-pity when he compared himself to his married friends.*

It is important not to fall into the trap of making value judgments concerning the client's goals in therapy. Not only is this patronizing and blaming toward the client, it also takes the responsibility away from the client for setting goals and effecting them.

Often, and especially with passive–submissive and active–submissive clients, acknowledging that the client has the right not to change has a paradoxical effect, although this is not the primary objective of the CAT therapist here. Clients who covertly want the therapist to talk them out of a no-change position, presumably as other people have repeatedly in their lives, are surprised when this does not occur. They then are left by the therapist to make their own decisions—a corrective experience in and of itself. Used to rebelling against what they are told by others, they now are stuck (at least temporarily) taking the change position.

Fifty-five-year-old Marie often complains to her therapist that she will never change, that her therapist cannot help her, and that she doesn't know why she comes to therapy at all. She also refuses to set clear goals for her therapy, as she maintains that she won't attain them anyway. The therapist responds that, while she enjoys working with Marie, maybe Marie is right. If Marie doesn't want to set any goals and feels so pessimistic about therapy, maybe therapy is not for her.

Marie gets angry at this, saying, "You're supposed to help me, not agree with me," and she sulks for the rest of the session. However, she continues to attend her sessions regularly. Her active participation increases and her complaining decreases somewhat after this session.

Forty-eight-year-old Robert calls his mother every morning to complain and express confusion about how to handle something in his life: his "cruel" boss, what doctors he should see, whether he should take the subway to an event in a different part of town or stay home, etc. His mother then gives him her opinion, as she always has done, and Robert often does the opposite. Robert tries to do the same thing with his therapist. The therapist not only points out that he is repeating his interaction with his mother in therapy, but also asks Robert, "What do you want to do about this problem?" When Robert gives him his answer, the therapist replies, "That sounds like an excellent idea to me." When Robert then shifts his opinion to the other side, as he sometimes does, the therapist expresses faith in however Robert decides to

solve the problem, and he stresses that he has total faith in Robert's ability to
make the right decision.

LEARNING HOW TO SET APPROPRIATE
BOUNDARIES WITH OTHERS

Self-respect also comes from setting appropriate boundaries with others. Clients, especially passive–submissive ones who avoid feared conflict or who play out longstanding patterns of placating and then resenting others, often fail to say no to the influence of others when they should. These clients are left feeling weak, used, and resentful, and feel little respect for themselves as agents in the world. We, therefore, help clients to define situations where doing what others want will violate their self-respect and to say "no" to others in appropriate ways. In the preceding example from Richard's session, Richard helped his client, using a modified gestalt technique, to say to her mother "Don't call me today."

In order to be able to set a much-needed boundary or limit with another, a person must (1) identify what has stopped him/her from doing this in the past—familiarity with the passive role or fear of the other's response, for example; (2) learn how to calm down these fears (which we will cover in the "Emotional Self-Care" section of chapter 8); and (3) practice setting these boundaries in firm and appropriate ways using role-play in therapy. With regard to the latter step, the therapist often asks the client to role-play the person with whom he or she is having difficulty setting a boundary and the therapist assumes the role of the new-and-improved client.

This is done for three reasons. First, it avoids the embarrassment the client may feel at being put on the spot to do something that he or she has previously had great trouble doing. Second, only the client knows how the other person behaves and what he or she says. The client can enact this role more accurately than the therapist. Third, this gives the therapist an opportunity to model various assertive responses and for the client to learn from observing this. Usually, when the role-play reaches a point where the therapist stymies the client, then the therapist-as-client has successfully set a useful boundary with the client's role-played "oppressor." Finally, the therapist will often switch roles with the client and have him or her practice setting boundaries with the oppressor.

In addition to role-playing boundary-setting, we model assertively setting boundaries to our clients via how we behave during sessions. We do not allow clients to speak disrespectfully to us; in many cases, we disallow showing up to sessions late or failing to call to cancel an appointment (if this is a pattern for the client); and, occasionally, we "fire" clients from therapy who repeatedly violate these basic rules. We also act in a self-confident manner around our clients during sessions and in the waiting room.

ENCOURAGING COMPETENCE

Self-respect is naturally gained through feeling competent and becoming competent at a variety of activities. Passive–submissive clients, in particular, depend on others to do many things by claiming that they are incompetent or that tasks are just too daunting or complex for them. They, therefore, have developed a variety of ways to rely on others to take care of them, but this also prevents them from feeling self-respect and self-confidence. Passive–submissive female clients often claim "technological incompetence" to maintain their dependence, saying that they just "can't" learn how to operate a computer, a VCR, and other common gadgets.

The therapist must encourage these clients to learn basic skills, be they technological or otherwise, by not accepting "I can't" or "I'm too weak" or "I'm too dumb" statements from clients and by relating such thinking to the client's passive–submissive personality style. Often, one of these client's parents was a caretaker while the other dependently pulled the first parent to do for him or her. The therapist must also make this connection for the client.

Clients who maintain that they are too scared to learn a new skill or get too anxious while trying to do so must learn that they will never feel competent, confident, and self-respectful unless they take some risks, and that failing to succeed initially while learning is natural and to be expected.

AN EXAMPLE OF WORKING ON SELF-RESPECT

A 40-year-old male client says that he wants to work on his procrastination problem. He has to write brief articles as part of his job, and he almost always waits for the last minute to hand them in or he hands them in late.

Client: I really want to finish the articles on time at work, but I just— every time I sit down to do it, something else comes up and I just don't do it. And then I feel badly because Nancy [his co-worker who coordinates the articles] *gets on my case.*

Therapist: So what do you get out of her getting on your case? [This is a question we use often (a) to suggest that such behavior is intentional, even if it is not experienced as such, and (b) to highlight the motivational aspect of security-seeking behavior and personotypic affect—that there is a nonconscious purpose to behaving and feeling this way.]

Cl: What do I get out of it? [Pause] *Well, then I can feel put upon by Nancy and angry at her, and I can feel like I've screwed up.*

Th: And what do you get out of that?

Cl: Well, I feel that way a lot. You know, like … But the predominant feeling is [angrily] *"Why are people rushing me?"*

Th: *And what's the feeling?*

Cl: *Well, I guess I feel like a victim. Sorry for myself and angry.* [The therapist has highlighted the personotypic affects, anger and self-pity, that result from the security-seeking behavior of procrastination.]

Th: *Who with?*

Cl: *With Nancy, in this case. And, in general, with anybody who's on my case. I–I get really angry.*

Th: *So you do this. So what's the problem?*

[This comment highlights that the therapist is being nonjudgmental—that this is simply what the client does. The therapist then asks the client if this behavior is disturbing to the client.]

Cl: *Well* [pause], *I guess I'd like to be more efficient and not put myself through this. You know, I don't really take it out on other people, but I might, in some ways. I don't want to put anybody else through this.*

Th: *So what stops you from being the way you want to be?*

Cl: *Um … well, I just don't seem able to change it. I tell myself I want to be different and then I just do the same thing.*

Th: *Well, yes, sure. I could tell myself I want to be different and be the same way, too. You've got to take some action. What stops you from taking action?*

[These comments hold the client responsible for change and explore how the client's security-seeking behavior works against his assuming responsibility.]

Cl: *Well, I know I stop myself, but I guess I don't catch myself at it.*

Th: *So, you're kind of oblivious? You don't notice what you do?*

Cl: *Yeah, I think I make myself oblivious. I get wrapped up in a lot of stuff that I'm doing in my life.*

Th: *Do you come from a self-centered family?*

[The therapist now links the client's behavior and the narcissism inherent in his passive–submissive behavior to his parents' personality styles.]

Cl: *Uh, yeah.* [laughs] *Both my parents were self-centered in their own ways.*

Th: *You sound very tied up in yourself and there isn't much concern for Nancy in all of this.*

[The therapist uses empathy training, which we will discuss in chapter 11, to cut through the client's narcissistic involvement in his personotypic affect and justifying cognitions.]

Cl: *No, that's true. It's all about my own —*

Th: *I mean, she's just trying to do her job.*

Cl: *I know. I know.*

Th: *You have an authority problem.*

Cl: *Yeah, I do.*

Th: No, actually, you don't have an authority problem. You have a reality problem. You see, in the real world, you've got to be responsible and do what you say you're going to do. In your fantasy world, you don't have to. In your fantasy world, you don't even have to notice that you're not doing it.

[The therapist highlights that many clients hold on to an unrealistic view of the world to avoid assuming responsibility and to fuel personotypic affect of rage and self-pity for the world's not living up to their expectations.]

Cl: That's right.

Th: There are five behaviors that I often talk about with clients: binging, whining, pleasing, procrastinating, and avoiding. Which of these do you do?

Cl: [Pause] All except binging.

Th: What do you get out of all of those?

Cl: That's what I've always done! So did and does my mother. It's all I know.

[The client becomes aware of the familiarity of his personotypic affect and justifying cognitions.]

Th: It's your engine's fuel. It's what feeds your engine.

[The therapist points out the motivating property of personotypic affect.]

Cl: My motivation in life. [Pause] OK.

Th: So you'll have to get mad at Nancy since you're feeling angry.

Cl: Well, I can't do that since it's not rational anger. She hasn't done anything to make me angry; I know that.

Th: So why can't you do this irrational thing along with all the others?

Cl: [laughs] That would be public.

Th: You're only privately irrational.

Cl: That's right. I'm only irrational in my spare time, in private.

Th: Let me check out one thing. Did you agree to give Nancy something?

Cl: Yes.

Th: Was this a voluntary agreement or did she torture you into saying yes?

Cl: Well, it's part of my job, but it's sort of optional, on the side. I guess it's voluntary, really, since if I didn't do it, someone else would and there wouldn't be any repercussions at work.

Th: So you don't keep your word.

[This emphasizes the lack of responsibility on the client's part. It moves the client away from his narcissistic justifying cognition that he is Nancy's victim and focuses him on his effect on Nancy—that he broke a promise. This now becomes a moral issue.]

Cl: To some extent.

Th: How does that feel, to be a person that lacks integrity?

[The therapist highlights the client's guilt to break through his narcissistic self-pity and anger and to highlight his having mistreated a colleague.]

Cl: Well, now you put it that way, pretty lousy. I'm feeling guilty about it. And ashamed of myself.

Th: *OK, good. If you don't want to continue to feel that way, then you better do what you say. Or you could continue to feel ashamed, if you want to. It is a choice, you know. I'm not here to make you a good guy. I'm here to point out what you do. It's up to you.*

[The therapist highlights that the client is responsible for changing or not. While the therapist has implicitly shared his values with the client— that he should have integrity—he also gives the client the message that he will not criticize or negatively judge the client for acting otherwise.]

Cl: *Right.*

Th: *I won't criticize you if you still go on and procrastinate. It's OK by me. But if you do agree to do something, do it cheerfully.*

Cl: *So I don't set anybody up then.*

Th: *That's right. Especially yourself. Then you can be a man of integrity.* [Pause] *Do you know, I sense you don't value sacrifice. I have a feeling that you don't value discomfort. That you don't see the good of it.*

Cl: [Pause] *I suppose not. I suppose I resent it. I do it, but I resent it.*

Th: *I think you need to look into that. You know, you only feel competent when things are difficult. You don't feel competent cooking dinner. You feel competent dealing with difficult situations and people effectively. You don't seem to have that model.*

[The therapist now teaches the client about what it takes to feel self-respect and satisfaction—a model different from the one held by the client.]

Cl: *Yeah, I bite the bullet rather than saying, "This is good" or "This is a challenge."*

Th: *You might look into that; developing challenge skills. Enjoying a challenge. You'll feel pleasure from meeting a challenge. You might feel pleasure from handing in an article to Nancy on time or even early.*

Cl: *I probably would.*

SETTING THE STAGE FOR CAT: CREATING A NONSHAMING THERAPEUTIC ENVIRONMENT

Before we explore the foreground of CAT and, in particular, spend time looking at interventions aimed at personotypic affect and the emotional setpoint, we want to describe the therapeutic environment that we establish to enable CAT to be effective. In CAT, we usually spend much time and attention exploring clients' shameful feelings. Talking about shame and also admitting to self-pity can potentially lead to further feelings of embarrassment and humiliation for clients, and clients, therefore, run the risk of shutting down or not returning to therapy. Moreover, as you can see in our last clinical example, we are often exceedingly honest and direct with our clients in a way that could be experienced by them as challenging. Since we teach, express our opinions, and are an active presence in the therapy, we do not also want clients to feel one-down with us, like we are the masters and they the humble students, which would, naturally, foster further shame, anger, and self-pity.

To avoid this scenario, we create a nonshaming, nonblaming, nonjudgmental therapeutic environment. Yes, we may hold clients responsible for their actions, but we do not blame them for their behaviors. In fact, we don't blame clients' parents either, although they might have unintentionally been the cause of problems in our clients. Most parents genuinely love their children and try to do a good job of parenting, but many were not given the tools by *their* parents to parent effectively. They cannot be blamed for this.

We also express our values to clients and point out the negative effects that some of our clients' behaviors have on others. But again, we do not judge our clients' values, unless they are causing great harm to others. Instead, we may agree to disagree if our clients choose not to concur with or adopt our value system. Many of our clients come to us, especially those in couples therapy, unable to accept different values that others in their lives hold. They are highly critical of others and even more critical of themselves—vulnerable to shame if anybody even questions their own values. It is, therefore, therapeutic to clients who hold values different from our own to maintain a good working relationship with a therapist who nonjudgementally accepts their different standards.

Once shame and blame are banished from the therapy room, clients can begin to experience a new sense of self-respect and acceptance from another. Blame, judgmentalness, and criticism are the fuel of shame, self-pity, and rage-ful anger, and an absence of these fosters self-respect, empathy for others, receptivity to others' caring, and self-confidence. We now turn to the specific components of CAT's nonshaming therapeutic environment.

THERAPIST SELF-DISCLOSURE

Shame can be reduced greatly with therapist self-disclosure (Wessler, 1993a; Wessler & Hankin-Wessler, 1986). When clinically relevant, the therapist can join with the client by self-disclosing similar experiences and similar feelings. Every therapist, at one time or another, has experienced shame, rage, and self-pity and has thought him-herself to be incompetent, unloved, and/or ineffectual. Moreover, we all struggle with the shortcomings of our particular personality style (yes, every personality style has some) as they play out internally, at work, or in our relationships and friendships. When a client has a personality style similar to that of the therapist, or client and therapist share some similar aspects of personality (and this almost always is true), therapist self-disclosure can again strengthen the alliance and reduce shame in the client. Sharing similar feelings, thoughts, and behaviors with clients turns the therapist into a well-informed colleague rather than placing clients in the shame-inducing position of disclosing embarrassing shortcomings to a distant "expert" on high.

> For example, in the CAT parent-training groups that I (Jonathan) conduct, I often share with group members a problem I have had in raising my children, and I try to do so with humor, to give the message, "It's not a big deal here to share personal shortcomings." Also, by linking my parenting problems to how I was raised, I set the stage for parents doing this later in the group. One example that I use frequently involves my son Christopher when he was an infant.
>
> My mother, while well-intentioned, panics easily when she believes something is unsafe, for herself, for me, or now for my children—and she believes that many objects, behaviors, and situations are unsafe. She herself was the youngest of three children in a poor family with a single mother who worked 20 hours a day during the Depression. She describes herself as a somewhat lonely, fearful "latchkey kid," so it is not difficult to imagine how she might have grown up feeling lonely, afraid of the world, and longing to have her fears soothed by another. Nevertheless, while growing up, I used to resent her many fears, her sometimes leaning on me to take care of them, and her valuing safety and security above all else. I swore that I would never be excessive in my worries like her, and that I would not impose them on others.
>
> When Christopher was 9 months old, he took my glasses off of my head, which he occasionally did to amuse himself. This time, however, he appeared to poke himself in the eye with one of the sidepieces. I immediately shouted "ooh, ooh" (exactly what my mother says in similar situations), froze, and did absolutely nothing that was helpful—much as my mother, paralyzed by her fearful helplessness, might have done. I handed my son to my wife, who I assumed would be better equipped to handle the situation. After seeing that Christopher was, in fact, fine (although he was crying, surely in reaction to my shouts), my wife looked at me with her and-you-call-yourself-a-child-psychologist look. I realized at that moment that I had internalized not only my mother's fearful beliefs but, more centrally, her underlying shameful belief that I was an incompetent parent incapable of preventing danger from befalling my son. (And my highly competent wife, on whom I must depend, is worthy to care for him.)

The therapist must be careful not to play up how far he or she has come from the days when or she struggled with a problem similar to the client's so as to avoid having the client feel one-upped by the therapist. Conversely, the therapist must not give the client the impression that he or she is still mired down in his or her problems, as this will inspire no confidence in the client in the therapist's own mental health and competence. And certainly, we avoid self-disclosing out of our own needs or out of narcissism, although we do let clients know that we are pretty much an open book and they can feel free to ask us anything about our lives whenever they want. This, too, fosters mutual trust and the client's feeling close to the therapist in a colleagial rather than a hierarchical relationship. It also models to shy and withdrawn clients how to self-disclose to foster closeness in a relationship. Therapists who do not self-disclose, and this includes therapists from the majority of orientations, must ask themselves if they are ashamed or embarrassed to do so, either because they do not want someone else knowing about them or because they are afraid of relating to the client as another person not that much unlike themselves.

THE SHARING OF NOTES IN THERAPY

Another way that therapists can exclude and patronize clients is to take notes in front of them—notes that the client never sees again. The stereotype here is of the ever-silent analyst, scribbling away on a small pad, who makes no contact with the patient whatsoever as he or she talks on and on. The "profound" scribblings are never shared with the patient, nor do the scribblings affect what the analyst does—or more likely doesn't do—in the therapy. The note-taking sends out a message: "I am writing profound thoughts, sometimes judgments of you, that are only for my all-knowing eyes. You could never possibly understand them."

The mystery of the notes can also influence some clients' in-session focus and behavior. I (Jonathan) recall that, when I was a psychology intern, I participated in psychodynamic psychotherapy. The therapist clearly paid careful attention to me, as I could tell by his intense and penetrating gaze, but he often said very little. However, when I recounted a dream (which I thought I should do, since the therapist was analytic, after all), the therapist would get an excited look on his face (or so I thought), grab a pad lying near him, lean forward in his chair, and furiously write. Being a people-pleaser in those days (and being as obedient as Skinner's pigeons), I found myself recounting more and more dreams of greater complexity in therapy. I tended not to remember most of my dreams before starting this therapy and, after ending the therapy, I returned to forgetting most of them, but I would faithfully dream a whopper the night before my therapy sessions. This also attests to the interpersonal power of note-taking for some clients.

In CAT, we do not believe in excluding clients. Therefore, we give our session notes to our clients at the end of each meeting. Naturally, we compose our notes with the client in mind, often making comments about personotypic affect, justifying cognitions, security-seeking behaviors, the influence of parents, and what to do about them. We take a smaller piece of paper from a pad, put carbon paper behind it, and clip it to a regular-sized pad. In this way, we can write notes on the smaller paper for the client, keep a copy for our records, and also write notes for ourselves (mostly facts like people's names, dates, and medications being taken) in the margins on the larger piece of paper.

Here are some examples of notes that we have given to clients at the end of our sessions:

> #1:
> Father —
> Never prepared you for independence
> But tries to FORCE you into it
> Barrages of criticism—you do this to yourself (like he did), generating shame—this needs to be eliminated
> Avoidance of a relationship (men as rejecting, critical, abandoners) makes you "choked up" and scared
> Anxiety=fear of victimization in the future
> #2:
> Doing what's right but not what makes you happy—this is the adult approach to life
> Your anxiety makes you narcissistic—you have to be "marketable" to another
> Food calms you down and indulges you when you feel deprived and lonely—like a baby with a bottle
> Deal with your feelings when you reach for food—calm down your anxiety and fears
> Eating to take you out of the dating game?
> Fear motivates you
> Be afraid: think about [your boyfriend] dating a beautiful 25-year-old to motivate you to work out
> #3:
> Your not working turns [your wife] into your dissatisfied mother
> Doing something (work) you don't want to do, but that's right
> You've made your bed, now accept it and get a job—no whining, no anger
> You feel unworthy (your dad) but you know you're not—ignore the feelings, they're from your past, not a reflection of Reality
> You have romantic (unrealistic) views of what life is and what work is/should be—generates rage and self-pity
> Use the fear of [your wife] leaving you to motivate you to get up and out in the morning
> #4:
> Always yearning to be cared for—taken care of—even by doctors—this really hurts you, as no one does this except for their kids

Slipping into childlike dependence—sickness pulls assistance
What you need hurts you—calming reassurance helps feelings like pills do
Desperate for people to comfort you—you do not FOCUS ON SELF-COM-
FORT
The "what-if" game is a self-pity and fear-creator
#5:
Anger awakens people—an activating emotion
(1) Dreading criticism
(2) Yearning for affirmation
(3) Pleasing others to avoid the first and achieve the second—This policy
fails, in that pleasing, needy behavior is passive and "invites" disrespect, cre-
ating shame, self-pity, and anger
A philosophy of blame enrages you—EMPATHY for others works
Stress—an emotional overreaction to a difficult situation
Stress= ANGER & SELF-PITY

We simply hand these notes to clients at session's end, without specifying if or how they should be used. Some clients keep our notes in a notebook or binder to refer back to them or study them between sessions. Certainly, for borderline clients who need to form a close relationship with the therapist initially but also need to hold on to something concrete to do so, just the act of giving them the notes is quite helpful.

Before meeting his future in-laws, one client copied a few suggestions for how to handle his feelings around them from his notes of that week onto a 3×5 note card. When the going got rough during the dinner with them, he excused himself and went to the bathroom to review these notes. He reported that this was central to his not feeling ashamed of himself in front of his fiancée's parents and not acting out of this shame. One adolescent asked the therapist to write down a role-play that they had done in which the boy asked his parents for a favor rather than tantruming angrily, as usual. He practiced this "script," then behaved accordingly at home, and had a great success in interacting appropriately with his parents.

Many clients ask us to write down comments that either we or they have made during a session in our notes, and sometimes clients have us write down homework assignments that they themselves have come up with. When clients actively participate in the note-writing, then the therapeutic alliance (and a relatively egalitarian one at that) is significantly strengthened.

We have found this form of note-taking particularly helpful to us as therapists. Knowing that we must produce notes that serve as an intervention, focused on personotypic affect, justifying cognitions, etc., has caused us to increase our focus on what the client is saying and to keep our theoretical underpinnings always in mind during sessions. The notes help us to integrate

CAT with the process and content of the session, to always think about what will be helpful to the client, and to boil down our CAT thinking into succinct, understandable communications.

GIVING EMPATHY, NOT SYMPATHY, TO CLIENTS

As mentioned in chapter 4, clients who pity themselves and who (sometimes nonconsciously) want others to take care of them—namely, passive–submissive and passive–dominant clients—pull forth sympathy from others. As such, the therapist who feels sorry for the client's plight and the therapist who does not confront the client's own sympathy-seeking, is reinforcing the power of the client's self-pity and dependence. The therapist is also undoubtedly playing the complementary role in the client's interpersonal security-seeking behavior.

Giving sympathy to the client also places him or her in the one-down position (as the weak, downtrodden one, talking to a stronger, more stable other) and, therefore, increases the risk of the client's feeling ashamed or embarrassed in front of the therapist. If one wants others to pity him-herself, then the implication is that he or she is unable (inadequate, weak, etc.) to stand up to others, and this inadequacy breeds shame. Additionally, if the therapist decides to comment on the client's self-pity, the acknowledgement of this emotion frequently causes the client to feel embarrassed or ashamed of him-herself.

We therefore strongly recommend not giving any form of sympathy to the client. Instead, we encourage therapists to react empathically (in an understanding, sometimes compassionate way) toward the client. Here is the difference:

> Thirty-nine-year-old Lucy is the mother of an 8-year-old girl and is in a relationship with a sweet, caring man. She has frequent panic attacks, especially in the subway, and therefore she does not take the subway. She is overweight. She comes to her third therapy session and sits in a very proper, erect fashion, with her knees together and a tissue carefully folded in a square resting on them. She has a wide, drawn smile on her face throughout the session. She speaks in a soft, singsong, weak, almost "little girl" tone of voice. She begins:
>
> "Hi. How are you? [pause. sighs.] I have been thinking about all of the things we have been talking about and I really resent being a mother. You know, I want to be such a good mother, but, you know, I have to stay home and take care of my daughter. Rollo, you know, my husband, he's so nice, but he tells me I'd feel better if I were working, but you know, I was thinking of going to work in the summer, but at the same time...
>
> "So, I was thinking, I get up in the morning, if I prepare one more bagel and butter it, I'm going to go crazy. But if I go to work, then I'm going to have to come home and ... Rollo, he has the best deal. You know where he is today? Atlantic City. You know, he can take off with his co-workers and they're all in

Atlantic City. I have to take my daughter to a picnic for mothers and their children, and I don't want to do it. But you know, she's a kid, and I have to take her. I don't want to go, and I feel guilty. What kind of mother will I be if I don't take her? You know? I resent my husband. He has a good life. He can come, he can go. I have to stay home, you know?"

Now, the therapist may make a comment such as, "It really sounds like you have it rough" or, trying to be "supportive" (a concept that is not used in CAT), the therapist says things such as, "You really have sacrificed a career to be a devoted mother and wife" or "I really feel for you. It must be so difficult watching everyone else have fun and success while you stay in the background supporting them." These statement may increase the client's self-pity and give her further justification for feeling this way.

Conversely, some therapists who want to "play tough" with the client, and who, in fact, find the client's whining aversive, may confront her with, "Your life really doesn't sound so bad; it seems to me that you have the same caretaking responsibilities as the rest of us." Naturally, the client will feel unheard and may feel even more sorry for herself now in the therapy relationship: "Here's yet another person, my therapist, who doesn't understand the sacrifices I make in my life. If anybody should understand this, it should be my therapist."

Instead, the CAT therapist may first reflect back or elicit from the client how this situation makes her feel, empathically remark upon how terrible that must feel to her, and then explore why she is choosing to conduct her life in this way:

Therapist: So how do you feel about this, Lucy?
Client: Like I'm trapped; like nobody cares about me?
Th: And how does that make you feel?
Cl: Sad, hopeless and angry, and resentful toward others.
Th: That sounds pretty terrible: walking around with all that hopelessness, anger, and, I think, self-pity.
Cl: What do you mean self-pity?
Th: Well, feeling sorry for yourself that your life isn't different and that others don't treat you with more respect and understanding.
Cl: Yes, that's true. I never thought of it as feeling sorry for myself but I guess I do.
Th: Have you felt these feelings about yourself and your life for a long time, even before your daughter and husband came into your life?
Cl: Well, I suppose so. Well, yes.

The therapy is now off and running. The therapist was able to underline Lucy's self-pity without giving in to or validating it, was able to empathize with her feelings without encouraging them, and, finally, is on the way to having Lucy link her current feelings and situation to those of her family of origin as the first step to having Lucy take responsibility for repeating these childhood feelings in her current adult relationships. The therapist has done so empathically and without infantilizing Lucy by agreeing with her self-pity.

Therapists should be aware of their own self-pity and nonconscious desires to be cared for by others. Therapists who tend to feel sorry for themselves to a great degree may tend to feel sorry for their clients and ratify their self-pity.

EXPLORING HOW THE CLIENT WAS PARENTED WITHOUT BLAMING ANYONE

Non-blame can arise from exploring how the client's parents influenced their current personotypic affect, justifying cognitions, and security-seeking behaviors. Feelings and thoughts in reaction to others can be likened to those either elicited by the client's parents or modeled by them. Personotypic affect, justifying cognitions, and security-seeking behavior can then be attributed *not* to the client but to the way the client was raised. Once clients begin to see that their shame-eliciting thoughts and behaviors were learned in childhood— when a child has no other choice but to accept and thrive on the type of attachment offered by the parent—then the client's self-blame and rage can begin to abate. And the client also will not feel judged by the therapist, who now knows where behaviors that could be embarrassing or humiliating came from.

> *Randall, a 45-year-old man, was initially extremely embarrassed to discuss his cross-dressing with his male therapist. However, in discussing how he had grown up with a very strong, aggressive, and domineering mother and older sister, and a weak father who all but abandoned the family after the parents divorced, he began to see how, as a young child, he came to equate power with being female. Moreover, as his horrible self-image and self-confidence developed, he longed to be more powerful and self-confident and the only way he had been taught to access these feelings was by being female. Thus, Randall put on dresses to feel the self-assurance and sense of power that he had not learned to experience as a male.*
>
> *Once he and his therapist had explored this, Randall's embarrassment and shame in discussing these issues—and in cross-dressing itself—melted away. His understanding that cross-dressing developed as a way of experiencing power and self-confidence had been learned (unwittingly, by him) in his family of origin. It was, in fact, the best way that he knew of feeling self-respect, given his early family dynamics. He now came to understand that, if he wished, he could seek out greater self-confidence in other ways. More importantly, he now felt no shame or embarrassment in therapy concerning these behaviors.*

156

Recall the case of Lucy, described in the last section. The therapist had just discovered from Lucy that she has often felt deprived, sorry for herself, angered, and like a martyr throughout her life. By exploring some basic facts about Lucy's family of origin, the therapist learned that Lucy's mother wanted Lucy to "always be there" for her, to constantly take care of her. Her father, on the other hand, was volatile—the only one in the family who was allowed to express anger, which he would do frequently. He was also described by Lucy as highly critical, guilt-inducing, self-involved, and nasty. Lucy's older brother left the family directly after college and appears to be the most well-adjusted of all. Lucy resents the fact that, even before he left, her brother kept a distance from the parents and left Lucy to care for her mother and bear the brunt of her father's rage and criticism.

It became clear now to both client and therapist that Lucy was simply replaying personotypic affect from her family of origin in her roles as wife and mother, even though neither her husband nor her daughter treated her the way her parents and brother had. At this point, not only does the client begin to attribute some of her thoughts and feelings to the past instead of to the current situation (see Chapter 8, "Breaking Emotional Ties to One's Parents" section), but she also comes to understand that she was taught this world-view and self-view simply by growing up in her family. She is not to blame for her viewpoint but she is responsible for changing it.

SETTING FIRM BOUNDARIES IN THERAPY: AFFECTS ARE DISCUSSED, NOT EXPRESSED

Many therapeutic orientations, especially experientially based ones, believe that the strong expression of affect is a significant change agent. Therefore, these therapies do everything possible to encourage clients to display strong emotions. However, such a display can often lead clients to feel a great degree of embarrassment, not only because some have been taught that showing feelings is a sign of weakness, but also because they have expressed a part of themselves that they know is irrational or childish. Even clients who repeatedly act out childish emotions as part of their security-seeking behavior feel humiliated after-the-fact by this affective display. This humiliation can actually damage the therapeutic alliance if not processed carefully. Safran and Segal (1990) note that the therapist should not only discuss with the client the feelings that he or she has displayed, but the embarrassment or humiliation felt by the client in front of the therapist should also be processed.

There is another alternative, however, one that is less embarrassment-inducing to the client and perhaps more corrective. For clients whose frequent display of intense emotions may be part of their emotional setpoint and security-seeking behavior—in particular, those whom we called Acting-out Clients in this book's Introduction, passive–submissive clients who get taken care of by expressing their feelings, and passive–dominant clients who become the center of attention via their emotionality—the therapist's disallowing the expression of affect in sessions can be extremely helpful and can avoid the experiencing of shame. We do not mean that clients are not allowed to discuss their feelings in sessions; they simply are told not to cry so much or so hard or not to stir up their anger to the point of going on tirades or tantrums during sessions. Similarly, clients who passively sulk or brood as a way of expressing anger and self-pity are disallowed from doing so. All of these modes of emotional expression are developmentally stuck in childhood, often around the age of 3 or 4 but sometimes adolescence. The enraged borderline experiences the global anger of a 3-year-old; the sobbing histrionic also is trying to attract attention in the manner of a 3- or 4-year-old.

As it is the job of the parent to teach his or her child how to calm affect and express feelings appropriately (Greenspan, 1992; Taffel, 1999), so too does the CAT therapist help clients to learn how to soothe strong, potentially inappropriate affect and to explore and express feelings maturely (i.e., through discussion). We will address this at greater length in the Emotional Self-Care section of chapter 8. Children experience the expression of strong affect without the parents' calming influence as frightening and out of control; so do these clients, without the calming, limit-setting influence of the therapist. Moreover, if a therapist can avoid such affective expression, he or she can also help these clients to feel less embarrassed of affective displays in therapy and in general.

We do not, of course, extend this intervention to clients who have difficulty understanding and/or expressing their feelings. For them, experiential interventions of exploring and heightening feelings like those described by Greenberg, Rice, and Elliott (1993) and Safran and Segal (1990) can be most helpful.

WELCOME TO OUR "MA AND PA STORE"

Another method we employ to defuse clients' shame and embarrassment is the atmosphere we create in our group practice setting. The three authors, our colleague Mildred Borrás, and our secretary Maureen Coveney all work in adjoining rooms in our practice, which is operated more like a house than an impersonal, generic workplace. (This is pretty easy to create, since, in fact, our offices occupy one floor of a townhouse, owned and lived in by Richard, Sheenah, and their family.) However, more important than the physical space is our effort to create a warm, family-like atmosphere, what we sometimes refer to as our "Ma and Pa Store."

We make it a point to introduce new clients to those of our colleagues who might be present, and to engage clients sitting in the waiting room in informal chats, conversations about current affairs and politics, and general joking. We do this to give clients the messages: there is nothing to be self-conscious or ashamed about in being here; we're all people here; and this can be a home-away-from-home for you (especially for those clients who grew up in angry or cold family environments).

We believe (from having worked in such environments) that offices that "respect the patient's privacy" by having clinicians ignore patients in the waiting room, having separate entrances and exits so one patient never has to see another, and creating a generally somber, impersonal tone send the messages to clients: since we go to great lengths to pretend you are not here in the waiting room, you should be embarrassed to be here; since we walk around with serious demeanors, therapy is a grave, humorless, lifeless process. Naturally, these messages are a veritable petri dish for breeding shame and self-pity in clients.

We have found that almost all of our clients, even fairly shy and socially anxious ones, enjoy the environment we have created in our office and most willingly participate in the waiting room banter, introductions, and discussions. For those few who remain put off or withdrawn in such a setting, we naturally use our sensitivity and tone down the volume and intensity of our interactions. However, it is often quite significant when one of these clients, sometimes after as much as a year of sitting in our waiting room without talking, comes out of his or her protective shell and interacts with one of us. We gleefully report to the colleague who is treating such a client that so-and-so finally smiled, made eye contact, and said hello to us, or that such-and-such a client made a humorous comment. In these instances, the client's social anxiety and underlying shame, rage, and/or self-pity clearly have diminished.

ADDRESSING PERSONALITY

GENERAL CONSIDERATIONS

We will demonstrate at length in chapter 11 how we adjust our therapeutic stance to match a client's personality style. However, at this point, we want to highlight our general approach to working predominantly with personality style as opposed to focusing mostly on particular Axis I disorders.

Our general principles for shifting maladaptive personality styles are: (1) modify extremes on the active–passive and dominant–submissive personality dimensions; (2) move the client's interpersonal stance from hostile (alienated) to friendly (attached); and (3) modify extremes of personality styles by helping "feelers" to become "thinkers" and thinkers feelers. We assume that a maladaptive personality style is one experienced by others as abrasive or off-putting in some way and this, therefore, leads to a client's not getting what he or she consciously wants from others. An abrasive personality is one that is extreme—that is, one that does not conform with what social rules define as acceptable and normal. The more extreme, the more abrasive one's personality is to others. In attachment terms, the more avoidantly and ambivalently attached one is to others, and the more disorganized one is, the more he or she will be experienced negatively by others—until one finds an equally avoidantly or ambivalently attached and disorganized other, that is.

Moving clients away from personality extremes and from a hostile to a friendly interpersonal stance basically helps them to become securely attached to the world. Within each of the four combinations of dominant–submissive and active–passive personality styles there lies a securely attached (i.e., friendly) variant. Therefore, therapists cannot change people's basic personality styles, but they can shift clients from unhealthy extremes to a more flexible, and therefore adaptive, personality middle ground, and they can help hostile clients to treat others in a more empathic, welcoming fashion. Recall that one of the goals of interpersonal psychotherapy is to increase the client's flexibility when interacting with others, as interpersonal and personality rigidity is significantly correlated with maladjusted behavior (Kiesler, 1996).

Therefore, we work to move the highly active–dominant client toward a less rigid and domineering interpersonal stance; the passive–dominant client to become less self-centered and, in some cases, to pull for less caretaking from others; the active–submissive client to be less attention-seeking and people-pleasing, more self-sufficient and empathic toward others; and the passive–submissive client to be less dependent, to play helpless less, and to be more self-confident and self-sufficient. We work with all hostile clients to instill in them a greater empathy toward others by diminishing the rage and self-pity that fuel their hostility and by helping them to understand the negative, often self-defeating consequences of their hostile interactions.

Third, as we will discuss in the "Emotional Self-Care" portion of chapter 8, we help overly intellectualized clients to understand and effectively express their feelings, and overly emotive clients to soothe unhelpful, highly pitched personotypic affect and, in some situations, to express it more appropriately. Our work with the former type of client is not specific to CAT. Many therapeutic approaches, from experiential to psychodynamic, help clients to better understand what they are feeling and to learn how to express their feelings. However, our work with overly emotive clients is more unique, as many therapeutic orientations do not teach therapists how to help clients rein in their affect. It has long been a misconception, among therapists and nontherapists alike, that venting one's feelings—"catharsis," as Breuer called it over a century ago (Fancher, 1973)—is curative. This venting is actually countertherapeutic to many personality-disordered clients (e.g., borderlines and histrionics) and to those clients with emotive personality styles. Instead, we teach these clients a variety of strategies to help them understand and effectively calm down their feelings so they can react appropriately and helpfully in situations that push their emotional buttons, so to speak.

How we shift clients from personality extremes and move them from a hostile to a friendly interpersonal stance is central to almost all of the interventions described in this chapter. It is important to note here that this goal of CAT finds a kindred spirit in interpersonal theory and psychotherapy. Kiesler (1996, p. 245) states that the principal objective of interpersonal psychotherapy is to "facilitate an increased frequency and intensity of interpersonal actions with significant others from segments *opposite* on the [circumplex] to the segments that define the patient's pattern of maladaptive interpersonal behavior." The therapist must, therefore, not play into the complementary interpersonal stance pulled for by the client.

Instead, after having a solid alliance with the client, the therapist must take what Kiesler terms an anticomplementary stance in order to disrupt the client's typical interpersonal stance. For example, using the categories from Kiesler's interpersonal circumplex, a hostile–dominant client normally pulls for hostile–submissive responses from others. Instead, the therapist should take a friendly–submissive stance with such a client. The client's aggressive and provocative statements should be met with warmth, nonchalance, and trust by the therapist instead of with competition for dominance or hostility on the therapist's part. Conversely, a friendly–submissive client normally pulls friendly–dominant responses from others; however, here the therapist should respond in a hostile–dominant way, although Kiesler notes that the therapist should quickly move away from a hostile stance so as not to drive away the client from the therapy.

In a similar vein, Safran and Siegel (1990) use as a cornerstone of their therapy experiential disconfirmation of the client's cognitive–interpersonal cycle using both out-of-session and in-session exploration. The former occurs when the therapist explores with the client what are some of his or her core beliefs and feelings that feed the cognitive–interpersonal cycle with significant and not-so-significant others. Such an exploration often makes it clear to the client that such feelings and thoughts are merely assumptions on his or her part, and interpersonal flexibility is increased with the realization that other ways of thinking and feeling are available to the client.

Second, disconfirmation can occur when the therapist facilitates an exploration of the cognitive–interpersonal cycle as it occurs in-session between client and therapist. This often makes the cycle come alive for the client. Additionally, the therapist then shares what he or she is actually feeling—often something quite different from what the client expects—or reacts in a way that does not coincide with the client's expectations of the therapist, and this disconfirmation of the client's core beliefs then elicits a shift in the cognitive–interpersonal cycle. Even though Safran and Segal's approach is constructivist, in that it does not have a theory of personality types or styles, it too fosters interpersonal flexibility via interpersonal disconfirmation.

SUMMARY

1. CAT makes its change-promoting values explicit to clients. These include (a) taking responsibility for our actions; (b) self-respect and self-confidence are gained through personal responsibility and doing what is right at any given moment; (c) people should do what they deem right (within moral and ethical bounds) rather than pursuing hedonistic ends; and (d) no self-blame (unless one has unjustly hurt others) nor blame of others.

2. CAT builds self-respect and self-confidence by encouraging clients to learn (a) to do what is right as they understand it (personal rules of living) at this moment; (b) that self-respect is earned, not inherited; (c) to understand their personal rules of living and follow them rather than justifying cognitions; (d) to be satisfied with effort instead of achievement; (e) to accept that change can be uncomfortable; (f) to understand that responsibility leads to self-respect; (g) to blame and judge neither oneself nor others; (h) that changing is their choice; (i) to set appropriate boundaries with others; and (j) to become competent rather than helpless.

3. CAT creates a nonshaming therapeutic environment by (a) disallowing blame during therapy; (b) using therapist self-disclosure to diminish the client–therapist hierarchy; (c) sharing our notes with clients each session; (d) giving empathy, but not sympathy, to clients 99% of the time; (e) exploring how clients were parented in order to remove blame from them for their difficulties (and also, in most cases, without blaming their parents); (f) discussing, but not expressing, affect (for some clients); and (g) creating a "Ma and Pa Store" environment in our office.

4. CAT shifts maladaptive personality styles by (a) modifying extremes on the active–passive and dominant–submissive personality dimensions; (2) moving the client's interpersonal stance from hostile (alienated) to friendly (attached); and (3) modifying extremes of personality styles by helping "feelers" to become "thinkers" and thinkers feelers.

CHAPTER **8**

Affect-based Interventions

A cornerstone of CAT is not only how we conceptualize affect, but also how we then help clients to understand and manage it. Most personality extremes are intertwined with emotional extremes, so our clients experience intense degrees (high setpoints) of shame, rage, and self-pity. It is not surprising, therefore, that these clients have not learned how to manage such feelings, let alone understand them, and that they often become consumed and drained of energy by them. Before discussing how we work with shame, rageful anger, and self-pity with our clients, we turn to a general description of CAT interventions which promote an increased ability to take care of one's maladaptive and difficult personotypic affect. We call this ability emotional self-care.

EMOTIONAL SELF-CARE

Wessler and Hankin-Wessler (1997, p. 183) define emotional self-care as consisting of "soothing one's feelings, reducing their intensity, and reassuring oneself." In CAT, this can be divided into (1) learning to calm down one's personotypic affect; (2) strengthening the influence of logical thoughts over personotypic affect and justifying cognitions; and (3) breaking one's emotional ties to one's parents.

SOOTHING PERSONOTYPIC AFFECT

The first step in calming down unhelpful personotypic affect is learning how to identify such affect. In the early portion of therapy, the CAT therapist focuses the client on his or her feelings in order to help him or her understand what they are exactly. We do so somewhat selectively, focusing more on shame, rage, and self-pity than on other emotions. We also begin to reframe feelings, such as anxiety, in terms of anger, shame, and self-pity in order to demonstrate to the client how a combination of these three negative feelings is dominating the client's emotional life. We also discuss the emotional setpoint with clients in order to show them how they are driven to habitually recreate the same emotional pitch across situations. Over time, the CAT client comes to understand his or her emotional life and motivation in terms of personotypic affect and the setpoint.

Once this has been achieved, clients learn how to identify their personotypic affect and setpoint in many situations, and how to differentiate personotypic affect from more situation-specific emotional reactions. For example, with regard to the latter, a client whose boss has chewed him out in front of his coworkers may be able to differentiate the familiar rage that he has felt in many situations where he has pulled angry responses from authority figures from the angry embarrassment he feels at his boss's having handled the situation poorly by failing to address the issue behind closed doors.

Clients are then typically asked to think of statements which will calm their shame, anger, and self-pity in a variety of situations. We sometimes ask clients to close their eyes (if they want to) and think of someone in their life who has been successful at calming them down while they were experiencing those feelings—to imagine what they said and how they said it. Sometimes, clients say they have never been soothed by another person, so we will ask them to imagine what they *would have liked* someone to say to them and then to stay with this fantasy for a while. We then ask clients to have their imagined person generate other soothing statements and to practice saying these.

I (Jonathan) often ask clients to practice soothing affect as they go to work in the morning, either on the bus or subway, as they walk down the street, or as they drive to work. I offer the following explanations: (1) retraining your brain takes a lot of practice, just as reshaping your body by working out does not happen overnight; it requires much work to see small, incremental changes in muscle tone; (2) "strike while the iron is cold," a reworking of the saying that I borrowed from Fred Pine's (1985) work with children. I use this to highlight the fact that most people cannot soothe intense, longstanding feelings successfully at first. They need to practice repeating soothing statements when they are not upset or when they are minimally upset. I ask some clients to think about, but not experience, a personotypic affect as they go to work, and then to generate and repeat statements with a calming influence.

> Twenty-eight-year-old Bob said that his mother was too self-involved and his father too dependent on him to ever take note of or calm down his feelings. Bob realized that he did not want to imagine either parent soothing his feelings, as he still felt too angry at them, but instead wanted to conjure up a "personal trainer" who could serve as a mentor, coach, and cheerleader for him. Once this trainer could be imagined by Bob, he could easily generate a series of statements and ideas that he could say to himself to manage his angry, fearful feelings.

We also might help a client to raise his or her affect using a two-chair technique (see, for example, Greenberg et al., 1993), and then practice calming it down. For example:

> Client: I wanted to strangle that guy when he talked to me in that sarcastic, belittling way. He talked to me like I was crap.
> Therapist: What were you feeling when he spoke to you that way?
> Cl: Enraged.
> Th: And what did you do?
> Cl: Well, that's the problem. I ranted and raved at him and, ultimately, made myself look like a fool. He was treating me like a fool and I guess I obliged him by acting like one.
> Th: It was hard for you to calm down your rage to the point where you could speak forcefully, but rationally, to him?
> Cl: Right. When I get that angry, I usually either lash out or leave the situation out of fear that I might explode and hurt someone.
> Th: Let's practice calming down your anger. Imagine that that guy is talking to you now, in this room. Hear him say something demeaning to you. Can you see the expression on his face and hear his put-down tone of voice?
> Cl: I sure can.
> Th: What's he saying to you?
> Cl: You little piece of shit. You're nothing to me.
> Th: What are you feeling?
> Cl: I want to kill him.
> Th: What are you feeling?
> Cl: Enraged. I only want to curse him out. [Raising his voice] Hey, fuck you, buddy.
> Th: Who's good at calming you down when you're angry?
> Cl: My sister's good at this. She knows what to say usually.

Th: Such as?

Cl: "Don't let him get the better of you. It will make you look like a fool. Brian, chill out. Think of summers at the lake. Imagine you're on the lake fishing. That always calms you down."

Th: OK. Let's try that. Sit over here and imagine that this guy has chewed you out.

Cl: OK. I'm angry again. [laughs] It doesn't take much to get me there.

Th: Voice your anger.

Cl: I hate you. How dare you treat me that way? I'd like to rip your head off.

Th: Now, sit over here. What would your sister say now?

Cl: Stop it, Brian. Don't play the fool. Then he's won. You're better than that. Calm down by thinking of fishing.

Th: Does that work? Is it that easy?

Cl: No, I'm still pissed off. Actually, I'm feeling angry that I can't control my anger.

Th: So sit over here. Voice what you're thinking.

Cl: I'm pissed off at myself. "Why the hell do you have to blow up all the time? I hate you for doing that."

Th: Sit over here now. What do you say back to that?

Cl: You're trying to change that. You're doing the best you can. Be patient with yourself. One step at a time. Don't be a hard-ass like Dad and expect too much too soon. Just try to calm down.

Th: Does that work?

Cl: A little, but I'm still a little angry.

Th: Too angry to speak rationally to the guy?

Cl: Still a little.

Th: OK. Sit over here. Voice your anger.

Cl: I still want to kick you ass, you clown.

Th: Sit over here. What can you say back to yourself now?

Cl: I hear my sister's voice. She's laughing. "Don't be such a big shot. Mr. Swagger. Just tell what's on your mind calmly. You're good at expressing yourself when you want to."

Th: Sit over here now. How do you feel now?

Cl: Better. That helped.

Th: And what do you say to the guy?

Cl: I'd appreciate it if you wouldn't talk to me that way. If you have a complaint about me, let's sit down like two adults and try to solve the problem.

Th: How do you feel saying that?

Cl: [laughs] Like the adult that I should be. And also, like I'm better than he is because I expressed myself maturely and he really didn't.

Th: So how do you feel now?

Cl: Pleased with myself.

It should be noted that this process is different from some cognitive–behavioral approaches which stress "rational coping thoughts" to debate the automatic thoughts that emanate from feelings. For example, in a cognitive–behavioral parenting group, Evans and McAdam (1988, p. 230) had parents respond to the automatic thought, "Why can't I control my child?" with the self-statement, "I can control him a lot of the time." However, it is our experience that people will not be able to do this when their feelings are flowing at full power. Feelings must first be addressed before thoughts can be debated logically. For this reason, Taffel (1991) has acknowledged that angry parents may need to remove themselves from a heated conflict with their child, calm themselves down, and return to the situation later (essentially giving *themselves* a time-out) if they cannot successfully calm down their feelings in the moment.

No two clients are the same in this respect. The CAT therapist must work with each to come up with various statements and various ways of learning to soothe personotypic affect. The therapist must also dispel in some clients the belief that learning to soothe personotypic affect can be given to them by the therapist in a generic, formulaic package (e.g., "Now just learn how to count to ten and take a deep breath, and you'll feel fine").

LOCKING THE "INNER CHILD" IN THE CLOSET

It has become popular to speak of taking care of one's feelings in terms of taking care of one's "inner child," but it is really more important to take care of the adult. Thus, emotional self-care encompasses taking care of one's feelings in an adult manner. We advocate doing so by "locking one's inner child in the closet."

First, we list three popularly used wrong ways to take care of one's feelings—ways which only serve to reinforce one's self-indulgent inner child. The expression of emotions, including strong emotions, in an inappropriate manner, heads the list. Some holdover spirit from the heyday of the humanistic psychology movement still leads some people to advocate the unrestrained expression of feelings. Some people, especially histrionic types, believe that it is unhealthy to restrain the free expression of emotion, and other people believe that they have a human right to express emotion. We live in a civilized society that provides ways and means for the appropriate expression of feelings and emotions. Anger, for example, can be expressed by speaking out against what offends us, without name-calling, profane language, or physical violence.

Adults express feelings in a civilized manner. They also know not to express feelings when the potential return is negative. They can, and at times should, suppress the expression (but not the experience) of an emotion. They find other outlets for feelings or simply let them dissipate.

Another damaging technique for dealing with one's feelings is to soothe them in self-handicapping ways, including overindulgence in food, alcohol, drugs, sleep, leisure, shopping, and gambling. The overindulgence in some of these pleasures is not only physically debilitating but can also result in shame about the habit or addiction; the shame is then soothed with more overindulgence which, of course, produces more shame.

Yet another wrong way to soothe feelings is the frequent and exclusive turning to others to soothe and care for one's own feelings. Children are dependent in this way, and for them it is a necessary part of the developmental process. However, adults who speak often of wanting and needing "support," "nurturance," and someone to "be there" for them often handle their feelings in a childlike manner. They need to turn to themselves instead of others for support and comfort.

Four "right" ways to take care of one's feelings are developing one's logical voice, positive self-deception, realistic self-praise, and the comforting of negative feelings. The first of these methods asks clients to split themselves into what can be called their "feeling part" (personotypic affect and justifying cognitions) and their "logical part." After having both parts describe themselves, the logical part then responds to the feeling part with mature and/or helpful statements that set limits on and debate the childlike (and childish) statements of the feeling part. This process often resembles experiential techniques such as splits and the two-chair dialogue described by Greenberg, Rice, and Elliott (1993) and Greenberg and Safran (1987), but rather than using these techniques to enhance affect, *here affect is softened as cognition is strengthened.*

A typical dialogue between a client's logical and feeling parts might go as follows:

> *Feeling Part: I'm so tired of trying to discipline my kid without results.*
> *Logical Part: Don't sacrifice your child's development to your own feelings.*
> *FP: I don't care!*
> *LP: You're acting like a spoiled child. You know that if you keep trying, you'll have some success. You just can't expect immediate results, like a little kid would. Be patient!*
> *FP: I don't think I'll make it.*
> *LP: You're just assuming that to feel sorry for yourself. You don't know if you'll make it or not. Just hang in there—it's worked for you in the past. Now—get to work!*
> *FP: But I don't want to!*
> *LP: Then don't expect anything to change. And then don't complain about it.*

There is no "cookbook" method by which clients can calm down personotypic affect and replace it with logical thoughts. Just as young children are different in how they can be soothed effectively (see Greenspan, 1992), so too are

clients different in what stops or diminishes the expression of their personotypic affect. Some clients find it helpful in calming down personotypic affect
to access the voice of someone else who can or could calm them down when
upset (e.g., a friend, a relative, a teacher, or coach). Other clients need to yell
at themselves ("Just cut it out already!") to diminish personotypic affect.
Others access a helpful image, such as a picture of themselves as a wimpy,
tantruming child, which embarrasses them out of feeling personotypic affect.
Still others use humor to joke themselves out of the melodramatic feelings of
rage, shame, and self-pity, while others make themselves feel guilty for
indulging in having such unhelpful, self-involved feelings. (I, Jonathan, used
to access an image of myself as the crying Pagliaccio, pathetically beating a
drum, when I was wallowing in melodramatic self-pitying thoughts—an old
emotional habit of mine. The melodrama and absurdity of this image stopped
these justifying cognitions extremely quickly.) Finally, other clients sometimes
find it helpful to say to themselves, "I sound just like my mother/father. That's
the last thing I want!" to use cognitive dissonance to shock themselves out of
experiencing personotypic affect.

It should be noted that, although we call it the Logical Voice, this voice
does not necessarily assume the constricted, intellectual, Aristotelian voice
encouraged by some cognitive therapists (i.e., "You are not always a loser. I'm
sure that you think of some times when you had a success"; "What you are
thinking is irrational. Try to take your mind off of it and think of a more positive thought."). Our Logical Voice basically uses any strategy and any communication that works to quell the Feeling Voice, much as a parent who is
dealing with a tantruming child will almost always not give a textbook
response but will try many things spontaneously to handle the situation. A
Logical Voice might simply respond, "Oh, shut up! I'm so tired of your whining!" to a Feeling Voice. This response is far from elegant; however, if it
works, then we encourage its use. (We only discourage overly self-critical or
demeaning statements from the Logical Voice, such as, "You're such an idiot
for whining like that.")

The second means of emotional self-care is positive self-deception. This is
a phrase that I, Richard, coined some years ago to describe a kind of encouragement we can give ourselves if not overly concerned about facts. For
instance, I was once blocked in a writing assignment and thought that several
other people could write the piece better than I could. I even named who they
were. I got unstuck by telling myself that I could write that article at least as
well as anyone else and, perhaps, a great deal better. No one could do better!
Realistically, the last statement was probably not true, but it did the job, and I
finished the task with enthusiasm. Positive self-deception is useful to counter
overly realistic thoughts; scientific thinking is a fine way to do science but a
poor way to create optimism and enthusiasm.

Positive self-deception can also act as a counterbalance to a habit of negative self-appraisal. Once the CAT therapist uses other interventions to help clients understand that their reality is subjective—based on the beliefs handed to them by their family of origin—then clients can understand that they can just as easily *choose* to be optimistic as pessimistic. We call this optional optimism since it stresses that optimism and pessimism are not reactions to reality but choices that one makes.

Some clients who have been pessimistic their entire lives experience optimistic thoughts as too artificial or Pollyanna-ish. There is another alternative: neutrality. Asking questions such as, "How would you feel if you felt only neutral about this?" or, "Rather than predicting a negative outcome, how about waiting to see what the outcome will be?" are often easier to accept for these clients than questions such as, "Why not expect something positive rather than negative to occur?"

Another important self-care technique is realistic self-praise. This technique corrects for overlooking one's efforts and achievements. It is a form of reinforcement, or self-feedback, and it can be helpful to encourage and remoralize oneself. It is especially recommended for people who habitually ignore or denigrate themselves and their efforts. Excessive humility may be socially approved and its lack condemned as bragging or blowing one's own horn, but the individual has to find the right balance between appearing acceptably humble and remaining privately honest about efforts and achievements. As we noted in a previous section, effort is the best basis for self-respect, but success, if one has some, can do wonders for morale.

A fourth adult self-care procedure is to comfort negative feelings. This is typically done by reciting the facts, especially those that have been overlooked, and reassuring oneself that one will feel better and that things will work out. Note that one need not be too careful about the facts in attempting self-comfort. When we try to bolster others, we accentuate the positive, eliminate the negative, and omit everything in between. Although we risk accusations of bias in offering the following generalizations, we believe that women are better at comforting feelings than men (and, certainly, the parenting literature, e.g., Clarke-Stewart, 1978; Lamb, 1982; Bridger, Connell, & Belrug, 1988, support us here). Men typically try to solve people's problems in order to relieve distress, and to solve problems requires scrutiny of the facts and available options. To hope that everything will turn out well requires the suspension of belief, which is harder to do when faced with facts. Naturally, it is all right to dwell on facts if they are encouraging, but not otherwise.

When speaking to clients about soothing their personotypic affect in an adult manner, we typically ask, "How would you soothe a distraught child?" Clients often respond with variations of "offer reassurance, make the child feel safe and cared for, and remain calm and encouraging." "How," we then ask, "can you do this for yourself?" We do not accept a simple answer from our clients, as it often takes more than one strategy to successfully soothe person-otypic affect. We ask, "And then, if that doesn't succeed in soothing your feel-ings, what could you try next?"

What do parents say to children that helps to soothe their feelings? Parents explain situations to children and encourage them to think and act differently. Ideally, they acknowledge and accept the feelings of the child but also offer new information, perspectives, and interpretations, often based on their own experiences. In essence, they do a form of cognitive psychotherapy. (I, Jonathan, have often thought while working with parents that I am essentially teaching them how to become cognitive–interpersonal–developmental therapists to their children.) They support the notion that thinking and talking to oneself are effective ways to cope with distressed feelings and that reasoned actions are the best ways to alter (or remove oneself) from situations that cause distress. Thus, the message to clients is, trust your thinking, not your feelings, as a basis for decisions and actions.

Recall the excerpt of the session conducted by Richard earlier in Chapter 7. When the client states that she feels guilty for appropriately saying no to her mother, Richard responds, "Every time you feel guilty, you should feel good. 'I must be doing something right. Look how guilty I feel.'" This remark makes the point to the client: listen to your logic, not your feelings—that her guilt here signals correct thinking, so she should not alter her behavior to diminish her guilt.

We should note here that calming one's personotypic affect does not involve only soothing statements. Parents soothe children when they are feeling sad, frustrated, and, sometimes, angered. However, when a child is tantruming, for example, the most helpful calming response from a parent is most probably not soothing. Instead, the parent needs to cut the tantrum short, either by ignoring it or by setting a limit on it (e.g., by shouting "Enough! Stop now!"). Similarly, enraged clients, or, for that matter, self-pitying clients, may choose to diminish angry or whiny affect by setting firm limits on their feelings (e.g., by saying to themselves a more adult variation of "Enough! Stop now!" or, as Sheenah often says, "Get over it!").

WORKING WITH SHAME, RAGE, AND SELF-PITY

The dissatisfaction and lack of fulfillment of virtually all clients are derived from the personotypic affect of shame. Self-pity and/or rage may arise in some clients as well, both in reaction to how the individual's parents raised him or her and as a defensive reaction to painful shame. As such, the CAT therapist must heighten the client's awareness of the personotypic pull of his or her underlying shame and then the therapist must help the client to develop behavioral and cognitive strategies to diminish the motivating property of shame.

Clients who are dominated by rageful anger must first understand this personotypic affect and then link it to their shame (i.e., come to understand that their rage is, in part, an "attack other" reaction to the pain of shame). Clients who mostly feel sorry for themselves will become enraged if the therapist focuses first on their self-pity, as this is an embarrassing emotion to own up to. Instead, the therapist must unearth and empathize with clients' underlying shame.

In working with shame, the CAT therapist first helps the client to understand what this consists of in his or her life (feeling inadequate, unloved, unlovable, like a loser, etc.) and how this has affected his or her thoughts and behaviors. The therapist highlights the motivational pull of this personotypic affect. The therapist then helps the client to build his or her self-respect as outlined in the "Self-Respect-Oriented Interventions" section of Chapter 7. This includes not only increasing one's self-respect but also insisting upon respect from others by setting limits on their disrespectful treatment, as also outlined in this section.

The therapist also works with the client to have experiences that disconfirm the client's shame-evoking beliefs about him or her. One typical example of this occurs when a client complains, "Nobody finds me interesting or attractive. Everybody ignores me." The therapist then discovers that, because the client believes himself or herself to be unacceptable to others, he or she avoids eye contact or initiating conversation with others. In short, he or she unintentionally gives off the signal, "I'm not interested in you. Stay away from me." Rejecting behavior is therefore elicited from others by the client—not because the client is undesirable, but because he or she shows no interest in or involvement with others. The CAT therapist can highlight this and urge the client (if he or she is not passive–aggressive) to try to make eye contact with others, smile at them, and initiate pleasant conversation, even though he or she does not believe that it will lead to successful results. "Try it anyway," says the CAT therapist, "even though you don't believe it will work. Think of it as nothing more than a scientific experiment." When clients succeed in doing this, they invariably evoke warm responses from others and begin to understand that their shame-invoking assumptions are nothing more than that—subjective assumptions and not reality. What they do, rather than what they believe, makes all the difference.

We also disallow shame-ridden clients from making derogatory comments about their weight, attractiveness, gender, age, or race, and from labeling themselves or their behaviors as pathological (e.g., "I'm so crazy"; "I guess I acted that way because I'm a depressed, dysfunctional person."). We point out that this only fuels their shame habit. Additionally, we discourage clients from focusing on weight, attractiveness, gender, age, or race at all, even to the extent of making positive comments such as, "You lost weight; you look good." Such a focus reinforces the idea that one's worth is based on such external factors, many of which clients cannot control (weight is an exception, of course).

We also attempt to diminish the power of shame by having clients explore its roots in their upbringing and primary attachments. Once clients come to see that their shameful feelings are not Truth but subjective perceptions and feelings based on how they were raised, clients can begin to unhook themselves from this feeling—to hand it back to their parents and their past, in essence. We will describe some interventions we use to do this in the "Breaking Emotional Ties to One's Parents" section that appears next in their chapter.

Here is an excerpt from a session where the CAT therapist identifies and works with an adolescent client's shame:

> Client: I get so stressed out sometimes. My friends all comment on it.
>
> Therapist: How do you look when you're stressed out?
>
> Client: I say to myself [in a very animated, loud tone of voice], "Oh my God, I can't believe I acted that way. Now my friends will all think I'm totally weird," and I'll say this to myself over and over again, and I'll say this over and over to my friends, too.
>
> Th: When you say that you're totally weird, what do you mean?
>
> Cl: That everybody thinks I'm a loser.
>
> Th: And being a loser means what to you?
>
> Cl: That I'm ugly; that I'm not as interesting to others as some of my friends.
>
> Th: And what will your friends do then?
>
> Cl: Not want to—not want to be around me. Reject me, basically.
>
> Th: So you're not really stressing. There's no such thing as stress, you know. Stress is just how one reacts to a situation.
>
> Cl: You mean, by getting so emotional?
>
> Th: Yeah. Exactly. And by assuming something negative—that people are rejecting you for being a loser—that is not true.
>
> Cl: But maybe it is true.
>
> Th: Well, let's see. Have you ever been rejected by any friends or acquaintances before?
>
> Cl: Well, sometimes kids who I want to be friends with don't talk to me and don't want anything to do with me.
>
> Th: Did they do this after you were friendly with them?
>
> Cl: Well, no. Not really. I was afraid they would think I was a loser, so I didn't talk to them or look at them. Protecting myself, I guess.
>
> Th: So you didn't talk to them and they didn't talk to you? Do you think if you had been more welcoming, they might have acted friendly toward you? We won't know for sure, but what's your best guess?

Cl: I think, yes, they might have been friendly to me. Usually when I'm friendly to others, they're friendly back.

Th: So, let me understand this. You're not friendly to kids who you think will reject you, then they reject you because you're not friendly to them—not because you're a loser but because you don't pay them any attention—and then you go around making yourself feel like a loser?

Cl: [laughs] Yeah, that's about right. Why do I do that? That's crazy.

Th: It's not crazy; it's what a lot of people do. Here's what I think. You don't get stressed out. You have a shame habit.

Cl: A what?

Th: A shame habit. It's my belief that people make themselves feel certain ways over and over again, not because it feels good to have these feelings but because it feels _familiar_. It's how we've always felt since early childhood and how we unconsciously—totally unintentionally—make ourselves feel over and over again, unless we become aware of doing this. It sounds to me—tell me though if this doesn't feel right to you—it sounds to me that you might be using certain situations to make yourself feel like a loser over and over again. The feeling that goes with believing you're a loser is shame.

Cl: It does feel right to me, what you say, but where would that have come from in me?

Th: I don't know. You tell me.

Cl: Well, my mother can get really dramatic, like me, when she's upset. We even joke about how similar we are that way—two drama queens.

Th: So you learned to rev up your feelings when you're upset from her. It feels familiar to you.

Cl: Totally. But why shame? My mother has pretty good self-confidence. [The client's father left the family when she was six.]

Th: Was she very critical of you or of others when you were growing up?

Cl: Not at all. Just the opposite. She always praised me and my brother. Said we were absolutely perfect. I stopped believing it after a while because nothing I could do was wrong or bad. I also stopped believing it because I told myself, "She's my mother. Of course, she's going to say things like that."

Th: She never punished you for doing anything wrong?

Cl: Not really, when I was young. When I was 10 or 11, she must have realized that she was spoiling me and she became stricter.

Th: How did that go?

Cl: Well, of course, I didn't like it at first, but we reached an understanding, and I pretty much did what she asked of me.

Th: Did your mom make sure you did your work, chores, and responsible stuff like that?

Cl: Pretty much, at least since I was 10 or so.

Th: So here's my theory. You have to tell me if it sits right with you.

Cl: OK.

Th: I think your mother unintentionally set you up. She clearly was being loving and accepting of you, but her always praising you made it really difficult for you to deal with the real world, since the real world isn't particularly supportive or ready with praise. If you always expect praise, then when you don't get it from friends and others, you flip to feeling like you're a loser.

Cl: That's interesting. My mother's mother was incredibly critical of her, put her down, like, all the time.

Th: Do you think she made up for that with you? Swore she would never criticize you?

Cl: Definitely.

Th: Maybe she went too far.

Cl: I think you may be right there. So, I'm still not sure why I'm so insecure, though.

Th: I'm not either. It may have to do with the fact that you had it pretty easy at home, with your mother, and that the world is not as easy, so you feel unprepared and unable to deal with it.

Cl: That's exactly how I feel about school. When school was easy, I could get by on my intelligence. Bluff my way through. But now that high school is pretty hard, I'm stressing out.

Th: You mean, you're afraid that you can't handle it, that you're incompetent.

Cl: Yes. Maybe I can do the work, but because it's hard, I'm convincing myself that I can't do it, that I can't handle it. And basically, that I'm a loser.

CAT's work with clients experiencing self-pity focuses on (1) drawing a connection between the client's self-pity and shame—that it is less painful to blame others than to blame oneself and so the client chooses to feel victimized rather than ashamed; (2) exploring the underlying shame first; (3) pointing out how the client makes him-herself feel and/or be victimized by others and consequently sorry for him/herself; and (4) highlighting that self-pity is a choice the client makes based on how he/she was raised; it is not a reflection of reality.

As we have previously discussed, the CAT therapist decreases self-pity by disallowing blame of any kind; by disallowing crying and attempts to gain the sympathy of others by these clients; by distinguishing actual versus psychological victimization for these clients; and by (playfully) labeling these clients' self-pity habit as Ripped-Off Disorder. Furthermore, we do not allow these clients to make negative predictions about the future (see our previous discussion of optional optimism), nor do we permit them to dwell on regrets about the past. We disallow statements concerning "what might have been" or "if only…," as they only rev up self-pity and serve no helpful purpose whatsoever. Similarly, those clients who repeatedly dwell on and ruminate about a past failed relationship (repeatedly saying things like, "I don't understand how he could have treated me so poorly"; "If only I had treated her differently"; "If only I could have another chance") are not allowed do this. We disallow it in sessions as well as out-of-session, as it is unproductive (and actually avoids the client's dealing with his or her core issues) and fosters self-pity.

Many self-pitying clients are resentful caregivers and people-pleasers. In part, they care for and please others because they want to be taken care of and pleased in a similar fashion by others. Typically, they attract people who like to be taken care of or pleased and who do not give this back to others. As a result, the self-pitying client can complain, "I give and give and give to others, and they give nothing back to me. Oh, why can't anybody take care of me the way I take care of others?" We point out to these clients that they care for and please others simply to rekindle their self-pity (security-seeking behavior). We label their caretaking as selfish, since they are doing it for themselves, to rekindle personotypic affect, rather than for others, and we point out that they can truly respect others by (like a good parent) letting them learn to care for themselves.

We work similarly with the enraged client, since virtually all of these clients experience the rage of someone who has been mistreated, disrespected, victimized, etc. A predominantly self-pitying client blames others but focuses more on his or her sorry state, while an enraged client also blames others but focuses outward, on others' horrible actions, rather than on his or her state. Again, we point out to these clients that their rage is longstanding and motivating rather than a legitimate reaction to various situations. We explore the client's underlying shame and vulnerability and highlight how the client has been taught (by parents) to attack others rather than experience more painful shameful feelings. We help enraged clients to become less judgemental toward others and, therefore, more empathic; to not personalize others' actions and use them to fuel their rage; and also to stop feeling victimized and sorry for themselves.

BREAKING EMOTIONAL TIES TO ONE'S PARENTS: DIFFERENTIATING THE PAST FROM THE PRESENT

As we discussed in chapter 2, personotypic affect and the primary parental attachment(s) are intertwined. It is, therefore, quite useful in diminishing the strong grip of personotypic affect and the emotional setpoint to help clients identify when they are feeling about themselves and others now as they felt about themselves and their parents in childhood. Clients can then be helped to stop relating to others currently as they did to their parents, and they can also be helped to stop relating to their parents in the present as they did in childhood. In essence, we work to break the link between Malan's (1979) self–parent and self–other links of his interpersonal triangle, and we also work to distinguish between the self–parent relationship of the past versus that of the present.

Clients who are particularly ruled by personotypic affect and their emotional setpoint tend to be more entrenched in old relationships with their parents, just as it has often been remarked how more severely personality-disordered individuals tend to be more developmentally immature in their thinking and interpersonal relationships (e.g., Westen, 1991). It is, therefore, essential in teaching these clients emotional self-care to promote a new way of relating to their parents (either their actual parents, if they are still alive, or the internalized parents) and, therefore, a new way of relating to others that is not infiltrated by the parental ghosts of their childhood.

We encourage many clients to think and behave differently with their parents in the present by breaking away from the personotypic affects and emotional setpoint that are intertwined with their parental relationships. Some clients interact with parents in a way that reinforces security-seeking behaviors, justifying cognitions, and personotypic affect; others have little or no literal contact with parents but they are still influenced by internalized parental "voices" (in the form of justifying cognitions and personal rules of living). We, therefore, help clients who interact with their parents to (1) create new, self-respecting, adult personal rules of living and behaviors; (2) replace childhood rules and behaviors with these new ones, both with parents and others; and (3) learn to calm personotypic affect in order to follow new personal rules while interacting with parents. We do the same with clients who have little or no contact with their parents, but instead we (1) identify personal rules, security-seeking behaviors, justifying cognitions, and personotypic affect that are derived from the beliefs and actions of the parents during the client's childhood; (2) help the client to differentiate between the present situation and his or her childhood circumstances; and (3) help the client not to perceive and interact with others now in terms of how the client interacted with his or her parents during childhood.

We have already covered how we sometimes use a modified two-chair technique to teach clients how to soothe personotypic affect. The only variation when addressing the influence of one's parents on one's thinking and feeling would be to identify the thoughts as belonging to one's parent and having a dialogue between the client's adult voice and his or her parent's voice (i.e., between his or her logical and feeling parts). Here is an example of such a dialogue:

> *Therapist: What do you say to yourself when you have difficulty being assertive with others?*
>
> *Client: I usually say something like, "Oh, don't even bother. It won't do any good"*

Th: Where did you learn to think those thoughts?

Cl: Oh, I'm not sure. Well, probably from my father.

Th: How so?

Cl: He was always giving up pretty easily. When my mother would get angry with him, which was often, he'd just shut down. When she'd ask him to stand up to other people, his boss or our annoying neighbors, he'd often say something like, "It won't do any good," and then, of course, she'd just get angrier at him and he'd retreat even further. God, I hated that.

Th: And now you're doing it too.

Cl: God, I am.

Th: Let's try this. Sit over here and voice your father's helpless thoughts. Some typical ones that you might have, too.

Cl: OK. "It's no use. Why bother? It's hopeless."

Th: What are you feeling as you say this?

Cl: Hopeless. Weak. Sad.

Th: OK. Now sit over here. Picture you father in the other chair having said that. Can you see him?

Cl: Yes. He looks like a wimp right now.

Th: What do you want to say to him?

Cl: Stop it! Man, you're not weak. You just think you are. I'm so disappointed in you when you're this way. You can do it; you can.

Th: Sit here. What does he say back to you?

Cl: Let's see. "I can't. I'm too weak."

Th: Sit here. What can you say back?

Cl: You just think you are. You just think you are. Get out of that chair and do something!

Th: Sit over here. What happens?

Cl: Nothing. He just sits. I never saw him be assertive or active, so I can't even imagine it.

Th: Is there anything you can say to yourself so you don't have to follow in his footsteps?

Cl: Yes, maybe. You don't have —

Th: Wait a second. Sit back over here.

Cl: You don't have to be like him. Just because he's a wimp doesn't mean that you have to be. You can cut it out, even if he can't.

Th: Can you say that to him too?

Cl: I don't have to be like you. I mean, I love you, but I can be stronger than you. I can be assertive. Stop influencing me, man. Go away!

Th: How do you feel now?

Cl: Bad. Guilty. Like I'm somehow betraying him or something by being stronger than him.

Th: What can you say to yourself about that?

Cl: Hmm … You can still love Dad, even if you're not like him. You need to be different from him to be successful in life. He'd be proud of you if you were different from him. He didn't like being a wimp, so he'd be proud of you for standing up to yourself.

Th: How do you feel now?

Cl: Fine. OK, actually. But I can't say all this to myself when I need to be assertive.

Th: No, you can't. But perhaps you can have this conversation with yourself from time to time to remind yourself that you don't have to act like your father, and that you can still love him. And you can also extract a few of the statements you made to yourself and say those to yourself when you need to be assertive. Only you can choose which of these statements will be the most effective for you. You'll have to play around with it.

The basic model for helping clients to break longstanding patterns of interacting and feeling with parents has already been demonstrated in the excerpt from Richard's session with the client whose demanding mother was in the hospital. He helps her to strengthen new personal rules of living ("I am not a bad daughter if I can't always do what my mother wants. A responsible person and parent takes care of themselves and their own children before their parent.") and to ignore the guilt and perhaps shame that are associated with ignoring old personal rules ("I am a bad daughter and a bad person if I don't do what my mother wants all the time.").

We also often use ourselves as role models in role-plays by modeling to clients how to set boundaries and be assertive with parents whom we have previously allowed to treat us like children. Remember here: we don't blame the parent for doing this. It is the adult child's responsibility to give the message to the parent, "You must treat me differently now, like an adult, to maintain a suitable relationship with me."

Client: It's really hard for me to stand up to my mother. She makes me feel so guilty when I don't do what she wants?

Therapist: She doesn't make you feel guilty. You make yourself feel guilty. But it sounds like you have a very difficult time standing up to her.

Cl: Definitely.

Th: OK. Let's play out a situation where you have difficulty setting boundaries with her. You play your mother, since you know only too well how she sounds and what she says. I'll set some boundaries with her.

Cl: Meg, you have to come over and help me move those boxes. You know they're too heavy for me and I'm all alone.

Th: I'm not going to be able to do it. Why don't you pay someone who works in your building to do it?

Cl: You're my daughter. You're supposed to help me out when I need you. I took care of you all those years, and it's —

Th: [Firmly] Mother. I'm going to stop you now. You must do this for your-self, and that's the end of our conversation about this.

Cl: You don't love me. If you —

Th: I will end this conversation now unless you change the subject. It's up to you.

Cl: [Pauses] I don't know what my mother would do next.

Th: That's a good sign. It means that I've tried something new that might work. What's your reaction to this role-play?

Cl: I loved what you said, but I don't think I could do it?

Th: How come?

Cl: First, I feel too guilty to say things like that, even though I'd like to; and second, it's just so different for me to do.

Th: The second part you'll just have to get used to—the strangeness of behaving differently. You'll get used to it the more you do it. But I think we should talk more about your feeling guilty when you stand up to your mother.

Cl: I feel like, here's this weak, lonely woman. And she raised me. How can I not take care of her?

Th: Is your mother very weak and infirm?

Cl: Well, no, not really. [laughs] She believes that she is, though, and there's no persuading her otherwise.

Th: So you're colluding with her delusion about herself. In the role-play, as you played her, she actually seemed quite feisty and strong to me, very adept at putting forward what she wants from you.

Cl: She is, all right.

Th: So what do you get out of believing that your mother is so weak?

Cl: Well, only that I've believed that practically forever.

Th: It defines your relationship with her. To not believe this means that you'll lose the relationship you've always had with her, lose the familiarity. Now, the question is: do you want to sacrifice what is healthy for you, your self-respect and your individuality, to maintain this relationship as it is, or do you want to take a risk and change the relationship—not lose it, just change it—to do what's best for you?

Cl: I'd like to change and grow myself. Not changing is killing me. It's why I'm here.

Th: Well, then, you have to be willing to disappoint your mother some-times and to change the relationship. You know, you'll only strengthen her if you let her down sometimes.

Cl: What do you mean?

Th: Well, right now you're coddling her; you're spoiling her by allowing her to think that she is weak, she needs to be taken care of, and only you can do it. Sometimes a parent has to allow a child to struggle as she learns to do something by herself. If the parent does everything for the child, the parent *handicaps the child, even though sometimes it's easier to do for a child than to give in to her tantrums when she doesn't get her way. You need to allow your mother to grow up, to take care of herself by learning how to solve her own problems without always relying on you. Are you willing to stop crippling your mother's growth as a person?*

    Cl: [laughs] *I guess I can make that sacrifice.* [pause] *I see what you mean.*

We sometimes have clients who need to have these conversations or express unfinished business to parents who are deceased. We suggest that they bring in a picture of their parent and have such a conversation with them. This can be extremely powerful emotionally for the client. We may also have clients write a letter expressing how they feel or conveying their new, adult personal rules to a parent who is deceased. We also do this with clients who are unwilling to work these issues out with a parent who is alive, but who feel more comfortable addressing these issues as they affect the clients' own personality at present. And sometimes it is just inappropriate to confront a parent who may have changed significantly over the years but toward whom an adult child harbors old feelings.

Concretely, we suggest to clients that they limit time spent with parents, as almost anyone who visits a parent for too long will revert back to old patterns of feeling, thinking, and interacting. Visiting a parent for too much time is a security-seeking behavior, as it inevitably rekindles personotypic affect. We also urge clients not to be overly self-critical if they revert to old behaviors around parents. It takes much time to break old habits, we tell them. It is especially difficult, thanks to state-dependent learning, to do so around our parents, perhaps in the same environment (the family home) in which we developed them in the first place. Clients should implement new personal rules, methods of soothing personotypic affect, and behaviors to set boundaries and foster self-respect with parents, but they should also not expect too much too soon. Again, they should feel satisfaction with their effort and not depend on the impact it has had on a parent. It's sometimes a very gradual process to retrain our parents!

SUMMARY

    1 A cornerstone of CAT involves helping clients to improve their emotional self-care, which consists of (a) calming personotypic affect; (b) strengthening the influence of logical thoughts over personotypic affect and justifying cognitions; and (c) breaking emotional ties to one's parents.

    2 Clients are helped to soothe personotypic affect by (a) understanding this affect, its motivating properties, and the emotional setpoint; (b) learning to

comfort negative feelings and practicing this using a variety of strategies; (c) developing a strong "logical voice"; (d) using positive self-deception (unrealistically playing up one's assets) when possible; and (e) using realistic self-praise (paying attention to one's effort rather than one's achievement).

3 Shame is addressed by (a) understanding what it consists of and how it affects one's thoughts and behaviors; (b) helping clients to have shame-disconfirming experiences; (c) disallowing self-critical comments; and (d) pinpointing the roots of one's shame in how one was parented in order to depersonalize one's shame.

4 Self-pity is addressed by (a) first identifying and exploring the underlying shame; (b) showing how one's self-pity can pull caretaking and ultimately annoyance from others; (c) defining self-pity and victimization as the client's choice rather than as reality; (d) exploring how the client's parents fostered this self-pity.

5 Rageful anger is addressed by (a) showing how the "attack other" stance really defends against the pain of underlying shame; (b) exploring this shame; (c) differentiating mature anger (assertiveness) from immature anger (sulking and tantruming); and (d) exploring how the client's family modeled the "attack other" stance.

6 Clients are encouraged to break negative emotional ties to their parents by (a) replacing childhood personal rules of living and behaviors with new, self-respecting adult ones; (b) learning to calm personotypic affect in order to follow new personal rules while interacting with parents; (c) helping the client to differentiate between the present situation and his or her childhood circumstances, and to behave accordingly.

CHAPTER 9

Additional Interventions Involving Cognition, Behavior, Adjunctive Medication, and Therapeutic Impasses

UNDERSTANDING COGNITION AND BEHAVIOR

Frequently, throughout therapy, clients return to unrealistic thoughts, such as "I am an idiot." Such thoughts clearly lack a factual basis, but it does little good to remind clients of what they have achieved professionally and/or personally, nor is it helpful to rationally debate such unrealistic thoughts. Clients short-circuit rational debate by readily agreeing that, in fact, they are not idiots, but they still *feel* like idiots. As we mentioned in chapter 3, when people say that they believe their feelings to be a guide to the truth, that feelings as evidence outweigh what can be consensually validated, or that feelings are to be trusted as bases for decisions, they provide clues to their justifying cognitions. The justifying thought is not prompted by external events but by personotypic affect.

> *The intervention here is not to debate the justifying cognition. One of my (Jonathan's) clients came to me from a rather well-known RET therapist, who had been somewhat successful with the client, but then came to an impasse. After the client had learned to dispute irrational thoughts (he could do a better job at this than I), he still persisted in feeling the same feelings and relat-*

ing to others in the same way. He told me that, at least as he perceived it, his
therapist was becoming increasingly frustrated with him: if he could dispute
so well, why wasn't he carrying it over to his behaviors? Additionally, he
thought that maybe he wasn't so good at debating if he still felt the same way
about himself. The client had an extremely critical, perfectionistic father who
was almost always disappointed in him, and he came to believe that his thera-
pist now felt the same way—intensely disappointed in him. He never men-
tioned this to the therapist and, since the therapist knew very little about his
past, the therapist never made this connection, nor was the therapist–client
relationship addressed. He left therapy feeling only half-helped.

Instead, the CAT therapist shows such clients that feelings cause thoughts (a "bottom-up" process) and that such thoughts are not to be trusted. We explain to clients that thoughts like "I'm an idiot" were created in their non-conscious minds so that they will feel bad (i.e., ashamed). We do not ask clients to disbelieve these thoughts, since they already disbelieve them, but to disregard and dismiss them as nonconscious attempts to bring their feelings back to a familiar place, in both intensity and type.

In other words, people develop distorted ways of processing information, through either direct or indirect learning, or because they are consonant with self-schemas. Distortions that were learned directly can be treated with educational methods common to cognitive therapy ("top-down"). Distortions that were acquired in other ways, including the rationalizing of affective experiences, must be treated with an approach that does not assume faulty learning or a need for reeducation.

We address security-seeking behaviors in a similar way. We do not formulate behavioral programs for clients or, in most cases, try to talk clients out of behaving as they do. Instead, we help clients to link security-seeking behaviors to their personotypic affect (our question "What do you get out of doing this behavior?" addresses this) and to understand that such behaviors are derived from those intrinsic to the parent(s)–child relationship. This implies that clients are in control of such behaviors, even though they often experience them as "just happening" to them. We might, at times, also discuss the appropriateness of such behaviors, given current social and societal norms and expectations. For example, we might say to a client who is prone to angry temper tantrums in public, "You can go ahead and express your anger in this way, but I don't think that people will want to be around you if you do, nor will they treat you with much respect, since public temper tantrums are often experienced by others as frightening, childish, or inappropriate." (See our chapter 11 discussion of how counseling and advice-giving, in addition to psychotherapy, are also functions of the CAT therapist.)

We also focus on our impressions of the client and on the client–therapist relationship to highlight for the client his or her interpersonal stance and security-seeking behaviors. Additionally, this focus mitigates against harmful ruptures in the therapeutic alliance by the client's security-seeking behaviors in the therapy. (See Safran and Muran, 1995, for a discussion of how the therapist's here-and-now focusing on the cognitive–interpersonal cycle as it plays out in the therapy relationship can break ruptures in the alliance.)

> For example, in an early session, one client pedantically lectured the therapist on what depression is and, while saying that he wanted to work with this therapist to explore how current patterns of behavior were influenced by his childhood, he vigorously dismissed any attempts by the therapist to link current with childhood experiences. The therapist then commented (as might a therapist following Safran & Segal's, 1990, interpersonal–experiential approach) that he was feeling "put-down and insulted" by the client's comments—lectured to and dismissed as if he were an Introductory Psychology student. The client responded by saying that many people in his life have distanced themselves from him because he unintentionally comes across as arrogant and dismissive, much as his own father had seemed to him growing up. This then led to a conversation about how this stance might not only be familiar to the client, but may also serve to push others away, rekindling feelings of not being loved enough by his father, as well as avoiding the tremendous shame the client feared he would feel if he made ongoing contact with another. Most importantly, the client stopped this dismissive stance in subsequent sessions, and, instead, acted more warmly, collaboratively, and spontaneously with the therapist.
>
> Here is another example of our focus on the therapist–client relationship to highlight the client's interpersonal stance and security-seeking behavior. A 25-year-old woman was considering breaking up with her boyfriend, by whom she felt "pressured" to get into a more serious relationship after having dated for almost a year. She described no out-of-the-ordinary behaviors by her boyfriend, who appeared to be a well-meaning, attentive, caring individual. During the session, a typical interaction went thus:
>
> Therapist: So you're thinking you'll break up with him.
>
> Client: [with an angry tone of voice] Look, there's nothing I can do to feel differently.
>
> Th: You sound angry as you say that.
>
> Cl: I've tried everything. I can't change myself enough at this point, and I'll actually be relieved to not have to deal with this relationship anymore.
>
> Th: So, you're ending it.
>
> Cl: I don't know. What do you think?
>
> Th: It's really up to you. I think —

Cl: I know it is, but I just wanted to get your opinion.

Th: It seems to me that there are two parts of you. One part that wants the relationship and another part that is really scared of it.

Does that feel right to you?

Cl: [angrily] I just can't do it anymore. I'm not ready for an adult relationship.

Th: You sound angry at me as you say that. Like you have to defend yourself to me.

Cl: No. [angrily] I'm just saying that it's too much for me right now.

Th: It might very well be too much for you right now, and that's certainly your choice. But you sound angry with me—like I'm forcing you to stay in the relationship, and —

Cl: I just don't want to stay in this re —

Th: Let me finish. You see, I think, and this is only a guess on my part, I think that what we're doing here is very similar to your relationship with your boyfriend. You feel forced to do something—"pressured." And I'm not trying to force you to do something. It's your choice. I just want to let you know that I have confidence in your ability, and I have confidence in our ability, to make a good choice for you.

Cl: [laughs] Maybe I am feeling defensive. Like I'll disappoint you if I don't make this work.

Th: My opinion is, it's up to you. I won't judge you one way or the other. But where did you learn to assume that I'll be disappointed in you for making the wrong choice?

Cl: What do you mean?

Th: Well, it seems you've cast me in the role of somebody who's pressuring you and disappointed in you. Is there someone else in your life who's played that role, someone besides your boyfriend?

Cl: Well, you know, my mother.

A conversation then ensued wherein the client described her mother as a highly critical, intrusive woman by whom she has always felt pressured, helpless, and "never good enough." The link, therefore, has been made between the client's in-session behavior in regard to the therapist, her boyfriend, and, most importantly, her mother, in order to highlight both the nature of the client's security-seeking behavior and where and why it originated. (Recall Malan's [1979] triangle of Parent–Therapist–Current Other.)

In addressing personal rules of living, the therapist must first infer what they are from what the client says and does over time. Like any adept cognitive therapist, the CAT therapist's ear should be attuned to implicit assumptions the client makes in what he or she says or does. The client who constantly berates himself for not doing a good enough job may hold the assumption: "If I do not do a perfect job, then I am worthless." The client who constantly pleases others may assume: "If everybody doesn't love me, then I am a freak." The client who has a predominantly angry demeanor may believe: "If one lets his guard down, then others will take advantage of him." And so on.

One of the jobs the CAT therapist has early in the therapy is to help the client put some of his or her personal rules of living into words in order to gain insight into these rules. While the session notes that we typically give clients involve all aspects of CAT, here is a copy of notes which focus exclusively on personal rules, given by Jonathan to a client after the second session. The language is mostly hers:

1. *"I should be happy all of the time" (from your father)*
2. *"If I'm not a strong, always competent, in-control person, then there's something wrong with me" (from your mother)*
3. *Dramatic thinking ("My life will always be like this," etc.)*
4. *"I want to be with my family members who are away from me, so that I'll feel calmer, since then I'll know that nothing bad is happening to them"*
5. *"I want people to calm me down when I'm worrying"*
6. *From being a younger sister: "I don't want to be left out—I want what she has or to go where she goes." (Now, you do this with your husband and his work.)*

After clients gain an awareness of many of their personal rules, we then invite them to modify these rules. We do this in several ways: by sharing our own philosophy for living, which may provide an alternative perspective for the client; by modeling behaviors which disconfirm some of the client's rules, and by helping clients trace the origins of their rules.

I (Jonathan) had a client who frequently thought, "There's no meaning to life. Probably some terrorist group will drop a bomb and the world will end. What's the use?" He then would use these thoughts to stay in bed all day and not go to work. I said that I agreed with him: Personally, I don't believe in God. I don't believe that, beyond some laws of nature, there's a purpose to being here; and that, who knows, maybe we will be bombed some day. However, I use these same thoughts to comfort myself: If there's no purpose to life, then don't worry about it so much; don't take it so seriously. And if we're going to be bombed one day, then I better get as much out of life as I can before it ends. I added that I didn't expect the client to share my philosophy, but I wanted to show him that, from the same assumptions he was making about life, he could, if he wanted to, find some peace and satisfaction. It was up to him.

While this type of intervention certainly has a cognitive flavor to it—debating the beliefs that shape one's decisions in life—we also try to personalize it. That is, we present our alternative stance as our own, as our personal philosophy and, unlike many cognitive therapies, we offer it to the client as one other possibility for him or her, rather than as some ultimate rational and logical "Truth" that must be accepted.

We also disconfirm personal rules of living by modeling behavior during sessions that contradicts such rules. To the client who believes, "People will only think I'm smart if I behave very seriously and intensely," we use humor and playfulness. To the client who believes, "I am a very sick and crazy person, and people treat me as crazy," we respond in a very casual, nonplussed and, if appropriate, playfully humorous way. A client described a habit of killing small animals when upset, a practice which had shocked and horrified past therapists. As the client had a good but underused sense of humor, the therapist responded to this news calmly and with humor, helping the client to devise new and inventive ways to dispose of small creatures—and this behavior stopped quite rapidly. This client believed that she was "crazy" and nonconsciously pulled confirming reactions from others. The therapist disconfirmed the client's security-seeking behaviors, self-perception, and related personotypic affect. To the client who believes, "I am only worth something if I make others laugh and entertain them," we might pay rapt attention to the few serious comments this client makes and ignore his or her entertaining behaviors.

Finally, we have spoken at length about the importance of linking current feelings, thoughts, and behaviors to those of childhood. Suffice it to say here that personal rules may be linked to the beliefs held by the client's family of origin and to the beliefs the client developed by reacting to his or her childhood environment. In order to drive home the point that personal rules are not objective reality but subjective, personal assumptions, the therapist points out the continuity of earlier beliefs with current ones. Once the client understands this, he or she is usually quite able to replace old personal rules with new ones that are more germane to living productively in an adult world.

THE USE OF ADJUNCTIVE MEDICATION

Currently, there are no medications that treat personality and personality disorders (see, for example, Cornelius, Soloff, Perel, & Ulrich, 1993). We recommend the adjunctive use of medication to help to contain the affect that, when overpowering, can interfere with a person's ability to function adaptively and with a client's ability to use therapy productively. Clients' affective states may prevent their entering into a collaborative therapeutic relationship or interfere with their ability to attend to and/or process in-session communications. CAT focuses on more than information and counseling; it involves removing the barriers that prevent the person from benefiting from new experiences, barriers which include excess levels of affect.

DISRUPTIVE AFFECTS

Agitation is an obvious example of affect that has disruptive consequences for interaction. When clients are agitated and feeling subjectively distressed, it is difficult for them to focus on very much other than their own feelings of agitation. The psychotherapist then gives too much time and attention to the client's distressed feelings and does not have the time to address disordered aspects of personality. Time that should be spent on the aforementioned modification of personality traits goes instead to calming the client, with only transient results. Psychotherapy contacts become occasions for managing the client's feelings, which can again become unmanageable soon after the session ends. The role of psychotherapy, then, is only supportive, and the psychotherapist is not allowed to function as the agent of change in the client's life. Listlessness, poor attention and concentration, and sleep disturbances are other examples of disruptive processes that handicap the effort of both client and psychotherapist to alter personality patterns.

Serotonergic agents, in our clinical experience, enhance opportunities for altering personality patterns and for acquiring new, more adaptive response patterns (Wessler, 1993b). They significantly enhance circumstances necessary for cognitive and behavioral therapy to take place by reducing excess affect that impedes psychological interventions. A reduction of symptoms facilitates the client's readiness to make use of the social learning aspects of psychotherapy (Weisman & Klerman, 1991). This is especially important because deficits in social functioning are characteristic of most personality disorders.

Serotonergic agents may be particularly useful in reducing rageful anger, which is an especially disruptive emotion in therapist–client interactions and which causes many angry clients to be categorized as "difficult" by their therapists. Clients who complain in a whining fashion can usually be endured and arouse few feelings other than impatience in others. Angry clients, however, are difficult to manage and stimulate a variety of strong feelings in many clinicians. Typical feelings include guilt that one is not performing competently, resentment at accusations angry clients can hurl, and reciprocal anger, because most people have an unwritten personal rule that says, "You shall not get angry at me without sufficient justification." Enraged clients are difficult and, at times, impossible to calm down, and they seldom respond to reasonable suggestions and persuasive attempts that rational professionals prefer. Because of the strong feelings they evoke in others, angry clients decrease their chances of getting better treatment.

Even if enraged clients were not so provocative, they are still less likely to benefit from a therapist's interventions because they are so preoccupied with, even flooded by, their own feelings. We refer here not only to the clients who express rage externally, but also to those who are filled with shame and/or self-pity and who convert these painful feelings into anger turned inward.

Emotional responses are not only mediated by cognition and appraisals, but by biological mechanisms as well. Serotonergic agents, in our clinical experience, are effective in reducing excessive levels of anger, whether induced by shame or self-pity, and enable psychotherapy to proceed productively. The reduction of anger makes it possible to work on cognitive distortions, exaggerated negative appraisals, and the personotypic affects that are ubiquitously present in the individual's everyday life.

SOME RESEARCH FINDINGS

There are some empirical studies that are consistent with our clinical observations. Several investigators (Klar, Siever, & Coccaro, 1988; Roy, Virkunnen, & Linoila, 1990; Soloff, 1990; Simeon, Stanley, Francis, Mann, Winchel, & Stanley, 1992) reported inverse correlations between serotonin levels and aggressive impulsivity, especially irritability and assaultiveness. Gunderson and Phillips (1991) raise the possibility that impulse dysregulation rather than affective dysregulation is primary in the borderline personality disorder, and suggest the possible efficacy of serotonergic agents in the treatment of borderline personality disorder.

Not surprisingly, therefore, serotonergic agents have been found to decrease aggressive impulsivity and affective instability in borderline clients (Chengappa, Ebeling, Kang, Levine, & Parepally, 1999; Hollander, 1999a,b) and they have also been found to significantly decrease self-mutilation and suicidal behaviors (aggression toward the self) in this population (Chengappa et al., 1999; Sonne, Rubey, Brady, Malcolm, & Morris, 1996).

In reviewing studies to date, Soloff (1990) found: "There is no empirically defined 'medication of choice' for a personality disorder itself, nor is it possible to define one. ... Target symptoms for drug treatment of personality disorders must be restricted to those specific biological processes or trait vulnerabilities that underlie loss of control over affect, anxiety, cognition, or impulse" (p. 234). He concludes that while medication does not cure character—which is more than the sum of its biological vulnerabilities—it can regulate the neurochemistry of instability of affect, anxiety, cognition, or impulse, and may modify its biological basis in the long-term pursuit of change.

More recently, Soloff (1998) has formalized his viewpoint into algorithms for the pharmacological treatment of personality dimensions. In particular, he has developed algorithms for the treatment of cognitive–perceptual symptoms, affective dysregulation, and impulsive–behavioral dyscontrol for personality-disordered clients. In a similar vein, Hirschfeld (1997) has divided the symptoms of borderline personality disorder into four groups: affective, impulsive, ego–interpersonal, and psychotic. He then uses various MAOIs, SSRIs, and the newer antidepressants (e.g., venlafaxine) to treat the severity of the symptoms of each of these groups, rather than treating the overall disorder.

In addition to any direct effects on personality symptoms, medications may help regulate affect and enable psychotherapists to proceed (Koenigsberg, 1991). Whether serotonergic agents directly affect personality traits is not the issue here; it is hypothesized that such medications free the client to work on interpersonal behaviors, social relations, and occupational endeavors in his or her everyday life. There is little point or hope of success in giving therapeutic feedback and corrective emotional experiences—the common operational characteristics of psychotherapy—to persons who are too agitated or too listless to employ them. At best, latent learning may occur, possibly to be utilized at some future time when the client no longer experiences excessive affect. However, such a procedure is inefficient and wasteful, and, at this time in the history of mental healthcare, efficiency and conservation of resources are expected and may be mandated.

A NEED FOR INTEGRATION

A need for integration is apparent because neither pharmacological nor psychological approaches to the treatment of personality disorders has demonstrated superiority. The borderline personality disorder is a case in point. At present, there is no consensus about the role of medication in its treatment (Koenigsberg, 1991). Since more research exists into the borderline diagnosis than any other except the antisocial, it seems warranted to conclude that the role of medication in the treatment of less severe personality disorders is also an open issue.

It may appear obvious that pharmacotherapy and psychotherapy can be used in a complementary fashion in treating personality, but their use is not readily accepted by all. Klerman, Weissman, Rounsaville, and Chevron (1984) wrote: "The major difficulties in combining drugs and psychotherapy does not lie in understanding the pharmacology of drugs or any specific problems of treatment. They have to do with patient and therapist attitudes... For therapists and patients alike, attitudes toward the use of medication not only involve larger social issues but affect the meaning that the use of drugs has for the individual" (pp. 185–186).

Although a survey found that the use of medications during psychotherapy is common in psychiatric psychotherapy (Chiles, Carlin, Benjamin, & Beitman, 1991), it still may be viewed by some clients and therapists as a "crutch" and not as part of an integrated treatment plan. Nonmedical psychotherapists may resist making referrals for medication review because it implies sharing or surrendering power to manage one's own case. This is unfortunate for clients and, in some instances, unethical, and exposes the clinician to possible legal action.

Many mental health professionals, both medical and nonmedical, enter a particular school of thought from which they never graduate. They align themselves with a certain biological, psychological, or sociological perspective and tend to reject or denigrate other approaches to treatment. When competition rather than collaboration rules the day, opportunities for integration get passed by in favor of divisiveness expressed as a belief for or against drugs or psychotherapy. But beliefs are a matter of ideology (Klerman, 1991); ideology is supported by faith and not by empirical or pragmatic demonstrations of what works effectively. One unfortunate consequence of competitive ideologies is that the unique and positive contribution each perspective has to offer gets lost.

There are an increasing number of outcome studies which include combined pharmacotherapy and psychotherapy as an independent variable. The psychotherapy most commonly studied is one or another type of cognitive or behavior therapy. These studies have concentrated on certain Axis I disorders, including anxiety, phobia, and depression (summarized in Beitman & Klerman, 1991). In general, no negative results have accrued from any combination of pharmacotherapy and psychotherapy, and there are indications that medication yields quicker results, while psychotherapy may contribute to long-term prevention of relapse and remission (Rush & Hollon, 1991).

Pharmacotherapists, who are perhaps more accustomed to diagnosing and treating Axis I disorders, should attend to Axis II personality factors. These relatively enduring traits of personality represent a major aspect of the client's vulnerability to Axis I disorders, both now and in the client's future. Personality traits that require therapeutic attention are almost certainly involved in cases where the client improves according to diagnostic criteria, but claims to feel no better. Medication can relieve symptoms but cannot lead people into rewarding, happy, satisfied lives, nor should it be expected to.

A NEED FOR MODERATION

While clinicians should not shy away from referring clients with personality difficulties for medication, especially for the specific symptoms outlined by Hirshfeld and Soloff, conversely, psychopharmacologists should not overuse medications. Again, if the use of medication is viewed as a way to get clients past a roadblock to making productive use of therapy and the change that it promotes, then its long-term use should, in many cases, not be essential.

More critically, we have noticed that the long-term use (more than six months to a year) of some of the more recent generation of SSRIs may be having serious emotional and behavioral consequences. The most obvious of these is not new: that more dependent clients come to rely on medication as a way of not taking responsibility for making changes in their lives. In this sense, then, medication becomes counterproductive to therapy.

More subtly, we have noticed that some SSRIs (most prominently, Prozac) and Xanax tend to *disinhibit* clients over the long run. One of the positive effects of Prozac most commonly reported in therapy is the acquiring of an "I don't care" attitude, where previously the client's incessant worrying and negative thinking led to both depressive and mood-disordered symptoms. However, for those clients taking medications for a prolonged period, and for those who never before had an "I don't care" worldview, the taking of these medications may result in a significant lessening of impulse control and responsible behavior.

> One of our clients had been treated for years for major depression, which co-occurred with a diagnosis of borderline personality disorder. She had been on Prozac and Xanax practically since the former was approved by the Federal Drug Administration. She began to shoplift frequently and, ultimately, had serious run-ins with the law, almost resulting in a long-term incarceration if not for the intervention of her therapist. This client had no long-term history of kleptomania, and no therapeutic intervention was successful in stopping this behavior. While certainly her personality style involved much self-pity and a feeling of being "ripped-off" and deprived by the world—key emotional underpinnings of shoplifting—no comments by her therapist along these lines were helpful to her.
>
> Her therapist ultimately suggested to her pharmacologist that she be taken off her medication to see if that might alter her kleptomania. It did; the behavior ceased almost immediately, never to return, and no subsequent symptom substitution occurred.

This clinical illustration shows a need for research on the long-term side effects and consequences of the recent SSRIs, as the use of these drugs is too new. However, Kindler, Dannon, Iancu, Sasson, and Zohar (1997) reported on three depressed clients who experienced kleptomanic behavior during treatment with SSRIs. They hypothesize that, although the SSRI treatment and the kleptomania data are as yet only correlational and not clearly causal, their subjects "experienced the kleptomanic behavior during remission of their depression and when they were in a euthymic state. Therefore, it is difficult to explain this behavior as a feature of their depression" (p. 126).

We have seen similar phenomena occur in some of our clients who, in retrospect, may have been taking SSRIs for too long. Formerly responsible clients have stopped paying utility and charge card bills on time, formerly faithful clients have started to cheat on their spouses, and so on. We urge researchers to perform carefully constructed studies on the long-term disinhibiting effects of the SSRIs. Until then, we urge their use more as temporary measures to help clients make better use of therapy, to get them through particularly difficult life experiences (e.g., the death of a relative, a divorce), and to diminish particularly overpowering affect until the clients have learned, via therapy, to do the work for themselves.

AVOIDING THERAPEUTIC IMPASSES: THERAPIST, HEAL THYSELF

To avoid therapeutic impasses, it is very important for the therapist to know his or her own personality style and to understand with which clients this style may clash. We, therefore, recommend that, when the therapist is becoming acquainted with a new client, he or she anticipate: (a) how the client will recruit the therapist using security-seeking behaviors to reexperience personotypic affect and justifying cognitions during sessions; (b) how the therapist, given his or her personality style and personotypic affect, will react to the client's security-seeking behaviors; and (c) how, in general, the therapist's personality style will mesh with that of the client.

As we have previously noted, we endorse Kiesler's (1996) belief that clients' maladaptive interpersonal cycles can be broken and greater interpersonal flexibility attained by the therapist's taking an anticomplementary (and therefore disconfirming) interpersonal stance during therapy. Kiesler advises that, to foster an anticomplementary stance, the therapist can discontinue his or her complementary response. Therefore, "The therapist who has been enticed to provide answers and advice must withhold these responses. When the therapist has been pulled to be entertained, he or she must stop enjoying the entertainment. When pushed into feeling cautious and constricted, the therapist must find a way to be more spontaneous. When trapped into protecting the patient from more intense emotion, the therapist must begin to help the patient face the feared feelings" (Kiesler, 1996, pp. 246–247), and so on. A complementary match may be useful to establish rapport and form a therapeutic alliance with a new client. Afterwards, it is counterproductive.

During the assessment phase of therapy, the therapist determines the client's personality style and, as we have outlined elsewhere, how that style expresses itself interpersonally. The therapist must also know his or her personality style, as we discussed in chapter 5. Then, the therapist must determine, given the client's personality style, what an optimal (anticomplementary) client–therapist match will be for that client and what an unhelpful (complementary) interpersonal match will be. The therapist must then determine how he or she can move his or her personality style toward that in the optimal client–therapist match.

Figure 9–1 depicts various client–therapist mismatches (i.e, complementary interactions) which only serve to reinforce clients' security-seeking behaviors, personotypic affects, etc. It can be seen that therapists should not take an active–dominant stance with a passive–submissive client, or become passive–submissive themselves with an active–dominant client. Similarly, a therapist should not be passive–dominant with an active–submissive client, nor should he or she be active–submissive with a passive–dominant client. Additionally, a friendly stance on the therapist's part only reinforces friendly interpersonal behavior—which is fine unless the client's friendliness is to placate and please others to avoid conflict or being assertive, or if the client is friendly to avoid experiencing and expressing his or her angry feelings. And a generally hostile stance by the therapist only pulls for more hostility from the client.

Our formula for optimal client–therapist matches is as follows:

1. *Along the active–passive personality dimension, therapists should always be active,* as this level of involvement and modeling being assertive and proactive are central in CAT to helping clients change.

2. *Along the dominant–submissive personality dimension, therapists should remain in the same quadrant as the client.* Therefore, the therapist should be submissive with a submissive client and dominant with a dominant client. Taking the complementary position (submissive with a dominant client and dominant with a submissive client) simply reinforces the client's interpersonal position in the world.

3. *Be friendly with a hostile client and hostile (i.e., anger-provoking, challenging, or nonaffirming) with a friendly client.* The latter can only be done, as Kiesler also points out, after a solid therapeutic alliance has been forged. To do so, complementary positioning (friendly with a friendly client) on the therapist's part can then give way to an anticomplementary stance.

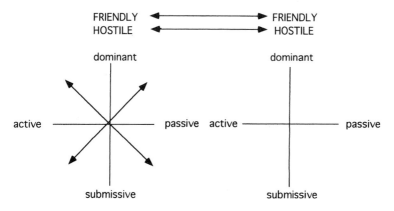

FIGURE 9–1 Mismatches of client and therapist personality styles

Active–dominant clients can be controlling or, more hostilely, cruel. The therapist cannot be passive–submissive in these instances, as this will only reinforce the client's interpersonal stance ("I am safe from shame if I intimidate and dominate others."). Instead, the therapist must come across as equally strong, tough, and competent, but also begin to highlight empathically for the client how he or she converts shame into the "attack other" tactic.

Likewise, the therapist cannot allow a passive–dominant client to use passive power as an interpersonal stance. Clients who make unreasonable demands of the therapist (e.g., continually show up late or miss sessions) must be stopped. We often threaten to "fire" clients from therapy who do not show up promptly and consistently to sessions, who do not interact appropriately, and who do not work hard during sessions—and this almost always has an immediate positive effect on these clients.

Active–submissive clients often try to win the therapist's praise and sympathy by entertaining him or her or by melodramatically seeking his or her sympathy. Here, we recommend becoming more passive—not being entertained; not feeling sorry for the client, although calmly empathizing with the client's situation.

Passive–submissive clients are looking to be taken care of and/or guided through life. Here, we become submissive, helping clients to understand their interpersonal stance and their expectations of others, rather than giving suggestions and guidance or feeling sorry for them.

Friendly, people-pleasing, placating clients sit on large deposits of festering anger and resentment, but they feel too embarrassed, fearful, or guilty to express their feelings or even to be appropriately assertive. We, therefore, provoke such clients into becoming angry as a way of forcing them to acknowledge this hidden emotion. And clients who are hostile usually induce others to be hostile with them. We remain friendly (although firm) with such clients, both to model for them another interpersonal option and to neutralize their interpersonal expectations ("I have to be aggressive because everybody else is hostile and mean" and "Eventually, everyone gets angry and fed up with me and rejects me").

Chapter 11 focuses on how we use various anticomplementary stances to help personality-disordered clients change their interpersonal perceptions and behaviors.

To ask therapists to shift their typical interpersonal style, especially when faced with a difficult, hostile client, is asking much. Just as we acknowledge that it takes hard work and patience for our clients to modify their longstanding personality styles, so do we realize that this process may be quite difficult for therapists as well, and especially for those therapists who grew up in families that modeled rigid coping styles and constricted emotional range. As such, we recommend that all CAT therapists participate in some form of group supervision, where their peers can serve as coaches. Therapists can become aware and be reminded of their own personality styles, as we outlined in chapter 5. Then, therapists can assess how their personality styles may present problems across clients and how to deal with clients that are particularly mismatched and challenging to the therapist, given his or her particular personality style.

In our own weekly peer supervision, composed of the authors and their colleagues Mildred Borrás and Vincent Minetti, we often do one of three things. We either role-play new or "difficult" clients, with the therapist assuming the role of the client and the other therapists taking turns doing therapy on the "client." This often gives the therapist new directions to go or new conceptualizations of the client. Second, we play an audiotape of a session and ask peers for feedback on our therapeutic style with that client. And third, we might ask for help with a general issue which occurs across clients (e.g., being too much of a "caretaker" to clients, being afraid of clients' anger, feeling frustrated when working with clients who do not share our values). The second and third of these activities almost always lead to the group's making a connection between the therapeutic difficulty and the therapist's own personality style, family of origin-related issues, and personotypic affect. We know each other's personality styles and therapeutic issues extremely well and we can lovingly, but honestly, challenge each other to identify these styles as they play out and suggest ways to prevent these styles from impeding the therapeutic alliance.

SUMMARY

1. CAT works with security-seeking behaviors by (a) linking them to personotypic affect; (b) showing how they are derived from the client's relationship with his/her parents; and (c) exploring how the client, at times, uses the relationship with the therapist as a security-seeking behavior.

2. CAT works with personal rules of living by (a) making them explicit; (b) disconfirming them by the therapist's sharing different personal rules about the same phenomena, encouraging the client to engage in disconfirming behaviors, and exploring the roots in the parent–child relationship of these rules.

3. Serotonergic agents do not affect personality style and personality disorders. They do, however, decrease symptoms (e.g., anger, agitation) that can prevent clients from using therapy productively and, therefore, are recommended for brief time periods so that clients can overcome affective barricades to making use of therapy.

4. Therapists should anticipate "difficulty" in therapy by predicting (a) how the client will recruit the therapist using security-seeking behaviors to reexperience personotypic affect and justifying cognitions during sessions; (b)

how the therapist, given his or her personality style and personotypic affect, will react to the client's security-seeking behaviors; and (c) how, in general, the therapist's personality style will mesh with that of the client.

5. CAT's "formula" for an optimal client–therapist match includes (a) the therapist's always taking an active stance; (b) the therapist's being dominant with dominant clients and submissive with submissive clients; and (c) the therapist's being friendly with a hostile client and hostile (i.e., anger-provoking, challenging, or nonaffirming) with a friendly client (only after a solid therapeutic alliance has been forged).

CHAPTER 10

The Process of CAT (Case Studies)

INITIAL CONSIDERATIONS

The basic process of CAT is simple to outline. It begins with assessment and, in ideal outcomes, ends with plans for the client's continuing to improve while maintaining at least a symbolic relationship with the therapist. Termination is not a final separation; the therapist hopes to continue to be a resource and a significant figure in the client's life, even if they have no further contact.

The first step in therapy and counseling is the establishing of rapport that will evolve into a therapeutic relationship. Interpersonal skills for establishing rapport are essential, and a therapist without such skills is like a surgeon without fine finger dexterity. These requisite skills are not unique to CAT, but are characteristic of good psychotherapy in general.

We recommend that therapists try to find something in common with each client, and mention their shared characteristics. To do this effectively, the therapist can self-disclose (see chapter 7). Unlike very traditional psychoanalytic approaches, CAT advocates self-disclosure rather than mystery. We do not strive to create a blank screen for clients' projections; we do strive to create a collaborative, mutually respectful, person-to-person relationship.

We also recommend trying to find something to like about each client. This might be the same as identifying the characteristics they share with us, but it might not. The therapist who can convey a genuine liking of some aspect of a client promotes a positive therapeutic climate within which to work. Liking implies a certain degree of respect for a person, and we want to create a respectful relationship. Interpersonally, liking pulls liking; and it is often one of our goals to move clients from the hostile toward the friendly quadrants of our personality style circumplex. While getting clients to like us as therapists is not a goal in itself, it contributes greatly to a close and productive working relationship.

The characteristics of the therapist and of the relationship described by the Rogerian school of thought are present in CAT. These include warmth, genuineness, and positive regard for the client. We try to represent ourselves as concerned for the client's well-being, not as experts who only apply techniques. We bring good humor to our sessions and conduct ourselves as humans, not scientists.

We see psychotherapy not as an art or as an application of science, but as a craft. It is a craft we learned as apprentices and developed through experience. We believe that a therapist comes to be adept not by seeing a few clients each week, but by working with many. Only then can he or she gain an understanding of the patterns of personality and individual differences, and of how to work effectively with these patterns.

The basis of our work is an understanding of human conduct (the theoretical aspects of CAT), and the wisdom we have acquired during the course of our personal and professional lives. To help people with their lives, we work to keep our own lives in order.

OVERALL TREATMENT STRATEGY

The first session with a client focuses on the nature and extent of the psychological problems. The authors are in the general practice of outpatient psychotherapy. Our first task in meeting new clients is to discover whether psychological interventions are appropriate for them, or whether some other form of intervention (or none at all) would be better.

Psychiatric terms get tossed about by laypersons and professionals alike, often without regard for what the labels stand for. A client's self-diagnosis of, say, depression, may not resemble a textbook description of clinical depression. A health professional's diagnosis may not be any more accurate and, of course, all diagnoses are subject to error. Therefore, the first task is to know what can be treated.

As we have said throughout this book, we do not focus primarily on the current clinical condition (Axis I diagnosis). However, if someone is severely depressed, a referral for a medication review is appropriate and ethically required. Similarly, if there is evidence of organic pathology, substance abuse, or other Axis I conditions that cannot be treated in an outpatient psychotherapist's office, such cases need to be referred elsewhere. The large numbers of remaining clients are ones wherein the Axis I diagnosis is a personality-related disorder, and among these will be difficult clients.

While it is accurate to say that assessment continues throughout therapy, most of it takes place in initial sessions. In CAT, longstanding patterns of thoughts, feelings, and interactions—personality patterns—are identified. These will be the targets of change. Personality modification is the goal, not total personality change. More specifically, the objective is to modify those personality patterns that are or have been implicated in current or past episodes of anxiety, depression, and other clinical conditions, and/or in problems of living, such as marital conflict and career dysfunction. Personality patterns predispose individuals to vulnerability to psychosocial and other stressors. When attending to clinical conditions alone fails to produce either the intended changes or lasting outcomes, it is not optional but essential to focus on personality variables.

It is not necessary to make a formal diagnosis of personality disorder. Indeed, such diagnoses are often overlapping and lack reliability, and may be misleading and confusing. On the other hand, if a client's patterns fit the descriptors for a particular personality disorder, it is convenient to use that label to summarize the information. For example, if a client has a pattern of chronic low self-regard, pessimistic thought habits, and joyless interpersonal relationships, it is convenient to use the diagnosis of depressive personality disorder.

CAT is more concerned with personality styles than with personality disorders. Rather than puzzle over whether a person matches the necessary number of DSM or other criteria to justify the label of a personality diagnosis, we think of personality patterns or styles (see chapter 4) and speak of them using diagnostic terms. For example, we speak of a person who is self-preoccupied, conveys a sense of entitlement, and shows little empathy for others as a narcissistic personality or narcissistic style. As we have stated, strictly speaking, we do not treat personality disorders; we attempt to modify personality patterns that contribute to Axis I disorders and other forms of human misery.

In peer coaching sessions (peer supervision), the authors role-play new clients for the others to assess. (We prefer to think of supervision, particularly peer supervision, as coaching sessions.) Coaches, in fields ranging from athletic to vocal, try to improve someone's performance even though they themselves may not be able to do better than or as well as the performer. So it is in therapy: a coach can point out what he or she thinks will improve a therapist's performance, and can do so without an attitude of I-can-do-better. The coach can function as an expert—an expert in helping others improve performance.

When coaching, a therapist can think of things to say and do that he or she might miss when face to face with a client. In this sense, we are all better coaches than we are therapists.

The identification of broad personality characteristics can be done quickly in peer supervision. These conclusions form the beginning of a therapy plan. The role-playing also provides feedback and verification of the presenting therapist's impressions of the new client's personality characteristics.

Here is an example of how we present, role-play, and then formulate a new case in peer supervision. This is a 32-year-old woman with whom Jonathan had met twice. He role-plays this woman to Sheenah, Richard, and our colleagues Mildred Borrás and Lori Neuschotz.

> *Jonathan: [In a rapid, anxious, dramatic tone of voice] I suffer from these panic attacks. Oh, they're terrible. They're terrible, these panic attacks.*
>
> *Lori: Ellis is coming to mind. "Awfulizing!" [All laugh.] I'm sorry. Go on.*
>
> *Jonathan: These panic attacks are terrible. They're mostly triggered in social situations where I'm sitting—it's like, I'm sitting around and listening to a conversation and then I'll say something, and then I'm thinking to myself, "Everybody's looking at me. Oh man, everybody's looking at me and I'm going to screw up somehow and that's it." So I have them in a lot of social situations. I'm a pretty social person but I'd rather—I'm just more comfortable being alone. I don't have to deal with all of this stuff. So I'm here for that. I also desperately want to get married. I desperately want to get married. I want to get married so badly that I push every guy away. I know I do that because I'm —*
>
> *Richard: You're overeager.*
>
> *Jonathan: Yes, I'm overeager. And maybe I'm a little too honest for my own good.*
>
> *Richard: You mean you tell too much about yourself too soon?*
>
> *Jonathan: I show too much of myself too soon. I get very temperamental. I'm a temperamental person.*
>
> *Richard: What does that mean?*
>
> *Jonathan: Well, I'm very demanding. I've always been that way. I was a spoiled kid. And so I learned to be very demanding. And I think too early I just get very demanding of my boyfriend.*
>
> *Richard: That might not work out too well later either. Have you thought that maybe that's the problem?*
>
> *Jonathan: I don't know. I haven't gotten that far in a relationship. They haven't gone on for more than maybe 5, 6, or 7 months, but that's about it. I haven't thought about that.*
>
> *Richard: What sort of things do you demand?*
>
> *Jonathan: Oh, everything.*
>
> *Richard: Oh, wow. [All laugh]*

Jonathan: Yeah, I mean, it could be something little like, "We're not going to see that movie; we're going to see this movie." Or I mean, the bigger things are like, "We're going to take a trip here, not there. This is how our weekend trip will be. I want it this way."

Richard: You're really set on getting your own way.

Jonathan: Yes, I am. I don't even realize I'm doing it. It's just I've been doing it since I was a kid. And afterwards, I feel guilty. And I sometimes, I tell the person "I'm sorry," but I'm still doing it.

Richard: You feel guilty about what? About wanting to get your own way?

Jonathan: After I realize what a tantruming, spoiled child I sounded like to my boyfriend, I just feel really guilty about it. "How can I be acting like that?"

Richard: It sounds to me like you're not so guilty as you are ashamed of yourself, that you did such an inappropriate thing, that you're such a spoiled kid.

Jonathan: No, I don't know what you mean by ashamed. I feel humiliated sometimes.

Richard: That's a good word for it.

Jonathan: Yeah, I see what you're saying. I feel really embarrassed.

Richard: Is that the same kind of embarrassment you feel when you're in these social situations?

Jonathan: It is kind of similar, now that I think about it. I mean, mostly in social situations I'm afraid of feeling that way. I don't feel that way, but I'm afraid of it. I'm like afraid of feeling that same feeling: "I did something wrong and screwed up, and people are going to think something bad about me."

Richard: It sounds like you really don't trust yourself to say and do what's acceptable and appropriate.

Jonathan: Yeah, sometimes. That's true. Sometimes.

Richard: So you worry about what kind of reactions you'll get, and how people will criticize you.

Jonathan: Yeah … I mean, I have a lot of faith in myself sometimes. I can go in and be very confident, like at work and in certain situations, but sometimes I'm afraid that I'll screw up. And I have sometimes, that's for sure.

Richard: How would you like to be different?

Jonathan: I'd like not to panic. I'd like, I guess, not to be afraid.

Richard: Of people?

Jonathan: Of going around thinking I'm going to mess up somehow. It's more about I'm going to do something than it is about other people.

Richard: You'd like to have more confidence that you're going to be OK and that people think you're OK.

Jonathan: Yeah, yeah. I don't want to have this background—like, this static in my head that says "Oh, people are going to think you've screwed up somehow." I guess, I want to find a man, I guess I have to be less demanding. I know that.

Richard: Well, we can get to that later. What's that stuff going on in your head that you referred to?

Jonathan: Well, it's just what I said. It's that voice saying, "People are going to think you did something really bad and they're not going to want to be around you. You know what it is? It's this voice inside of me saying, "I'm going to be all alone. I'm going to be all alone." That's what it really is. "Everybody's going to leave me and I'll be all alone." I know it doesn't make any sense.

Richard: Does the voice tell you why?

Jonathan: No, but it has something to do with my … Maybe, I'll do something and push people away.

Richard: Where does that voice come from?

Jonathan: Well, I was adopted.

Richard: What's that got to do with it?

Jonathan: I don't know, people tell me that that has a lot to do with my personality and my problems, that I was adopted.

Mildred: How old were you?

Jonathan: Oh, I was very little, practically a newborn. A couple weeks. I don't know; I don't know. I've had a lot of deaths in the family recently. My brother died and my sister died. I was very close to my mother, extremely close to my mother.

Mildred: Did she die?

Jonathan: No, no, she's still living in California. I mean, we're still close. I speak to her on the phone a few times a week, and that's OK, but, so, I don't know where that feeling of "You're going to be alone" really comes from other than a lot of losses.

Richard: Did you have it before these losses?

Jonathan: [Pause] Not so strongly. Maybe a little, but I wasn't so aware of it. My sister committed suicide 6 years ago.

Richard: Is she your biological sister?

Jonathan: No, no. She was also adopted but not from my—from a different family, and there's about a 5-year difference. We were kind of close growing up. Not super-close but not distant either. And I think since then, I've been thinking a lot about loss and about being alone and everything.

Richard: Sure. That's quite understandable.

Lori: How old were you at that time?

Jonathan: I was 26, and I had been living here in New York for a few years at that time. So a lot of things were new for me.

Sheenah: You were on your own here. Alone really.

Jonathan: You should know too that, shortly after her suicide, I started taking pills, antidepressants. I wasn't really getting them the right way. I got the original prescription through my regular doctor, my internist, and I never went to a psychiatrist. I just knew people who I got them through, and I was taking a lot of pills. Abusing them. And I finally I went back to—quite a while later, about three years—I went back to California and I checked myself into a rehab program and I got clean and I've been clean ever since, but I think that the pills definitely had to do with what her suicide stirred up in me. I just couldn't deal with it. I was getting big panic attacks, and feeling very sad.

Richard: Let me pause the role-play for a moment —

Jonathan: [As himself now] There's something I didn't say yet that's relevant. Her father was an extremely cold and critical parent whose love she craved but never really got. He was a gambler who had lots of affairs and never had much time for his family. In fact, her grandmother, her mother's mother who lived with the family, often said to her growing up, "Be nice to your father. If you'd only be nice to him, then he'd love you." And he never did show his love, so she assumed, growing up, that it was all her fault.

Sheenah: You've got an attachment difficulty here. She's insecurely attached, craving contact but pushing people away.

Richard: Are you going to use psycho-glue to fix the attachment? [Laughter]

Mildred: It's interesting because when you were playing the client, I would have gone maybe in a different direction. I got caught up in something she said, about her being a child who was very demanding, and now she does the same thing. I would have wanted to know what it felt like as she was being so demanding. What the demanding feelings were, and if she's demanding, she's not getting something, and therefore she felt she had to demand it.

Sheenah: I would have said that, too.

Richard: I wouldn't have done that so early. Remember, we're trying to figure out what her problem is. I don't like to jump in and make those connections so soon.

Mildred: But this is the third session.

Richard: No, this is the demonstration of a first session.

Jonathan: Yeah, I've seen her twice but I was playing her like it was the first session.

Richard: What was I trying to do? What was I trying to uncover? Well, first of all, I was trying to discover the meaning of panic for her. I know it's not a true panic attack —

Sheenah: No, it's not.

Richard: It's social anxiety, maybe even social phobia, at times, with an underlying avoidant personality style, which is much more important in working with her. Don't get sidetracked by the "anxiety." At the same time, this demanding stuff is a much more assertive, self-centered kind of thing. So we have a curious paradox in this woman of the spoiled kid, that's the narcissistic personality style, and the avoidant type. Somehow, she hasn't reconciled the *two, maybe they can't be reconciled or oughtn't be. The connector about the humiliation is interesting, since it suggests that she does have this low self-regard, and that probably goes back to what we commonly find in people who have social anxieties, because they fundamentally criticize themselves. They feel not good enough in some very significant way. So, that's what I was trying to explore at the beginning, to begin to find the ballpark to put it in.*

Jonathan: I think now the narcissism and the avoidance are very linked, because she kind of becomes demanding and ends up pushing people away. And then she can feel rejected and also avoid contact.

Sheenah: It's that kind of childish narcissism which is related to an insecure attachment with others.

Jonathan: I gather that she also picks guys who feed that insecure attachment. She was asking me if it was too demanding when she objected that her boyfriend booked a first-class air ticket for himself and a coach ticket for her.
[Laughter]

Sheenah: I've heard that before.

Richard: You know, it may also be the case that she's not as demanding as she portrays herself.

Sheenah: I think she may have been told that she's demanding if she asked for anything.

Richard: That's right.

Jonathan: You know, it's true. I don't think she's given me a good example of being unreasonably demanding, now I think about it.

Sheenah: Her mother told her she was a bitch when she asked for things, quite possibly.

Jonathan: I think her father did.

Sheenah: But, you know, if you have this degree of insecurity, it's got to be both of them, that's my belief. If her mother's truly loving and her father's distant and critical, the insecurity is not going to happen to this extent. It's both of them.

Jonathan: But could it be, and I still have to explore her mom more with her, that her mom overprotected her to the point where it kind of fostered —

Sheenah: She coddled her.

Jonathan: Yes, right. I see that combination a lot, where one parent is distant and critical and the other is coddling and maybe even dependent.

Sheenah: That's one of the classic shame-producing patterns.

GOALS

It is easy to specify goals when working with a medical model of psychopathology. The goal is to reduce or eliminate symptoms, preferably by eliminating the underlying causes, thereby restoring the client to adequate social and/or occupational functioning. Presumably, both client and therapist tacitly agree that these goals are the ones to be pursued, and that the psychotherapist or pharmacotherapist has the expertise needed to reduce or eliminate symptoms and to restore adequate functioning, and that the client will cooperate by complying with the treatment regimen.

Difficult clients either do not cooperate or do not respond well to standard and accepted treatment practices, or both. While such clients may just be "resistant," other explanations may account for their difficulty.

One of these is a misunderstanding of the process of therapy. People need orientation to become clients. From movies and television, clients may get the impression that therapy consists of talking about whatever one wants to, while a therapist listens, nods occasionally, and offers compassionate understanding. The media also convey the impression that the client can and should express strong emotions, especially anger and grief, and possibly mistreat the therapist, who is supposed to take abuse without comment.

Clients also have misunderstandings of how therapy is supposed to work to benefit them. Some believe that the mere act of talking will produce profound changes, and express frustration and annoyance when they do not feel better after several sessions of the "talking cure." Others expect advice and directions about what to do, how to do it, and how to live.

The problem of orientation is compounded because we do three different overlapping activities:

1. *Psychotherapy*—that is, we apply psychological principles to favorably alter patterns of acting and emoting.
2. *Counseling*—that is, we inform others about the way things are and the way things work.
3. *Advice*—that is, we recommend certain courses of action and caution against others.

A case in point: a man in his 30s had, on three occasions, become engaged to be married, whereupon he would find significant flaws in the woman he chose and end the relationship (the Jerry Seinfeld Syndrome). When the same pattern arose upon his recycling the engagement ring for a fourth time, he consulted a psychotherapist. His fears of being trapped and at the mercy of a dominating wife soon emerged, and appeared to relate to the type of relationship he continued to have with his mother. His understanding of this pattern led to his deliberately separating from his mother's influence and her forcefully delivered, unsolicited (but usually followed) advice.

The counseling mode was employed to clarify his misconceptions about the nature of family life. His dependence on a dominant mother was consistent with the view that this was the typical and desirable pattern of family life, even though he disliked it. Information about other ways to be in a family helped him see that his family of origin, though hardly dysfunctional, was not typical nor a style he was obliged to duplicate.

Finally, direct advice was offered in the form of asking him to continue his current relationship rather than breaking it off due to some contrived dissatisfaction. He was advised to think of the engagement as "going steady" instead of "planning to get married." (He was also advised to keep this cognitive reframing to himself and not worry his fiancée with it.) Unlike his mother, the therapist provided a full rationale for the advice, and made it clear that his decision to follow or reject the advice would not affect the therapeutic alliance. The three-fold strategy worked well, enhanced, in all likelihood, by the fact that the therapist told the client which of the three he used at any given time.

PUTTING IT TOGETHER: FORMULATING A CAT TREATMENT APPROACH[1]

Our specific treatment approach focuses on clients' unique patterns of affect, behavior, and cognition (the components of their personality style) as outlined in Figure 6–2. To illustrate how we formulate a treatment approach, we use the case of Silvia. Refer to this case as we first presented it in chapter 6 to acquire the necessary background information.

The starting points for CAT treatment are the goals the client has identified. Two questions we ask every client are, "What do you want?" and "What are you willing to do to get what you want?" Silvia indicated that she wants to be a good wife and mother. What is she willing to do to reach these goals? This question implies that she *can* do something, and asks her to assume responsibility and give up the self-defined status of helpless victim. Self-proclaimed victimhood is reduced when people recognize self-pity as a habit—a habit that eventually angers sympathizers.

In identifying what she will do to change, Silvia also identifies what she believes is right, implicitly stating a prescriptive personal rule of living (i.e., a belief about how things ought to be). This is important, in that fulfilling one's personal values by doing what one believes is right is the basis for self-respect.

On what basis are people to evaluate themselves positively? This is an ethical and moral question. It should have an ethical and moral answer. Therefore, we give one: positive self-appraisals should only be made when one acts ethically and morally. Since one's actions are under one's control, one has control over self-appraisals. Silvia can control her self-appraisals, therefore, by doing what she thinks is right. However, like the rest of us, she may have difficulty doing this consistently; so many of us are tempted to do what *feels good*

---

[1]This section is based on Wessler (2001).

rather than what is *right*. A self-respecting life comes not from pursing hedonistic pleasures, but from acting morally and ethically.

Therefore, Silvia needs to make a commitment to her husband and children, and resolve to improve relations at home, with her family of origin and with her husband's family. Similarly, she needs to learn how to set respectful boundaries for family members and how to control her own children, particularly the two younger ones. Silvia needs to understand how and why she pulls criticism and rejection from other people—that it is not just that they are critical and rejecting people, but that she *acts* in ways they find offensive. (Perhaps her in-laws, too, have noted how she falls short as a wife and mother and perhaps their so-called criticism is an attempt to induce more responsible behavior.) Whether or not she gains full and perfect understanding of her own actions, she can forgive her mother-in-law for the accusing remarks and begin anew in the search for a better relationship. She might do this by admitting that her carefree and fun-loving ways could have easily given the impression of promiscuity, and that she could have been seen as having trapped her husband into marriage by becoming pregnant. Looking at herself from others' perspectives is a form of empathy, and this very self-focused young woman could benefit from increased empathic understanding of others.

Cognitive and emotional changes are instigated in behavior. Here are some of the behavioral changes we pursue in CAT. Silvia needs to treat her in-laws as equals rather than as oppressors. She will require considerable coaching on how to relate to her in-laws, especially her mother-in-law. She can seek respect from them. She can have a policy of politely ignoring their advice unless it is requested (and it should not be requested very often), tolerating no criticism from them, and not reporting her daily activities to them (nor to her own mother). Having done nothing to earn anyone's respect, she must conduct herself well and make continued contacts with her and her children contingent on their behaving politely toward her. Similarly, she can learn to stand up to her father and not permit criticism and bullying. She needs to be taught what to say and how to say it, and how to deal with anyone who treats her disrespectfully. Her message to everyone needs to be: "If you want to have a relationship with me and my children, you must treat us respectfully."

Silvia needs to separate from her own mother by acting more independently, relying on her own judgment, and taking responsibility rather than expecting others to do for her. This part of our treatment approach attacks her passive dependence on others (i.e., her hostile–passive–dependent personality style) and her reluctance to take adult responsibility. She can be taught to expect to make mistakes in judgment and not to criticize herself for them. She will be urged to act like a computer and simply correct errors without self-recrimination. Respect for self based on expressing her own values and doing what is right as she understands it would be emphasized as her new way of evaluating herself.

Silvia can be encouraged to work at improving her marriage by making time for her husband, who seems overworked and probably feels unappreciated, and, in self-pity, turns to his mother for solace. More attention to him could improve their life together.

Sex-by-prescription, an intervention that is perhaps unique to CAT (see chapter 14), could also improve their relationship: Have sex once a week whether you feel like it or not. Silvia's so-called loss of sexual desire is due to anger, although the medication she takes for depression may also be a major ingredient contributing to her disinterest. Lack of sexual relations is both symptomatic of the breakdown in the marriage and a contributing cause to maintaining the rupture. Leave the kids with the mother or mother-in-law and recapture some of the passion of the past—but practice some acceptable form of birth control! (She already has three children under the age of 7 and an unstable marriage.)

Silvia's husband may not be receptive to a resumption of sexual relations because of her weight, although the case is silent regarding how long she has been overweight. Overeating, the presumed cause of her being overweight, is often an attempt to soothe one's feelings (see chapter 12). As Silvia becomes less self-pitying and enraged, it is likely that she will eat less and lose weight.

THE POWER OF THE SETPOINT

In CAT, we urge clients to stop complaining and blaming, and to take action and responsibility. Once they understand these options, they can choose to indulge in characteristic emotional habits and interpersonal patterns or to work against them.

The formula is simple but the application is not necessarily easy. Because shame, self-pity, and rage are so prominent in Silvia's life, we regard them as habitual rather than reactive. People become addicted to feeling certain ways, even when the feelings are aversive, and addictions have powerful motivational properties. In CAT, we assume that people have nonconscious rules about what they should feel, and that the need to feel the ways a rule specifies motivates both thought and action. Silvia's efforts to change will be countered by thoughts and actions prompted by a nonconscious need to reexperience certain emotional feelings, namely, self-pity, rage, and shame. Therefore, as positive changes appear, they are likely to be countered by justifying cognitions and security-seeking behaviors that return Silvia to familiar and accustomed modes of experience.

THE PROCESS OF CAT: THE CASE OF CAROLINE

In this next section, the case of Caroline, adapted from Hankin (1997), illustrates in greater detail the process of CAT-style psychotherapy, counseling, and advising to favorably alter longstanding personality patterns.

Caroline was a 46-year-old, unmarried, female college teacher. She described her father as verbally abusive and demanding—a very hostile individual, feared by his neighbors for his violent outbursts. Her mother was hysterical and complaining, fearful of her husband, and regularly retreated to psychiatric hospitals for treatment of chronic depression. Both parents demanded services from their children on the grounds that they had done so much for them by raising and educating them—a guilt-driven family system.

Caroline, who seemed very anxious and described herself as depressed, had been referred by a physician with whose help and encouragement she had lost 60 pounds. She had severe binge–purge cycles until two years prior to the initial interview, had been overweight since she was 12, and, finally, felt attractive for the first time in her life. She was saddened to find that her depression did not lift after losing weight, and despite nearly 12 years of analytic therapy with a psychiatrist whom she was still seeing. She felt hopeless about future happiness—trapped as her parents' nurse and housekeeper, and bored with her job. The only achievements in her life she claimed were weight loss and the purchase of her own house, which she had decorated herself and described as "a haven from the world." When asked why she chose to possibly change therapists, she passively replied that her doctor had told her that she needed a new approach. She was too scared to tell her psychiatrist she wanted to leave.

Caroline had been a victim of physical violence and verbal bullying by her father. Her mother was extremely self-centered, yelling at her husband for upsetting her and screaming at her three children for upsetting him. In contrast to their behavior, the parents told the children of their extreme good fortune in having such caring parents, and how selfish and ungrateful they were for being upset and miserable so much of the time. They were never allowed to express anger.

ASSESSMENT

The majority of assessment data in CAT are obtained during each therapy session, especially the initial interview, and the process of assessment continues to be updated throughout the course of treatment. The MCMI scores indicated a guarded response style, consistent with self-reports that Caroline should not reveal personal information. Nonetheless, there were significant elevations on three scales: depressive, self-defeating, and anxiety. The MCMI scores described an individual who was chronically self-critical and felt powerless, and who believed that, despite whatever efforts she might make to fulfill her dreams, she would not succeed. The interpretation of the anxiety scale is straightforward. In addition, there were modest elevations in scales (schizotypal and thought disorder) that reflect nonpsychotic peculiarities in thought processes, such as those found in persons who are socially isolated and prone to idiosyncratic thinking.

CASE CONCEPTUALIZATION

CAT employs concepts of personotypic affects, security-seeking behaviors, justifying cognitions, and personality style to portray personality.

Personotypic Affect

Caroline presented a history of depression but could describe no other feelings. After an initial interview and analysis of the MCMI and BDI, it was clear that her familiar emotional experiences were:

Shame, feelings of inferiority and inadequacy for being overweight for most of her life, and unmarried. The cognitive correlate of shame is self-criticism, and she viewed other people as superior to her.

Anger, from which she dissociated, a habit she developed as a protection when she was beaten and threatened by her father and terrified during her parents' frequent raging battles.

Guilt, resulting from a constant litany of reminders from her parents, whose message was, "You have only one father and mother, and if you do not take care of them, you will be sorry when they die."

Fear of reprisals, if she were to express her anger and dissatisfaction. She feared that her father would injure her—which she did not rationally believe—and that her parents would die following her being "nasty" to them.

Self-pity, the strongest of Caroline's personotypic affects, is essentially passive in its expression. Caroline would ruminate privately about how miserable and unbearable her life was and then slip into feelings of shame. She expressed these feelings cognitively by saying, "Because I am worthless, I get what I deserve." Caroline spoke of herself in a concrete, childlike manner, "If life is good and I am treated well, then I am good; if not, then I am bad." Her so-called panic attacks—internal temper tantrums—are seen as unexpressed rage overloading her ability to calm herself down.

Security-seeking Behavior

Caroline's predominant security-seeking behaviors were:

Eating disorder   She would binge and purge, consuming vast quantities of high-carbohydrate and high-sugar foods.

Passivity   Caroline seldom stood up for herself, asserted herself, or set boundaries for others. She compulsively overworked, relying on perfectionism to avoid censure, and went to great lengths to please and placate others due to fear of their criticism and rejection. Her two long-term covert sexual affairs were with married men who made advances she felt she could not refuse, despite feelings of guilt and shame at complying with an arrangement she did not morally agree with.

Avoidance   may seem to be only a defensive maneuver, but it also served Caroline as a security-seeking pattern. She avoided social contact except for two girlfriends who, like her parents and love-partners, were extremely critical and self-centered. She had little in common with them, but made herself available at their bidding, doing what they wanted to do.

Justifying Cognitions

Caroline's main justifying cognition was: "I am useless, a failure in life—no good." When asked what made her no good, she said that she did not really believe this self-description; that she was, in fact, kind and well-intentioned and tried to please people. Yet, she also believed that she was worthless because her parents told her so and, therefore, she "felt" that way.

Personal Rules of Living

Caroline believed that anger was evil. She also believed that she was too weak and frightened to change anything and that her life would always be the way it had been. This thought also changed from a personal rule of living to a justifying cognition: when she believed that she was a victim of her own life, the thought maintained her feelings of self-pity, deprivation, and powerlessness.

Personality Style

By referring to Table 6–2, we can see that Caroline's father fits the Cruel parenting style (hostile–dependent–active), while her mother fits the Whining and Complaining parenting style (hostile–submissive–passive), with a touch of the Nasty style (hostile–dominant–passive) as a secondary style. The parents' styles perfectly complement each other, and leave Caroline feeling passive, dependent, whiny, complaining, perfectionistic, and caretaking of her parents, while also enraged and resentful. These elements, as well as her predominant thoughts, behaviors, and feelings, combine to give Caroline a *sub-*

missive–passive personality style. While her presentation to others is mostly friendly, as she has assumed the perfect, pleasing, placating caretaker role, there certainly lurk great hostility and resentment beneath her friendly interpersonal facade.

Problems to be Treated

The following *goals* were identified for Caroline's treatment:

- To understand, reevaluate, and change the interactions between Caroline and her family, her friends, and her colleagues in order for her to feel less self-pity and to give up self-blame (shame and guilt) for asserting herself.
- To examine her values and promote independent thinking about matters of right and wrong. In learning to think for herself, Caroline could develop an individuated self, instead of remaining dependent on her parents to furnish a rulebook to live by.
- To help Caroline reduce the levels of emotional intensity, especially of fear, shame, self-pity, and unacknowledged rage, which had precipitated both depressive episodes and a serious eating disorder.
- To generally ensure that Caroline's actions were active and in her own interests and not passive and based on the desires and wishes of others. Passivity invites disregard and disrespect from others and from oneself.

BASIC SEQUENCE OF TREATMENT

I (Sheenah) sought to establish a warm, respectful relationship in which Caroline was not seen as sick or defective but as having strengths and attributes that she might not be aware of or wish to acknowledge. I was positive and expressed a belief in her capacity to make positive changes.

From the outset, Caroline talked easily of her situation—after all, she had been in therapy for over a decade and was accustomed to talking to a therapist. After learning about her father, I reciprocated and disclosed information about my own father—he was both an alcoholic and a bully—a means by which to promote a sense of commonality and understanding (empathy), and a feeling of closeness of fit between client and therapist. Disclosure by the therapist seems to increase the degree of disclosure by the client, especially in early sessions. At the end of session one, Caroline told me that she both felt closer to me and had told me more than she had the psychiatrist, from whom she still had secrets.

I encouraged her to inform him that she would not see him again. Passive and terrified, she role-played with me responses to his anticipated objections and it was clear that she would cave in if pressured—she was so fearful of criticism and confrontation. Instead, she composed a letter and delayed her next appointment for a month, when she hoped to be able to be more honest. (She was.) My support of Caroline in this endeavor created an environment of safety and the beginning of a trust on which we could build a solid, warm working relationship.

BEGINNING THERAPY

In the initial session, it is important to achieve some small specific change quite quickly. I asked Caroline what she would like to do more or less of:

> Caroline: I would like more time for myself. I am sick of being a servant. Last night, I spent two hours ironing his [her father's] shirts.
> Sheenah: Is that what you would like to give up?
> C: Yes, but I can't. He would have a fit.
> S: How would you feel if he did?
> C: Scared—and guilty.
> S: Of what? Would he hit you?
> C: Oh, no! He would just scream and rage and tell me how ungrateful I am. And that he has done so much for me.
> S: Does he always react this way?
> C: Always. I can't face it!
> S: Let's see if you can. Let's role play. You be your father and I'll be you.

> During the role play she responded as she believed her father would—viciously and with much blame. When I suggested he send his shirts to the laundry, Caroline (as her father) yelled, "You are no good! A lazy bitch! If I die, you will be sorry. I can feel another heart attack coming on." She truly feared that he would die if she upset him, and she expected to feel eternal guilt as a result.

> Using typical cognitive therapy interventions, we looked for evidence that Caroline could cause her father's death by upsetting him. Of course, there was none, and she was amused by the idea that verbal conflict can kill people. Accepting that she might be able to refuse without undue guilt helped her to get in touch with a lot of rage she was only vaguely aware of: "I hate him! He has made us [three children] feel so scared and guilty and made us his slaves. I wish I could change this but I think I will have a panic attack if I try."

In the final part of the initial session, I focused on the moderation of Caroline's affect, so that she could "survive" an argument with her father. We planned that (1) she would make a clear statement ("I will no longer do your laundry and ironing. You can send it to a laundry service."); and (2) she would *not* discuss her decision with him—her boundaries were to be defended, not negotiated. To calm Caroline's feelings was a difficult task for us and by far the most challenging. Making the behavioral change and the cognitive shifts were much simpler than assisting her to manage her emotions.

To help her manage her affect, I asked her not to cry. This request *not to express feelings* is the opposite of what many clients expect to do in therapy and what many approaches to treatment advocate. The expressing of emotion can be essential to the therapy process provided it is done appropriately by putting feelings into words. Merely sobbing or flying into a rage increases levels of emotion and the number of histrionic justifying cognitions that serve to fuel it. Therefore, in CAT we discourage *prolonged* crying. Instead, I practiced with Caroline some new methods of emotional self-control:

Question the justifying cognitions   Avoid all those that are not firmly held to be true by consensual validation. Subjective reality is not adequate proof that a belief is true: "feeling" that a statement is true is not the same as proving it.

No self-criticism   If you betray your values, stop and live in accordance with your personal rules of living, I told Caroline. Do what is right for yourself—the central axiom of self-respect.

Firm self-regulation   I elicited statements from Caroline which pertained to containing her affect. "I will not panic. I am angry and can express it." "I will not cry." "I fear facing my father but neither of us will die. I can get through this." These coping self-statements were intended to help her contain affect and remain behaviorally on target.

At the end of the session, I gave her a note I had been composing during the session. It reinforces all the work accomplished in the session and clients keep them as a kind of personal self-help book. Caroline's note said:

> *Guilt is about wrongdoing, not about disappointing your father. Anger does not kill people.*
> *Panic is often unexpressed anger. When you feel scared of him, remember how angry you are, how angry you have been all your life.*
> *Laundry—facing father*
> 1. *make a statement of your intention*
> 2. *Do not discuss this*
> 3. *Walk out and go home when he gets insulting and abusive. Remember to calm feelings*

Feelings:
Be encouraging, not critical
No crying
Disallow childlike fears. He cannot hurt you. When Caroline returned the following week, she had accomplished her mission and it was not as terrible as she had predicted. Her father backed off and never mentioned laundry.

MIDDLE SESSIONS

It was more difficult for Caroline to see the role her mother had played and continued to play in her life. Caroline saw her as sick and sad, and she had spent her life trying without success to cheer her up and, in fact, mothering her mother and feeling too guilty to express her resentment.

I used the same format for dealing with this relationship as I had with her father. Cognitively, she came to see that, after 48 years of marriage, her parents were attached to each other and to their hostile relationship. As Caroline understood this fact, she could accept that their problems were not her problems. She further realized that her mother avoided responsibility by being sick and psychologically weak. Caroline planned to limit her interaction with her mother to what she felt was self-respecting and appropriate. For example:

> C: *My mother called me at midnight to come over. My father had screamed at her and refused to cook her dinner. She was hungry.*
> S: *What did you decide to do?*
> C: *I thought about our last session. She pays no attention to me or my feelings. So, I decided that she will not die of hunger—she could get something for herself.*
> S: *How did you feel?*
> C: *Two things. Guilty, but I calmed it down by saying, "I can get used to being an adult and disappointing people." Angry—but anger actually helped. I thought, "Leave me alone. This is inconsiderate."*
> S: *What action did you take?*
> C: *I told her, "Do not call me like this. It is inconsiderate. Never call me after 10 p.m. And I will not discuss your fights with your husband."*
> S: *What happened?*
> C: *She tried to make me feel guilty. She burst into tears, "You don't care that I'm hungry. He abuses me!" I told her to stop! Said goodnight and hung up the phone.*
> S: *How did you calm your feelings?*
> C: *I reassured myself but I do not feel so badly anymore. I felt good!*

END OF THERAPY

We worked together in an active, collaborative manner on all of Caroline's relationships. She found new friends who were respectful and undemanding. She came to see responsibility as important to one's self-respect. As self-respect increases, self-pity and shame decrease, and the need to indulge oneself likewise decreases as there are fewer negative feelings to manage.

There were, of course, setbacks. Every challenge to a personotypic affect weakens the emotional habit and promotes a new sense of security. My role was to provide encouragement, motivation, and reassurance. Humor was very helpful; I teased her about my being wrong and told her she should really act as her parents' servant. Why not get a maid's uniform? Laughing together was a check on reality.

Caroline began to see me less often as she altered her patterns, every two weeks at first, and then every three. Termination of treatment is a client-directed process, mutually agreed upon by both parties. A relationship of value is not normally terminated. Feelings of connection and affection are still present when regular meetings are no longer necessary. Like many other clients, Caroline comes in to see me occasionally just to check in. I intend to be a presence in my clients' lives as long as necessary and to be of service to them.

THE CASE OF MICHAEL: THE LONG AND THE SHORT OF IT

I (Richard) saw Michael on three occasions; the number of contacts was limited by his insurance carrier and the fact that he was involved in a costly divorce action. Michael was an actor who, unlike the majority in his profession, was steadily employed. He did not command a star's salary, but he was paid above scale and his work promised continued employment.

The divorce prompted him to seek psychotherapy, upon the recommendation of his internist. He was generally distraught and agitated, and reported feeling anxious, depressed, and physically tense in reaction to the unpleasant divorce action. He knew that his time with me was limited and so he got right to the point. He had been happily married for several years and had fathered a child. However, married life began to change when his wife became devoutly religious, something neither of them had previously thought about, and she recruited him into her church. Try as he might, he could offer only lip service to his "conversion," and soon felt estranged from his wife and from her new style of living.

Circumstances befitting a soap opera had him cross paths with a woman with whom he had had a relationship many years earlier, and who now lived in another part of the country. They began an affair, and since he traveled in his work and she in hers, they met several times as he became more infatuated. Meanwhile, he reported, his wife had drastically reduced sexual activity as a result of her new religious outlook.

No philanderer, he became more and more guilty about the newly revived relationship and more and more hopeless about the future of his marriage. Then, unexpectedly, the woman ended the relationship; she explained that she was only interested in short-term affairs and it was time for her to move on. In despair, Michael turned to his wife for comfort and forgiveness. She offered neither; instead, she called a lawyer.

Despite the brief therapy structure, I tried to understand his personality patterns and did so as quickly as I could. I intended to share my understanding with him so that he might avoid getting himself into future difficulties, and stop blaming himself for his "stupidity." His self-blame soon became our focus, for this habit, which was not new in his life, compounded the sadness over the loss of three relationships (both women and his child).

Further, his actions and demeanor were consistent with a dependent (i.e., passive–submissive) personality style. Evidence: he joined his wife's church, even though he did not truly agree with their teachings; he became involved with an old flame at her urging; and he meekly left his house when his wife told him to go. He passively sought to please others by going along with them and squelching his own desires for fear of antagonizing or alienating others.

Here is an excerpt from the second session:

> Michael: I've messed up everything in my life. I can only do my job because it's easy. All I have to do is say what somebody else wrote and pretend to be somebody else.
>
> Richard: You're putting down your own accomplishments. You know that most actors don't earn a living, and you earn a pretty good one. Sounds like you're feeling sorry for yourself.
>
> M: What's wrong with that? My girlfriend dumped me, my wife threw me out, and I've got no place to live.
>
> R: You're not homeless, and there's plenty wrong with self-pity. It leads to anger and inaction—passivity. This is a time to work on your future, not wallow around in your feelings.
>
> M: What can I do?
>
> R: Stop feeling sorry for yourself. It only makes it easier for you to feel like a helpless victim. Second, what do you want?
>
> M: What?
>
> R: Your goals, objectives. What do you want?
>
> M: I don't know. I never thought about it.
>
> R: You've talked about it. You want a good relationship, you want to be a good father, you want to leave that church of your wife's, and you want to enjoy your career.

M: Yeah.

R: Now, what are you willing to do to get what you want?

M: Anything!

R: Let's be realistic. I wouldn't do anything to get what I want, and you wouldn't either. The point is, you need a life plan—a resume of the future. You need to accept responsibility for making the future.

M: My fate is in my hands?

R: Not completely. You can only control what you do, not the outcomes or results. But if you don't take initiative, you'll end up as a victim and feel sorry for yourself again. What feelings could stop you from taking initiative?

M: Guilt. I don't deserve better.

R: Guilt should stop you from doing wrong, not from doing right. If you've done wrong, correct it and move on, and, of course, don't do it again. Are you saying you should be punished?

M: Yes.

R: How?

M: I don't deserve to get what I want.

R: You mean, your child shouldn't have a good father?

M: No.

R: And one he can be proud of? A success?

M: No.

R: This sounds like your wife and her church talking. "Wrongdoers must be punished!"

M: They believe that.

R: Do you?

M: Not really.

R: "Go and sin no more." You've heard that?

M: Yes. And it's what I believe.

R: So do I. Reform. It's what forgiveness is for. Do what's right and respect yourself for it. You've tried to reconcile with your wife, but she won't agree. She's made the decision about divorce, not you. Focus on what you can do— your decisions are about what you can do.

How much could be accomplished by describing him to him? He seemed to understand himself well, and could relate my description of his relationships to earlier ones with his family of origin. He himself declared what he must do in the future, indicating that he had an idea for action, if not a fully developed plan. He knew what he wanted to assert and resolved to do so.

Follow-up information confirmed that he had psychologically survived the marital breakup and was relieved not to be part of his wife's church. She was unrelenting, despite his assertive reminders about godly forgiveness, and involved herself even more in church activities. The benefit of her involvement was that he could spend more time with his child, and could see himself as a good and responsible father. He noticed that he was less dependent on colleagues' approval of his work (although he still lived for applause), even though we had not dealt at all with work issues. Although it is an exaggeration to say that his personality changed, he became more aware of his patterns (and of the emotional setpoint that prompted his enacting them), and, therefore, was able to work against them more effectively.

The process of psychotherapy and its pace depends on several client variables, especially clients' willingness to speak and reveal themselves, and their knowing what to reveal and how to put thoughts and feelings into words. And on several therapist variables, especially our ability to keep the client focused on psychological material (affect, behavior, cognition) and away from storytelling, and our ability to listen empathetically without losing the ability to hear and connect that which is psychologically meaningful. In both the client and the therapist, maturity level is critical. The more developed the ego or character of the person, client or therapist, the more effective and quickly the therapy can proceed. We offer these hypotheses, supported by our clinical and supervisory experience, as propositions for other therapists and supervisors to contemplate.

THE CASE OF GEORGE

George was a middle-aged man who had an anger problem, according to his own description. Just how it was a problem was not clear, because George did not explode or suffer somatically; if angered, he simply withdrew until he felt better. He had discovered how to do a form of cognitive therapy on himself, but did not understand "what I say to myself to get angry," or why he seemed to get angry over very little.

I (Richard) explained that anger was his response to his own perceptions that other people had violated his personal rules (i.e., demands that they do as he wanted them to do). George seemed very satisfied. He liked the emotional setpoint theory and related it to his younger days when he had a bit of a drug addiction problem. He said that drugs made him feel good at first, but that later, he felt worse. And when he tried to stop, he would lapse after a while. He understood his lapses as related to his personal setpoint—to return to how he should feel—that is, the "worse" feeling. Without knowing it, he wanted counseling and instruction. As an investment banker, he liked formulas. Over the course of 6 months, he came to understand himself better and resolved two difficult relationships in his life.

One of these was with his wife, with whom he had an indifferent relationship; the other was with another woman with whom he shared business-related interests and sexual passion. His was the classic triangle, in which he would not choose, nor could easily choose, between two women. During our work together, he expressed anger toward his wife for not "keeping up" with him. They had been married for 12 years and had no children, but their once-close relationship waned as he became more successful.

The other woman appeared to be a more rational choice of mate for him, he opined, but he could not commit himself to her. As he spoke of her during subsequent sessions, he became increasingly angry at her for not being the ideal woman he wanted.

His was not a problem of low self-respect. His passive–dominant (i.e., narcissistic) personality style included the expectation that others would do as he wished. Therapy focused on the relationship between a personality trait (narcissism) and a feeling (anger at not getting what he wanted). However, before such a focus could occur, George spent several sessions discussing the relative merits of each woman and what made the decision difficult for him.

We had to cut through considerable psychobabble he had acquired from extensive reading and from friends. "Commitment phobic" was one layman's diagnosis of George's problem. "Emotionally shut down" was another, due to his tendency to withdraw rather than overtly express his feelings, especially anger.

Beneath each cliché is an implicit theory of psychopathology that must be addressed if client and therapist are to share working assumptions about human nature. George, like most clients, had his own ideas about people, but he respected the expertise of his therapist and was willing to learn some new ideas. While CAT is not explicitly an educational model of therapy, there is some teaching of basic principles involved, just as there is in any psychotherapy. Insight is a form of learning, as clients learn how concepts and propositions fit their own lives.

George wanted to learn. He would ask questions about himself and about people in general. Far from flinching when the meaning of narcissistic was explained, he reacted with, "Yes, yes, that's me." He did not suffer from low self-respect, so he could absorb information about his personality traits and their role in his life without any defensiveness. Instead, his response was a pragmatic, "What can I do about it?"

Later discussions focused on his having realistic expectations about himself and other people. As he attempted to change his expectations, he was pleased to discover that he felt less dissatisfied, less frustrated, and, therefore, less angry. He became more tolerant of both women in his life and stopped discussing what decision he should make. His work emerged for a while as the main topic of sessions, until one day when he said, almost casually, that he had stopped seeing the other woman and was getting reacquainted with his wife.

He reported that he had benefited especially from an analogy about anger I had used. I described feelings of anger as a smoke detector. The alarm signals that something is wrong and should be put right. Now, when he got angry with people, he stopped to ask himself what was wrong and what he could do about it. He used angry feelings as a motivational message to get busy and stop complaining.

George ended therapy on a happy note, declaring his intention to write a book on how to handle anger. To the best of my knowledge, he never fulfilled his intention, although he did write and publish quite a different book, a fictional adventure story.

CONCLUSION

The point of these case reports is to give to each, according to his or her need. Psychotherapy is not easily manualized when it is the person who is the focus of treatment instead of, say, depression or anxiety. While we do not advocate the ignoring of clinical conditions, we highly recommend trying to understand the person (client), even in a short time. We take as a working assumption that when therapists understand their clients and can assist clients in understanding themselves, the results are more satisfying for both and the client leaves therapy better prepared for the many vicissitudes of life. After all, this is how we want to be treated, and you, the reader, probably also want to be treated as a person and not as a symptom.

PART **III**

Applications of CAT

CHAPTER **11**

CAT with Personality-disordered Clients

The treatment of personality disorders has gained steady acceptance in the cognitive and behavior therapies, whereas before such clinical conditions as anxiety and depression were the main focus and concepts of personality were not addressed. Thorpe and Olson (1997) observed that, "until recently, behavior therapists have questioned the very existence of pervasive, long-standing personality characteristics or 'traits'" (p. 232). Cognitive therapists, formerly ignoring personality traits, have now given them closer attention (Pretzer & Beck, 1996).

There are several reasons for this change. First, some clients did not make or maintain therapeutic gains, and personality variables were hypothesized to be the cause or contributing factor. Second, medications increasingly became the treatment of choice for anxiety and depression, due to their relatively low cost and convenience. Psychotherapists had to look elsewhere for opportunities to contribute to client improvement. The personality disorders are an obvious alternative.

Third, the study of personality, which had been dominated by psychodynamic theorists, practitioners, and researchers, turned to less abstract ways of conceptualizing personality and its disorders. The chief proponent of a social learning perspective on personality is Millon (1996), who described cognitive, emotional, interpersonal, and other patterns for each personality disorder. These patterns furnish fairly specific cognitive, affective, and behavioral targets for intervention, rather than trying to deal with such vague and nonoperational theoretical constructs (see Rotter, 1954; Rotter & Hochreich, 1975) as oral or anal character.

While this chapter speaks of treating certain personality disorders, in reality, it addresses attempts to modify certain personality traits or longstanding patterns of cognition, affect, and interpersonal behavior. Each individual has distinctive traits that are less adaptive than they could be. In this sense, every client—and person—has a personality "disorder".

PREVALENCE

Clients with diagnosed personality disorders make up a significant proportion of persons treated by mental health professionals (Brooks, Baltazar, McDowell, & Munjack, 1991; Maier, Lichtermann, Klingler, & Heun, 1992; Oldham, Skodol, Kellman, & Hyler, 1995; Shea et al., 1990; Spitzer & Forman, 1979). Studies dealing with the impact of personality disorders on the outcomes of treatment of clinical syndromes consistently show poorer outcomes when clients are diagnosed with one or more personality disorders (Mellman, Leverich, Hauser, & Kramlinger, 1992; Ronningstam, Gunderson, & Lyons, 1995; Shea et al., 1990). There are data that suggest that the severity of a personality disorder, rather than its mere presence, is prognostic of treatment outcome in generalized anxiety (Beaudry, 1991), panic disorder (Shear, 1991) and agoraphobia (Mavissakalian, 1990).

The focus of psychological treatment of personality disorders is longstanding patterns of behavior (or psychological traits that may be inferred from behavior) that interfere with social and occupational adjustment, or that impede recovery from depression and other clinical syndromes. Although there are more than a dozen personality disorders described in the DSM–IV, most abnormal psychology textbooks focus on two—the antisocial and the borderline. The severely psychopathic antisocial personality disorder has attracted much research attention and the borderline has stimulated a great deal of theorizing. And both disorders have garnered much publicity in the media, due to such movies as "The Silence of the Lambs" for the antisocial personality and "Fatal Attraction" for the borderline (or, rather, an exaggerated, melodramatic version of this personality disorder). Antisocials almost never voluntarily seek treatment and, like borderlines, have a reputation of being difficult to treat. Because of this, there is an impression that all personality disorders are difficult to treat. This is not so, and this chapter is devoted to treating some of the "other" personality disorders—often the majority of clients in a clinical practice—using CAT.

The following treatment guidelines were derived from our clinical experience. They are the results of well over a decade of extensive work with personality-disordered clients by Wessler (1993a), Hankin (1997), and Stern (1996). This approach combines our adaptation and extension of Millon's descriptions of personality prototypes to establish targets of change with CAT principles for overcoming resistance to change.

WORKING WITH DEPENDENT PERSONALITY-DISORDERED (PASSIVE–SUBMISSIVE) CLIENTS

The distinguishing features of a dependent personality disorder, according to DSM–IV criteria, are a pervasive and excessive need to be taken care of that leads to submissive behavior and fears of separation. The individual looks to others to make decisions and assume responsibility for most of his or her life.

Our formulation of the dependent personality style, not unlike Millon's, involves an individual who is primarily *passive and submissive*. Dependent persons are essentially passive and seek to get along with other people by pleasing them. The reinforcement they desire is approval from others, and the consequence they fear is disapproval. The person sees him-herself as weak and helpless, and engages in submissive, deferential interpersonal behaviors to ensure approval and lack of censure. They are agreeable to an extreme; it is a rewarding tactic, for if one agrees with what others say and want, there is little possibility that others will disapprove. Severe dependents offer no opinions of their own, make no decisions, and always follow, never lead. Pleasing others is their way of getting by in the world.

Dependent persons are prone to anxiety, as they worry about avoiding disapproval and fear criticism. They become depressed when they fail to receive positive comments from others or when they have no one stronger to rely on. Relationships are valuable to them as a source of comfort, reassurance, and guidance. Independence is both alarming and depressing. Episodes of depression occur when the dependent person has no one on whom to rely and must face the vicissitudes of life alone. Anxiety that they might have to act independently is almost always with them; hence, they are prone to generalized anxiety disorder. The personality style itself predisposes the person to chronic anxiety and recurrent depressive episodes. The personality characteristics, therefore, must be a focus for treatment. Treating the anxiety or depression alone will not be sufficient to prevent their recurrence.

The dependent person presents special problems for therapists, especially therapists who have a take-charge educational approach. Eager to please the therapist, the dependent will agree with everything and send the subtle message: "I am harmless and helpless—take care of me." To further insure that the therapist will be exceptionally helpful, the dependent will present him-herself as especially troubled, and clearly a helpless victim of some real or vague tormentor. However, the dependent will not really follow the therapist's advice, for to do successfully what the therapist says means that the dependent will change and becoming independent is too threatening. Consequently, he or she will "yes" the therapist and not really work hard to change, and the take-charge therapist will ultimately end up feeling frustrated, thwarted, and disobeyed by the dependent. Angry responses from the therapist, even subtle ones, may bring about a sense of security for the dependent, as most caretakers of dependents end up feeling burned-out and resentful of their roles as perpetual caretakers of people who do not really want to be on their own.

The overall strategy for working with dependent persons is to encourage them to be less passive and more active on their own behalf, and to focus on pleasing themselves more than pleasing other people. Simply explaining this goal to a client is a good beginning. Then, every instance of passive, pleasing behavior can be pointed out by the therapist. The client can be encouraged to take risks outside the therapy session by asserting himself or herself, offering opinions, and making decisions. Certain tactics of CAT are helpful in carrying out this strategy.

1. *Do not feel sorry for the client* or express any attitude that might convey pity. As a passive, self-defined victim, the dependent person desires sympathy and wants the therapist (and most other people) to reinforce the self-image of weakness and disadvantage. Therapists who describe themselves as "nurturers," "caretakers," or "earth mothers" are most likely to increasing dependent clients' self-pity, as they openly express sympathy for this client's self-pity and they instill the dependent belief that the love of a "supportive, nurturing" (i.e., more powerful) other will heal them.

> *Client: Nobody at work cares about how my boss treats me. They just go about their jobs and let her boss me around and demean me.*
>
> *Therapist: What would you like them to do?*
>
> *Cl: To talk with me and make me feel better when I feel so demoralized. To be more supportive of me. Heck, I'd really like them to give my boss a piece of their minds on my behalf, but I know that that's not going to happen.*
>
> *Th: Sounds like you feel angry at your co-workers for not being there for you and sorry for your having to work with your boss.*
>
> *Cl: I guess you could say that. Well, wouldn't you feel like that, too? Having to put up with my boss's indignities? She practically gets off on torturing me. You don't understand. You don't care.*

Th: *I do care, but I don't see it the way you do. I believe that there are things you can say and do at work, if you want to, that will make you feel like less of a victim.*

Cl: *You just don't understand.*

Th: *I know that you feel taken advantage of and all alone at work, and that stinks. You probably feel that I also am callous to your needs, just like your boss and your co-workers. So, in all these situations, you feel like the uncared-for victim, longing to be better taken care of. And that leaves you feeling angry at others and sorry for yourself that nobody cares enough about you.*

Cl: *That about sums it up.*

Th: *It's you that's going to have to change in order for you not to feel that way anymore—not the world. The world is too big an entity to change, but you're not.*

2. *Do not let the client please the therapist.* Dependent persons will be especially compliant, ready to accommodate and defer to the therapist. Beginning and insecure therapists are particularly susceptible to allowing this behavior, as it mollifies their own shame-based fears. The frustrating of dependent clients' attempts to please and ingratiate themselves will weaken these responses.

Cl: *Man, I'm so glad you're my therapist. There are so many lousy therapists out there and I'm so fortunate to have you.*

Th: *Well, thanks.*

Cl: *How did you get to be so good?*

Th: *Let me stop you for a minute. You seem to be wanting to please me an awful lot by praising me. What do you believe would happen if you didn't praise me?*

Cl: *[Pause] Gee ... well ... I don't know. Maybe you'd think I didn't like you or appreciate you, and you wouldn't want to work with me or think that working with me is a real drag.*

Th: *So, if you please me, then I'll like you and, what? Maybe I won't criticize you or reject you in some way?*

Cl: *Hurt me in some way, I guess.*

Th: *And, you know, there's actually something annoying about your praising me. It seems put-on and not so genuine; even if you believe it, it doesn't come across that way to me. And it's a bit excessive, so that also makes it feel phony, like you're sucking up to me. I don't think that your praise necessarily has the effect on others that you think it does. It might actually irritate them and make them suspicious of you*

Cl: *Thanks for pointing that out. I really appreciate it*

Th: *See, there too you thanked me in a kind of deferential way. It's part of your deferential, must-please-others pattern.*

3. *Do not take responsibility for fixing the client's problems.* Skilled at getting others to solve their problems and make their decisions, dependent persons expect therapists to do the same. They define the therapist's role as one of authority and of helping (i.e, as the complementary active–dominant stance); therefore, they feel justified in asking the therapist to manage their lives. To do so, of course, merely reinforces the pattern of dependence and is antitherapeutic. Therapists who are self-styled "fixers" and teachers are most likely to accept this active–dominant role and, therefore, reinforce the dependent's passive–submissive stance.

> Cl: I really don't want to go to work tomorrow because I'm feeling sick, but I've already taken a lot of sick days. What do you think I should do?
> Th: What do you think is best in this situation?
> Cl: Well, I don't know. That's why I'm asking you.
> Th: There's really no right or wrong here, as I see it. The most important thing for you is that you learn to make decisions by yourself, without depending on another to give you advice. To trust your own good judgment and opinions.
> Cl: So, you think I should stay home.
> Th: You really want to depend on me rather than depend on yourself. How do you feel, that I'm not making up your mind for you?
> Cl: Well, look, I understand what you're saying, but I hate it. It's difficult to make these decisions. What happens if I make a mistake?
> Th: You're right. It is difficult to make these decisions. If you make a mistake, then you pick yourself up, dust yourself off, learn from the experience, and move on. The point is, you take responsibility for your mistakes and for your triumphs. Don't give the power to someone else, unless you want to remain dependent on others for the rest of your life, which, of course, is your decision to make.

4. *Incite anger.* This tactic may seem surprising, but it is based on the observation that passive people harbor unexpressed resentment. They are afraid to express any negative feelings for fear of offending and alienating others and, thus, being left alone. And they often give in to the desires of others and spend a lifetime not getting what they really want. Much repressed anger and resentment results. In the safety of the therapy setting, the therapist should attempt to elicit negative feelings, anger, in particular.

There are several ways to do this. The frustrating of attempts to be taken care of and to please the therapist has already been discussed. The therapist can also make this strategy more anger-provoking by openly expressing annoyance at the client's sympathy-seeking and/or people-pleasing behaviors.

A more novel tactic is to defend the person the client complains about, since dependents complain about what displeases them rather than taking effective action to correct what they perceive as undesirable. Therapists can evoke anger by disagreeing with the client, but the anger may remain covert unless its expression is encouraged. To get the client to express anger responsibly, the therapist can comment on how the client appears angry (often by commenting on body language) or the therapist can infer anger from the client's spoken language. Often, dependents who don't openly express anger have a tight smile or grin on their face when they are expressing seemingly neutral statements that really contain a lot of underlying rage. The therapist can comment on this as well.

> *Client: My son doesn't care about me. He's changed so much since he's been married. I always thought he was a caring human being, but he's changed so much. He has so little time for me. Sees me maybe once a week; sometimes, a little more, but he's looking at his watch the whole time.*
>
> *Therapist: How do you deal with his not paying you too much attention?*
>
> *Cl: Well, I tell him. I have to or I don't think he'd even realize he was ignoring me.*
>
> *Th: How do you discuss this with him?*
>
> *Cl: Well, I keep bringing it up. Many times. Hoping against hope that he's come to his senses.*
>
> *Th: You know, I'd probably be distant toward you too and look at my watch. I'd be thinking, "Here she goes again, for the millionth time. She's not satisfied with what I'm giving her, not acknowledging or accepting that this is as good as it gets. It's so unpleasant to be around her constant nagging and dissatisfaction. What a downer. I could be having a pleasant evening with my wife or my friends instead."*
>
> *Cl: So, you're taking his side! I don't believe this! You're just like him.*
>
> *Th: What I'm saying is: how do you think your behavior affects your son? How does it make him feel?*
>
> *Cl: This is outrageous! I thought you were trying to help me! You don't care about me either! I'm furious!*
>
> *Th: So you're getting angry at me for not agreeing with you, just like you do to your son. You know, not seeing things the way you do is not the same as not caring about you. But when somebody, me, your son, disagrees with you, you feel uncared-for and get enraged.*
>
> *Cl: Well, it's only natural.*
>
> *Th: How does it affect the other person?*
>
> *Cl: I don't know. That's not the point.*
>
> *Th: Sure it is. If you keep bothering and nagging your son that he doesn't give you what you want—that he's a disappointment—you're progressively*

pushing him away, out of your life. Take responsibility for this, rather than blaming it on your son.

A paradoxical intervention can also evoke anger. The therapist can agree with the client who expresses hopelessness or unwillingness to change. This intervention, like any good paradoxical intervention, must be based on the therapist's honest belief: that any client who believes his or her ability to change to be hopeless will, in fact, not make any significant attempts to change. His or her chances of change are, therefore, legitimately hopeless. This intervention also challenges the dependent person's wish that other people or environmental conditions must change if he or she is to change, and it can also lead to the client's expressing unexpressed anger.

> *Client: It's really hopeless. [Pause] I'll never change. It seems that nothing you do gets me to change and nothing I do helps me to change. Why bother with therapy?*
>
> *Therapist: Well, maybe you're right. Maybe you're not going to change.*
>
> *Cl: What do you mean? How can you say that?*
>
> *Th: If you don't believe in the possibility of your changing, then you won't change yourself. Only those who have some hope of progress or change really change.*
>
> *Cl: [Long pause]*
>
> *Th: I notice that you are smiling, which certainly doesn't match the mood of our conversation. Your foot's also shaking furiously.*
>
> *Cl: It's just a nervous habit.*
>
> *Th: It's just an angry habit. You're sitting on your anger at me like you always sit on your anger. You know, it's OK to show it in here. It's healthy for you, a sign of change.*
>
> *Cl: [Pause] How can you say that there's no hope for me? How can you do that to me?*
>
> *Th: I'm not doing anything to you. If you're not going to believe in your ability to change and really work to change, then you won't change. It's as simple as that.*
>
> *Cl: I guess I am sort of angry at you for saying that.*
>
> *Th: Sort of angry? You're enraged!*
>
> *Cl: [Laughs] Yeah, maybe.*

5. *Ask the client to be his or her own therapist.* "What would you do if you were your own therapist?" or "How would you feel if you were your own therapist?" are the general questions to pose. This tactic asks the client to assume responsibility and gets the therapist out of the unhelpful active–dominant role of expert. It is also a tactic that can be used to evoke anger in the client if he or she is steadfast in the desire for the therapist to be the all-knowing problem-solver.

6. *Assume that the client mislabels at least some anger as "anxiety."* So-called "panic attacks" are sometimes anger attacks. Passive persons misconstrue negative subjective feelings, especially anger, as anxiety since anger seems so unlikely to them—they are (as they see it) weak and "nice" people who want others to like them. Further, they may fear giving any indication of anger or negative feelings, as these feelings will not please others and pull caretaking from them, and these clients, therefore, focus on their fear and "anxiety" rather than on their anger. Finally, some of these clients have come from anger-avoidant families as well, and they are simply not versed at identifying, let alone expressing, anger.

Recall that panic attacks can also really be expressions of fear of not being able to take care of oneself in a "cold, cruel world." In other words, panic attacks stir up feelings of shame and self-pity, dominant personotypic affects in the dependent personality. Not far behind these feelings lies anger; in this case, anger at the perceptions that the world is so cold and cruel and that the dependent cannot always be sheltered by others from outside assaults.

We suggest redefining panic attacks for the client as either "anger attacks," if the predominant unexpressed feeling is rage, or as "dependence attacks" or "self-pity attacks" for those clients who fear not being able to care for themselves successfully.

7. *Help these clients set boundaries in their interpersonal relations.* People-pleasing individuals let others do and say whatever they want and never object directly to others, even when they feel imposed upon. To set a boundary means that the person will not let others impose on them or treat them with disrespect. After clients understand that indiscriminately pleasing others is a central feature of their personality pathology, then they can be encouraged to refuse to be imposed on or treated disrespectfully. Since they may not know how to do this, the therapist can demonstrate and then allow practice within the session. Role-playing, a familiar behavioral and experiential technique, is an excellent way to practice boundary-setting skills.

Role-playing can also be used to elicit unexpressed feelings, such as those dependent persons often have toward their parents. People-pleasing dependents usually have or had one or more critical parent(s)—that is how they learned to become dependent. (See chapter 4.) They learned that compliance and placating were effective ways to avoid criticism and then continued this habit into adult life. Role-playing brings out the underlying anger and related feelings that occur when these clients are being compliant to their parents, and at the same time the client can use role-playing to rehearse new ways of dealing with old tormentors.

8. *Use self-disclosure to counter the client's dependent maneuvers.* Therapists have feelings too and can use them to help clients. In this case, the therapist might disclose irritation at the client's whining and complaining, or express

discomfort at the client's attempts to be "nice" and to ingratiate (as in the dialogue under (2) of this section). Self-disclosure encourages the client to disclose via modeling, and establishes a climate of honesty in which both therapist and client can express feelings. This sharing of feelings between two somewhat equal people is especially helpful with dependent clients, who often relate to others in an unequal, one-down way and often are guarded for fear of being criticized by the other.

DEPENDENT PERSONALITY VARIANTS

Three variations of the basic dependent personality style are compulsive, passive–aggressive, and dependent–avoidant. Most typically, dependent people are disorganized and ambivalent. In this way, they pull others to take care of them—to organize their lives, to make decisions for them. At the extreme, disorganized dependents are substance abusers. Not only do they depend on alcohol or drugs, but use of these substances is the ultimate cry for help from others. The opposite of the disorganized dependent is the compulsive personality. While the disorganized dependent often openly wallows in shame, the compulsive dependent attempts to avoid shame through order. As the perfectionist avoids shame by attempting to have no flaws to criticize, the compulsive greatly fears being exposed to others and, therefore, attempts to please others by being perfectly prepared and perfectly organized. The disorganized dependent might calm down his or her feelings by abusing substances, while the compulsive dependent does so by organizing, ordering, and "doing things right." As the avoidant personality runs away from contact with others, which causes him or her to confront shame-based feelings, the compulsive runs away from depending on others and letting others down by being in control and organized. At rock bottom, the compulsive is motivated to not let others down and be criticized by them.

The major difference in working with a compulsive person is that the therapist does not have to teach him or her how to be responsible. Instead, the CAT therapist helps the compulsive to learn how to calm down and soothe "out-of-control" feelings in new ways, without now depending on compulsive behaviors to mollify affect. In particular, the therapist might ask the compulsive to imagine calming down an upset (angry or sad) child or friend. As the compulsive generates solutions to calm down this individual, the therapist then asks him or her to practice using the same strategies on himself or herself. With the noncompulsive dependent, who already treats himself or herself like a child, this strategy will only lead to increased self-indulgence and coddling. It is also helpful to reframe compulsivity as dependence. Once the centrality of what others think about them is highlighted and related to underlying shame, the compulsive person can begin to reevaluate the usefulness and meaning of his or her compulsive behavior.

Passive–aggresives come from families who not only fostered the client's dependence but also either did not express anger appropriately themselves and/or discouraged the direct expression of anger from the client. (To the child's angry outburst, the parent replies, "We don't do that here" or "You're overreacting," or the parent may simply ignore the anger.) While the CAT therapist works with the passive–aggressive in the same way as with a basic dependent personality, the difference lies in highlighting how enraged the person is and how he or she inappropriately expresses anger. The therapist again helps the client to learn to express anger appropriately by being more assertive, by setting appropriate boundaries with others, and by learning to stop feeling victimized and put upon by those who try to get what they want from the client.

The dependent–avoidant personality (see also Millon, 1996) belongs to the individual who desperately wants to attach to another but fears "giving over" and "losing" his or her personality to the other. This individual typically has at least one parent who was and may still be extremely overintrusive and domineering in the person's life—domineering to the point where the individual chooses to adopt the parent's personality rather than risk conflict by developing his or her own independent personality. Consequently, this individual becomes so dependent in relationships that he or she lets the partner make all decisions and even feel for both of them. The dependent–avoidant, therefore, feels totally submerged in a relationship. To counter this frightening feeling, the dependent–avoidant spends much time alone, although he or she longs for (and fears) a relationship. The therapist frequently hears this individual say, "I often only feel like myself [or like I'm being true to myself] when I'm on my own. The minute I'm in a relationship, I forget who I am. My partner takes over my personality and my decision-making." The therapist mostly needs to help these clients understand that the avoidance of others is due to an inability to set boundaries in the relationship to maintain one's sense of self. The therapist also helps the client learn how to say no to partners and to say and get what he or she wants in the relationship, as well as not to feel guilty or afraid of harsh criticism for having interests and goals apart from those of one's partner.

The therapist should also comment on how this pattern plays out in the therapy relationship. In particular, if the client avoids closeness with the therapist or too readily goes along with what the therapist suggests or expresses, the therapist should comment on this. In contrast to the client's parent(s), the therapist should make it clear that he or she is not critical nor demanding of the client; and the therapist should encourage the client to actively set some of the agenda for the therapy.

WORKING WITH HISTRIONIC PERSONALITY-DISORDERED (ACTIVE–SUBMISSIVE) CLIENTS

The DSM–IV criteria for the histrionic personality disorder describe a pattern of excessive emotionality and attention-seeking. The style of interpersonal behavior is expressive and dramatic, using physical appearance and often a seductive or provocative manner to become the center of attention. The histrionic person seems to be putting on a performance or show, and expresses feelings in an exaggerated manner. Casual acquaintances are referred to as friends, friends as close friends or best friends.

The DSM–IV includes the histrionic personality disorder in the same cluster as the antisocial, borderline, and narcissistic. They share a common characteristic of appearing dramatic, emotional, or erratic, but there are more psychological differences than superficial similarities among these disorders. The histrionic person does not typically engage in antisocial behaviors, does not exhibit the emotional chaos and rage that characterize the borderline, and does not express the feelings of entitlement of the narcissistic personality.

According to Millon (1996), the histrionic has more in common with the dependent personality discussed in the previous section. Both dependents and histrionics are *submissive;* they seek to obtain approval and to prevent disapproval from others; both aim to please others and thereby avoid potential shaming criticism. However, in contrast to the dependent person's passive stance, the histrionic is *active* in his or her attempts to gain favor. The dependent passively pleases; the histrionic actively entertains. Other persons form an audience for whom the histrionic person performs, and he or she alters each performance to suit each audience.

Histrionic persons encounter interpersonal difficulties when their performance becomes irritating. Their theatrically expressed feelings are transparent misrepresentations of their true feelings, and others come to see them as disingenuous, insincere, or simply too "high maintenance" as friends or colleagues. They are given to emotionality rather than reasoned arguments, which makes discussions with them troublesome or unpleasant for many. Interpersonal relations thus become strained, and occupational difficulties may follow.

Their histrionic actions defend them from criticism, and from feelings of inferiority and shame (self-criticism) stimulated by others' comments. Thus, there is the potential for shame should their performances fail, the fear of which is often experienced as anxiety; and there is the potential for depression should others tire of their company. Histrionic clients pose certain problems for therapists that can affect the outcome of treatment for anxiety or mood disorders.

1. The fundamental problem for the therapist is to *establish rapport without reinforcing the histrionic behavior.* This can be done by initially showing the

interest and attention the histrionic person seeks, in order to establish the alliance. Once rapport is solid and a therapeutic alliance formed, the therapist can shift to a more empathic approach and reflect the feelings the client truly has rather than the overly dramatic ones he or she portrays. This is not done to expose the histrionic person's defensive style—that might induce shame and halt therapy before it begins—rather, it is done to let the client know that the histrionic performance is not necessary to secure the relationship or to fore-stall criticism.

> *Client: After I left the party, I actually made a list in my mind of those people who did not laugh much at my jokes. I thought I would absolutely die when I was talking to them*
>
> *Therapist: So you were making your funeral arrangements after the party?*
>
> *Cl: What? No, silly. Alright, I wasn't going to die but I was mortified that I hadn't made everyone laugh. Or that some people at the party were too thick-headed to appreciate my wit.*
>
> *Th: Sounds to me like you were ashamed of yourself when people weren't entertained by you.*
>
> *Cl: I was devastated*
>
> *Th: Yes, it must have scared you, that people were not seeing you as won-derful. That you failed somehow and were not being praised But did you feel that there was something wrong with you, or that these un-entertained people thought there was something wrong with you?*
>
> *Cl: I thought they thought I was a bore and … and, I guess, and an idiot.*
>
> *Th: And how do you feel that they thought this of you?*
>
> *Cl: Humiliated. Like I'm nobody Like…like…like I'm a failure.*
>
> *Th: That must feel very painful.*
>
> *Cl: Yes, painful. Extremely painful.*

2. *Help the histrionic client to stay calm.* Because histrionic persons can be amusing and entertaining, with interesting experiences to report and captivat-ing stories to tell, the therapist can easily become a willing audience. Worse, the therapist may subtly encourage the client to tell more and more interesting stories and divert him or her from examining the client's affects, behaviors, and cognitions. In other words, the interaction can easily become social rather than therapeutic.

While all therapists may be susceptible to an entertaining client, those who are most so may be therapists who feel sorry for themselves and "put upon" by their work. Thus, they may think, "My job is so demanding, with all the atten-tion and intense concentration I have to pay to people's depressing problems. How refreshing it is to have an entertaining client. I deserve to be entertained for a while."

When the client is sexually provocative in appearance, dress, and manner, the therapist may get excited and, without violating any ethical codes, create a climate of titillation, not therapy. Anger when expressed in an histrionic manner can stimulate anger in the therapist, so the best advice is to understand the client's affective expression in terms of his/her histrionic personality—and *stay calm*.

3. *Carefully use humor to deflate the client's melodramatic style.* The histrionic client is likely to magnify small events into big ones, disappointments into tragedies, and minor criticisms into major insults. Innocent flirtation may be described as attempted rape. Humorous remarks must be aimed at what the client says, not at the client, and should be used with the goal of bringing perspective to the client's exaggerated account in a playful manner. Naturally, such interventions should not be attempted until a firm therapeutic alliance has been forged, until the client knows the therapist well enough to understand his or her particular brand of humor, and until the therapist understands what kind of humor he or she can use effectively with that specific client.

A client discusses how, after breaking up with her, a former boyfriend responded to a letter she sent him asking if perhaps they could reconcile their differences and get back together again. (Therapist and client have been working together for about four months at this point and have a solid alliance.)

> *Client: I'm extremely nervous that I'm going to blow it with Jim. He left a message on my machine saying, "Maybe we can have lunch sometime to discuss what you said in your letter. Give me a call." Oh, my God! I'm so nervous. I don't want to blow it! My life will be over if I do something wrong to scare him away again. I have to get my phone message back to him exactly right or, I know it, that will be it. What do you think of this message: "Hello, this is Rita. I'm —"*
>
> *Therapist: What! You're going to start your message with "Hello"!?*
>
> *Cl: Oh, my God. What do you mean?*
>
> *Th: You're actually going to say "Hello" to him at the beginning of your message?*
>
> *Cl: You've made me so nervous! What do you mean?*
>
> *Th: Maybe you should say "Hi" instead of "Hello."*
>
> *Cl: OK, OK. "Hi, this is Rita. I got your message and I'd really like to get together with you. Please call me back and let me know when it's convenient for you to do so. Take care."*
>
> *Th: "Take care"? You're going to say "Take care"!?*
>
> *Cl: Oh ... my ... God. You are making me so nervous. I'm going to blow it, aren't I? I just know it. What should I say?*
>
> *Th: How about, "You take care now" instead of "Take care."*
>
> *Cl: What? I don't get it. What difference does that make?* [Starts to laugh.] *You're joking with me.* [Laughs more.] *What's going on?*

Th: I'm pulling your leg. Look, I know that this is very important to you, but I think that sometimes you get too wrapped up in the details of what you're doing. It's almost as if, if you say one word wrong, you're going to turn him off and chase him away. It doesn't work that way.

Cl: It doesn't? Why not?

Th: Well, you're giving yourself way too much power over him, which you don't have anyway: If you say one word wrong, you'll lose him; or one word right, and you'll have him back. Like you're a magician with a magic spell.

Cl: [Laughs] OK, I get it. But when should I leave the message, today or tomorrow?

Th: Tonight at exactly 2:34 a.m.

Cl: What!? [Laughs] Oh, be quiet. But why do I obsess like this?

Th: What would you be thinking and feeling if you weren't obsessing about getting it just right?

Cl: I'd be thinking, "He's not going to want me. I blew it. I'm undesirable. I'm incapable of having a relationship."

Th: Pretty shameful thoughts. So maybe your obsessing distracts you from your feelings of shame. Let's talk more about these feelings and how to manage them better. Then Rita the Magnificent will turn into Rita the Self-Confident.

Cl: [Laughs] I'd like that very much.

4. *Keep the client in touch with reality.* Clients may not know that they give exaggerated accounts of events and their reactions, or they may know it but believe that others expect more colorful versions of reality than actually exist. One way to bring a realistic perspective is to use self-disclosure. The therapist can tell the client how he or she would think or feel were he or she in the same situation or event. (This tactic assumes that the therapist is not histrionic, or at least is not uninformed about his or her histrionic tendencies!)

Cl: I was absolutely mortified when everyone was looking at me at the staff meeting, waiting for an answer that I couldn't give them. You know what I was thinking?

Th: What?

Cl: That I was going to resign then and there. How dare my boss ask me that question! How dare he!

Th: Was it unreasonable of him to ask that question then?

Cl: Well, it was an appropriate question at that particular meeting. It wasn't unreasonable, but he should know that I don't like to be put on the spot like that.

Th: I might have felt embarrassed in that situation, annoyed with myself that I came unprepared. In fact, I remember a case conference meeting at the hospital where I used to work, when I didn't prepare a case presentation sufficiently. Thought I'd wing it. And it came out pretty lame.

5. *Try paradoxical statements to help reduce the degree of catastrophe and to keep the client in touch with reality.* When using this tactic, the therapist magnifies the client's already magnified statements.

> Cl: *When my husband forgets to buy something at the supermarket or at another store, I get so angry, like he doesn't care about me, and I want to kill him. I feel so angry, like I want to murder him.*
> Th: *With an ax or a gun?*
> Cl: *What? What do you mean?*
> Th: *Would you like to cut him up into pieces when you're angry or simply put a hole in his head?*
> Cl: *Yuck! I'm not really that angry at him. Just miffed that he doesn't listen to me when I give him a chore to do.*
> Th: *Oh, you sounded like you actually wanted to do him in, you were so enraged.*
> Cl: *No, I didn't. It just bothers me so much.*
> Th: *Makes you feel uncared for?*
> Cl: *Yes. Like I'm not important to him.*
> Th: *Then let's talk about why you feel uncared for rather than how you're going to dispose of your husband.*
> Cl: *[Laughs] OK.*

Like all paradoxical interventions, care must be exercised. Clients may believe therapists who say that there is no hope for them or that their story is the worst ever told. When clients take paradoxical statements too seriously, therapists must quickly explain the nature and purpose of the intervention, and possibly even admit that it was ill-chosen. Even then, the client may well get the point of the intervention; that he or she has a presentation that is overly dramatic to others.

6. *Reframe client's statements and explain their effects on other people.* Histrionic clients have a mistaken idea about other people, especially about how critical they are. In the histrionic person's past, there are usually one or more very critical people whom the client learned to deal with by cleverness and charm. (See chapter 4.) Often they have had one or two histrionic parents and lived in a family where dramatic emotional expression was common and approved of. Learning to adjust to such a family is poor preparation for living in a world where such displays are not welcome.

The histrionic person typically believes that his or her form of expression is not only appropriate but a right. Further, he or she often believes that the inhibiting of emotional expression is psychologically and, perhaps, physically harmful. What this client fails to realize is the impact of his or her style on others after the initial entertainment value wears off. While exercising their "right" to complain, they draw the very criticism they want to avoid, or they get others to reject them (another shame-based fear). The therapist can reframe complaining as "over-informing" others—too much information for them to handle. This tactic helps this client see that his or her behaviors are ineffective without criticizing him or her.

WORKING WITH NARCISSISTIC PERSONALITY-DISORDERED (PASSIVE–DOMINANT) CLIENTS

The narcissistic personality disorder, according to DSM–IV, is characterized by grandiosity, need for admiration, and lack of empathy. Such persons are extremely self-centered and uninterested in other people. Their grandiose ideas may be confined to fantasy and never get put into action. This suggests that they have a distorted view of reality, with their own fantasies substituting for socially validated facts. Thus, no one else may think them as important as they themselves do, but instead of using this information to correct their self-image and harmonize it with social consensus, they arrogantly reject others' opinions when they differ from their own. Of course, if others have favorable opinions, such expressions are readily accepted. This heavy reliance on idiosyncratic views of reality comes close to paranoia; however, narcissistic persons are only convinced of their own importance, not that others oppose or persecute them.

Narcissistic personality disorder has several theoretical explanations. One is that the narcissist compensates for feelings of unimportance and inadequacy by unconsciously adopting the opposite self-image and behaviors; this is defensive narcissism. The other explanation is that the person was repeatedly reinforced within the family for his or her narcissistic attitudes.

Millon (1996) gives this account based on social learning theory: the person grows up without having had to develop the skills necessary for obtaining gratification. This is due to parents' anticipation of the child's needs, and their gratifying those needs with no effort by the child. When this pattern continues into adolescence and early adulthood, the narcissistic personality is formed. There is no defensive compensation for inferiority; the person truly believes that he or she is superior to others!

This pattern, Millon says, is self-centered, self-pleasing, and passive. In the CAT personality formulation, the narcissist is *passive–dominant*. Having never had to make efforts on their own behalf, narcissistic persons come to feel entitled to get what they want without having to take action. The pattern is passive like the dependent, but self-centered rather than other-centered, and it is dominant interpersonally, as the narcissist expects to be catered to and admired by others, rather than submissive. Narcissistic persons tend toward depression when their style fails to pay off, when the environment fails to furnish the reinforcers the individual feels entitled to, or when others expect the person to perform some act or service in order to receive reinforcement. Feeling deprived and helpless, they are prone to depressive episodes.

The challenge for the therapist is to help them become less self-centered and more active on their own behalf. To do so, the therapist has to deal with the client's sense of entitlement and his or her demand, often expressed, that the therapist act as the active agent of change—for this is the type of service the narcissist expects.

1. *Try to impress the narcissist.* People with a grandiose sense of importance want only the best, including the best therapist. The therapist has to feel confident and convey this to the client. In addition, a few well-chosen statements about one's competence are called for. This is one circumstance where modesty is counterproductive and immodesty therapeutic.

> *Client: How do I know that you'll be able to help me?*
>
> *Therapist: I'm glad you asked me that. You're a person with very special concerns and I'm the best therapist to help you. Many therapists won't understand your unique struggles but I have specialized in understanding such concerns and, quite frankly, I'm the best in town to work with you and to give you the special understanding that you require.*

Certainly, therefore, therapists who are struggling with shame-based concerns of their own, who lack in self-confidence, and who cannot fake having greater self-confidence than they actually have may have difficulty being accepted by narcissistic clients.

2. *Discover whether the client is a "defensive" narcissist or a "true" narcissist.* The defensive version has underlying low self-confidence and covers up feelings of inferiority. The "true" narcissist lacks empathy and is self-involved. The defensive person requires work on improving self-appraisals, and needs to understand how he or she overcompensates for such poor self-confidence by coming across as highly self-centered and, perhaps, arrogant to others. The true narcissist already has more than enough self-regard. The goal in each case is the same: to achieve more realistic self-appraisals, but the starting point is not the same. The defensive narcissistic must explore how he or she puts himherself down and where this comes from, while the true narcissist needs to understand how he or she inflates his or her importance, where this comes from, and how this affects others in ways the narcissist is not aware of.

3. *Select reducing shame or increasing empathy as a target for change.* The defensive narcissist has a shame problem, as people who think themselves inferior always do. Getting at the shameful thoughts and feelings is not easy, due to the facade of superiority the client erects. One novel way to penetrate the shield is to raise the client's anger. This can be done after a working alliance has been formed because it involves pointing out the client's deficits; this tac-

tic stimulates shame which results in anger as the client tries to intimidate his or her "tormentor" (the therapist) into stopping the remarks. This tactic also presents an alternative version of reality, one that challenges the client's private version.

> Client: Those brainless morons at the Department of Motor Vehicles just stood there looking at me as if I were speaking Swahili, and then didn't help me a bit. Naturally, I became short with them and called them more than a few names.
> Therapist: It sounds to me like you weren't making yourself clear from the beginning.
> Cl: What do you mean?
> Th: These people have worked at the DMV for years and know people's car-related problems inside and out. They may not always have the most friendly demeanor, but they clearly understand what people say to them. Maybe you weren't being clear enough with them.
> Cl: Nonsense!
> Th: Hypothetically speaking, how would you feel if, in fact, you did screw up at the DMV?
> Cl: But I didn't!
> Th: Hypothetically speaking.
> Cl: [Long pause] Like a complete idiot. Like a total fool. But I did not mess up at the DMV!
> Th: So, perhaps it's easier for you to blame and put down others than it is for you to admit a mistake. You are extremely self-critical, so it's easier for you to get angry at others' shortcomings than it is for you to experience the intense pain and self-criticism that go along with admitting a mistake that you have made, even the smallest of mistakes.
> Cl: Well, maybe. I don't know about that.

However, if lack of empathy is the target, which it inevitably is with the true narcissist, then the tactic is quite different. In-session client–therapist interactions provide opportunities for empathy training. Therapist self-disclosure is required. The therapist repeatedly asks, "What am I feeling now?" A true narcissist will have little, if any, idea about the therapist's feelings or how he or she might have affected these feelings, and the client may object to the question— all questions and statements are supposed to pertain to the client, not the therapist! Discussions of what others think and feel in various situations also sensitize the client to other people. Merely learning how one's actions affect other people, including the therapist, is significant progress for a narcissistic person.

> Therapist: It sounds like you're feeling really angry.
> Client: [Sarcastically and annoyed] Duh. Of course, I'm angry. That's pretty obvious.

Th: *How do you think I'm feeling right now?*

Cl: *What?*

Th: *How do you think I'm feeling right now?*

Cl: *I don't care. This is my session, not yours.*

Th: *I don't care if you care. I want you to answer the question: how do you think I'm feeling right now?*

Cl: *I honestly have no idea.*

Th: *Your sarcastic remark left me feeling put down and demeaned by you.*

Cl: *Look, this is my therapy; it's my money. Let's talk about me.*

Th: *You are sitting in a room with another person with feelings, and I think you need to know how you influence my feelings as well.*

Cl: *Well ... why?*

Th: *Because you can't maintain relationships with people if you don't know how you affect their feelings. You're going to be an extremely lonely person, pushing everybody away from you.*

Cl: *Are you saying you don't want to work with me anymore?*

Th: *No, I'm not. But you need to understand that there are consequences in the world to your actions. If you don't see how you affect others, how you make them feel, then you'll never get what you want from them. Your actions will backfire. For example, you want me to understand what you've been going through, but you push me away with your sarcasm. That's self-defeating, unless, of course, you ultimately want to feel uncared for by me.*

Cl: *No, I don't want that.*

4. *Use self-disclosure to create dissonance between the client's private version of reality and the therapist's socially appropriate version.* This is a less directive approach than directly confronting the client with his or her distortions and, therefore, should be met with less anger. By sharing his or her thoughts and feelings, the therapist disconfirms the client's false assumptions. Shared thoughts and feelings here are not in response to the client's behavior but instead are used as examples of how the therapist might feel in a given situation.

For example, if the client is discussing how he yelled at a waiter for bringing the check 5 minutes too late, the therapist could remark, "Wow, if I were a waiter and someone yelled at me like that, I would not only think that the customer was acting like a spoiled child but I might also feel really angry and demeaned." Or, if a client is discussing how she yelled at her mother for trying to help her solve a problem, the therapist could remark, "I might feel really hurt if I were trying to help someone, going out of my way to show caring and concern, and they rebuffed me. I might even give up on that person if it continued repeatedly. I certainly would have wished that, if the person did not want my help, they could tell me so calmly and respectfully."

5. *Get the client to be more scientific when drawing conclusions about other people's thoughts, feelings, and motivations.* This is a standard cognitive therapy

tactic involving the collecting of empirical data to test one's assumptions about reality. (See, for example, Beck, Rush, Shaw, & Emery's, 1979, work on modifying assumptions.) Grandiose thinkers often fool themselves by believing facts that are not true; they are the person's own invention. Questions such as, "How specifically do you know you are right?" or "What concrete proof do you have that supports this belief?" will irritate narcissistic persons, for they think that what they believe to be true is self-evident and requires no proof. However, this challenge to beliefs can be effective if the client is committed to change and to the process of therapy.

6. *Train narcissistic clients to be more powerful.* Since they are not accustomed to engaging in instrumental acts, narcissists feel powerless. Indeed, they may be powerless and they may require social and practical skills training. The aim is to encourage them to feel responsible, self-reliant, and capable of getting what they want without exploiting others.

In addition to the practical advantages of self-reliance, this tactic works against the self-pity that powerless people feel (and most narcissists feel unappreciated and misunderstood by "inferior" others—a form of self-pity). People who feel powerful do not see themselves as victims and do not feel sorry for themselves and depressed. Self-efficacy is a potent antitode to the self-pity that results when self-styled entitled persons fail to have their needs met by others. (For a more detailed discussion of how CAT teaches clients to be more self-reliant and powerful, refer to chapter 7.)

WORKING WITH AVOIDANT PERSONALITY-DISORDERED (EXTREMELY SHAME-AVOIDANT) CLIENTS

The DSM–IV describes the avoidant personality disorder as a pervasive pattern of social inhibition, feelings of inadequacy, and hypersensitivity to criticism. There are extensive fears of ridicule, shame, and humiliation with the result that the person avoids interpersonal contact.

The Millon description of this disorder coincides with that of the DSM. There is a simple reason for this: Millon created the diagnosis. He says (Millon, 1996) that avoidant personalities actually want social contacts and the pleasurable rewards that derive from them. However, their fears of rejection or criticism outweigh their desires, and in this classic approach–avoidance conflict, avoidance wins because it reduces anxiety. The distinction between the formerly mentioned dependent–avoidant and the purely avoidant personality is that the former fears the loss of his or her identity and power in a relationship and so avoids it, while the latter fears feeling intense shame in a relationship and so avoids it.

Because they are devoid of the benefits of good interpersonal relations, avoidants tend to depression. They often present a mixed picture of depression and anxiety, especially social anxiety, but reveal strong desires for normal human relations. (And do recall that here anxiety is really a shame-based fear of rejection and criticism in a relationship.) Their social isolation is similar to the schizoid personality disorder, but in that disorder, according to Millon, there is an absence of social motives and a markedly reduced capacity to experience either pleasure or pain. Avoidant persons, on the other hand, feel anguish exquisitely.

Their pattern of avoidance has mixed consequences. It is adaptive in that it reduces anxiety, but maladaptive when it results in depression. Further, this pattern closes off certain other potentially rewarding activities and occupations. Fortunately for the avoidant persons of the world, cyberoffices and working with computers rather than with people has made it easier to pursue a living and maintain some marginal but, nonetheless, meaningful contact with people

Avoidant persons are difficult for therapists because they isolate themselves. Urging them to do behavioral homework, especially homework that involves social contacts, raises anxiety and is not likely to be performed. Avoidant persons almost always have passive–aggressive traits characteristic of people who fear others. The passive–aggressive feels angry because he or she feels victimized by others, or fears this, and also because he or she spends a lifetime not getting what he or she consciously desires. Afraid of criticism or rejection by others, the avoidant sits on this anger, however, and so becomes passive–aggressive.

The keys to psychotherapy with avoidant persons are to win their trust and then reduce shame by increasing self-acceptance. The overall strategy is to promote self-understanding with special emphasis on understanding that theirs is basically a problem of fear and shame, even when the self-diagnosis is depression.

1. *Define the problem as fear of humiliation.* The gigantic fear of criticism that the dependent person deals with by moving toward people and pleasing them, the avoidant deals with by moving away from people. Others are seen as malevolent to some degree; an examination of the client's past usually reveals critical parents or family members from whom he or she learned the lesson that all people are potential critics who scrutinize each and every word and deed. In the early stage of therapy, the client usually believes that his or her problem is anxiety, or more likely depression. Therefore, careful exploration of fears of rejection, criticism, and humiliation should be undertaken, and anxiety and/or depression should be recast as "fear of humiliation."

2. *Break the self-criticism habit.* This tactic is based on the hypothesis that all shame is due to self-criticism. Already convinced of their own inadequacy,

avoidant persons have a self-criticism habit that extends well into their past. It is projected onto others—they see others as critical, as most likely their parents were. However, criticism from other persons only stimulates self-criticism.

By framing the problem this way, the avoidant person may realize that he or she has the potential to change. Breaking the self-criticism habit is necessary to overcome the fear of being criticized by others. It is possible to change the habit into a choice—to criticize or not to criticize oneself.

> *For example, after therapist and avoidant client have explored the client's intense self-criticism and have ascertained that the client learned this from his critical parent(s), the therapist may then remark: "So, your fear of being humiliated in front of others is really just an offshoot of your own intense self-criticism, a habit you've had since your father taught it to you in childhood. In essence, you use your fear of humiliation in front of others to feed your self-criticism habit. But, you know, habits can be broken. If you want to break your self-criticism habit, then your fear of what others think of you should melt way. So let's break your addiction to self-criticism."*

3. *Show the client that the ideal state of affairs in which he or she is never criticized is unrealistic.* Comments on behavior are commonplace; everyone makes them and everyone is the object of others' comments. Avoidant persons typically believe that they should not be criticized because they are so sensitive or because the world should not be this way. They want to eliminate their problem by eliminating criticism from others. A good question to ask to unearth these beliefs is, "Why shouldn't you get criticized by others?"

> *Client: I hate that others can be so critical.*
> *Therapist: Why shouldn't they be so critical?*
> *Cl: But it's not right; it's not fair. People should be nice and respectful toward each other. People should care.*
> *Th: Maybe so, but that's the way things are. We can't change the world. So, what do you get out of holding onto the belief that the world should be different when it can't be, in reality?*
> *Cl: Nothing.*
> *Th: That's not true. Holding onto this belief does something for you.*
> *Cl: It makes me want to run away.*
> *Th: Yes, and how does it make you feel?*
> *Cl: Really angry that the world can be so cruel.*
> *Th: Anything else?*
> *Cl: And hurt by it. Hurt in the sense that people can do this to me.*
> *Th: Sounds like maybe you're feeling sorry for yourself in that you have to live in a world where people can be critical of you.*
> *Cl: Yes, that's, that's right.*

Th: So, what you get out of clinging to the belief that the world should be different from the way that it is is feelings of anger and self-pity. The more you're upset by others' criticisms, the more you feel angry and sorry for yourself.

Cl: And I just want to run away from it all.

Th: That's right. It's easier to deal with a reality you don't like by running away from that reality. But this hasn't worked for you. You're left feeling lonely and unfulfilled.

Cl: I know, I know.

4. *Point out the self-centered assumption that one can know what others are thinking.* This is called mind reading. Further, point out the folly of acting upon these untested assumptions about people, that others are carefully scrutinizing everything about the client and making silent judgments. Avoidant individuals are usually very skillful at avoiding criticism. They do this primarily by social isolation. However, even though criticism is democratic—we all give and receive it—it is not as prevalent as avoidant persons imagine. They are so sensitive that they do not have to hear criticism; they *infer* it from how people look or from the mere presence of other people in the environment.

5. *Help the client understand that it is he or she who is judgmental, not necessarily others.* It is perhaps ironic that self-critical people are so critical of others. It can be useful to introduce a little therapeutic guilt by highlighting the client's judgmental attitudes toward other people and by inducing him or her to eliminate the habit.

Client: I just know that Maura [her friend] was thinking something nasty about me, and I didn't want her to be my friend anymore.

Therapist: What did she do to show you that she was thinking something nasty?

Cl: I could just tell.

Th: We need concrete evidence to support your assumption; otherwise, it's just that: an assumption on your part.

Cl: Well, the way she looked.

Th: How did she look?

Cl: All distant and better-than-me.

Th: What about her look was distant and better-than-you?

Cl: Oh, I don't know. I can't think of it.

Th: Is it possible then that you just assumed that she was thinking these things?

Cl: Maybe. [Laughs] It wouldn't be the first time.

Th: You know, it sounds to me like you felt better-than-Maura. You're not giving her credit for being a good friend to you and you're falsely assuming that she's a pretty catty person. You were really the critical one in this interaction. Based on some possibly false assumptions that you made about what

Maura was thinking, you were going to end the friendship? That's not being a very good friend.

    Cl: You're making me feel really bad.

Guilt can also be used when it is discovered that the client lies to others about his or her thoughts and feelings in an effort to evade their criticism. Honesty is difficult for socially anxious people, but it is the only way avoidant people can learn that they will not be dealt with harshly if they speak up.

> *Therapist: So, let's see, you told June [the client's friend] that you didn't mind her showing up at your job when, really, you didn't want her there.*

> *Client: That's right. Remember, I told you what June can be like. If she feels rejected, which she can feel a lot, then she's relentless. She keeps on confronting and confronting. "Why, why, why did you not want me around? What's the matter with you?" I didn't want to deal with it.*

> *Therapist: So, to avoid June's anger and disappointment, you lied to her.*

> *Cl: Well, I think it was a pretty white lie.*

> *Th: That's pretty self-centered: taking care of your own feelings and not the friendship.*

> *Cl: Um … I…*

> *Th: When she came over to your job, was she, was June aware of how angry you were underneath, do you think?*

> *Cl: She's got radar for rejection, so I'm sure she picked up on my displeasure, and I also, as you certainly know, have a way of subtly broadcasting my anger to others, sometimes even when I'm not aware of doing it.*

> *Th: So, basically, she came over and you took it out on her by sulking or being angry in other ways.*

> *Cl: Yeah, that's, that's pretty much it.*

> *Th: So, in essence, you did take your anger out on June, but in an immature way, by giving in to her and then sulking. Do you think this was fair to her?*

> *Cl: But she can be pretty relentless when she feels rejected.*

> *Th: Again, you're putting your own feelings first and not working to improve the friendship by being more up-front with how you feel and what you want. If you can't take her reactions, then you either ask her to change, accept her the way she is, or end the friendship. But brooding and sulking and fearing her are not the stuff of a solid friendship. Besides, you're giving June very mixed messages—I want you around, but I don't. No wonder she gets angry at you and feels insecure.*

> *Cl: I never saw it that way before. Maybe I'm contributing to her feelings of rejection around me.*

> *Th: I think you are.*

> *Cl: Maybe I'm actually adding to her anger toward me.*

Th: *That's very possible. Either you learn how to handle your friend's reactions to your honesty or you continue to be dishonest in the friendship, basically to protect yourself.*

6. *Use role-playing and behavioral rehearsal to prepare the client to take the risk of interacting honestly with people.* Standing up to others is not something an avoidant personality does very often. Avoidants may not know how and may need skills training. Even if they do know how, they still need practice to gain confidence that they can do it in the real social world. If they come from a critical family, as they usually do, then they need practice confronting the criticism they have received for so long. Simple statements such as, "I do not want to be criticized any longer. If you persist I will leave," can be very helpful in developing better interpersonal relations. Similarly, the anger that remains covert can be expressed in socially acceptable ways and, in this instance, role-playing and behavioral rehearsal can also be helpful.

REVIEW

The basic outline for treating personality disorders is simple. First, longstanding patterns of thought, feeling, and interaction are identified. One or more interviews are often sufficient for this task, along with the administration of the MCMI. Second, cognitive and behavioral interventions can be directed at these target patterns. A typical cognitive intervention is to present disconfirming evidence to convince the person to surrender misconceptions or, at least, to create enough dissonance to produce some attitude changes. When these efforts fail or the changes do not last, another approach is needed.

In CAT, it is assumed that people have nonconscious rules about how they should feel, how well they should perform, achieve, find acceptance from others, etc. These covert rules define an emotional setpoint; deviations from the setpoint will be resisted. The person will engage in so-called self-defeating behaviors (security-seeking behaviors), distorted perceptions, and thoughts that lack bases in reality (justifying cognitions) but serve to restore a steady state around the setpoint.

Third, we explain this hypothesis to the person to promote self understanding. Failure to change or maintain change can then be seen as a natural process, something to be expected as part of attempts to change. The person is not blamed or labeled as hopeless, but is encouraged to continue efforts at change.

Each personality disorder presents its own challenges to the therapist and, therefore, calls for a different therapeutic stance and different interventions from the therapist. We summarize these interventions and interpersonal stances in Table 11–1 for each of the four personality disorders we addressed in this chapter.

TABLE 11–1   Summary of CAT Interventions with Four Personality Disorders

(I) *Dependent Personality Disorder:*
   (1) Therapist's anticomplementary stance:
     (a) Do not feel sorry for the client.
     (b) Do not let the client please the therapist.
     (c) Do not take responsibility for fixing the client's problems.
     (d) Use self-disclosure to counter the client's dependent maneuvers.
   (2) Interventions:
     (a) Incite anger.
     (b) Ask the client to be his/her own therapist.
     (c) Relabel (at least some) anxiety as anger.
     (d) Help the client to set boundaries in his/her interpersonal relationships.

(II) *Histrionic Personality Disorder:*
   (1) Therapist's anticomplementary stance:
     (a) Establish rapport without reinforcing histrionic behavior (reflect client's true underlying personotypic affect rather than overly dramatic shows of emotion).
     (b) Help the histrionic client to stay calm by remaining calm.
   (2) Interventions:
     (a) Carefully use humor to deflate client's melodramatic style.
     (b) Keep the client in touch with reality.
     (c) Use paradoxical statements to reduce catastrophizing and keep client in contact with reality.
     (d) Reframe client's statements (as over-informing, emotionally draining to others, etc.) and explain their effects on others.

(III) *Narcissistic Personality Disorder:*
   (1) Therapist's anticomplementary stance:
     (a) Impress the client.
     (b) Self-disclose to create dissonance between the client's private version of reality and the therapist's socially appropriate version.
     (c) Ask the client, "What am I feeling now?" to increase his/her ability to empathize.
   (2) Interventions:
     (a) Discover whether the client is a "defensive" or a "true" narcissist.
     (b) Reduce shame for "defensive" narcissist.
     (c) Increase empathy for "true" narcissist.
     (d) Get client to be more scientific (provide concrete evidence) when drawing conclusions about others' thoughts, feelings, and motivations.
     (e) Train the client to be more self-reliant and powerful (social and practical skills training).

(IV) *Avoidant Personality Disorder:*
   (1) Therapist's anticomplementary stance:
     (a) Win the client's trust by understanding and empathizing with his/her shame and shame-based fear.
     (b) Do not assign behavioral tasks or homework.
   (2) Interventions:
     (a) Define the problem as fear of humiliation.
     (b) Break the self-criticism habit.
     (c) Show the client that his/her ideal state of affairs, in which he/she is never criticized, is unrealistic.
     (d) Point out the self-centered assumption that one can know what others are thinking.
     (e) Help the client understand that it is he/she that is judgmental, not others.
     (f) Prepare the client to interact honestly with people (use role-playing and behavioral rehearsal).

In chapter 9, we discussed various therapist–client mismatches (see Fig. 9–1) and outlined our rules for how the therapist should position him-herself to maintain an anticomplementary (i.e., change-promoting) stance with the client. This bears repeating here. Therapists who have an active–dominant personality style will have difficulty working with dependent (passive–submissive) clients. Instead, they should strive to be active–submissive, actively encouraging and enabling the client to become his or her own therapist. Therapists with a passive–submissive style will have difficulty working with antisocial (active–dominant) clients, as they will cede their power to the client. Instead, these therapists need to take an active–dominant stance with such clients, becoming equally as strong, competent, and charismatic as they.

If a histrionic (active–submissive) therapist works with a histrionic client, then emotionality, mutual people-pleasing, and avoidance of the underlying shame-based issues will rule the day in the therapy. Therapists must instead assume a more passive stance, in so far as they act calm and do not get hooked into the drama and overstatements of the client. (However, therapists should remain very active participants in therapy, especially in not getting pulled into nor allowing the entertainment value of these clients. Narcissistic (passive–dominant) clients require a therapist who is active–dominant, in that the therapist must be as self-assured as the client but more empathic and less entitled. Passive therapists will be rejected by true narcissists as not good-enough to work with them and passive–submissive therapists may end up catering to and resenting the narcissist's demands without being able to confront his or her lack of empathy and demanding nature.

Finally, avoidant clients need a therapist who can slowly, patiently, but persistently work to build a close and trusting relationship. Avoidant or passive therapists will not engage sufficiently with these clients and will only reinforce their belief that people don't care about them. However, very active–dominant therapists may be so impatient or charismatic as to frighten away these clients before they feel safe enough to begin trusting the therapist. The optimal therapeutic stance with these clients, then, is to be moderately active and moderately dominant while empathizing with their extreme degree of shame.

WHAT WE DO *NOT* VARY ACROSS DIFFERENT PERSONALITY STYLES

There are two simple strategies we employ that do *not* vary with personality style. The first step to modifying a client's personality style is insight, helping the client to understand what is his or her personality style and how he or she expresses it in thought, feeling, and action. With the help of the MCMI, we actually present the client's personality style to him or her in the first few sessions of therapy. Yes, we often tell a borderline client that he or she is borderline, a histrionic client that he or she is histrionic, and so on. Although every personality has many more shadings (apparent in our three-dimensional model of personality), we present the two or three dominant chords of a client's personality style to him or her. We have *never* had a client who is shocked by this and fails to return to therapy. Instead, clients often are relieved that their problems are understandable and have a name (and can, therefore, be treated), grateful that we are being honest and forthcoming with them, and/or understood by us, as they have already suspected that they have their particular personality style. For clients to whom our description of their dominant personality style is news indeed, we may spend many sessions highlighting how certain behaviors, thoughts, and feelings are evidence of their particular style.

Second, we make interventions that match a person's interests so as to form a solid alliance with them. We use Wall-Street language with a stockbroker client ("Here's a cost–benefit analysis of your personality style"); theater terms with actors ("Perhaps we could do a dress rehearsal during this session of your newly found assertiveness"); and so on. We also directly share similar interests that we have with our clients to foster the alliance and cut through differences in interpersonal styles.

SUMMARY

Table 11–1 presents a comprehensive overview of the interventions discussed in this chapter. The reader is referred to this table for a summary of this chapter.

CHAPTER 12

Working with Borderline Personality-disordered Clients

We suspect that the words "difficult client" and "borderline" are virtually synonymous in the minds of many mental-heath professionals. We further suppose that the diagnosis of borderline personality disorder (BPD) is often made simply because a person is difficult (i.e., angry and uncooperative). It should be clear by now that we do not consider all difficult clients to be borderline nor all borderlines to be difficult. Many borderlines are difficult, many are not; however, we must treat them regardless of whether they are difficult and how difficult they are.

Borderlines have a reputation for being difficult to manage—unpredictable in affect and behavior, self-mutilating and suicidal, and prone to creating conflict. Their reputation includes dividing and pitting professional against professional (a process commonly called splitting) and hurting, or at least hurting the feelings of, the dedicated helpers who work so hard to treat them.

Perhaps the main reason that borderlines are so difficult to work with is that they are almost always in a state of emotional turmoil—so much so that the *state* of turmoil is more like the *trait* of turmoil. With low capacities for managing their own feelings, they look to other people to contain and control them. However, they resent these attempts to modulate feelings and resent the people who make the attempts.

EMOTIONAL CHAOS

Emotional chaos occurs when a person is utterly consumed by emotional experiences. Nondestructive methods for calming and soothing oneself are absent, leaving only destructive ones, including substance abuse, eating disorders, and other forms of self-harm.

Filled with humiliation about their unworthiness, "I am not worth the space I take up on this earth," is a common statement we hear BPD clients express. Their personal lives are tumultuous, as are their relationships. Many are so self-abusive that they self-mutilate or overmedicate with any combination of prescription medications, over-the-counter drugs, illegal substances, and/or alcohol in an attempt to calm down affect that they cannot soothe successfully. Many are suicidal.

Finally, they complain of intense anxiety, and CAT interprets this anxiety as self-pity which results from the prediction "bad things will happen and I will be rejected, fired, hurt, and/or humiliated." The BPD individual's world view is both negative and filled with danger—the danger experienced by a young child who cannot find his or her parents (or who cannot be comforted by them) and who cannot take care of him-herself.

Research supports this clinical observation. As Diamond and Doane (1994) point out, quality of attachment and affect regulation appear to be intertwined: "Children classified as securely attached were able to modulate negative affects in a constructive way, whereas children classified as insecurely attached displayed more negative affect and hostility in reunion episodes with their parents (Kobak & Sceery, 1988) and in preschool settings (Sroufe, 1983)." Diamond and Doane's own studies (1994) found a significant relationship between expressed emotion (EE), affective style (AS), and attachment type. In particular, they found that high EE and a negative AS within families are significantly correlated with problematic attachment styles (and appear to be passed down intergenerationally).

We have found that this affective overload seems to weaken the immune system, at least temporarily. Many BPD clients have a range of psychosomatic illnesses from the top of the head (migraine headaches) through gastrointestinal difficulties to severe back pain. BPD individuals are noticeably more susceptible to viruses and infections, and we have seen a great degree of urinary tract and yeast infections in our female BPD clients. Certainly, people with other diagnoses also suffer from somatic problems, but the emotional discontrol apparent in the BPD client contributes to long-term illness that is reformulated with new labels. We have noted labels such as hypoglycemia, chronic fatigue syndrome, mitral valve prolapse, and Epstein–Barr virus. Most recently, some BPD clients are being labeled with adult attention-deficit disorder, we believe.

RAGEFUL ANGER AND FEAR

The two main emotions that borderlines find so hard to manage within themselves are fear and rageful anger. Fear may be experienced as overwhelming anxiety and tension, or disruption of sleep, physical health, and concentration. Anger may be experienced as overwhelming rage and tension, or disruption of sleep, physical health, and concentration. In other words, when strongly felt, these two emotions may be indistinguishable to the client. Their interpersonal effects, however, are quite different. Fear leads to dependency and prompts help from others. Rageful anger, whether expressed directly or indirectly, prompts rejection from others.

TUMULTUOUS RELATIONSHIPS

The fear/anger ambivalence takes its toll on interpersonal relationships. Thus, we look for a history of tumultuous relationships as an indicator of the borderline condition. Individuals with BPD can be quarrelsome to the point of physical danger or dependent to the point of being exploited by another person. Their relationships with therapists are similarly fraught with tension and ambivalence.

A SENSE OF "EMPTINESS," OR LACK OF A SELF

BPD individuals often feel a chronic emptiness within, derived undoubtedly from their insecure attachments with their parents. Longing for a secure attachment, the BPD never matures to the point of self-definition. The emptiness of the borderline is a feeling that almost everyone has experienced at one time or another. We can remember feeling extreme *homesickness* as children— a combination of the fear of being alone and abandoned and of anger at a person or the world for not responding to our neediness and loneliness. It might have been called school phobia, separation anxiety, or just plain homesickness in our youth. It is a feeling of profoundly missing one or more persons with whom we have a close relationship. Homesickness is a feeling of yearning and emptiness, a result of being cut off from a significant person in one's life.

In other words, as homesick children we briefly experienced the powerless feeling of vulnerability that BPD people live with every day—that of looking for someone to nurture and care for them, while not trusting that there is anyone to do so. They are left to exist in a world of fear, hoping for comfort that never appears.

EXTREME DEPENDENCE AND A LACK OF SEPARATION FROM PARENTS

Recall from chapter 4 that, following from Millon (1996), we view BPD as *a more dysfunctional variant of the submissive personality styles,* which include both the histrionic (active–submissive) and the dependent (passive–submissive) personality styles. In fact, we conceptualize our BPD clients in terms of *histrionic borderline* and *passive borderline.* By "more dysfunctional," we mean that these clients are more developmentally arrested than the typical histrionic or dependent client, and, therefore, they behave in an even less adaptive, flexible, mature manner.

Noshpitz and King (1991) point out that many studies have concluded that, although childlike, the BPD client's personality traits do not relate back to any single developmental stage of childhood. Nevertheless, the BPD individual, like a child, has not developed sufficiently along various dimensions of personality that are central to coping maturely with day-to-day life, let alone with adversity. BPD clients, like young children: (1) have great difficulty modulating their intense affect and, therefore, express intense rage and self-pity inappropriately and immaturely (e.g., by tantruming and/or sulking); (2) see things in extreme, black-and-white terms; (3) are often impulsive and have poor frustration tolerance; and (4) are highly dependent (a combination of wanting others to care for them because they believe that they cannot care for themselves and believing that the caretaking of others is not good enough).

Two findings from attachment theory research pull together the four aforementioned relatively unique factors of BPD. First, researchers have hypothesized that children with a disorganized attachment to their caregivers may be experiencing a precursor to BPD (Fonagy, 1996; Fonagy et al., 1995; Main, 1995). Disorganized attachment behavior consists of disorganized or disoriented behavior in the infant, including at least one of the following: sequential display of contradictory behaviors (e.g., a strong attachment behavior followed by a strong rejection of the caregiver); simultaneous display of contradictory behavior patterns (e.g., sitting on parent's lap while gazing away); undirected or misdirected expressions (e.g., crying loudly when a stranger leaves the room); and/or direct indicators of apprehension regarding the parent (e.g., fear expressed when parent enters, backing toward parent with head averted) (Main, 1995). Mothers of disorganized infants become alarmed and disorganized in distressing situations, giving the infant nowhere to turn and no way to calm down his or her dis ress—either the infant remains alone and distressed or joins the mother's upset and disorganization. One can well see from these findings how this affective lose–lose paradigm may develop into BPD's difficulty with affect regulation and modulation, as well as its black-and-white thinking.

Second, Sack, Sperling, Fagen, and Foelsch (1996) found that BPD adults consistently report an avoidant attachment with their fathers and an ambivalent attachment with their mothers. The authors conclude that BPD individuals may typically have a father who is disinterested, disapproving, and uninvolved, and a mother who "typically demonstrate[s] a pattern of negative overinvolvement" (p. 98). The BPD father is, therefore, designated as the rejector, while the mother is considered the rescuer. (We should note here that, in our clinical experience, we have often found that one BPD parent is critical, abusive, and/or rejecting, while the other is passive, self-pitying, and, at times, overinvolved, but the former does not necessarily have to be the father nor the latter the mother.) One can, therefore, see how this parental combination fosters a powerful dependence in the BPD person, who is caught between feeling ashamed of him-herself via the paternal attachment and incapable of taking care of him-herself via the overprotective maternal attachment.

If it did not sound so benign, the word "immature" could easily substitute for the term "borderline." The clients we call borderline do not function very well as adults They eschew responsibility for their actions, their future, and their welfare. They relate to others in a dependent manner rather than pursue life independently. They crave emotional caretaking rather than taking care of themselves (but they often find the caretaking of others to be lacking). They feel justified in engaging in angry outbursts, especially temper tantrums, rather than moderating their feelings and patiently pursuing goals.

THE BPD CLIENT AND THE THERAPIST

It is, therefore, a combination of the characteristics we have described—and what they typically pull from and evoke in the therapist— that makes therapists consider these clients to be "high maintenance" and threatening. And it is the individual therapist's reactions, given his or her own personality style and related issues, that will intensify his or her reaction to BPD clients.

In other words, if a therapist resents having to work "too hard", then he or she will resent the idea of a "high-maintenance" client. If a therapist freezes when confronted with a client's rage or intense anxiety/fear, then he or she will come to dread working with a BPD client. If a therapist recoils from having a client express intense neediness and dependence, then he or she will not respond therapeutically to the borderline's numerous requests. If a therapist, given the emotional setpoint in his or her own family of origin, is thrown off by a histrionic borderline's rage or a passive borderline's emotional withdrawal, then the therapist will not teach the borderline how to modulate and express affect appropriately. And, of course, if a therapist easily experiences shame, then the BPD client's security-seeking behaviors, which often involve denigrating or withdrawing from others, will elicit much shame in this therapist.

The very feelings experienced by BPD clients—rage, either actively demonstrated or passively concealed; shame or humiliation; feelings of unworthiness and the self-pitying fears of being victimized or mistreated—are also the feelings they nonconsciously pull from the therapist. As all clients unintentionally pull the therapist to play a complementary, personotypic affect-reinforcing role in their lives, so, too, is the therapist pulled to enter the emotional world of the borderline. The inexperienced therapist is left asking the question, "Why do I feel so crazy/enraged/out of control/scared when I meet with that client?"

BPD clients generate anxiety in the therapist. We often dread their next session, not knowing if the client will be needy and dependent or hostile, rebellious, and disrespectful. Some anxiety is fear of future failure and, ultimately, of shame and/or self-pity. Future failure can consist of persecution or victimization ("That BPD client will treat me like crap and abuse me") or of either guilt ("I'll screw up the next session, just as I did the last. I'll fail the client") or shame ("I can't work with this client. I'm a lousy therapist").

Highly immature developmentally, some BPD clients regress into needy infantile behavior and see us, at least temporarily, as their savior: we will be the all-caring, ever-concerned, all-powerful parent they never had. We make a serious error if we are flattered by this devotion (as some particularly insecure therapists are) and allow this desperate, needy person to become special to us, much as a child is special to its caretakers. Not only does this error reinforce the BPD client's neediness and dependence, but also it sets up the therapist for a fall from grace in the borderline's eyes, as the borderline will quickly shift from idealizing to devaluing us.

THE THERAPEUTIC ALLIANCE

A solid relationship is requisite for working with any client. The borderline is no exception, and the task of building a working relationship is more challenging. Instability of relationships is one of the key criteria for diagnosing borderline personality disorder, and, therefore, therapists can expect to encounter a highly variable working relationship.

At times, rapport with a BPD is as good as it gets with any client. At other times, the atmosphere can be distant, hostile, and downright combative.

Instability implies unpredictability, and BPD clients can be very unpredictable, which usually echoes the climate in which they were raised. One week, they offer excessive praise of the therapist's skills and efforts, and the next week, they put down the same skills and efforts they had previously praised. When negotiating a relationship, it is best to keep in mind how volatile it can and, most likely, will be.

Because of its instability, the relationship with a BPD client can be deceptive. The connection may appear to be closer and more solid than it really is, especially during the first few sessions. Early in therapy, the client may want to impress the therapist; this is particularly true of clients who complain about previous therapists (and perhaps wish to sue them, a not uncommon theme among BPD clients). Wary of all relationships, borderline clients often believe they must appear reasonable and pleasant in order to avoid nonacceptance. They may attempt to ingratiate themselves with therapists in the hope that they will be accepted and liked, and, therefore, treated (and perhaps rescued) successfully.

Behind the façade of acceptability, borderline clients do not trust the new therapist any more than they trusted former therapists or anyone else in their lives. As mentioned in the beginning of this chapter, BPD clients have enormous difficulties with attachment. It might be noted here that *all* personality-disordered clients have attachment difficulties. Estrangement from others is, in our opinion, the characteristic that separates disordered personalities from their normal counterparts. They lack a feeling of solidarity with others; they are deficient in what Adler called *Gemeinschaftgefühl*. The challenge to therapists who work with borderlines is to build a relationship of trust with someone who is fundamentally mistrustful.

Therapists who have exceptional interpersonal skills already know how to create conditions for working relationships. They show interest, competence, kindness, and strength. Which of these traits should be emphasized depends upon the individual client. Matching the style of the client is very helpful. If the client is hostile, the therapist should show strength and not appear intimidated. A dominant but empathetic stance tells the client that the therapist will not put up with inappropriately expressed hostility. By contrast, a passive borderline with a pleasing style of interacting needs kindness and interest emphasized and strength de-emphasized.

A good question for therapists to ask themselves is, "Why should anyone trust me? How can I let people know that I will not harm them, can help them, and will respect their confidences without making a speech in which I claim these as personal facts?" Therapists, of course, can make these representations about themselves, but it is much better when clients get the right impression without their therapists writing personal ads. Trust, in everyday life, is ordinarily earned through experience. There is no reason to think it is different in psychotherapy, especially with borderlines.

EXPLAINING BPD TO CLIENTS

Honesty can contribute to rapport, provided it is expressed empathetically. Speaking frankly about the borderline's condition is a form of honesty. Unlike approaches that keep diagnoses secret (and, therefore, make them appear shameful), we explain what a borderline personality disorder is. We recommend to many clients the book *I Hate You; Don't Leave Me* (Kreisman and Straus, 1989), which reviews the different components of BPD and clearly describes the experience of being borderline. While we do not agree with some of their theoretical explanations and interventions, our clients have found the book helpful in making sense out of their experiences as borderlines. This book also drives home the point that BPD is not a genetic or biological condition, but a developmental one. Clients are not crazy; they can improve.

We encourage clients to opt for optimism and believe that they can and will improve. It will take time to modify personality styles, but positive changes can be expected. Offering realistic hope is another way to promote a good working relationship.

We speak honestly about setbacks. The chart of improvement is seldom, if ever, a gracefully rising curve. There are zigs up and zags down, with plateaus in between, but the overall picture is one of steady improvement. Setbacks are predictable, both from clinical experience and from CAT theory, and are, therefore, a normal part of the therapy process. CAT says that people are driven to seek their emotional setpoints and reexperience personotypic affects and the sense of security they bring. Setbacks, then, are simply attempts to get back to feelings that are familiar to an individual—the same feelings he or she consciously tries to avoid.

The explanation of setbacks as normal and predictable gives reassurance and hope. We are good at inspiring people to believe that they can get better—that what once was does not have to be. This is an essential point in CAT. BPD clients seem to hold more tenaciously to negative but familiar feelings than do others. They are frightened to change, to remove the mantle of discomfort they wear, and enter a new and unfamiliar world. Thus, we expect progress to be slow and setbacks to be frequent.

MEDICATION AND AFFECT

To comfort themselves, borderline clients typically turn to methods that are partly satisfactory, partly destructive. Alcohol, street drugs, and prescription medications are used to ameliorate the bad feelings, but all of these can be addictive and lose their power to comfort. However, we do not recommend removing these chemical supports, at least, not at first. Instead, we tell them to moderate their use rather than eliminate them entirely. BPD clients may simply not be able to function without help. Prescribed medication is not different from self-medication except that prescriptions may be seen as saviors, whereas alcohol and street drugs are not spoken of in this way.

When we refer BPD clients for medication review, it is with the knowledge that the prescriptions will not help very much and that there is a risk of over-medication. Further, clients may have unrealistically high expectations that the medicine will do for them what nothing else has done—the magic pill. A 3- to six-month trial of antidepressant medications often helps clients until they can learn to moderate their feelings without medicine. But there is no medication that will make borderline clients feel good and function better for very long. A different focus is needed.

WORKING WITH EXHAUSTION

Because they have grown up feeling massively inferior, some borderlines compensate for these feelings in a classic way: they overcompensate for their presumed shortcomings. They become compulsively organized and perfectionistic in many areas of their lives. One result is chronic exhaustion. Constant attention to details and frantic efforts to make sure everything is right eventually saps energy and creates fatigue. Their over-efforts never pay off for long, and borderline clients do not get the good feelings (or relief from bad feelings) they seek from the strategy of perfectionism.

Over-emotionality is another source of exhaustion for borderlines. It is well known that BPD clients experience emotions more exquisitely than do other people. Daily high levels of anxiety and attempts to ameliorate the anxiety take their toll and wear the person down.

While these two sources of exhaustion must be addressed in order for treatment to be most successful, the exhaustion itself is the initial focus. Psychotherapy with a fatigued client is extremely difficult. One early goal, then, is to get these clients to take care of themselves by resting more than they are accustomed to do. Their sleep patterns are often awry, sleeping when they should be awake and unable to sleep at the appropriate times. We try to get them into regular habits of rest and to reestablish conventional sleep patterns. Even if they cannot at first regulate sleep, rest itself is important. Rest periods allow recovery from exhaustion and prevent further compulsive efforts that produce additional fatigue. Serious psychotherapy should be postponed until the client is more rested.

A physiological event that has problematic effects on female borderline clients is premenstrual syndrome (PMS). (We are using the term PMS in the loose, popular sense rather than as a medical diagnosis.) It is a problem for borderline clients in that it magnifies and amplifies affect. Therapists should know their clients' menstrual cycles because they can distort reports of problems and of affects and cognitions, and make therapeutic interventions very difficult.

EMOTIONAL SELF-CARE

Emotional self-care is a central theme in working with borderline clients. Borderline clients lack skills to comfort themselves, and many report not getting much comfort when distressed as a child. If they have recollections of receiving comfort, we try to build on these. We also point out to them that children are given physical comfort, but as they grow older verbal reassurances, explanations, and encouragements replace physical contact as the main method of providing comfort. (CAT is not a "touchy-feely" therapy but sometimes a hug does feel good and is just what is called for, although we do not recommend such physical contact between clients and therapist.) If clients cannot recall a person who comforted them or how they were comforted, we may ask them to imagine what someone could do to soothe them. Although their images are about external sources of comfort, our intention is to shift these to internal, self-caring methods of comfort. We also try to remain realistic about the effects of self-comfort—clients should not expect to turn distress into joy, but to reduce and moderate affects they find so distressing.

Metaphors about retraining the brain to bring comfort can be helpful in "selling" the idea of self-care and self-comfort. And the metaphor is not inaccurate; new neural pathways are laid down as old habits are replaced with new ones, including habits of feelings and thinking. Thus the question, "What would make you feel better?" is really about developing a new approach to easing one's distress. The techniques may be physical, such as exercise, walks, hot baths, etc., or mental, such as reassuring oneself and opting for optimism. These are comforts in themselves, but they also retrain the brain to make it easier in the future to turn to self-comfort more automatically.

Prominent emotional habits of borderline clients include shame and self-pity and the angry defenses against them. Insight into one's shame and self-pity helps explain the rumbling anger of borderline clients, and that insight can be used as a means of self-comfort. Similarly, insight into the yearning homesickness of the BPD client can be reassuring to the client ("No one before has ever pinpointed how I feel."). CAT theory assumes that clients "need" to experience certain familiar feelings in order to preserve or restore a sense of psychological security. When shame and self-pity are personotypic affects, clients will unwittingly seek them out. They will "collect" shameful experiences and put themselves in potentially shaming interpersonal situations. They will "collect" self-pity and manage to get themselves victimized by others.

Humor can be used to highlight the emotional habits of BPD clients. Respectfully delivered comments about the joys of collecting shame and self-pity can make the point with good humor, and maybe even elicit a laugh. "Congratulations on setting yourself up to feel sorry for yourself. It's the best I've heard this week. A winner!" The ability to laugh at oneself without self-put downs is a fine way to reduce shame and self-pity, a fine way to stop taking yourself so seriously. A word of caution. Humor has to be used carefully. The borderline client is very vulnerable and sensitive to criticism.

FOSTERING INDEPENDENCE AND MATURITY

It is helpful to think of the borderline personality as massively immature. The task of therapy is to provide maturing experiences. The goal is to promote an independent and responsible adult. We look into the client's family for clues that explain why the client failed to mature. We often find that clients' relationships with parents and siblings (and, perhaps, other family members) are excessively dependent. Parents (or at least one parent) are feared and rule by threatening anger and inducing guilt. The client does not dare to function independently, as someone might disapprove, and comes to fear making independent decisions as something that is overwhelmingly difficult.

Criticism heard from parents during the formative years (and later) becomes internalized as self-criticism. Self-deprecation is common, although some clients do not feel they have a self to deprecate. While narcissistic clients were usually overly praised by well-meaning parents, borderline clients were (are) overly criticized by parents whose intentions were not necessarily benevolent or benign.

Separating clients from the families in which they are enmeshed is a key strategic intervention in CAT treatment of BPD clients. We help them to learn to say no with respect and firmness. Adults say no when they mean it; immature adults fear saying no and conform but feel resentful. The dramatic way to represent this process is to call it "standing up for yourself." Separation also involves making one's own decisions instead of relinquishing choices to others. A fundamental idea in CAT is that self-respect should be based on doing what is right, as the person understands what is right. It is imperative, therefore, that the individual make his or her own decisions.

Clients who are financially dependent on their parents present special issues. Receiving financial support places clients in a vulnerable position and makes separation all the more difficult. The old adage, "Who pays the piper calls the tune," applies to such cases. In exchange for money, parents, not necessarily unreasonably, expect compliance to their wishes. Money comes with strings attached. Independence means giving up parental funds and, perhaps, accepting a lower standard of living. For borderlines who are unable to work, the problem is even more acute. However, we recognize that they are negotiating a fine line between genuine independence of thought and action and family welfare.

We also urge clients to keep their own counsel. By this, we mean that they need not reveal personal information or private thoughts and feelings to anyone against their wishes. It is not uncommon amongst our borderline clients, especially women, to have several telephone conversations each day with one or both parents, who ask about details of their daily lives and offer comments, criticism, and directive advice. Such a practice is inconsistent with the independence borderlines must achieve, and we actively discourage it. We teach clients simple replies to inquiries, replies that draw a line between what they will discuss and what they will keep private. Examples are, "I don't want to talk about that," and "That topic is off limits."

Similarly, we work with enmeshed clients not to tolerate disrespect. "I will end this conversation if you criticize me or put me down," is one way to signal intolerance for disrespect. Self-respect, though based on doing what is right, cannot be maintained unless one rejects disrespect from others. Of course, the rejecting of disrespect must be done politely and in a respectful manner or else the client would show disrespect, thus encouraging disrespect in return.

The goal is not to dissolve all family ties. It is, instead, to create a new, adult relationship with others in the family—a relationship based on mutual respect. Closer connections are sought. The clients' responsibility is to stop blaming others, especially family members, and to be aware of how they pull anger from people with their own hostility. Clients who are married or in a committed relationships may displace their anger onto partners and treat them in an insulting manner. This, too, needs to be monitored and moderated along with indirect, passive–aggressive expressions of anger in which fearful clients engage.

BPD AND SEXUAL ABUSE

The mood swings of BPD can strongly resemble certain symptoms of post-traumatic stress disorder. (Indeed, mood swings may lead to a confusion of BPD with bipolar disorder, even though the abrupt changes so characteristic of BPD are not at all typical of bipolar disorder.) Mood swings are an alerting clue that the client may have experienced significant trauma in the past. We recommend careful inquiry into the client's history for instances of trauma, especially physical violence or sexual abuse.

The inquiry has to be done without "planting" answers or false memories of childhood events. The inquiry need not be done in one session, and, certainly, should not be undertaken until a solid working alliance is in place. The purpose of uncovering such information is not to confirm a diagnosis or to reveal all such memories in order to attain catharsis; instead, it is to allow the client slowly to confront his or her own shame and self-blame about childhood experiences.

The key question to ask is, "Do you think you have a history of sexual or physical abuse?" This question can be asked of anyone, but it is especially important to inquire of clients who have difficulty making or sustaining relationships, and/or who either avoid sexual relations or are promiscuous. It is likely that such clients already have an inkling of past traumatic events. There may be partially remembered sexual abuse or memories of violence in the family that are reawakened by potential sexual encounters or contemporary violent behaviors. The brain calms and soothes us by forgetting, but the associative memory can be rekindled.

When the answer to the question about one's past is yes, there is plenty to explore. When the answer is no or the question produces only silence, it is often useful to switch to imagery. Ask the client, "If your father (or some other family member) were sitting close to you on the couch, how would you feel?" The answer may be verbal, but the client may also jump away, cover the face with hands, and appear fearful and disgusted, as many of our clients have. *Disgust* as a way of experiencing shame may be unique to the sexually abused person. While sexual abuse is not confined to BPD clients, it has been estimated that over half of female BPD clients have been sexually abused, usually over an extended period of time.

Explicit physical contact with children is clearly sexual abuse. A more insidious sexualizing of children occurs when one (usually, the opposite sex) parent or both, in some instances, are voyeuristic and/or flirtatious. He or she or they may comment on the child's maturity or compliment his or her physical attributes or inquire into his or her sexual thoughts and experiences. As children, and later as adults, clients tend to blame themselves for provoking sexualized comments from parents or other family members, not realizing that it was the adult who had the prurient interest, not they. Kids look for attention, but they do not flirt. Instead, they repeat behaviors that result in consequent attention, and, as adult clients, they can be helped to understand and accept this fact. Until they do, their sense of secure attachment is damaged and they find it difficult to trust authority or attachment figures.

Another clue that the client may have a traumatic background is difficulty sleeping and nighttime terrors. They may be afraid to be alone at night. They may go to a hospital emergency room to feel in a safe place. Either consciously or nonconsciously, they associate a bedroom at night with someone coming into the room to abuse them.

It can be helpful to ask about siblings, especially of the same sex. Do they have similar BPD problems? Do any claim sexual or physical abuse?

Memories, we have found, tend to return in short spurts rather than all at once. They create self-pity and rage, and thoughts of or actual acting-out to get revenge. BPD clients with passive–aggressive traits will make decisions and take actions that are contrary to the family's ethical, moral, religious, or social class standards. As mentioned previously, the bolder BPD clients engage in promiscuous sexual activities with same or opposite sex partners, or both.

It is not necessary to exhaustively remember each and every instance of abuse. It does *not* "all have to come back" in order for therapy to proceed effectively. Clients need to talk about what they remember, facing their feelings, especially those of shame and fear. Dreams are often important (another similarity to PTSD), not for their content but for the feelings they contain. Discussing dreams can help the client become aware of feelings of shame and fear and to confront them.

The therapist's attitude toward the parents is critical. The therapist must be on the side of the client and talk about the parents as culpable but without severe condemnation. In the typical case, the father, stepfather, or other male relative was the abuser and the mother passively ignored the facts or did nothing to intervene and protect the child. (We have also worked with atypical cases where the mother abused and the father did nothing.) Abusing children is a crime and should be spoken of accordingly.

We do not recommend the client's confronting the parent(s), because such confrontation usually leads to denials and gets nowhere. Confrontation is not a cure. Instead, the client can write a letter to express feelings, but the letter should not be sent. It, too, is likely only to provoke denials. The psychodrama/gestalt technique of the empty chair can be helpful, especially to confront the overall disrespect that abusive parents showed the client. Sympathetic siblings can be good confidants, particularly if they were also abused and are symptomatic.

When the abuser was an outsider, e.g., a babysitter or priest, we point out that they may be subject to criminal charges, and we help the client decide whether to pursue them. In one instance, a client recalled as an early teenager having had sexual contact with his priest, but he could not confront him because he had died; however, the priest's superiors believed the story and reimbursed him for therapy.

Getting over the self-blame is crucial. We encourage the client to have empathy for his or her younger self. The experiential technique of talking to the young child has been helpful. The memories will emerge slowly, in most cases, so the process of self-empathy (not self-sympathy) may have to be repeated several times.

We encourage clients' comforting their own feelings. They need to be alert, as does the therapist, for signs of self-pity and feelings of powerlessness. Clients sometimes take the irresponsible route by saying they are nothing but victims, that they were abused, and are now borderline, and, therefore, can do nothing to help themselves. Group therapy can be very helpful in this regard. By working with others, these clients come to understand that they are not alone or unique—it happens to others, too.

Although physical and sexual abuse has been the central theme of this section of the chapter, it is an essential, but not a central, theme of therapy with BPD clients. It can be a recurring theme, and the feelings dealt with bit by bit as memories emerge or evocative contemporary situations are encountered. Difficulties in new relationships may stir up old associations, thoughts, and feelings. In this process, as in every aspect of working with a BPD client, patience is the watchword.

WORKING WITH SUICIDAL GESTURES AND SELF-MUTILATION

Borderline clients have a reputation as "manipulators," as if the rest of the human population were not. Everyone takes actions that are likely to lead to payoffs, and our knowledge of behavioral principles alerts us to look for a payoff even when there seems to be none. To do a proper functional analysis, one must be ready to discover idiosyncratic reinforcers.

Attempts to kill oneself fall into the category of nonobvious reinforcers. The obvious payoff is relief from the agony of life. However, many people make what appear to be inept suicide attempts. These botched attempts are known as suicidal gestures.

The layperson's response to them is to become alarmed. Even professionals might label them "cries for help." Indeed, suicide attempts do call attention to the person and may elicit offers of aid and assistance. Such attempts can also induce guilt in friends and family, and even in professionals, who believe they should be able to prevent self-inflicted death.

The therapeutic response is to view the suicide attempt dispassionately. The client who is determined to end his or her life will find some way to do so. No amount of persuasion or surveillance will prevent it. Unsuccessful attempts, or gestures, are usually based on feelings.

A constant theme in CAT is not to trust your feelings. By this, we mean that feelings are not a good basis for either knowing reality or making decisions about one's life (especially whether to continue life or not). Kids respond to affect—little kids. Feeling like ending it all (i.e., feeling fed up with life, as we know it) is not a sound basis for deciding to die. It is highly self-centered and uncaring about other people with whom the client is connected.

The therapist's position, then, is to convey disapproval of suicide—it's a cop-out. It is the way out sought by a self-styled helpless victim. But can the therapist stop it? No, although ethical standards require therapists to try and to take the proper steps regarding notification, etc.

Contracts in which clients pledge not to kill themselves are not used in CAT. The contracts are not enforceable in an outpatient setting; the therapist's sole power is to stop seeing the client and refer the case elsewhere. The contract, therefore, poses a threat to the therapeutic relationship. Further, the contract may encourage additional suicidal gestures, because it appears to impose restrictions on the client. (It cannot, in reality, because the "contract" is not binding or enforceable.) Clients do not want some other adult to tell them what to do, and they are likely to rebel and "prove" their power. Rebellion, of course, is counterconformity, not true independence. Because true independence is a primary goal for borderline clients, we discourage opportunities for rebellion. Therapists should not get into parental roles by telling dependent clients what to do and what not to do. True independence does not arise from further dependence.

Self-mutilation is one of the diagnostic criteria for borderline personality disorder. As with suicide, no contracts against self-mutilation are negotiated. Instead, we try to offer clients an alternative. We recognize that cutting and other forms of mutilation represent a point of desperation. It is the ultimate angry response. However, it is passive anger directed at self because the client cannot cut the other person. Punching a pillow is less harmful but also less satisfying.

The therapeutic response is to remain calm and not get angry at the client, and to try to furnish a new way to acknowledge and understand anger. When a client feels like cutting, that is the time to call the therapist. It is perhaps the act of making contact rather than anything specific the therapist says that helps. The dialogue is usually the same: "What are you angry about?" This question may be repeated several times; the client may not readily acknowledge anger. Eventually, the cause comes out, and it may seem trivial to anyone except the client, but to him or her it is very important—some infringement of his or her self-respect. The telephone contact is not the time to deal with the problem in great detail; that is postponed until the next therapy session. However, the telephone contact helps relieve the tension and anger, and gives the client something else to do other than self-mutilation, and it changes the focus from cutting to feeling. And the feelings are almost always rage and self-pity.

Since the whole goal of CAT with borderline clients is to push independence and maturity, always give them choices. We prefer to see them twice a week initially, but the choice is theirs to accept this schedule or ask for another. Unlike authoritarian therapists who require a certain schedule, we say, in effect, do what you need to do; you know then that you can do what you want. You always have a choice in life, including the choice to cut yourself. To underscore the last point, we may offer first-aid advice: how to clean the wound, what type of bandage to use (butterfly bandages work well). We also point out reality: go to the hospital with a self-inflicted wound and get hospitalized for a suicide attempt. Having to take care of their own wounds seems to get people to stop doing it.

The main point is, the therapist has to be the solid person in the client's life, the one who does not panic or become histrionic over highly unusual behavior. By not being frightened, the therapist acts differently from others in the client's life. The so-called "manipulation" cannot work with the therapist as it most likely did in the client's family. Looking at the cut marks may even promote bonding. The client–therapist alliance is strengthened by the I-care-about-you-and-I'm-not-intimidated-by-your-actions approach.

SETTING BOUNDARIES WITH BORDERLINE CLIENTS

Maturity involves more than choices, it involves responsibility. Caring for oneself, including dressing self-inflicted wounds, is a responsibility many people, borderline clients especially, try to avoid. It is easier (and more fashionable these days) to appear as a helpless victim rather than a responsible adult. Taking responsibility requires a large measure of self-discipline, i.e., doing what you don't feel like doing.

To promote self-discipline, clients need to observe a few simple rules of therapy. One of these is to speak respectfully to the therapist (as the therapist does to the client) and to express feelings in a socially acceptable manner. Another is to appear promptly for the beginning of the therapy session and to leave without lingering when it is over. The rule of promptness is necessary with borderline clients, especially passive–aggressive ones who are chronically late. Lateness shows disrespect for therapy and for the therapist—as well as for oneself. Lateness may be seen as listening to feelings and letting them make decisions, rather than facing the challenge and making decisions that are in the person's interests. Promptness can be specified as a condition for continued treatment.

THE MYTH OF SPLITTING

Splitting is a jargon word that can mean splitting the treatment team (assuming at least two professionals working with the same client; in our practice, a therapist and psychopharmacologist), or it can mean an internal process—the splitting of self. The latter definition comes from psychodynamic theorizing about the borderline condition and is not used in CAT. Instead, we note the powerful ambivalent feelings borderline clients have about many things, people and self, and how, like children, they have difficulty appreciating the complexity of human nature, preferring to simplify their concepts of self and others, summarize them with utterly inadequate global appraisals, such as good and bad.

Moreover, borderline persons have highly insecure, often disorganized attachments with others, which stem from the poor attachments they had with their parents. "Splitting" can be seen as nothing more than the borderline's attempt to recreate the family environment in the therapy (security-seeking behavior) and to rekindle the associated personotypic affects. BPD clients' ambivalence about relationships directly affects the efforts of professionals who work with them. If they connect and attach, they will want to reject, due to fears of closeness—of conforming to another's wishes, of enslavement. To avoid feeling trapped and dominated, they push people away. In anger, they may turn to other therapists or pharmacologists who, if they are ethical and insightful, will urge the client to go back to the original therapist.

To prevent clients from seeing us as perfect creatures (and potential saviors), we disclose personal information (the opposite of the "blank screen"). Therapists should be competent and confident and act as good examples for clients, but they cannot be perfect. Clients' conceptions of therapists are, nonetheless, distorted due partly to lack of information and partly to the habit of seeing other people, especially those in authority, in certain ways. The CAT therapist asks, "Why do you need to see me that way?" Getting to know the therapist as a person is an important way to replace fantasy with reality. Hence, while other approaches to treatment may forbid personal disclosures, they are an important feature of CAT.

REVIEW OF CAT TACTICS WITH BORDERLINE CLIENTS

CAT was developed for working with personality-disordered clients based on our experiences with borderline clients. What we do with them and with borderline clients is not really much different. More challenging than borderline clients are male antisocial personality-disordered clients, because they are more likely to be threatening and not to form a relationship with the therapist; they are more likely to attack than attach. Clients with predominantly passive–aggressive characteristics are challenging because they are sweet and nice but do not do much work in therapy.

Each of the tactics that follows has been discussed in previous sections of this and other chapters.

1. Explaining the client to him-herself. This is a powerful intervention because many borderlines do not know who they are. They have no sense of

self and vacillating identities. Their emotional life is a whirlpool they cannot sort out. We explain that they need to feel like victims, to feel inferior, and to elevate others in their lives, including their therapists.

2. Explanations also cover their ambivalence about relationships, and their closing and widening the distance between themselves and others. Treating the therapist badly is an attempt to regulate emotional closeness and to reexperience guilty feelings. Feelings of anger that accompany attempts to distance need to be expressed directly but respectfully. Real or imagined offenses by the therapist need to be clearly labeled by the client so they can be discussed.

3. Similarly, attempts to idolize the therapist are not allowed. We say in response to attempts to lionize, "I'm just a technician. The only one who can save your life is you. It's entirely up to you. You can use what I have to offer—it works. If you don't want to use what I have to offer, you don't have to. It's your choice. Implementing what we talk about is your decision." Seeing the therapist as perfect or exceptionally powerful or capable is a way of remaining a victim. It is a strategy to avoid responsibility and change.

4. "Working through" is a phrase that can take on several meanings. In CAT, it refers to discussing feelings over and over again. The point is not to discharge or exhaust feelings, but to understand them and to know how to lessen their impact. We ask, "How did you feel in this situation, and how could you have managed it differently? How could you feel differently?" Such reviews prepare clients to approach future situations with new sets of cognitions and behaviors, and to acquire new affective habits.

5. Feelings expressed toward the therapist are not seen as projections or transferences. Clients relate to therapists as they do most or similar people in their lives. They relate on the interpersonal dimensions discussed in chapter 4, i.e., they appraise the other on continua of friendly–hostile, dominant–submissive, and (pro)active–passive. Their self-images are complementary to their images of other people. Clarifying the self- and other-images are part of the explanation process.

6. That CAT is most compatible with a social learning approach to personality is evident from its emphasis on identifying reinforcers in clients' lives. What do clients' get out of being treated by others in the ways they are accustomed? Where does it get them to be victimized? These are the type of questions we ask clients, with the aim of their eventually asking themselves these questions.

ADVICE TO BORDERLINE BEGINNERS

You cannot work with borderline clients (or many others, for that matter) if you do not have a relationship in place, if you are afraid of them, if you are afraid of their running out of the office, or if you are afraid of losing the income. If you are insecure about your abilities as a therapist, then you will have trouble working with borderline clients.

Do not give them any power to be punitive or to treat you badly. Since they do not know how to relate to people, they are not going to relate to you very well, either. Go slowly and do not set up too many rules too soon, even though they need them to relate to people. It is better to be less directive than too directive. Give lots of explanations, making certain that they are reasonable ones.

Borderline clients will take advantage of the appearance of weakness, and the therapist will most likely get covertly angry at them. They will either exploit the weakness and anger, or simply consider the therapist a fool and not come back. Confidence is essential.

When and if borderline (or other clients) become enraged, try a time-out. Have them leave the office for 5 minutes or until they are able to control the *expression* of their feelings. If they do not comply, let them go home. If they threaten to leave treatment, say it's OK—call up if you change your mind. At times, therapists may have to leave sessions because clients will neither calm themselves nor take time out. (Incidentally, do not call it time-out—that's for kids, not adults.)

It is not necessary to discuss the incident at length ("process it") at the next session. A simple, "Have you thought about what happened last time?" is enough. It is better to look to the future, to how anger should be handled next time. ("Tell me that you can't take it anymore rather than blowing up.") And then move on; such episodes with borderlines can be ancient history to them by the time of the next appointment. Lengthy discussion risks shaming the client and making the therapist seem parental. The main point to emphasize is respectful expressions of feelings and mature, respectful relationships. The message: your anger doesn't bother me, but I will not tolerate disrespect.

Clients who are silent can be brought out with self-disclosure: "I get uncomfortable if people don't speak, because I feel like I'm not earning my money. So I'm telling you my feelings and I hope you'll tell me your feelings. Eventually, I might get annoyed, because I hate wasting people's money." A cup of tea, coffee, or a soda often loosens them up. It's a sort of benevolent guilt trip—do them a service or small kindness; it's hard not to please someone who has done something nice. Most people do not want to pay to have you stare at each other in silence.

THE FORMAT OF THERAPY WITH BORDERLINES

Twice a week is about the right frequency to see a new BPD client, especially one in great distress. Later, individual sessions can be supplemented with group therapy. A group is an excellent setting for encouraging clients to put into practice what they do in an individual session. They have to interact with people in a group, and experienced group members can become very sophisticated about the CAT model of shame, self-pity, and anger. Experienced group members also serve as living examples of people who have improved.

New group members can begin to empathize with others: "Oh, I know what that's like. I feel just like that." They begin to see others' problems and become less self-centered. They are expected to help other people. It may be necessary to do some explicit empathy training ("How do you think other people feel when you do that? How do I feel when you do that"?), and the group setting provides a forum for instant feedback.

There are no limits on the proportion of borderline clients in a group, provided some are socialized enough to help the others. Ages can be mixed, passive clients can be mixed with more histrionic ones. Same-sex groups work well because most borderline clients are women and women do well in same-sex groups.

Spouses or significant others can assist in the treatment of borderline clients, or might simply want to know how to survive while in a relationship with one. They can be invited into individual sessions; the client should do the inviting, as it is his or her session. While they may accept the invitation with the intent to complain about the client, they can benefit from some orientation from the therapist. They can improve their relating to the client by emulating what the therapist does—without the interventions. They can learn to insist on respect, not to accept blame, and not to make heroic efforts to please the client. They can walk out (give themselves a time-out) during periods of unchecked emotional (especially angry) expression.

They will find that borderline clients may use the diagnosis as an excuse. ("I can't help myself. I'm a borderline.") Or face a person who believes he or she is exquisitely vulnerable and unable to bear much responsibility. Or persons who hide behind physical illness, whose self-pity-based anger contributes to ailments by suppressing the immune system. As they come to understand the client better, they can learn to take a less active role in trying to put things right for the client, and allow the client to shoulder the responsibilities of an adult in an adult relationship.

IDENTIFYING THERAPEUTIC PROGRESS

The ability to function more successfully in the world is the best indicator of progress in any client. There should, in addition, be an ability to understand themselves and a certain degree of psychological sophistication that allows them to have better social relations. Most important for borderlines is the capacity to moderate their feelings, especially anger. If clients can manage anger well over a period of time in a variety of situations, they are well on the way to recovery. The absence of rages or sulks is a positive sign. This is not to say that clients will never experience anger; rather, they will use it effectively to put right what is wrong, and express feelings in a socially acceptable and respectful manner.

Behaviorally, the ceasing of procrastination is a very positive indicator. A mature person faces life's challenges and does not avoid them, as a child does. Ceasing to procrastinate means ceasing to avoid. Victims feel too weak and inadequate to face difficulties. While everyone needs help at times, mature adults feel equal to the task of solving problems in a timely and constructive manner.

Simply put, when the client is no longer stopped by the vicissitudes of life that stopped her or him in the past, the client is vastly improved.

SUMMARY

1. The BPD client is characterized primarily by emotional chaos, rageful anger and fear, tumultuous relationships, a sense of "emptiness," and extreme dependence and a lack of separation from his or her parents.

2. CAT treats the BPD client by: (a) slowly and patiently building a trusting relationship with the client; (b) explaining to the client what BPD is and that it is treatable; (c) explaining that setbacks involving BPD behavior are normal and to be expected; (d) initially urging moderation, but not cessation, of addictive behaviors. Cessation occurs after BPD clients have learned to adequately manage their affect; (e) decreasing the exhaustion brought on by BPD clients' overemotionality; (f) teaching and practicing the management of shame, self-pity, and rageful anger; (g) decreasing BPD clients' dependency on their families by encouraging the establishment of firm boundaries from their families of origin; (h) exploring the possibility of childhood sexual abuse, either explicit or indirect (e.g., voyeurism or flirtatiousness); (i) treating suicide attempts and self-mutilation dispassionately, calmly, and with disapproval, in order to foster clients' independence and maturity. Contracts are never made with clients, as they only reinforce self-injurious behavior; (j) setting in-session boundaries with clients by insisting that they speak respectfully to the therapist and express feelings in a socially acceptable manner; (k) reframing "splitting" as recreating the disorganized, insecure attachments of the BPD client's childhood. Therapist self-disclosure diminishes the client's tendency to idealize (and devalue) the therapist.

3. Therapeutic progress is indicated primarily by the client's ability to moderate his or her feelings, especially anger (rages and sulks), as well as to function successfully in a variety of life situations.

CHAPTER 13

Couples Therapy

INHERENT DIFFICULTIES

Several considerations make couples difficult clients. In working with a couple, the therapist is a player in a psychological ménage à trois. Each client hopes to be more influential than the other and to have the therapist "see my point of view." The therapist risks losing the trust of one or both clients. The therapist must keep track of the characteristics of each individual and of the relationship that emerges from the couple's interactions. An alliance with each person is necessary when both are seen as clients, and confidences must be kept when each is seen separately, if individual confidentiality is the therapeutic agreement.

Impairments in functioning experienced by one or both members of the couple and personality characteristics (longstanding patterns of affect, behavior, and cognition) that handicap a person in many social, work, and leisure pursuits can be expected to handicap him or her in a marital relationship.

The moral values and social principles in which each person believes—his or her personal rules of living—must not be ignored. Ethics is about how people *ought* to treat each other, and there is no more ubiquitous setting for acting ethically or not than a close relationship. There are daily opportunities to choose right over wrong, respect over disrespect, kindness over cruelty, or vice versa.

WHAT MAKES A DYAD A COUPLE

Throughout this chapter, we will speak of marriage and of spouses. This is a mere convenience. There are varieties of both committed and not-so-committed relationships that exist between two persons. Our labels cover legal marriages and living as a couple with a significant other, and heterosexual as well as homosexual couples. Experience has shown us that there are no practical differences in the problems and difficulties couples encounter regardless of their legal status or sexual orientation.

There are differences when there are children, for they transform a marriage into a family with additional responsibilities, duties, and obligations. When children are present, either in the home or out of it as a result of separation or divorce, we speak of a family and distinguish it from a marriage. Problems involving children and the family are discussed throughout this book; this chapter restricts itself to two-person relationships, even though the two persons may be parents.

Although marital relationships are our focus, many of the principles discussed here apply to other relationships as well. Thus, relating better to other family members, bosses, coworkers, subordinates, and clients can be approached using these methods.

A QUESTION OF VALUES

All psychotherapy rests on certain assumptions, usually tacit, about personal values derived from one's religion, family ethical system, and the culture at large. From Freud's ego ideal and superego concepts to behavior therapy's assertiveness training (it's good to be assertive and put one's interests first), psychotherapy and ideas about right and wrong cannot be separated. This statement is particularly true when working with couples.

Basic conflicts involving values include such questions as: Is the attaining of one's own goals to be favored over what is good for the marriage or family? To what extent should one be selfless with respect to one's spouse and one's children? Each spouse has a position on this conflict, as does their therapist. All three persons may have to discover the couple's individual orientations, but the therapist should know his or her own. Whatever it is, it will be communicated to the couple in some fashion.

Some therapists consider marriages disposable. If things aren't working well, divorce is an option. The happiness and fulfillment of each individual is what counts, and whether they remain married or not is of little importance. A therapist who believes in family values (in reality, the value of the family to children and society) is likely to work harder to preserve marriages, but, of course, would be doing a disservice to couples who believe that marriages are disposable.

A certain amount of subtle negotiation is needed to resolve any mismatch between a therapist's values and those of the couple. They should be resolved in favor of the couple's orientation, although when children are involved, the authors of this book will lobby for putting family first. Now you know our orientation; in the interest of self-disclosure, we will say that what we now believe is not necessarily what we once did.

THE SOCIAL PSYCHOLOGY OF MARRIAGE

Another way in which values are inevitably linked to couples therapy is in the expectations each person brings to a marriage. Each has an idea of the role of wife and of husband (and of mother, father, and male and female children), and these can vary widely, depending on one's family and cultural backgrounds. Diversity is a popular but controversial notion at the present time, hailed on college campuses as a mark of acceptance and sophistication, and condemned by those who see it as a threat to the dominant American culture. Whether one likes the idea or not, diversity is a source of serious conflict in marriages.

Specifying how a wife and a husband should behave within a relationship is a set of prescriptions—prescriptive personal rules of living. In sociological terms, these are role prescriptions—cultural and subcultural values so internalized by the individual that they seem normal and natural. They represent the *right* way to do things!

When both parties agree on the prescribed roles of husband and wife, there is no problem. However, not everyone marries the girl or boy next door. Especially in large urban areas, one's spouse may come from a very different background and, therefore, have very different expectations of self and of his or her partner.

To further complicate matters, each person also brings expectations about the proper role of one's own parents and in-laws. What one spouse regards as helpful, the other may regard as intrusive.

Kay came from a well-to-do family whose ethic included the philosophy that parents should help their children, including adult children. Stephen came from a more modest family that emphasized self-reliance and independence. When they married, Stephen thought that Kay's father would not offer financial assistance. Kay verbally agreed, but quietly assumed that her father could buy her gifts, as he always had, without violating the understanding she had with Stephen. When the first expensive gift appeared in her closet, the husband objected. Kay's reaction was to go underground; she accepted the gifts but kept them secret from Stephen. Stephen detected her deception and declared he could not trust her; she believed he was unreasonable.

On the brink of divorce after less than a year of marriage, they tried couples therapy. The fact that the wedding had been a lavish affair gave Kay justification to preserve the marriage. Honor was Stephen's justification. In fact, it was his honor as "the provider" that had been attacked by Kay's accepting expensive gifts from her father. As a result of therapy, Kay came to understand her husband's values. Stephen came to understand that gifts were just an ordinary part of life for his in-laws, and no insult was intended. With increased mutual understanding came greater mutual acceptance.

Why didn't they recognize their differences by themselves and resolve them? Like so many couples, they were "crazy in love" and believed that marriage was about love and nothing more. Even after several sessions together, they had difficulty accepting that while love is not irrelevant, it is not enough to ensure a good and lasting marriage.

The best time to counsel couples on values and their expectations about marriage is before they wed. Even better than premarital counseling is *preengagement* counseling. Before getting serious enough to contemplate marriage, a pair should discuss their personal values.

However, many, and perhaps even most, couples don't discuss what they want, how to get what they want, and their ideas of right and wrong. While they should get to know each other cognitively—including and especially their views on child-rearing—they are busy getting to know each other emotionally and physically. They may know a great deal about what makes them feel good, but very little about what they value and how it should be expressed in decisions and actions.

Any discussion about children, a topic basic to marriage, often gets deferred until after the wedding, honeymoon, and several years together. Even then, the discussion is usually about *having* children, not what to do with them once they are born. So much is either deferred or left to presumption, it is impressive that any marital relationship survives.

Couples therapy deals with *personal expectations and the individual's psychological reactions to them.* By assuming the role of anthropologist here to learn the ways of the local inhabitants, a therapist can probe for and reveal the personal rules of living each person has about the social (and, for many, religious) institution of marriage—beliefs about the way things are in marriage and how they are supposed to be. This process can ordinarily be done with both parties present, but can also be done separately, if necessary.

CAT RELATIONSHIP CONCEPTS

A cornerstone of CAT work with couples is the understanding of what emotional experiences people seek but are not necessarily aware of. CAT assumes that people find and stay with partners who provide the behaviors necessary to reexperience one's familiar emotional states (personotypic affects). People marry others who remind them of their parents in their ability to recreate emotional experiences, and, in this sense, "marry one's mother or father."

People seem to have an uncanny ability to spot raw talent—the talent to furnish opportunities to satisfy nonconscious needy emotional states. Over time, each partner refines the raw talent of the other into a set of skills that bring forth old familiar experiences with minimum effort. The talent to make a person feel a certain way is very valuable and highly prized in a relationship, and the relationship can, in some instances, become one big security-seeking behavior.

Many times, a partner does not have actually to act in a fashion that stimulates the other's personotypic affects. Ambiguity is sufficient, and the other's perceptual biases complete the task.

> Jay thought Juanita was very critical of him, and, in fact, she could be. However, countless times Jay felt criticized when Juanita had said something neutral or had not said anything at all. Jay's personotypic affects—self-pity and anger—dictated his interpretations of her remarks or lack of remarks.
>
> Personotypic affects also prompt verbal and nonverbal behavior. When Jay "felt deprived" of self-pity and anger, and thus lacked a certain degree of psychological security, he would say or do something that caught Juanita's attention and she would criticize him. He, of course, felt sorry for himself and angry with his wife for "being such a bitch." Juanita's emotional response to Jay's blunders was exasperation—how could he be so stupid and how could she be so stupid to be with him? Feeling oppressed by fate and helpless to change it were her complex of thoughts and personotypic feelings; their re-occurrence provided a psychological payoff. As miserable as they could be with each other, each had, in fact, married a reliable source of emotional satisfaction—not pleasure in the conventional sense, but satisfaction via familiarity nonetheless.

A goal in individual psychotherapy is to gain insight into one's personal rules of living and personotypic motivations. The same goal applies to couples therapy, but, in addition, each partner should gain insight into the other's mind. It is not unusual for couples to enter therapy convinced they know the other person better than he or she knows himself or herself. Many quarrels center on statements about what the other *really* thinks and feels, and his or her true motivations for saying and doing things. In CAT, we attempt to replace these attempts at mind-reading with more genuine understanding of self and one's partner, thereby increasing empathy.

Empathy is a misunderstood word. It is possible to be exquisitely aware of what the other person is experiencing without regard for that person. Such empathy may be destructive, and is best epitomized by the torturer and his victim: the torturer knows that his victim is suffering—that is the whole point of torture. Constructive empathy involves not only awareness of another's probable subjective states but concern for the person as well.

Understanding another's thoughts and feelings can be used to excuse the other's thoughtless, irresponsible actions, or it can be used to sympathize excessively with another, to pity that person. The insidious effects of pity for oneself have been discussed extensively throughout this book. The effects of pity for another person can be just as grave. When feelings of pity motivate one to help another, such feelings are appropriately used. When they are used to excuse the bad behavior of another, they are altruistic feelings gone wrong.

Empathic knowledge of another can also be used against that person. For couples, this often means using accurate psychological insights into one's partner as the basis for criticizing him or her.

> Carla knew Carl very well and vice versa. Unfortunately for the stability of the family, hostility was their common personotypic affect. The reasons for this could be found in the interactions of their respective families of origin, and each could tell the other's story in fine detail. Such recounting was not done with constructive empathy but rather was the grounds for hurling criticisms: "You're just like your mother, father, etc.", said with relish as the receiving spouse bristled with anger, poised to return the attack. The payoff for attacking the other was twofold: the attacker could feel superior and get a certain sadistic satisfaction for his or her efforts, and the person attacked could feel like a victim. Carla was an active–dominant attacker, and Carl was a passive–submissive one. Carla's insults were loud and direct, Carl's quieter and subtle. Both were expert at provoking attack, Carla by offering "helpful" suggestions that Carl found offensive, and Carl by botching his chores, which inconvenienced Carla. On the surface, they were unhappy, but each received an important satisfaction he and she found hard to give up.

SIX APPLICATIONS OF CAT

There are six ways spouses can be involved in Cognitive Appraisal Therapy. Each presents a different set of difficulties for the therapist.

1. *The spouse of the focal client can be included in one or more sessions.* There may be marital problems to address or there may not. The inclusion of the spouse is intended to help the focal client, not primarily to work on marital issues.

2. *The spouse of the focal client can be included to work on issues of child rearing.*

> *For example, Jim asked whether Joan could join him during his regularly scheduled session to learn how to deal better with their son's problems at school. She raised several questions Jim hadn't thought of and they left feeling more confident about their competence as parents. They realized that discipline is necessary for children and does not damage self-confidence, but makes kids feel more secure by living according to rules made by parents strong enough to keep them.*

3. *Relationship problems are commonly discussed in psychotherapy.* In all likelihood, most attempts to improve marital relationships do not involve both partners. The old saying that you can't change others, only yourself is *not* true. Clients can often learn how to deal with a spouse differently and produce outcomes more satisfying for both of them.

4. *Both persons as clients want to decide about continuing the marriage.* Couples are usually seen together, although, at times, one or the other may be seen separately. Joint sessions may evolve into individual sessions. At least some individual time spent with each person is appropriate when one or both explores and attempts to discover what he or she wants. This usually means whether to continue the relationship or to end it, and this is best done out of earshot of one's partner.

5. *CAT can be oriented toward finding maximum happiness for each partner, whether or not the couple stays together.* The decision to undertake such an orientation should be the couple's. If the therapist has another opinion, e.g., marriages should be preserved at all costs, he or she should recuse him-herself from the case. The therapist can work with each individual on plans for the future and how they can best raise their child(ren), though divorced.

6. *CAT works with couples in traditional marital therapy.* The relationship itself is the target for change, and each party commits to the improvement of the relationship, although, in reality, that commitment can be withdrawn at any time. Cases range from easy to nearly impossible, but with a commitment firmly in place, any marriage can be preserved and improved.

> *Holly had a successful career and earned more than Howard, who thought of himself as an artist and did not measure success in dollars. Holly came to accept his attitude and he hers, but they differed on household responsibilities. Their mutual caring was evident in the first session, and their commitment to their marriage and its improvement was easy to obtain. Therapy provided a forum for their listening to each other and, away from their two young chil-*

dren, they could appreciate each other more, and reach agreements that both found reasonable, rewarding, and, therefore, easy to keep.

A nearly impossible case was Kate and Bud. They had married young, matured at different rates, and found themselves with little in common except for three children. One of the only things they agreed on was that they would part if it weren't for the children. They asked the therapist if that were reason enough to stay together. Kate and Bud were surprised to hear a "yes" from their therapist, but the answer led them to think seriously about the welfare of the new lives they had brought into the world and their responsibilities. They were further surprised when their therapist said that their lack of love for each other did not matter, only their commitment to solving their problems and respecting each other did. Placing their children's future above their own present, they agreed to work together and later, to their further surprise, they revived loving feelings that had been masked by personotypic anger and blame.

IT'S ABOUT POWER

Whether they are married or not, two people living together find it more difficult than if they lived alone. The benefits of companionship or financial arrangements may outweigh the problems of adjusting to a routine with another person, but adjust they must if they are to live under the same roof. Just being a roommate involves personal rules of living that can be a source of distress for both self and other.

There are two ways of adapting to the behavior of another person: you can take the lead and try to modify the behavior of the other, or you can allow the other to lead and accommodate to his or her preferences. In egalitarian relationships, there is a balance between the two; at times and for some issues, one person's view prevails and for other issues, the partner's wishes are followed.

When taking turns at getting what one wants fails, a bid for power ensues. Nothing insidious is meant by the word power. It simply refers to one person's attempts to influence the other to comply with his or her wishes. Power may be exerted in a direct and obvious manner, or it can be subtle.

When couples come to therapy, seemingly trivial matters have usually escalated into serious conflicts. These are often mislabeled by the couple as "communication problems." In fact, there is rarely a lack of understanding of what the other wants or expresses. The "communication problem" is about power and influence. Lack of compliance with one's wishes is described as lack of comprehension, and the underlying assumption is, "If you understood what I want, you would give it to me." The other is portrayed as deaf rather than independent, dense (i.e., stupid) rather than self-directed.

Some people think that to love someone is to defer to them. Feelings of anger over lack of compliance then mix with feelings of rejection and self-pity brought about by rejection. The standoff is about power, not about communication. It's about getting what one wants, but disguised and glamorized with psychobabble about "communication." There are *four styles of exerting power* in a coupled relationship, two that are warm and positive and two that are cold and negative.

The emotionally positive styles are active and overtly controlling, and passive and self-sacrificing. While they are associated, respectively, with male and female stereotyped social roles, each can be assumed by either sex. They work best with partners who are typically accommodating. The spouse who takes charge, makes decisions, and even appears benignly authoritarian at times, typifies the active–dominating style. The more interesting style is the one that relies on passive power—self-sacrificing, guilt inducing, and, there is no other word, motherly.

There are two corresponding negative emotional styles: active and cruel and passive and nasty. "Cruel" needs no further elaboration; "nasty" means harshly critical. They too work well with partners who are accommodating, and even better with partners who are accommodating and reciprocate the negative emotional tone of their habitual interactions.

KEEP TRYING UNTIL YOU FAIL

Persons in long-term relationships settle into a pattern of behavior modification and accommodation. The couple Carl and Carla illustrates another sad fact of life in couples. When people's attempts at influence and power fail repeatedly, they keep trying the same approach! Getting people unstuck is the task of the therapist. It is easier to do when the therapist understands the psychological satisfaction that comes from failing—it enables a familiar feeling to be re-experienced.

Carl would try repeatedly to reason with his wife, who was not only unmoved by his logic, but angrily resented it. Carl then could feel superior and maintain his image of Carla as unreasonable, perhaps even incompetent to take care of herself without him. Carla habitually provoked noncompliance from Carl, who simply dismissed her wishes as emotional and unreasonable. Carla's failing to influence Carl led her to believe in his stubbornness and lack of caring.

The therapist's task was to unravel these strands of interaction that were woven so long ago. By feeding back impressions of their styles of interaction and pointing out the emotional payoffs each received from the other's noncompliance (i.e., the rekindling of personotypic affect), the therapist offered understanding of self and of partner. Where to go from there? A behavioral contract might seem in order, wherein each exchanges a specified behavior.

Instead, the therapist asked how each could get what he or she wanted without resorting to the familiar patterns. In other words, the clients were invited to work *against* their familiar patterns and the payoffs they typically provided.

A related intervention is to point out that each partner is an expert on what influences him or her. Just ask, "What is the best way to approach you? How can I make my wants and wishes known so that you are likely to say yes? How can we collaborate to solve the problem?" These questions are possible when the hostility that exists between spouses has been reduced or minimized.

> *Jack annoyed Jill by solving her problems for her and for the family without her or anyone's asking him to. She felt demeaned, as if she were an idiot. Jack, finding only benevolent motives within himself, could not understand her anger. They needed to define problems and seek solutions together, the model of egalitarian modern marriage. Jack was willing to try, but clumsily continued to annoy his wife. She was coached to react without annoyance, but simply point out Jack's behavior; Jack was coached to ask her to stop her angry outbursts and examine what, if anything, he had done to provoke them. No blame, no shame for either one; <u>shared responsibility</u> for changing their longstanding pattern of interaction.*

SEX AND MONEY

Sex and money are two common reasons people marry who they do. For men especially, sexual attraction and the prospects of continued sensual pleasure justify "forsaking all others." For some women, money and the security it represents are a good reason to favor one suitor over another. With so much at stake, it is not surprising that these attractions have such great potential for disappointment and become the source of divorce-threatening conflict.

Attitudes about money are the issue. Virtually no couple or family thinks it has enough, even if it does, by objective standards. One partner will want to spend more than the other does and roles of spendthrift and miser quickly emerge in the minds of each partner. These attitudes originate in their respective families of origin. Family myths can instill a fear of poverty, self-pity habits connected with fears of deprivation, and, on the positive side, a sunny outlook about there always being more where that (money) came from. People often use family beliefs about money to rekindle personotypic affect: self-pity with "No matter how hard I work, I never have enough money"; anger with "How come all those dumb bastards make more money than I do?"; and shame with "I just don't have what it takes to make a lot of money." Having power over the purse strings creates resentment in the one who lacks it, and this dynamic can feed personotypic affect (e.g., "How come she gets to spend all of my money?"; "He's such a cheapskate. Living with him is no fun."). Whose money is it, anyway?

The egalitarian answer to this question is, it's the couple's money, not either individual's. However, ideas about marriage, the roles within it, and who has power over what, vary considerably in a pluralistic society. Money is another topic for pre-engagement counseling, but, of course, it, like the raising of children, is usually deferred. Left without shared traditions to decide the question for them, each couple has to reinvent marriage and find what suits them.

Men are more likely to think it is their money rather than "our" money, and many women, following what they think is the "right way," agree. Women who go back to work after the kids are in school often see their earnings as pocket money rather than as a genuine contribution to family income. Many women seem ignorant about money, some confessing that they cannot balance a checkbook or perform other simple mathematical or financial tasks. Whatever shared power they might have in marriage they mentally sign away by thinking they are disinterested or incompetent to manage. Should they become divorced or widowed, they face a frightening prospect of dealing with the very issue they avoided in marriage at a time when they need all the acumen they can muster. In divorce especially, women are faced with an increased risk of poverty and reduction in standard of living.

By giving power away to the other person, one becomes weaker in the relationship. Lack of power means that a spouse can see him- or herself as a victim of the other, with all the accompanying familiar feelings of self-pity. The practical solution is to share decisions about money (i.e., share the power over money) and the psychological solution is not to define oneself as a victim and give up self-pity.

Sexual dissatisfaction is common among couples in therapy. Withholding sex is a form of power, the hoarding of a finite resource. The risk involved in withholding sexual contact is that the partner is more likely to seek it elsewhere. Both withholding and infidelity are threats to marriage. Sex, an inherently pleasurable activity, can become the source of anger within a relationship, both a symptom of marital breakdown and a contributing cause.

Sexual dysfunction and disinterest, when not physiological, are usually due to *anger* in couples who formerly had satisfactory sexual relations. Therapy for anger and self-pity, rather than sex therapy, is required.

In couples whose resolution of angry exchanges is to have sexual contact, hostility is almost always characteristic of their interactions. Look for the signs of a cruel or nasty spouse paired with a rejecting or whining and complaining one. There is a mutually sadistic quality about their interactions; in CAT, we say this is due to their personotypic affects, and if so, there will be evidence of a nonsexual nature to confirm this supposition.

Men and women who lose sexual interest in their spouses are usually angry, unless the spouse has done something to make him- or herself unattractive (e.g., become grossly overweight). We work to uncover the roots of this anger (i.e., is it personotypic affect or simply a reaction to not getting what one wants in the relationship?), and we help partners to express their anger more appropriately and productively.

Lack of sexual satisfaction within marriage weakens the bonds between partners. Getting a couple to resume sexual relations is not difficult; we simply tell them to do it. *Sex-by-prescription* requires the couple to have sexual relations at least once a week, whether they feel like it or not. Once into the physical contact, most persons respond, relax, and enjoy themselves. If it possible to have pleasurable sex with a virtual stranger, it is possible to have some measure of pleasurable sex with one's spouse, provided negative feelings do not get in the way.

INDIVIDUAL PSYCHOPATHOLOGY

Marriage offers the best opportunity for individual pathology to come out. A spouse is a convenient target of blame and anger, even when he or she has done nothing to provoke such feelings. Protection from and comfort for one's fears can be sought from a spouse, with the expectation that he or she is obliged to help. Spouses can be turned into oppressors (or, at least, perceived that way), intent on tormenting their helpless victims.

Feelings and how they are handled shape the marital relationship just as much as expectations and attitudes, perhaps more. There are five patterns of defensive maneuvers frequently found in marriage. Each represents an attempt at dealing with personal problems within the context of marriage, but can easily become a major source of dissatisfaction. These patterns can be dealt with either in couples therapy or individual therapy.

The Pleaser tries to get along by pleasing others. The personality diagnoses of histrionic (active–submissive) and dependent (passive–submissive) are the extreme variants of this style. A certain degree of mutual pleasing is necessary for both spouses to feel satisfied and fulfilled. However, Pleasers do not simply exchange good feelings; they please others to neutralize their fears of others' criticisms and putdowns. To avoid shame, they defer to others' wishes. Pleasers inevitably resent pleasing. Caught between their fears of humiliation and of being proven inadequate and their resentment at having to please others, Pleasers are chronically unhappy and find, often unwittingly, subtle ways to make their spouses unhappy, to pay for their "demands."

The Complainer feels entitled to the best of everything. The extreme variant is the narcissistic personality disorder (passive–dominant). Failing to get the best goods, services, treatment, etc., the Complainer speaks up, and their spouses may feel embarrassed by the Complainer's audible criticisms of nearly everything around them. Complainers feel victimized by others' incompetence or indifference, but instead of harboring self-pity, they get nasty. Of course, the spouse is often the target of their complaints, with all the resultant bad feelings.

The Procrastinator is a familiar figure characterized by uncooperative attitudes, unreliability, and neglect of responsibilities. It's not that they don't intend to do what they should, they just do it on their own timetable—and they may never get around to it. Theirs are passive–aggressive traits associated with several different personality styles. They have passive power in that their lack of action can control outcomes. Because they cannot be relied upon, they engender hostility. Spouses accuse Procrastinators of not pulling their weight and perceive them as burdens. Their habit of not doing what they have agreed to do in a timely fashion shifts more responsibility to their spouses, who feel unfairly treated. In couples therapy, Procrastinators are accused of being lazy and uncaring. Psychologically, this pattern may have several precursors, but most prominent is fear of criticism and shame about the possible discovery that one is inadequate. However, hidden feelings of entitlement—that one should not be required to do the normal things of life like everyone else—may emerge during treatment.

The Binger indulges himself or herself in order to calm feelings and provide some amount of self-comfort. This stance is related to the active and passive variants of the narcissistic personality disorder. Bingers rely on substances—food, alcohol, prescription and street drugs—instead of relying on spouses for emotional satisfaction. Self-pity is the main feeling. Spouses either support the Binger's addiction (known elsewhere as enabling) or criticize it, thus inflicting more psychological hurt on the person. Either spousal response diminishes the quality of the marriage. Because Bingers assume less and less responsibility within the relationship, their spouses feel more and more exploited and resentful.

The Avoider deals with social anxiety by social isolation. Like those with avoidant personality disorder, these persons fear others' criticisms and see them as sources of shame or shame mixed with pleasure. They usually have an elaborate fantasy life centering on isolation in paradise—escaping to an island where no one can bother them and only pleasures abound. Unfortunately for them, they live in the real world, not a fantasy world, and when the two worlds collide, they feel anxious and depressed.

In marriage, Avoiders try to coopt their partners into a compromise version of their island fantasy. They isolate, see only certain family members, and ignore friends, acquaintances, and neighbors. They try to get their spouses to do the same, to the point of neglecting business contacts and other career-enhancing socialization opportunities. Spouses come to feel stifled by them, as they either drag them reluctantly to social affairs or attend alone. Mothers with children can easily disguise social phobia by citing the need to care for the children. Whatever their excuse, they harm their marriage.

TIPS FOR A HAPPY MARRIAGE

Not all work with couples is therapeutic or remedial. The therapist can give good advice to enhance relationships or to get pre-engaged couples off to a good start. These ideas apply equally as well to relationships that need improvement or rejuvenation:

1. *Don't talk too much about problems.* If you don't like something, express your feelings very briefly and ask for specific change. Condemning, nagging, and preaching are counterproductive and usually result in begrudging compliance or open hostility.

2. *Commit to problem-solving.* If even sworn enemies can reach some understanding and agreement, so can supposedly loving couples. The biggest barrier to problem-solving is the refusal to modify one's position or to find common areas of agreement. Unyielding insistence on one's point of view gets nowhere. One's partner may give in, but it will be unenthusiastic acquiescence, not genuine agreement in which he or she has some personal investment.

3. *Don't fight, except to relieve tension or boredom.* (But look for better ways to get relief.) Fighting means exchanging hostile, demeaning statements that are heartfelt at the time, and perhaps afterwards as well. Except for couples who find reinforcement in hostile exchanges, fighting weakens emotional bonds. Fighting is about power (not problem-solving), and, in the best relationships, power is shared or divided more or less equally.

4. *Discuss values.* Know where each other stands with regard to children (having them and how to raise them), money (how much and how to allocate it), and sex (no further comment needed). In addition, in-laws, ex-spouses, and stepfamilies are common areas of disagreement. Agreement on what is right and wrong in each matter avoids most problems and makes solving the rest much easier.

5. *Respect one another.* Treat each other at least as politely as you would a stranger. A primary rule for damaged relationships is that of civility. Couples who intend to divorce but need to live together have followed this rule with great success. So can couples who want to stay together.

6. *Follow the rule of cheerfulness.* Don't agree to anything unless you can agree cheerfully. If you agree to do something, do it cheerfully. No whining! (A phrase we use in therapy is "sacrifice cheerfully".)

If your spouse has been unfaithful and you choose to remain with him or her, do so cheerfully. It was your decision to stay in the relationship. Do not use togetherness as an opportunity for revenge.

Remember that your spouse is only the best choice among all the available alternatives. He or she is not the ideal person, your "soul mate", or the creature invented in your fantasies or dreams. Be grateful for what you have, not carping and self-pitying for what you don't have. If you are not satisfied, take action.

CHAPTER 14

CAT Group Therapy[1]

THE REKINDLING OF SHAME IN GROUP THERAPY

THERE'S NO PLACE LIKE HOME

Many clients come to group therapy already feeling highly ashamed of their inability to be at ease socially, more assertive, better parents, nonaddicted, etc. Naturally, group therapy will be a countertherapeutic experience for these clients if their shameful feelings are enhanced. Moreover, if clients are primed by years of shame-seeking thoughts and behaviors to reinvoke shameful feelings, they often unintentionally use therapy to do so. Cognitive and cognitive–behavioral group therapies that are wed to a set "protocol" run the risk of enhancing clients' shame. Inherent in a behavioral or cognitive–behavioral protocol is the possibility that failure to comply or succeed with such a program indicates that one is not good enough, is incapable, stupid, etc. We hypothesize that shame-seeking clients may participate in such programs in order

[1] Parts of this chapter are from Wessler (1993c).

(nonconsciously) to fail. They can then get angry at themselves, fellow group members, or the therapist, feel sorry for themselves and/or, ultimately, feel like a failure, thus replaying old familiar feelings and interpersonal patterns.

Yalom's (1985) help-rejecting complainer is a case in point. This individual comes to the group and repeatedly complains, pulls sympathy and advice-giving from others, rejects all advice, and continues to complain, ultimately alienating and infuriating the other group members. This individual can then say to himself or herself (as well as to the group): "Just as I thought. You don't really care about me. Well, to hell with all of you"—and the complainer's personotypic affects and personal rules of living are once again verified. Certainly, the more rigid and task-oriented the group's agenda, the more opportunities the help-rejecting complainer has to fail to follow through with recommended tasks and assignments.

Group therapists who inflexibly use a protocol or agenda may also end up feeling angry, annoyed, or disappointed with clients who, week after week, do not comply with or succeed at the tasks at hand. The clients, therefore, can get these therapists in particular to play the complementary role of the judgmental, angry, disappointed other in the security-seeking behaviors they do in such groups.

Groups that are more interpersonal–experiential in nature also run the risk of enhancing members' shame, as well as anger and self-pity. Less active, structured therapists who allow the "group process" to unfold in order to understand members' interpersonal styles (e.g., the placater, the confronter, the avoider) and those who encourage group members to express their feelings toward one another "openly and honestly" may allow members to treat each other disrespectfully. An angry member may feel it his duty to "confront" or put down other members; a self-pitying member may whine to pull for the group's sympathy; and an ashamed group member may withdraw from others, who ultimately confront that member's silence in a way that further humiliates and shames him or her. While an adept group therapist can quickly head off these interactions and help group members to learn about themselves from these interactions, the format of these groups plays into the personotypic affect and security-seeking behaviors of clients who already arrive equipped with a suitcase filled with shame and interpersonal failure experiences.

OFFERING SYMPATHY RATHER THAN EMPATHY IN GROUP THERAPY

THE INNER CHILD OUTSHOUTS THE INNER ADULT

"Validation" and "support" from others can be important elements of a group therapy (Yalom, 1985); however, they can often be confused with sympathy (feeling sorry for another) rather than associated only with empathy (understanding how another feels). While it is important to acknowledge how difficult it can be to cope with certain difficulties and to alter one's cognitive, behavioral, and emotional patterns, a group therapist must not focus on this to the exclusion of having group members assume responsibility for their behaviors and feelings and for changing them.

Clients who are prone to feeling ashamed of themselves and pulling sympathy from others will attempt to do so in group therapy. Self-pity and rage (the voice of one's "inner child") may reign supreme. Instead, empathy (an adult behavior) should be given to these group members rather than sympathy, and self-pity should be discouraged or ignored.

We have found that groups for people who have undergone a traumatic life event (e.g., the death of a loved one, an assault or abuse) can unintentionally foster self-pity and increase the sense that one is a victim in life. "Poor me," sometimes a justifiable initial reaction to a life trauma, often turns into "poor us" when group members do nothing but sympathize with or try to top each other's suffering and misery week after week. Similarly, so-called support groups for a particular population (men's or women's support groups, gay and lesbian support groups) may focus on how unfairly others treat this population, and group members feed each other's rage and sense of being oppressed and victimized. An "us against the world" mentality results, and group members, already primed to see the world as hostile and rejecting, allow their rage to pull anger and rejection from others, thus "confirming" their self-pitying belief system. The sensitive group leader, while allowing group members to validate one another's experience, can then pose the question to the group: "If you feel rejected by the world, what can *you* now do to counteract this rejection? We can only change ourselves, not the world, so how are *you* going to solve this problem in a productive, nonangry and nonvictimized way?" In this way, *personal responsibility* becomes the group norm rather than self-pity and rage.

IMPORTANT COMPONENTS OF GROUP THERAPY

Group therapies range from those where the therapist interacts with one client at a time while the other members form a silent audience that simply observes this interaction to groups which focus exclusively on the here-and-now interaction between all group members. (Refer to Wessler, 1993c, for a review of this dimension of group therapies.) In this chapter, we restrict the meaning of group therapy to include only instances wherein individuals have a relatively high probability of interaction and engage in a fair amount of face-to-face contact.

GROUP PROCESSES AND EMOTION

Plutchik (1981) presents evidence to support the contention that group cohesion and emotions are very closely related. Sharing promotes group cohesion.

Sharing proximate positions in a hierarchy, sharing space and identity contribute to the feeling of belonging. Significantly, feelings do the same: "*the sharing of any emotion, pleasant or unpleasant, tends to increase group cohesion* ... this is also true in the group therapy experience, whereas groups of strangers become tied together—become cohesive—as a result of sharing emotions. That the crucial element is the sharing of emotions and not the exchange of information is evident from the fact that people who simply attend a lecture do not thereby become cohesive" (Plutchik, 1981, pp. 141–142; italics in original).

Plutchik's analysis suggests that most of the learning that takes place is a result of experiences within the group rather than intentional lessons taught by the therapist. Members learn about themselves as persons and about interpersonal skills. The goal is to function more effectively outside the group and not simply to be better group members. The key that makes group therapy possible is the sharing of emotional experiences, or self-disclosure.

Self-disclosure is a requisite in group therapy, as it is in individual therapy. The same psychological factors that inhibit free expression of information about oneself, one's personal life, and felt emotions in individual treatment are present in groups. Although many people can open up to a therapist in a one-on-one situation, they find it difficult to speak as freely and openly in a group. Shame and embarrassment cause them to defend by remaining quiet or closed about themselves. A measure of progress in a newly formed group is the degree to which persons disclose about themselves.

SHAME AND SELF-DISCLOSURE

Within a therapy group, one is expected to put into words what one would normally discuss only with persons very close to oneself—friends, relatives—or perhaps with no one at all. Although there are cultural and generational differences in regard to what is considered appropriate for disclosure, to whom and when, the key emotional correlate is shame: "I do not want you to know about me because I consider the information to be shameful." It is probably correct to assume that the way a person characteristically handles shame in everyday life is the way that the person will handle it in a therapy group, at least initially. Nathanson (1987) identifies four characteristic defenses against shame in his compass of shame (see also chapter 3) that have relevance for group therapy.

A common method for concealing shame is to avoid and withdraw. The silent members of a group take no risks and reveal little or nothing about themselves or their feelings. Such persons must be encouraged to participate and confronted if they do not.

Another typical defense against shame is to deny one's feelings by being active in the group but always keeping the focus on others and their problems and feelings rather than on oneself. Such persons may appear helpful, give advice and attention to others, and seem to be highly involved with the group. In fact, because group cohesion depends on the expression of emotions, such a group member is, sooner or later, seen as on the periphery, perhaps as trying to function as the therapist's assistant or replacement. The group and its therapist have the task of confronting the overtly helpful but covertly concealing member to deal with shame and to become self-disclosing.

A third way to handle shame is through humor. Even though some good humor is beneficial in not taking oneself too seriously, excessive reliance on humor is not because it conceals shame or other emotions. By making oneself the butt of one's jokes, a person preempts confrontation by others. The person discloses what he or she considers safe rather than exploring and revealing more risky feelings. The joker may be amusing at first, but unless the humor is accompanied by serious self-disclosure, the person will not integrate into the group, and will likely not benefit from psychotherapy.

Finally, anger may be a person's characteristic defense against shame. Rage often surfaces when shame has been provoked underneath. Shame-defended rage presents two problems for group therapy. First, unbridled rage is disruptive and inappropriate. Although the expressing of anger is desirable, it must be done according to social rules and conventions, and the leader must be ready to set limits if the group fails to enforce norms about appropriate expressing of feelings. In general, feelings should be put into words and not acted out. Second, fear and shame about expressing anger or other negative affects may produce evasiveness, silence, or passive–aggressive comments, as anger is leaked out in relative safety. Whether shame-related anger is hotly expressed or hidden under ice, neither group cohesiveness nor personal therapeutic benefit is likely to result because true feelings are concealed.

Therefore, for group therapy to be effective—for the individual to deal with and express his or her feelings—the group has to be perceived as "safe," which means that the group has to be a shame-free environment. If one is to surrender defenses against shame, one should expect to reveal shameful secrets in the safety of a noncritical setting. One way to do this is to give feedback with especial care.

Group members are instructed to give feedback about statements and actions, and not about the person. Feedback should be about specifics and not about abstractions and generalizations; it should be useful to the focal person and not catharsis for the speaker (Johnson, 1988). The model sentence is, "I feel this way about what you just said or did." Such feedback is clearly an expression of feelings, for which the speaker takes responsibility, expressed directly about a specific here-and-now behavior. The comment is designed to help the listener, not condemn him or her. Because the listeners are humans and not machines, even feedback that is optimally given may be taken as criticism. A result is further shame and a conclusion that the group is not a safe place to express intimate thoughts and feelings.

Feedback, because it consists of impressions, opinions, and feelings, promotes group cohesion, but because it can stimulate shame even when well-done, it can threaten group cohesion. Without feedback, there can be no therapy. Feedback provides opportunities for reality-testing concerning interpersonal interactions and reality-testing when exploring the accuracy of one's cognitive inferences and predictions. Feedback serves as positive reinforcers for desirable behaviors and as aversive consequences for undesirable ones. Feedback helps clarify one's social impact and allows the modifying of the self-image by hearing about impressions one makes on others. Feedback allows the person to learn to label feelings more accurately and to discover aspects of the self that are apparent to others but of which the individual is unaware. Without feedback, there is no therapy.

Group therapy offers opportunities for multiple sources of feedback. This provides, on the one hand, a variety of perspectives and, on the other, heightened impact when feedback is univocal. An individual therapist's impact can be minimized by thinking it is the opinion of one person. It is much less easy to disregard the consensus of several group members.

Personal change results from experiences of interacting with other people, experiences that are both emotional and resultant in cognitive understanding of self, other people, and interpersonal relations. Personal change includes shifts in thinking and acting, and relief from emotional distress. When emotional distress cannot be relieved because it is associated with some aspect of the person he or she is unwilling or unable to change (such as the emotional distress associated with remaining in a marriage one's values prohibit one from leaving), the person is, at least, more accepting of this reality.

In addition to this general purpose of effective group therapy, we offer the following as the primary goals of CAT group therapy:

1. to explore one's interpersonal stance (how friendly versus hostile, dominant versus submissive, active versus passive one is) by looking at how one interacts with group members and the responses that one pulls from these members;

2. to gain insight into one's shame, rage, and self-pity both by exploring how these feelings play out and are expressed in the group and by receiving feedback from group members concerning these feelings both when discussing out-of-group problems and via in-group situations;

3. to learn to take responsibility for one's actions, for how one affects others, and for change;

4. to gain insight into one's personal rules of living and to understand that they are subjective, implicit personal assumptions that one makes rather than Absolute Truth or Reality;

5. to create a shame-free, whining-free, respectful yet honest group environment which will enable the previous goals to occur.

One type of CAT group consisting of eight members and ran for ten $1^1/_2$-hour sessions. Longer closed-end CAT groups are just as feasible, as are open-ended groups. In an open-ended format, there is less use of formal feedback periods and more attention to personal issues presented by group members. The topics discussed in a group should arise from the members' lives rather than out of a topic list, as this often enables the group to focus on deeper personal issues and feelings.

In the 10-session CAT group, however, there are planned themes for each group meeting. These are:

Session 1: Introduction and initial presentation of self
Session 2: Feedback about first impression
Sessions 3 and 4: Current issues in each member's life
Sessions 5 and 6: In-depth understanding of past and present relationships
Session 7 and 8: open—to be used as needed by group members
Session 9: Member–member feedback
Session 10: Feedback to and from the therapist

SESSION 1

Group members introduce themselves and say something about their goals for therapy. The therapist encourages members to ask the type of questions that promote getting acquainted with each other, urging openness, dealing with issues of trust and confidentiality and other rules for the group.

SESSION 2

In this session, process is the focus. Each member gives feedback to each other member about his or her initial impressions, and describes feelings about each person. (These will be compared to feedback given during Sessions 9 and 10.)

The purpose of this procedure is to give each member an opportunity to discover the impact of his or her self-presentation on other people (one's interpersonal stance or personality style) and how he or she pulls responses from other people (security-seeking behaviors). This is also a time when members can learn about the expectations of other people that they bring to a new situation (personal rules of living), and they can compare their biases against reality as defined by each person (who can protest "I'm not like that") and, consequently, by the group ("We don't see the person that way").

SESSIONS 3 AND 4

There is time during each session for four persons to present problems on which they wish to work in therapy. These are here-and-now issues which the therapist will work on with the assistance of group members. Interventions featured are characteristic of CAT and, occasionally, of behavior therapy (such as the assigning of homework), of problem-solving therapy (Rose, 1989), and Rogerian counseling (the feeling of empathy and its communication).

Group members are told to be empathic and to share similar experiences, provided they have had any, but not to give advice or tell the focal person what he or she is thinking, feeling, or what his or her motivations are. The therapist stops an offending group member and uses the occasion to illustrate and model more appropriate responses, and to encourage compliance with the sharing-of-experiences rule.

In a similar vein, we disallow whining and complaining among group members when presenting their problems as a way to both highlight and begin to diminish self-pity and sympathy-seeking. We also disallow caretaking. Often, one group member wants to solve others' problems or make overly "nurturing" remarks, and avoid examining their own shame-based issues. Caretaking also fosters self-pity and anger in group members by enhancing their sense of helplessness and distress. We, therefore, mount an anti-caretaking campaign at this point in the group.

As group members discuss current issues, we work against fostering an "us against them" attitude among group members. We discourage blaming the absent person who is being discussed, and we do not allow group members to strengthen cohesion by siding against people who are not group members. For example, it is typical in a "support" group for a member to complain about his angry, demanding boss and then for other members to rally and make such remarks as, "Your boss is a bastard" or "Go in and stand up to him." Instead, the CAT group therapist poses questions such as, "If your boss is a bastard, how do you deal with bastards? You don't want to lose your job. It's not a democracy at work. Perhaps your boss has a problem—have a little empathy for him. What is your boss feeling underneath the anger? Perhaps he's ashamed of being out of control. It sounds to me that you are contributing to your boss's shame by being passive–aggressive with him. How can you not show disrespect for your boss and help him to calm down?"

SESSIONS 5 AND 6

Four persons per session explore in depth their present and, particularly, their past relationships. Each reviews his or her personal developmental history of interpersonal relationships and the interpersonal patterns that have resulted. For the focal person, the connections between the past and present are sought, with the gaining of insights into present attitudes and relationships. As we have discussed elsewhere, recurring interpersonal patterns highlight security-seeking behaviors that are variations of the primary attachments, and recurring emotions are inroads into understanding personotypic affect and the emotional setpoint. Present situations can be seen relatively quickly by group members as really being echoes of the past—and this insight can free up members to make new choices in the present. For other group members, this process is a time of discovering similarities between self and others.

The therapist encourages empathic relating by requiring each person to comment or question the focal member. Comments mat be in the form of feedback ("Something like that happened to me, too"). Questions are the least one can do to participate in the life of the focal person; even if one has had no similar experiences, one can seek to know more about someone else. By requiring full group participation, the therapist can work against the evasiveness that sometimes develops as an informal group norm; that is, group members sometimes handle shame by tacitly agreeing not to confront one another about anything that might produce shame. Since a tactic in CAT is to confront one's shame rather than avoid it, it is important to counteract this common tendency to "respect" another's privacy and not commit the social error of stimulating shame. Group therapy, however, is not an ordinary social situation, but a time to penetrate both individual and group defenses.

SESSIONS 7 AND 8

These sessions provide a break in the therapist-imposed structure and allow participants to return to a presentation of individual issues. Everything that has been developed within the group during the previous sessions can be used here. By now, most group members can address one another and give feedback by speaking about their feelings. Group members, in fact, usually become quite adept by this time at holding each other personally responsible for their actions and at calling each other on self-pity and unfair blaming of others, and they learn to do so in a respectful manner.

Issues within the group are less likely to be dealt with here than issues outside the group. However, since clients have had some opportunity to work on their problems during the prior several weeks, noncompliance, procrastination, oppositionality, and other forms of avoidance come up frequently. Group members are urged to express their feelings about a person's failure to work on his or her problems, but not to condemn him or her for it. Empathy and sharing are stressed, advice and scolding not permitted.

Sometimes at this point, one group member's issue is generalized so that the group as a whole can work on a related shared issue. This happens more frequently in the open-ended CAT group, where we do not have to focus equally on each member's specific topic in a circumscribed amount of time. We might, for example, use the focal member's discussion of his or her shame as a starting point to having all members pay a visit to the "Museum of Shame." We begin by stating that we all collect thoughts and behaviors that represent and stir up shameful feelings in us. We then have members "stroll through" various galleries in this museum, the "Hall of Ugly," the "Stupid Gallery," the "Loser Exhibit," the "Fat Atrium," and so on. Each member goes to those galleries that represent what they say to themselves to rekindle their shame (their justifying cognitions) and, in an atmosphere of good humor, they share these self-statements with the group.

In some groups, especially those that I (Sheenah) have run with women, we may focus at this point on women's passivity and how it fosters self-pity. Group members share examples of how they make themselves more passive than they need to in various situations, and how this results in their feeling weak, victimized, and sorry for themselves. We explore how women can actually (unintentionally) cause others to victimize them, by distancing from men (e.g., withholding sex), for example, and thus having others confirm their view of themselves as aggressed-upon victims. The goal here is to highlight that passivity is a behavioral choice that women make (to rekindle personotypic affect and affirm their personal rules of living) and that they are not "trapped" or "stuck" being passive. Instead, than can choose to break the self-pity habit and act more assertively and proactively in their lives.

Along with this focus on passivity, we may also have "anger week" in which group members take turns practicing expressing their anger rather than turning it into self-pity. Group members are encouraged to express anger at each other, but to do so in a respectful, assertive, but not aggressive or sarcastic, manner. Members often find that others in the group can hear their angry statements without lashing out in return or crumbling, and this disconfirmation that the expression of anger is negative often liberates group members from their passivity and self-pity, as well as from their personal rules of living concerning the expression of anger.

SESSION 9

As in the second session, feedback from each person to each other person is formally sought. Comparisons between initial and subsequent impressions are made, and the focal person can learn about his or her interpersonal style and about any attempts he or she made to modify it. The focus of this session is on changes (or lack of changes) each person has made. During this session in particular, strong feelings, either negative or positive, are expressed about others.

One intervention that occurs here, and that is used throughout an open-ended CAT group, is the disconfirmation of inaccurate interpersonal perceptions. Often, clients give feedback statements to each other that are distorted by their own security-seeking behaviors, personal rules of living, and personotypic affect. It is extremely corrective for these clients to become aware of such distortions.

> For example, Elizabeth continuously avoided confronting and contributing to discussions of Andrea's problems. This dynamic was addressed by the group during this feedback session. Elizabeth said that she perceived Andrea as unpleasant and authoritative, misunderstanding Andrea's more open expression of feelings as a sign of her feeling superior to Elizabeth. (Note the personal rule of living here: "It is arrogant and authoritative to strongly express one's feelings."
>
> Elizabeth was surprised to realize that Andrea reminded her of her mother. The therapist then suggested that Andrea role-play Elizabeth's mother and that Elizabeth coach Andrea as to how to accurately portray her mother. As a result of this role-play, which focused on a typical problematic mother–daughter interaction, Elizabeth clearly saw that Andrea was not at all like Elizabeth's mother and that Elizabeth had distorted her perceptions of Andrea to recreate this familiar family dynamic in the group. Therefore, Elizabeth, in essence, turned Andrea into her mother as a security-seeking behavior in the group. This example also illustrates the value of the group, as opposed to one-to-one therapy, for the recognition of personal rules of living and the rekindling of personotypic affect.

SESSION 10

Although this is nominally time for feedback to and from the therapist, in practice, the first portion of the session is used to finish comments from Session 9. The therapist has probably given continuous feedback to each member during their weeks together, but this is a chance to do so more formally, and to hear what group members' feelings are about the therapist. It is also a time for deciding on the future course of treatment for each person and/or the continuation of the group for additional sessions.

In summary, the CAT version of group therapy quite intentionally incorporates aspects from other therapeutic orientations. It does so because CAT is not only concerned with surface issues (a criticism, not altogether unfair, leveled at behavior and cognitive therapies) but with broader aspects of personality and of genetic explanation as well. However, CAT is also concerned with current events in people's lives, and so includes problem-solving and, at times, behavioral homework. In addition, should lack of emotional expression be a problem in a specific group, tactics to promote emotional expression, such as those associated with psychodrama and gestalt therapy, can be integrated into the procedures.

SUMMARY

1. Shame in group therapy members can be encouraged when (a) a group (often cognitive–behavioral) adheres to a rigid protocol that members can not easily follow and therefore fail; (b) a group (often experiential–interpersonal) encourages group processes that can reinforce a client's shame; (c) the expression of shame, self-pity, and anger becomes the group norm.

2. A shame-free group environment is created (a) by encouraging feedback about members' actions but not about the members themselves; (b) by making the group norm one of personal responsibility rather than self-pity; and (c) by disallowing a group process to unfold that leads to the reinforcement of shame in group members.

3. Goals of CAT group therapy are (a) exploring one's interpersonal stance/personality style; (b) gaining insight into one's personotypic affect; (c) taking responsibility for one's actions; and (d) gaining insight into one's personal rules of living.

4. A 10-session CAT group therapy was outlined which follows the aforementioned goals and guidelines.

CHAPTER 15

Working with "Difficult" Parents[1]

Many behavioral and cognitive–behavioral protocols exist to help parents diminish their children's impulsive, aggressive, and poorly regulated behaviors. These protocols have been found to be effective in achieving their goals, if and only if the parents are willing and able to implement them appropriately, consistently and firmly (e.g., Clark, 1985; Forehand & McMahon, 1981; Mash, Hamerlynk, & Handy, 1976). In doing parent training in conjunction with other treatment modalities, I (Jonathan) have found that parents fall into two groups: those who use behavioral tools effectively and those who say they want to use these tools but instead employ a variety of strategies to undermine their effectiveness.

The second group of parents seem as earnest as the first in professing that they want to improve their children's lot in life, as well as their own as parents. They often appear amenable, sometimes enthusiastically, to trying out the various behavioral strategies that I suggest to them. However, week after week, after many modifications and troubleshooting sessions, these parents are still unable to follow through with their prescribed assignments. Instead, they prefer to tell me of yet more horrendous terrorist tactics used by their 5-

---

[1] This chapter is based in part on Stern (1996).

year-old son; to berate me that I just do not understand how headstrong and downright frightening their child can be; to come up with many creative reasons why they were unable to implement the behavioral strategies we discussed; or to complain bitterly that all their lives they have been the overly responsible caretaker while everyone around them (including me, now) makes unrealistic and uncaring demands of them. Nevertheless, many of these parents keep on returning to therapy.

I remember that, as a naive and overzealous psychology intern running behavioral parenting groups, when I heard such complaints from parents I used to think, "I've given you all you need to know to change your kid's behavior. Damn it, why aren't you using it?" Now, when I hear parents make these statements, I think "Good. Now the therapy can really begin."

From hearing parents have such reactions to parenting protocols, I came to see that behavioral interventions can be effective in treating both the child's and parent's behavioral *symptoms,* but they do not address underlying *personality* characteristics in the parents, which can often sabotage their willingness to comply with behavioral assignments. I have also found that challenging illogical thoughts, as a rational–emotive therapist might do, is not enough to help some parents change, since personotypic affect dominates their logic and motivates their parenting. By dint of how they grew up and how they saw themselves in relation to the world around them, some parents (those whom Yalom, 1985, calls help-rejecting complainers) seem more invested in maintaining their roles as downtrodden, victimized, unappreciated, and ineffective parents than in changing these roles. Others prefer to maintain their roles as the rescuers of their "incompetent" children, as they covertly encourage their offspring not to change. Still others opt to be taken care of by their children rather than addressing the children's resulting problematic behaviors (e.g, school phobia, resistance to sleeping apart from the parent, psychosomatic symptoms).

It should be clear to the reader by now that CAT views these parents, whom many might consider to be "resistant" or "difficult," as motivated to seek out personotypic affect and their emotional setpoint and to avoid novel (and, therefore, uncomfortable) feeling states. They unintentionally are motivated to remain the same emotionally—predominantly enraged, victimized, or ashamed of themselves. They, therefore, experience behavioral and cognitive–behavioral interventions as highly threatening, since they require the parents to relinquish core personotypic affects and the emotional setpoint. In essence, these interventions are sending the message to parents: "Give up the bedrock of your entire emotional and interpersonal life." No wonder many parents bridle or withdraw from change and from such protocols.

Behavioral interventions also imply that parents themselves are in control of changing a self-image that they previously thought was immutable. Coming to the therapist mostly to see if he or she can change the child(ren), the parent is now faced with the notion that it is *he or she* that needs to do something differently—and, therefore, that it is he or she who is doing something wrong and needs to change. Parents who are already prone to feeling ashamed of themselves will experience this once again, and may well run away from the therapy—or return for more shame-inducing experiences without attempting to change.

> Joe, a 46-year-old father of three adolescent girls, felt victimized and help-less in his family. According to Joe, his wife would undermine any decisions he would make and harshly rebuke him in front of his children—all of which he would allow—and then his daughters would criticize and ignore him. In CAT parenting group therapy (see Stern, 2000), Joe came to see how this paral-leled his relationship with his highly critical mother, who would often set him up to fail and then berate him. For example, Joe recalled that when he was a boy, his mother would dress him up in white pants and shirt to play baseball with his friends. Naturally, Joe would be unable to keep his clothes clean as he was out playing with his peers all day long, and his mother would scream at him and spank him for not returning spotless. As he grew up, Joe passive–aggressively rebelled against his mother and, later, against his wife by drinking and having affairs. This behavior would naturally pull for more criti-cism and disapproval by his wife, as well as self-hatred.
>
> In the CAT parenting group, Joe came to understand this recurrent pattern and how he set himself up to be a victim. The group then generated some help-ful ways that he could devictimize himself—all of which he promptly ignored. The group got angry and frustrated with Joe, who would often talk over empathic remarks and suggestions from others with his incessant complaining, characteristic of the help-rejecting complainer (Yalom, 1985). The group then discussed how Joe was pulling anger from them and making himself the victim of their annoyed frustration. Only when Joe began to focus on and understand the affects (rage, shame, and self-pity) inherent in his victim stance and how he uses others to rekindle these feelings could he diminish these feelings using cognitive and experiential strategies, and then do the right thing as a parent.

In this chapter, we will describe how CAT can help "difficult" parents who "resist" using more traditional approaches to parent training and family problems. CAT can help difficult parents understand, in a nonshaming way, why they have difficulty accepting and implementing more traditional parenting techniques. It can also help them address the underlying personotypic affect which leads to their supposed resistance and then frees up these parents to employ more tradi-tional behavioral and development-based techniques with their children.

CAT AND THE PARENT–CHILD RELATIONSHIP

CAT's emphasis on attachment makes this approach very compatible with par-ent training. Using CAT concepts, it can be seen that a parent may fail to follow through with a behavioral assignment (which promotes the threat of change) in order to repeat familiar interpersonal patterns and related feelings. *The parent's own relationship with his or her parent(s) is now recreated in the parent's relationship with the child, the latter relationship becoming a security-seeking behavior for the parent.* More specifically, the parent's actions toward the child (e.g., affective presentation and availability, use of rewards and punishments, responsivity to the child, degree of closeness/distance, boundaries, and hierarchy) elicit responses from the child, which can then be interpreted by the parent according to longstanding justifying cognitions (e.g., "I'm unappreciated"; "I'm an ineffective caretaker"; "My child is a victimizing monster"; "I must shelter my weak child from a dangerous world") and personotypic affect (e.g., shame, rageful anger, fear, self-pity). A parent may replace the justifying cognition "I'm a bad son—I should be ashamed of myself" with "I'm a bad father—I should be ashamed of myself," or "I should be ashamed of myself for separating from my parent" with "I should be ashamed of myself for letting my child venture out into the cold, cruel world," or "I hate my father for never giving me the love that I needed" with "I hate my child for not showing me enough love."

A parent may not elicit problematic behaviors from a child, but still may interpret the child's normal behaviors in terms of the parent's justifying cognitions. A child who is acting appropriately can still be seen as uncaring, disobedient, overdemanding, self-centered, too weak, too strong, and so on (Brazelton & Cramer, 1990). Nevertheless, parental perceptions usually result in the child's responding in kind. Being repeatedly called a "bad child," for example, may sooner or later lead the child to feel so frustrated and angry that he or she ends up acting in a way that fulfills the parent's expectations.

All parents are motivated at times by personotypic affect, instead of their logic, while parenting. However, some parents are swayed by personotypic affect a majority of the time. We term these individuals *affect-driven parents,* and we define the affect-driven parent as: (1) motivated by familiar, longstanding, often negative, maladaptive feelings rather than by rational, logical thoughts; (2) having feelings which are derived from how the parent was parented, but not from the current parent–child relationship; (3) having interactions with the child that are driven by the parent's longstanding feelings rather than by what the parent logically thinks would be most helpful to the child (based on developmental principles and what the child is communicating to the parent).

Behavioral and cognitive–behavioral interventions that can alter parent–child interactive patterns become highly threatening to personotypic affect, the emotional setpoint, and justifying cognitions—in essence, threatening to reshape the parent's personality in significant ways and to loosen the glue of the parent's primary attachment to his or her parents. Affect-driven parents, naturally, are particularly wed to personotypic affect, and therapeutic interventions are especially threatening to them. Resistance to parent training may become yet another security-seeking behavior to preserve personotypic affect. Unless parents become aware of how their affect (a) is motivating their parenting behavior, (b) is consequently eliciting problematic behavior in their children, and (c) is working against their conscious, rational wish to improve their parenting skills, little progress can be made using behavioral and cognitive–behavioral strategies.

CAT AND PARENT TRAINING OUTCOME RESEARCH

It should be noted here that outcome studies have yet to be conducted to verify whether CAT is more effective than other approaches in working with "noncompliant" parents. However, in terms of CAT's being applied to impasses in parent training, some outcome research exists supporting our hypothesis that parental issues can block the use of behavioral tools. Griest and Forehand (1982) review studies which indicate that family variables (e.g., marital distress, maternal depression) can impede productive use of parent training. Horne and Patterson (1980) noted that 50% of the participants in their parent training program were not able to implement the requisite skills and needed up to a year of subsequent individual treatment to work through interfering conflicts and improve their negotiation skills.

The role that parents' emotions play in their noncompliance with parent training is still speculative; however, some research suggests that parenting can be improved by helping parents soothe interfering negative feelings. Joyce (1995) found that children's behavior problems were significantly reduced and associated with changes in their parents' irrational beliefs about their self-worth and ability to reduce stress 10 months after their parents participated in a rational–emotive parent education program. Nixon and Singer (1993) found a significant improvement in the parenting of children with severe disabilities by teaching parents to decrease their guilt, self-blame, internal negative attributions, and depression using cognitive–behavioral techniques.

THE CAT PROCESS WITH DIFFICULT PARENTS

Table 15–1 presents a summary of the elements of CAT applied to working with affect-driven parents (which can, for that matter, be used with non-affect-driven parents as well).

Carmen is the 50-year-old custodial caretaker of her daughter's five children. She came to therapy for her two grandsons, 11-year-old Joseph and 9-

TABLE 15–1   CAT with Affect-driven Parents

---

(1) *Assess the personotypic affect, emotional setpoint, justifying cognitions, and security-seeking behaviors in the parent–child interaction*
    (a) Observe a parent(s)–child interaction directly or indirectly
    (b) Explore what parents are experiencing (thinking, feeling) and doing before, during, and after this interaction—about self, child, and therapist
    (c) Assess the type of affect-driven parent (parenting style)
(2) *Create a nonshaming therapeutic environment*
    (a) Therapist self-disclosure
    (b) Explore how the parent was parented to foster empathy
(3) *Differentiate the past from the present*
    (a) Help parents to separate from their parents—experiential work, assertiveness
    (b) Teach parents to soothe feelings and strengthen the influence of logical thoughts over personotypic affect and justifying cognitions—two chairs, role-playing, *in vivo* dyadic work
(4) *Differentiate appropriate guilt from inappropriate shame*

---

year-old Marco, who often fought with each other and with their peers in school. Hardly a day passed when Joseph, in particular, was not fighting quite aggressively in school. Additionally, Marco had significant developmental delays, presumably due to his mother's copious drug use while pregnant with him. Marco had a history of soiling his pants without concomitant constipation since age 5. A gastroenterologist found no physical cause nor damage as the result of the soiling. Both boys also refused to do chores around the house, such as cleaning up their room and washing their dirty dishes, and if told to do so, they would tantrum angrily, scream, curse, cry loudly, and punch the walls. Marco would sometimes smear his feces on the bathroom walls when upset. At such times, Carmen would yell at them, punish them unrealistically (e.g., "Santa Claus will bring you no presents"), and then not follow through on these threats; or she would slap the boys on the legs with her opened hand. None of these approaches had short- or long-term impact on the boys' problematic behaviors.

The boys' mother, Eva, was living in the neighborhood with a new boyfriend, and both were apparently unemployed and drug-addicted. Eva would visit the house sporadically, mostly to ask Carmen for money, and the two would usually end up quarreling loudly. Eva had little to do with her children and Carmen described Eva as competing with her own children for Carmen's money and attention. The children's father had been in jail for the past 5 years, having killed a man in a drug-related incident. The family, believing the children would follow in their father's footsteps if they knew the truth about him, told the children that their father was in the army.

ASSESSING THE EXTENT TO WHICH PARENTS LINK THEIR FEELINGS, THOUGHTS, AND BEHAVIORS TO THOSE OF THEIR CHILDREN

I (Jonathan) often elicit from parents, in the initial intake session, their beliefs about how therapy for their child might be conducted (e.g., seeing the child individually versus involving the parents; expectations about the type and extent of parental involvement) and what kind of changes need to occur for their child to improve his/her behavior. As CAT focuses on parents' feelings, thoughts, and behaviors, this exploration usually gives some indication of how willing parents are to participate in their child's therapy, to include themselves as part of the pre-senting problem and to work on some of their own issues instead of remaining solely child-focused. Certainly, parents' ability to relate their own internal and interpersonal issues to those of their child bodes well for flexible parenting, the quality of parent–child attachment, and therapeutic change (Fonagy, Steele, M., Moran, Steele, H., & Higgitt, 1993; Newberger, 1985).

In my (Jonathan's) experience, few parents maintain that their actions have no impact at all on those of their children; however, many apparently do not connect how their feelings and thoughts influence the parenting choices they make. If a parent of a latency-aged child does not make this connection, I often will have the parent engage in unstructured dyadic interaction with the child à la Stanley Greenspan's (1992) "floortime." (See also Jernberg, 1989, for a sim-ilar and extremely useful *in vivo* method of assessing difficulties in the par-ent–child interaction.) Greenspan's ideal model for parent–child playtime interaction, that which allows the child to build self-confidence while acquir-ing the appropriate social–emotional developmental skills, has the parent allowing the child to take the lead in the play, with the parent serving as an interested, inquisitive, and noncritical commentator on the play action. The parent can mirror what the child is doing and can, especially in the case of a shy child, take the lead only occasionally in moving the play to the next level of interaction (e.g., after a parent repeatedly puts his doll next to the child's and notices that the child's doll is not engaging with that of the parent, the par-ent may have his or her doll say "hello" to the child's doll to attempt to initi-ate an interaction). However, during this assessment, the therapist does not coach the parent on how to be effective at floortime. Instead, he or she just observes the natural interaction unfold as parent and child interchange around play in a characteristic fashion. (Is the parent overly controlling or structuring of the play? Is the parent bored or distant during play? How does the child react interpersonally and emotionally to these parental stances?)

If the child is an adolescent, I will observe patterns of interaction between parent(s) and child, much as a family therapist might, as they discuss or try to solve a problem together. If the parent of a latency-aged child feels too embarrassed to engage in an interaction in front of me, we will draw up a behavioral parenting intervention to be implemented at home over the next few weeks.

Most commonly, some form of problematic parent–child pattern will emerge during dyadic interaction. This then gives the therapist an opportunity to explore with the parents what they were thinking and feeling during the interaction in reference to the child, each other, the interaction, and the presence of the therapist. Behavioral interventions at home also frequently repeat problematic parent–child interactions or are not carried out by parents, and this too gives the therapist an opportunity to explore how and why the parents reacted as they did to the child, to each other, and to the therapist's asking them to carry out a parenting task. (However, direct observation of the complex nuances of a parent–child interaction in the therapist's office almost always yields more information than the parents' reporting to the therapist of the interaction around a behavioral task done at home.) Parents can then to begin to connect their feelings and thoughts while parenting to their parenting choices and the reactions these choices elicit in their children. They can also begin to identify how they react to being observed or being given input and tasks to do at home by the therapist.

> In addition to weekly therapy for each of the boys with different therapists and bimonthly family therapy with the participation of all of the therapists involved, Carmen willingly attended parenting meetings with Jonathan. (Carmen's husband and daughter repeatedly refused to take part.) Over a series of parenting sessions, behavioral programs were established for Marco's soiling and for the boys' fighting at home. A star chart was also set up and rewards were offered to all five children for completing their assigned daily chores.
>
> However, over time, a clear pattern emerged: Carmen welcomed and even initiated some of the behavioral interventions and then was unable to follow through with any of them for more than a few days. Initially, Carmen said that she was "too busy taking care of five children" to consistently use these strategies, but then stated that she had great difficulty both negatively reinforcing (e.g., using time-outs, taking away television privileges) and rewarding the boys. As the thought of rewarding the children entered her mind, Carmen would begin to feel angry that her daughter, supposedly as retribution for having had an unhappy childhood, kept on procreating and had "made" Carmen take care of the children and give up her own career. It became clear that Carmen experienced great rage and self-pity, as well as the guilt-laden belief that she had been forced to care for these children (when other options were actually available).
>
> Additionally, anger emerged at her husband, whom she suspected was quite depressed after retiring recently, for parenting significantly less than she. (Carmen herself had given up a thriving and satisfying career as a beautician

to raise her grandchildren.) While Carmen displayed great interest in and caring for her grandchildren, the notion of giving rewards to them on top of all she had sacrificed for them triggered her rageful anger and self-pity. Furthermore, while she reported not feeling anger toward Jonathan for adding to her many responsibilities with his behavioral interventions (and for being, like her husband, "all talk and no action"), her noncompliance with any of his suggestions may have indicated the presence of anger or resentment.

FOCUSING EMPATHICALLY ON PARENTS' SHAME-BASED ISSUES

Unlike many systemic approaches to working with families which include parents as equal contributors to patterns of interaction (e.g., Papp, 1983), CAT actually shifts the focus to the parents at this point in therapy. If the parent cannot disclose intimate material *without feeling shame,* this shift in focus runs the risk of making the parent feel quite criticized and blamed by the therapist for the child's difficulties. Many parents, thus, pull out of treatment at this early point in the development of the therapeutic alliance (Kalmanson & Seligman, 1992).

As the therapist and parent begin to explore the parent's thoughts and feelings, a high degree of empathy *must* be employed by the therapist to decrease the parent's shame and possible anger at him-herself or at the therapist. A non-shaming therapeutic environment (Wessler, 1993a; Wessler & Hankin-Wessler, 1986) can be created in several ways. First, the therapist can join with the parent by self-disclosing similar experiences and similar feelings. Every therapist, at one time or another, has experienced shame, anger, and self-pity and has thought himself or herself to be incompetent or ineffectual. Most child and family therapists, let alone therapists who are parents, have experienced these feelings while interacting with children. As discussed in greater detail in chapter 7, sharing similar feelings and behaviors turns the parent into an equal rather than placing him in the position of supposedly being judged by a withholding, and therefore "superior," professional.

> *Jonathan shared with Carmen how he could relate to her feeling angry, overwhelmed, and sorry for herself as she parented the children. He told her how he tended to volunteer to take on too many responsibilities at the hospital where, at the time of the therapy, he worked. He initially volunteered with the best of intentions (consciously), but then ended up feeling angry and resentful that he is "given too much work to do." Thus, he came to realize that he nonconsciously sets up the work situation to elicit his personotypic feelings of self-pity and resentful anger and his passive–aggressive way of coping with them.*
> *He also outlined for Carmen how these feelings can subtly hurt his work with some of his clients; how he feels (justifiably) guilty, since this was unfair*

to these clients, who had absolutely nothing to do with the cause of his resentment; how he has come to realize that taking on too much work is his responsibility and not the fault of his bosses or clients; and how he, at that time, struggled not to take on too many responsibilities by more assertively saying "no" to others and not being such a "people-pleaser." This relevant self-disclosure, as well as similar others, was returned to throughout the therapy as Carmen began to acknowledge that she was responsible for her feeling "overwhelmed" and that she nonconsciously elicited from her grandchildren behaviors that perpetuated this feeling. Thus, both therapist and client came to discuss their passive–aggressive work/parenting styles in a collegial manner.

Second, nonblame can arise out of exploring how the parent's *parents* influenced his/her current parenting style. Feelings and thoughts in reaction to the child can be likened to feelings and thoughts elicited by the parent's parents during the parent's own childhood. In this way, not only are the parent's personotypic affects and justifying cognitions identified, but their psychogenesis can be attributed *not* to the parent but to the way the parent was *raised*. Once a client begins to see that his or her shame-inducing parenting style was learned in childhood—when a child has no other choice than to accept and thrive on the type of attachment offered by the parent—then the client's self-blame and the resultant anger at the child can begin to dissipate.

DIFFERENTIATING THE PAST FROM THE PRESENT

As the parent's personotypic affect and justifying cognitions are identified and interrelated, the therapist can help the parent to see how he or she uses interactions with the child as security-seeking behaviors. The parent comes to see that parenting decisions in the present are often made with the nonconscious goal of repeating situations and evoking feelings from the parent's own childhood. In addition to this insight, various interventions, described in chapters 8 and 9, can be used to confront personotypic affect and justifying cognitions.

During therapy, Carmen came to realize that she was "discipline-phobic" and was not willing to punish her children in any way, except by ineffectively yelling at and emptily threatening them. As a child, Carmen lived with an adoptive family who severely abused her physically. Punishments not only far exceeded whatever she had done, but she was often punished for no apparent reason—just to "keep her in line." Carmen had been burned by cigarettes, locked in a closet for hours, had her hair pulled and cut off, and punched repeatedly for such "misbehaviors" as not combing her hair "correctly," taking "too long" to complete her homework, and "looking the wrong way" at an adult. She also witnessed her half-brother chained to a radiator numerous times as punishment. Carmen then repeated this interpersonal pattern by choosing a husband who, before she took him to court, used to beat her and hold a gun to her head when she discussed separating from him.

As a parent, therefore, Carmen came to equate the impact on a child of *any* punishment, even appropriate negative reinforcement, with the abuse she had received as a child. This left her yelling at and threatening the children, but not following through with these threats—and, ultimately, rendered her "power-less" with the children. This apparent powerlessness left Carmen feeling angry at the children's "disrespect" for her, sorry for herself in that she had sacrificed her career for these troublemaking kids, and ashamed of her inability to control the children. She unrealistically believed that she was a "victim" of her grandchildren, as she actually had been a victim of her adoptive parents. Carmen's shame at not effectively impacting the children's behaviors and some of her anger at their supposedly victimizing her diminished significantly as she came to accept over time that her parenting decisions were powerfully influenced by her own childhood victimization and other resultant feelings that persisted and predominated.

TEACHING THE PARENT HOW TO MANAGE PERSONOTYPIC AFFECT

As discussed in chapter 8, emotional self-care can, arise in part, from "doing the right thing" in spite of what one feels. The therapist can help the parent to practice during sessions how to pay more attention to logical, appropriate parenting thoughts rather than to personotypic affect and justifying cognitions. Some parents need to be taught appropriate parenting skills at this point since they never had such skills modeled for them, while others already know the logical thing to do. Likewise, some parents (even parents who are, in general, quite competent) may need to be educated about normal developmental stages in children and teenagers, as parents might have unrealistic expectations of their children (e.g., reasoning with an acting out 4-year-old as if he/she were 10) or they may misinterpret behaviors that are healthy to a particular developmental phase as problematic (e.g., the sulky or explosive belligerence of the teenager; the high activity level of some 3-year-olds). The parent must also understand that personotypic feelings and related cognitions will not go away, but instead must be soothed, chided, or, at times, downright ignored.

Most parents, even those who never were soothed appropriately as children and are not appropriately soothing their child(ren), do know how to comfort others when upset. It is often helpful here to have a parent practice how he or she would comfort another who is feeling ashamed or enraged, and then to apply those comforting skills to his or her own feelings. If the parent, as a child, never had anyone comfort him or her and the parent does not comfort others, the therapist can ask the parent to imagine what he or she would have liked from someone to soothe and comfort his or her upset feelings. The parent can then practice saying these things to him-herself. As mentioned elsewhere, emotional self-care can consist not only of soothing and reassurance, but also of firmly and, at times, angrily cutting off one's unhelpful feelings. Certainly, the good parent knows when to soothe a child's upset and when to ignore it or even cut short the child's tantruming in an angry, firm tone of voice. So, too, can the parent manage his or her own unhelpful, out-of-control feelings in these ways.

Parents are sometimes asked to "split" themselves into what we call the "feeling part" (personotypic affect and justifying cognitions) and the "logical part." After having both parts describe themselves, the logical part then tries to comfort the feeling part, initially with the help of the therapist. Experiential techniques, such as splits and the two-chair dialogue described by Greenberg et al. (1993) and Greenberg and Safran (1987), can be used to enhance the impact of the logical part's managing of the feeling part. However, while experiential therapists most typically use these strategies to enhance affect and soften cognitions, they must be modified here to allow new cognitions to soften personotypic affects.

The parent is then ready to practice managing personotypic feelings and listening to his or her logical part in various parent–child situations. The parent is asked to reenact recent parent–child interactions as they actually occurred, voicing all accompanying feelings and thoughts. The parent then reenacts the interaction a second time and practices managing personotypic affect and following logical parenting thoughts rather than justifying cognitions. At times, it is helpful for the parent to take the child's role and the therapist to assume the parent's role, in order for the therapist to model listening to the logical instead of the feeling part (and for the therapist to experience and share with the client how difficult it can be to do so when placed in an actual parent–child interaction). After the parent feels quite comfortable in the therapy situation, it is helpful to bring in the child and coach the parent to conduct a new, logic-driven dyadic interaction with the child.

> While it initially "made sense" to Carmen that she was unwilling to implement new parenting strategies in order to elicit longstanding feelings which stemmed from her childhood, she had difficulty contacting these feelings as she was actually parenting. In sessions, some of the experiential techniques described by Safran and Segal (1990) were employed in order to intensify and understand such feelings. For example, Carmen described her frustration, anger, and sense of powerlessness in trying to get the boys to clean up their rooms on a daily basis. She understood the potential effectiveness of the behavioral protocol that we had designed, but was repeatedly unable to put it into

action. Instead, she yelled and pleaded with the boys and, ultimately, did their chores herself.

In several therapy sessions, Carmen was asked to imagine hearing and seeing the situation with the boys as if it were happening in the present. At one point, she began to cry and said that she felt helpless to change the situation and that the boys were more powerful than she. She then said she felt angry that they were "taking advantage" of her and "abusing" her time and attention. Jonathan asked if she had ever felt that way before and she connected the feelings first with her marriage and then with her adoptive parents. Jonathan next asked the question, "So why would you keep on doing the same things if they keep leading to such pain and anger?" Carmen responded that maybe she wanted to continue to feel this way but she could not think of any logical reason why.

Carmen then discovered that, as she was beginning to discipline the boys, she would say, "It's hopeless; they'll never listen to me." She then practiced calming down her "powerless feelings," as she called them, by accessing a logical, calming adult voice—and this was difficult for her, as she never had an adult model such a voice to her as she was growing up. The voice would say things like "I know you're feeling it's no use, but try setting consequences for the boys' not cleaning up their room anyway. It will be OK," and "Do your job as a parent; don't feel like a poor little child—you're not anymore." At times, Carmen said she heard Jonathan's voice saying these things as she practiced being logical while parenting.

Diminishing Inappropriate Shame while Augmenting Appropriate Guilt

In addition to helping parents manage personotypic affect, the therapist can also help them to distinguish appropriate (i.e., helpful) guilt from inappropriate (i.e., unhelpful) shame. The reader will recall that guilt is a helpful emotion in that it fosters adaptive self-correction in the individual: "I did something wrong and, therefore, must rectify my behavior." Shame, on the other, hand is unhelpful in that it leads to no self-correction, only painful self-punishment: "I am a bad person. It's hopeless. I can't change who I am." Guilt, therefore, can lead to positive behavioral changes and can coexist with self-confidence while shame cannot.

Affect-driven parents who are very shame-dominated often equate various elements of *effective* parenting with shame. Parents who were physically abused as children or who had parents who did not control their angry outbursts frequently equate any kind of discipline—even appropriate limit-setting and rewards-and-punishments—with abuse. Therefore, to avoid feeling the shame of being an abuser, this parent will shy away from using any kind of discipline.

Overprotective parents tend to overindulge their children since they equate depriving or upsetting their child with being a bad parent. Feeling deprived and sorry for themselves, they swear never to withhold anything from their child. Additionally, these parents are often afraid that, if they discipline their child, they will be judged unfavorably, rejected, and abandoned by the child.

Perfectionistic (and, therefore, compulsive) parents equate deviating even slightly from their personal rules of living that define "the good parent" with shame, failure, and incompetence. They rigidly and angrily control their child's every move, and get flustered and even angrier if the child does something that challenges their internal agenda of what perfect parent–child interactions should be. These parents lack the spontaneity, flexibility, and ability to really listen and respond to their child, which are so important to enhancing the child's sense of competence and identity.

It is, therefore, useful in therapy to empathically highlight how these parents' behaviors are shame-based and derived from their own childhood experiences. It is even more important to let these parents know that what they are doing is harmful to their child—sacrificing the child's healthy development to their own shame and misguided attempts to manage this feeling. Therefore, they *should* feel guilty about their parenting behaviors (but not ashamed of themselves as parents or as people).

The parent who is afraid of feeling like an abuser should learn to distinguish appropriate from inappropriate discipline, should learn how to soothe his or her shameful feelings when disciplining appropriately, and should understand that it is "abusive" *not* to discipline a child at all.

The overprotective parent should similarly learn that not disciplining a child constitutes an "emotional abuse" (what we often call "emotional welfare"), as the child will not learn how to take responsibility for his or her own actions, to problem-solve effectively, or to take care of his or her own emotions adaptively—all important components of healthy development (Greenspan, 1992). Overprotective parents should feel guilty about their overindulgence, which is really a form of narcissism rather than of altruism. Moreover, they should learn, when disciplining a child, to soothe their own shameful feelings and calm unrealistic fears of eternal rejection and abandonment by the child. "Learn to be unpopular—it's part of parenting," we tell these parents. "If you are out to win a popularity contest by overindulging your kids, then you are not helping them to grow up with a sense of competence and strength and, in the long run, you will be less popular with them for this."

And the perfectionistic, compulsive parent must come to feel guilty about not being a flexible, responsive parent while learning how to soothe feelings of shame and replace highly self-critical justifying cognitions with supportive, empathic self-statements. These parents should learn that they are perfection-istic to avoid shame, but their perfectionism is a security-seeking setup for shame and disappointment—unfair to themselves and to their child. Coaching these parents to become Rogerian human beings helps them develop empathy not only for their child, but also for themselves. And the coaching may involve a partly humanistic approach by the therapist to counteract the perfectionist's intense self-criticism. These parents also benefit from learning how to praise their own and their child's efforts more than the outcomes of these efforts.

> *Jonathan worked with Carmen on taking care of her own shame-based feel-ings related to thoughts that she was being "bad" and "abusive," like her adop-tive parents had been toward her, when she was disciplining her grandchildren. First, Jonathan helped Carmen to imagine some of the future consequences of her not disciplining the boys in order to increase her guilty feelings at not par-enting them in a helpful way. Carmen imagined (accurately so) that, if the boys remained the same as they matured, they would not be able to maintain a job; they would look for a quick way to earn money without having to work or follow rules—probably selling drugs or committing other crimes; and, ulti-mately, they would break the law without remorse and go to jail, as their father had done. Consequently, Carmen felt guilty when not disciplining the boys rather than ashamed of being an abuser when disciplining them. She realized, "I would be abusing them if I raised them to turn out like their father."*
>
> *Nevertheless, Carmen and Jonathan soon came to realize that, while saying these logical statements to herself helped diminish her personotypic feelings during sessions, it did not do so at home. Some way of decreasing the intensity of her feelings while parenting was still needed.*

DIMINISHING THE POWER OF THE PARENT'S PERSONOTYPIC AFFECT BY BREAKING AWAY FROM THE PAST

Often, parents are helped to override the power of their personotypic affect by finding ways of psychologically and/or literally detaching from their parents. In our experience, most affect-driven parents remain under the spell of their personotypic feelings, since they have maintained the centrality of their attach-ment to their parents. Clients who were overprotected and/or overindulged by their parents cling to the safety net of the knowledge that, if they mess up, somehow mom and dad will rescue them. Clients who are enraged with their parents find it extremely ego dystonic to move beyond adolescent anger toward mature understanding, acceptance, and/or forgiveness. The CAT ther-apist can bolster the power of the parent's "logical part" by helping the parent

let go of the importance of his/her relationship with his/her parents, and thus
move away from the "inner child" of affect-driven parenting toward the "inner
adult" of newfound logical parenting.

*Jonathan suggested that Carmen imagine talking to her adoptive parents
(who were long dead) and telling them how their parenting was harmful and
"sadistic" and how she will never let herself experience that kind of victimization again. She also practiced hearing her adoptive parents voicing the self-
defeating statements she would make to herself while parenting and then setting limits with her parents as they tried to weaken her resolve.*

*Carmen ended her "discussion" with her adoptive parents by stating that she
did not want to raise her grandchildren to be irresponsible and weak, as she
was raised by them, but instead wanted to punish the boys appropriately to
help them "respect and follow rules, and be strong in doing the right thing—
something that you did not teach me. I will not be your victim anymore." It is
important to note that Jonathan encouraged Carmen to speak to her parents
not with a high pitch of anger and blame, as some more cathartically oriented
approaches advocate, but with mature assertiveness, honesty, and firmness.*

*Ultimately, not only did Carmen's parenting improve, self-confidence
increase, and the power of her personotypic affect decrease, but the boys'
behaviors improved significantly. Both boys virtually stopped fighting; Joseph's
grades improved significantly and he was transferred out of special education
into a mainstream classroom, where he did well academically and interpersonally; Carmen helped to decrease Marco's soiling by implementing a behavioral
program (although he still soiled occasionally when angry); and both boys
began to do chores on a regular basis, reacting only with sulking expressions
sometimes rather than with acting out and angry oppositionalism. The family
could now talk more openly about previously held family secrets (e.g., father's
being in jail), and they were getting somewhat better at sharing their feelings
about their biological parents in a productive fashion.*

*Occasionally, Carmen would return to her old patterns. Jonathan encour-
aged her not to be self-critical or hopeless at these times, but instead to realize
that the old "victim part" of her was fighting for its life as it was being
squelched and that it would continue to do so from time to time. This was a
normal part of progress. Carmen seemed relieved by this explanation and continued on her journey of change.*

SUMMARY

In sum, we challenge parents who believe that parenting should be fun and
easy instead of involving hard work and sacrifice, and we challenge parents

who filter their parenting through unrealistic expectations and their own personotypic affect. We also hold parents solely responsible for the behavioral and emotional difficulties of their children and we rise to the challenge of confronting parents with this belief while still maintaining a solid therapeutic alliance and a nonshaming therapeutic environment.

A step-by-step summary of how CAT works with "difficult" parents is presented in Table 15–1.

REFERENCES

Ainsworth, M. D. S., Bell, S. M., & Stayton, D. J. (1971). Individual differences in strange situation behavior of one-year-olds. In H. R. Schaffer (Ed.), *The origins of human social relations.* London & New York: Academic Press.

Ainsworth, M. D. S., Behar, M., Waters, E., & Wall, S. (1978). *Patterns of attachment.* Hillsdale, NJ: Erlbaum.

Ainsworth, M. D. S., & Eichberg, C. G. (1991). Effects on infant–mother attachment of mother's unresolved loss of an attachment figure or other traumatic experience. In P. Marris, J. Stevenson-Hinde, & C. Parkes (Eds.), *Attachment across the life cycle* (pp. 160–183). New York: Routledge.

Alford, B. A., & Beck, A. T. (1997). *The integrative power of cognitive therapy.* New York: Guilford Press.

Andrews, J. D. W. (1991). *The active self in psychotherapy: An integration of therapeutic styles.* Boston: Allyn & Bacon.

Armstrong, T. (1995). *The myth of the ADD child.* New York: Penguin Books.

Bandura, A. (1977). *Social learning theory.* Englewood Cliffs, NJ: Prentice Hall.

Barkley, R. A. (1990). *Attention-deficit hyperactivity disorder: A handbook of diagnosis and treatment.* New York: Guilford Press.

Barlow, D. H. (1988). *Anxiety and its disorders: The nature and treatment of anxiety and panic.* New York: Guilford Press.

Bartholomew, K., & Horowitz, L. M. (1991). Attachment styles among young adults: A test of a four-category model. *Journal of Personality and Social Psychology, 61,* 226–244.

Bateson, G. (1972). *Steps to an ecology of mind.* New York: Ballantine Books.

Baumeister, R. F., Stillwell, A. M., & Heatherton, T. F. (1994). Guilt: An interpersonal approach. *Psychological Bulletin, 115,* 243–267.

Beaudry, P. (1991). Generalized anxiety disorder. In B. D. Beitman & G. L. Klerman (Eds.), *Integrating pharmacotherapy and psychotherapy* (pp. 211–230). Washington, DC: American Psychiatric Press.

Beck, A. T. (1976). *Cognitive therapy and emotional disorders.* New York: International Universities Press.

Beck, A. T., Freeman, A., & Associates. (1990). *Cognitive therapy of personality disorders.* New York: Guilford Press.

Beck, A. T., Rush, A. J., Shaw, B. F., & Emery, G. (1979). *Cognitive therapy of depression.* New York: Guilford Press.

Bedrosian, R. C., & Beck, A. T. (1980). Principles of cognitive therapy. In M. J. Mahoney (Ed.), *Psychotherapy process: Current issues and future directions.* New York: Plenum Press.

Beitman, B. D., & Klerman, G. L. (Eds.) (1991). *Integrating pharmacotherapy and psychotherapy.* Washington, DC: American Psychiatric Press.

Belsky, J., Rosenberger, K., & Cernic, K. (1995). The origins of attachment security: "Classical" and contextual determinants. In S. Goldberg, R. Muir, & J. Kerr (Eds.), *Attachment theory: Social, developmental, and clinical perspectives* (pp. 153–184). Hillsdale, NJ: The Analytic Press.

Benoit, D., & Parker, K. C. H. (1994). Stability and transmission of attachment across three generations. *Child Development, 65,* 1444–1456.

Berzins, J. I. (1977). Therapist–patient matching. In A. S. Gurman & A. M. Razin (Eds.), *Effective psychotherapy: A handbook of research* (pp. 222–251). Elmsford, NY: Pergamon Press.

Borden, K. A. & Brown, R. T. (1989). Attributional outcomes: The subtle messages of treatments for attention deficit disorder. *Cognitive Therapy and Research, 13*(2), 147–160.

Bowlby, J. (1969). *Attachment and loss. Vol. 1: Attachment.* New York: Basic Books.

Bowlby, J. (1973). *Attachment and loss. Vol. 2: Separation: Anxiety and anger.* New York: Basic Books.

Bowlby, J. (1980). *Attachment and loss. Vol. 3: Loss: Sadness and depression.* New York: Basic Books.

Brazelton, T. B., & Cramer, B. G. (1990). *The earliest relationship: Parents, infants, and the drama of early attachment.* Reading, MA: Addison-Wesley.

Brehm, J. W., & Cohen, A. R. (1962). *Explorations in cognitive dissonance.* New York: John Wiley.

Brickman, P., Rabinowitz, V. C., Karuza, J., Coates, D., Cohn, E., & Kidder, L. (1982). Models of helping and coping. *American Psychologist, 37*(4), 368–384

Brickman, P., Rabinowitz, V. C., Karuza, I., Coates, D., Cohn, E., & Kidder, L. (1982). Models of helping and coping. *American Psychologist, 37*(4), 368–384.

Bridges, L. J., Connell, J. P. & Belsky, J. (1988). Similarities and differences in infant-mother and infant-father interaction in the strange situation: A component process analysis. *Developmental Psychology, 24*(1), 92–100.

Brill, N. Q. (1967). Gross stress reaction: II. Traumatic war neuroses. In A. M. Freedman & H. L. Kaplan (Eds.), *Comprehensive textbook of psychiatry* (pp. 1031–1035). Baltimore: Williams & Wilkins.

Brooks, V. R. (1981). Sex and sexual orientation as variables in therapists' biases and therapy outcomes. *Clinical Social Work, 9*(3), 198–210.

Brooks, R. B., Baltazar, P. L., McDowell, D. E, & Munjack, D. J. (1991). Personality disorders co-occurring with panic disorder and agoraphobia. *Journal of Personality Disorders, 5,* 328–336.

Brown, G. W., Bone, M., Dalison, B., & Wing, J. K. (1966). *Schizophrenia and social care.* London: Oxford University Press.

Burgess, A. W., & Holstrom, L. L. (1974). *Rape: Victims of crisis.* Bowie, MD: R. J. Brady.

Burns, D. D. (1980). *Feeling good: The new mood therapy.* New York: New American Library.

Caro, I. (1996). The linguistic therapy of evaluation: A perspective on language in psychotherapy. *Journal of Cognitive Psychotherapy, 10*(2), 83–104.

Carson, R. C. (1969). *Interaction concepts of personality.* Chicago: Aldine Publishing.

Cashdan, S. (1988). *Object relations therapy: Using the relationship.* New York: W. W. Norton.

Cassidy, J., & Marvin, R. S. (1987/1992). *Attachment organization in three- and four-year-olds: Coding guidelines.* Unpublished manual, Psychology Dept. of Univ. of Virginia: Charlottesville, VA.

Chengappa, K. N. R., Ebeling, T., Kang, J. S., Levine, J., & Parepally, H. (1999). Clozapine reduces severe self-mutilation and aggression in psychotic patients with borderline personality disorder. *Journal of Clinical Psychiatry, 60,* 477–484.

Chibucos, T. R., & Kail, P. R. (1981). Longitudinal examination of father–infant interaction and infant–father attachment. *Merrill-Palmer Quarterly, 27,* 81–96.

Chiles, J. A., Carlin, A. S., Benjamin, G. A. H., & Beitman, B. D. (1991). A physician, nonmedical psychotherapist, and a patient: The pharmacological–psychotherapy triangle. In B. D Beitman

& G. L. Klerman (Eds.), *Integrating pharmacotherapy and psychotherapy* (pp. 105–118). Washington, DC: American Psychiatric Press.

Choca, J. D., Shanley, L.A., & Van Denburg, E. (1992). *Interpretative guide to the Millon Clinical Multiaxial Inventor.* Washington, D.C.: American Psychological Association.

Cicirelli, V. G. (1991). Attachment theory in old age: Protection of the attached figure. In K. Pillemer & K. McCartney (Eds.), *Parent–child relations across the life course* (pp. 25–42). Hillsdale, NJ: Erlbaum.

Clark, L. (1985). *SOS! Help for parents.* Bowling Green, KY: Parents Press.

Clark, W. M., & Serovich, J. M. (1997). Twenty years and still in the dark? Content analysis of articles pertaining to gay, lesbian, and bisexual issues in marriage and family therapy journals. *Journal of Marital and Family Therapy, 23*(3), 239–253.

Clarke-Stewart, A. (1978). And daddy makes three: The father's impact on mother and young. *Child Development, 49*, 466–478.

Cobb, C. (1993). *Patterns of attachment and family paradigms.* Unpublished doctoral dissertation. Department of Sociology, York University, Downsview, Ontario, Canada.

Cox, M. J., Owen, M. T., Henderson, V. K., & Margand, N. A. (1992). Prediction of infant–father and infant–mother attachment. *Developmental Psychology, 28*, 474–483.

Crittenden, P. M. (1985). Maltreated infants: Vulnerability and resilience. *Journal of Child Psychology and Psychiatry, 26*, 85–96.

Crittenden P. M. (1992). Treatment of anxious attachment in the preschool years. *Developmental Psychopathology, 4*, 575–602.

DeJong, C. A. J., van den Brink, W., Jansen, J. A. M., & Schippers, G. M. (1989). Interpersonal aspects of DSM–III Axis II: Theoretical hypotheses and empirical findings. *Journal of Personality Disorders, 3*, 135–146.

Diamond, D., & Doane, J. A. (1994). Disturbed attachment and negative affective stye: An intergenerational spiral. *British Journal of Psychiatry, 164*, 770–781.

Ehrenberg, D. B. (1992). *The intimate edge: Extending the reach of psychoanlytic interaction.* New York: W. W. Norton.

Ellis, A. (1962). *Reason and emotion in psychotherapy.* New York: Lyle Stuart.

Ellis, A. (1994). *A rational emotive behavior therapy approach to personality disorders.* Presented at the annual American Counseling Association conference, April 25, 1994, Minneapolis, MN.

Ellis, A. (1977). The basic clinical theory of rational–emotive therapy. In A. Ellis & R. Greiger (Eds.), *Handbook of rational–emotive therapy, Vol. 1.* (pp. 3–34). New York: Springer.

Emde, R. N., Klingman, D. H., Reich, J. H., & Wade, J. D. (1978). Emotional expression in infancy: I. Initial studies of social signaling and an emergent model. In M. Lewis & M. Rosenblum (Eds.), *The development of affect.* New York: Plenum Press.

Epstein, L., & Feiner, A. H. (1979). Countertransference: The therapist's contribution to treatment. *Contemporary Psychoanalysis, 15*, 489–513.

Evans, E. H., & McAdam, E. (1988). Training parents to be effective. In W. Dryden, & P. Trower (Eds.), *Developments in cognitive psychotherapy* (pp. 218–238). London: Sage.

Fancher, R. E. (1973). *Psychoanalytic psychology: The development of Freud's thought.* New York: W. W. Norton.

Feeney, J. A., & Noller, P. (1990). Attachment style as a predictor of adult romantic relationships. *Journal of Personality and Social Psychology, 58*, 281–291.

Festinger, L. (1957). *A theory of cognitive dissonance.* Stanford, CA: Standford University Press.

Fonagy, P. (1996). Attachment, the development of the self, and its pathology in personality disorders. *Plenary: Implications of research on attachment for psychotherapy.* Society for the Exploration of Psychotherapy Integration 12th Annual Conference (26th April, 1996).

Fonagy, P., Steele, M., Moran, G. S., Steele, H., & Higgitt, A. C. (1993). Measuring the ghost in the nursery: An empirical study of the relation between parents' mental representations of childhood experiences and their infants' security of attachment. *Journal of the American Psychoanalytic Association, 41,* 957–989.

Fonagy, P., Steele, M., & Steele, H. (1991). Maternal representations of attachment during pregnancy predict the organization of infant–mother attachment at one year of age. *Child Development, 62,* 880–893.

Fonagy, P., Steele, M., Steele, H., Leigh, T., Kennedy, R., Mattoon, G., & Target, M. (1995). Attachment, the reflective self, and borderline states: The predictive specificity of the adult attachment interview and pathological emotional development. In S. Goldberg, R. Muir, & J. Kerr (Eds.) *Attachment theory: Social, developmental, and clinical perspectives* (pp. 233–278). Hillsdale, NJ: The Analytic Press

Forehand, R. L., & McMahon, R. J. (1981). *Helping the noncompliant child.* New York: Guilford Press.

Freedman, M. B., Leary, T. F., Ossorio, A. G, & Coffey, H. S. (1951). The interpersonal dimension of personality. *Journal of Personality, 20,* 143–161.

Freud, S. (1895/1954). Project for a scientific psychology. In S. Freud, *The origins of psychoanalysis: Letters to Wilhem Fliess* (pp. 347–446). New York: Basic Books.

Freud, S. (1920). Beyond the pleasure principle. In S. Freud, *The standard edition of the complete psychological works of Sigmund Freud* (Vol. 18, pp. 3–64). London, UK: Hogarth Press.

Freud, S. (1924). The dissolution of the Oedipus complex. In S. Freud, *The standard edition of the complete psychological works of Sigmund Freud* (Vol. 19, pp. 171–179). London, UK: Hogarth Press.

Freud, S. (1926). Inhibitions, symptoms, and anxiety. In S. Freud, *The standard edition of the complete psychological works of Sigmund Freud* (Vol. 20, pp. 75–175). London, UK: Hogarth Press.

Goldberg, S. (1995). Introduction. In S. Goldberg, R. Muir, & J. Kerr (Eds.) *Attachment theory: Social, developmental, and clinical perspectives* (pp. 1–18). Hillsdale, NJ: The Analytic Press.

Goldberg, S., Muir, R., & Kerr, J. (1995). *Attachment theory: Social developmental, and clinical perspectives.* Hillsdale, NJ: The Analytic Press.

Gramzow, R., & Tangney, J. P. (1992). Proneness to shame and the narcissistic personality. *Personality and Social Psychology Bulletin, 18,* 369–376.

Greenberg, J. R., & Mitchell, S. A. (1983). *Object relations in psychoanalytic theory.* Cambridge, MA: Harvard University Press.

Greenberg, L. S., Rice, L. N., & Elliott, R. (1993). *Facilitating emotional change: The moment-by-moment process.* New York: Guilford Press.

Greenberg, L. S., & Safran, J. D. (1987). *Emotion in psychotherapy: Affect, cognition, and the process of change.* New York: Guilford Press.

Greenberg, L. S., & Safran, J. D. (1989). Emotion in psychotherapy. *American Psychologist, 44,* 19–29.

Greenspan, S. I. (1992). *Infancy and early childhood: The practice of clinical assessment and intervention with emotional and developmental challenges.* Madison, CT: International Universities Press.

Griest, D. L., & Forehand, R. (1982). How can I get any parent training done with all these other problems going on? The role of family variables in child behavior therapy. *Child and Family Behavior Therapy, 41,* 73–80.

Guidano, V. F., & Liotti, G. (1983). *Cognitive processes and emotional disorders.* New York: Guilford Press.

Gunderson, J. G., & Phillips, K. A. (1991). A current view of the interface between borderline personality disorder and depression. *American Journal of Psychiatry, 148,* 967–975.

Hankin, S. W. R. (1997). El proceso terapéutico en la terápia de valoración cognitiva. In I. Caro (Ed.), *Manual de terápias cognitivas* (pp. 261–278). Barcelona: Paidos.

Harlow, H. F. (1958). The nature of love. *American Psychologist, Dec. 13,* 673–685.

Harris, J. R. (1998). *The nurture assumption.* New York: Simon & Schuster.

Hazan, C., & Shaver, P. (1987). Romantic love conceptualized as an attachment process. *Journal of Personality and Social Psychology, 52,* 511–524.

Hazan, C., & Shaver, P. (1990). Love and work: An attachment-theoretical perspective. *Journal of Personality and Social Psychology, 59,* 270–280.

Heider, F. (1958). *The psychology of interpersonal relations.* New York: John Wiley & Sons.

Herman, J. L., Perry, J. C., & van der Kolk, B. A. (1989). Childhood trauma in borderline personality disorder. *American Journal of Psychiatry, 146,* 490–495.

Herman, J. L., & van der Kolk, B. A. (1987). Traumatic antecedents of borderline personality disorder. In B. A. van der Kolk, *Psychological trauma* (pp. 111–126). Washington, DC: American Psychiatric Press.

Hirschfeld, R. M. A. (1997). Pharmacotherapy of borderline personality disorder. *Journal of Clinical Psychiatry, 58,* 48–52.

Hollander, E. (1999a). Managing aggressive behavior in patients with obsessive–compulsive disorder and borderline personality disorder. *Journal of Clinical Psychiatry Monograph Series, 17,* 28–31.

Hollander, E. (1999b). Managing aggressive behavior in patients with obsessive–compulsive disorder and borderline personality disorder. *Journal of Clinical Psychiatry, 60,* 38–44.

Horne, A. M., & Patterson, G. R. (1980). Working with parents of aggressive children. In R. A. Abidin (Ed.), *Parent education and intervention handbook* (pp. 159–184). Springfield, IL: Charles C. Thomas.

Horowitz, M. J. (1976). *Stress response syndromes.* New York: Jason Aronson.

Horowitz, M. J. (1988). *Introduction to psychodynamics: A new synthesis.* Chicago: University of Chicago Press.

Izard, C. E., Haynes, O. M., Chisholm, G., & Baak, K. (1991). Emotional determinants of infant–mother attachment. *Child Deveopment, 62,* 906–917.

Jernberg, A. M. (1989). Training parents of failure-to-attach children. In C. E. Schaefer & J. M. Briesmeister (Eds.), *Handbook of parent training: Parents as co-therapists for children's behavior problems* (pp. 392–413). New York: John Wiley & Sons.

Johnson, M. M. (1988). *Strong mothers, weak wives.* Berkeley: University of California Press.

Joiner, T. E. (1996). A confirmatory factor analytic investigation of the tripartate model of depression and anxiety in college students. *Cognitive Therapy and Research, 20,* 521–539.

Joiner, T. E., Catanzaro, S. J., & Laurent, J. (1996). The tripartite structure of positive and negative affect, depression, and anxiety in child and adolescent psychiatric inpatients. *Journal of Abnormal Psychology, 105,* 401–409.

Joiner, T. E., Steer, R. A., Beck, A. T., Schmidt, N. B., Rudd, M. D., & Catanzaro, S. J. (1999). Physiological hyperarousal: Construct validity of a central aspect of the tripartate model of depression and anxiety. *Journal of Abnormal Psychology, 108,* 290–298.

Joyce, M. R. (1995). Emotional relief for parents: Is rational–emotive parent education effective? *Journal of Rational–Emotive and Cognitive Behavior Therapy, 13,* 55–75.

Kagan, J. (1989). Unstable ideas. Cambridge, MA, and London, UK: Harvard University Press.

Kalmanson, B., & Seligman, S. (1992). Family–provider relationships: The basis of all interventions. *Infants and Young Children, 4,* 46–52.

Kantor, D., & Lehr, W. (1975). *Inside the family.* San Francisco, CA: Jossey-Bass.

Kelly, G. A. (1955). *The psychology of personal constructs. Vol. 1, A theory of personality.* Englewood Cliffs, NJ: Prentice-Hall.

Kiesler, D. J. (1982). Confronting the client–therapist relationship in psychotherapy. In J. C. Anchin & D. J. Kiesler (Eds.), *Handbook of interpersonal psychotherapy* (pp. 274–295). Elmsford, NY: Pergamon Press.

Kiesler, D. J. (1986). Interpersonal methods of diagnosis and treatment. In R. Michels & J. O. Cavenar, Jr. (Eds.), *Psychiatry* (Vol. 1, pp. 1–23). Philadelphia: Lippincott.

Kiesler, D. J. (1987). Complementarity: Between whom and under what conditions? *Clinician's Research Digest: Supplemental Bulletin, 5*(20).

Kiesler, D. J. (1996). *Contemporary interpersonal theory & research: Personality, psychopathology and psychotherapy.* New York: John Wiley & Sons.

Kiesler, D. J., Anchin, J. C., Perkins, M. J., Chirico, B. M., Kyle, E. M., & Federman, E. J. (1976). The Impact Message Inventory: Form II. Richmond, VA: Virginia Commenwealth University.

Kiesler, D. J., Anchin, J. C., Perkins, M. I., Chirico, B. M., Kyle, E. M., & Federman, E. J. (1985). *The Impact Message Inventory: Form II.* Palo Alto, CA: Consulting Psychologist Press.

Kiesler, D. J., & Schmidt, J. A. (1993). *The Impact Message Inventory: Form IIA Octant Scale Version.* Palo Alto, CA: Mind Garden.

Kiesler, D. J., & Watkins, L. M. (1989). Interpersonal complementarity and the therapeutic alliance: A study of relationship in psychotherapy. *Psychotherapy, 26,* 183–194.

Kiernat, J. M. (1984). Geriatric therapy: Is mental health included? *Physical and Occupational Therapy in Geriatrics, 3*(4), 3–10.

Kindler, S., Dannon, P. N., Iancu, I., Sasson, Y., & Zohar, J. (1997). Emergence of kleptomania during treatment for depression with serotonin selective reuptake inhibitors. *Clinical Neuropharmacology, 20,* 126–129.

Kirsch, I. (1985). Response expectancy as a determinant of experience and behavior, *American Psychologist, 40,* 1189–1202.

Kirsch, I. (1990). *Changing expectancies: A key to effective psychotherapy.* Pacific Grove, CA: Brooks/Cole.

Klar, H., Siever, L. J., & Coccaro, E. (1988). Psychobilogic approaches to personality and its disorders: An overview. *Journal of Personality Disorders, 2,* 334–341.

Klass, E. T. (1987). Situational approach to the assessment of guilt: Development and validation of a self-report measure. *Journal of Psychopathology and Behavioral Assessment, 9,* 35–48.

Klass, E. T. (1990). Guilt, shame, and embarrassment: cognitive–behavioral approaches. In H. Leitenberg (Ed.), *Handbook of social and evaluation anxiety* (pp. 385–414). New York: Plenum Press.

Klerman, G. L. (1991). Ideoogical conflicts in integrating pharmacotherapy and psychotherapy. In B. D Beitman & G. L. Klerman (Eds.), *Integrating pharmacotherapy and psychotherapy* (pp. 3–19). Washington, DC: American Psychiatric Press.

Klerman, G. L., Weissman, M. M., Rounsaville, B. J., & Chevron, E. S. (1984). *Interpersonal psychotherapy of depression.* New York: Basic Books.

Kobak, R. R., & Sceery, A. (1988). Attahment in late adolescence: Working models, affect regulation, and representations of self and others. *Child Development, 59,* 135–146.

Koenigsburg, H. W. (1991). Borderline personality disorder. In B. D. Beitman & G. L. Klerman (Eds.), *Integrating pharmacotherapy and psychotherapy* (pp. 271–290). Washington, DC: American Psychiatric Press.

LaForge, R., & Suczek, R. F. (1955). The interpersonal dimension of personality: III. An interpersonal ckeck list. *Journal of Personality, 24,* 94–112.

LaForge, R., Freedman, M. B., & Wiggins, J. S. (1985). Interpersonal circumplex models: 1948–1983 (symposium). *Journal of Personality Assessment, 49,* 613–621.

Lamb, M. E. (1982). The father-child relationship: A synthesis of biological, evolutionary, and social perspectives. In L. Hoffman, R. Gandelman, & H.R. Schoffman (Eds.), *Parenting: Its causes and consequences* (pp. 55–73). Hillsdale, NJ: Erlbaum.

Lazarus, A. A. (1976). *Multimodal behavior therapy.* New York: Springer.

Lazarus, A. A., & Fay, A. (1982). Resistance or rationalization? A cognitive behavioral perspective. In P. L. Wachtel (Ed.), *Resistance: Psychodynamic and behavioral approaches* (pp. 115–132). New York: Plenum Press.

Lazarus, R. S. (1991). Cognition and motivation in emotion. *American Psychologist, 46,* 352–367.

Leary, T. (1957). *Interpersonal diagnosis of personality: a functional theory and methodology for personality evaluation.* New York: Ronald Press.

Lederer, W., & Jackson, D. D. (1968). *Mirages of marriage.* New York: W. W. Norton.

Lee, C. M., & Gotlib, I. H. (1991). Adjustment of children of depressed mothers: A 10-month follow-up. *Journal of Abnormal Psychology, 100,* 473–477.

Leventhal, H. (1984). A perceptual–motor theory of emotion. In L. Berkowitz (Ed.), *Advances in experimental social psychology*. New York: Academic Press.

Lewicki, P. (1986). *Nonconscious social information processing*. Orlando, FL: Academic Press.

Lewis, M. (1992). Self-conscious emotions and the development of self. In T. Shapiro & R. N. Emde (Eds.), *Affect: Psychoanalytic perspectives* (pp. 45–73). Madison, CT: International Universities Press.

Lewis, M., Sullivan, M. W., & Michalson, L. (1984). The cognitive–emotional fugue. In C. E. Izard, J. Kagan, & R. B. Zajonc (Eds.), *Emotions, cognition, & behavior* (pp. 264–288). Cambridge: Cambridge University Press.

Liotti, G. (1986). Structural cognitive therapy. In W. Dryden & W. Golden (Eds.), *Cognitive–behavioural approaches to therapy*. London, UK: Harper & Row.

MacLean, G., & Wessely, S. (1994). Professional and popular views of chronic fatigue syndrome. *British Medical Journal, 308*, 776–777.

Mahoney, M. J. (1985). Psychotherapy and human change processes. In M. J. Mahoney & A. Freeman (Eds.), *Cognition and psychotherapy* (pp. 3–48). New York: Plenum.

Mahoney, M. J. (1991). *Human change processes: The scientific foundations of psychotherapy*. New York: Basic Books.

Mahoney, M. J., & Mahoney, K. (1976). Self control techniques with the mentally retarded. *Exceptional Children, 42*, 338–339.

Maier, W., Lichtermann, D., Klingler, T., & Heun, R. (1992). Prevalences of personality disorders (DSM–III–R) in the community. *Journal of Personality Disorders, 6*, 187–196.

Main, M. (1995). Recent studies in attachment: Overview, with selected implications for clinical work. In S. Goldberg, R. Muir, & J. Kerr (Eds.) *Attachment theory: Social, developmental, and clinical perspectives* (pp. 407–474). Hillsdale, NJ: The Analytic Press

Main, M., & Cassidy, J. (1987). Categories of response to reunion with the parent at age 6: Predictable from infant attachment classifications and stable over a 1-month period. *Developmental Psychology, 24*, 415–426.

Main, M., Kaplan, N., & Cassidy, J. (1985). Security in infancy, childhood and adulthood: A move to the level of representation. In I Bretherton & E. Waters (Eds.), *Growing points in attachment theory and research. Monographs of the Society for Research in Child Development*, Serial No. 209, Vol. 50, Nos. 1–2, 66–104.

Main, M., & Solomon, J. (1986). Discovery of a new, insecure–disorganized/disoriented attachment pattern. In T. B. Brazelton & M. Yogman (Eds.), *Affective development in infancy* (pp. 95–124). Norwood, NJ: Ablex.

Main, M., & Solomon, J. (1990). Procedures for identifying infants as disorganized/disoriented during the Ainsworth Strange Situation. In M. T. Greenberg, D. Cichetti, & E. M. Cummings (Eds.), *Attachment in the preschool years* (pp. 121–160). Chicago: University of Chicago Press.

Malan, D. H. (1979). *Individual psychotherapy and the science of psychodynamics*. London, UK: Butterworths.

Mash, E. J., Hamerlynk, L. J., & Handy, L. C. (Eds.) (1976). *Behavioral modification and families*. New York: Brunner/Mazel.

Maturana, H. R. (1975). The organization of the living: A theory of the living organization. *International Journal of Man–Machine Studies, 7*, 313–332.

Mavissakalian, M. (1990). The relationship between panic disorder/agoraphobia and personality disorders. *Psychiatric Clinics of North America, 13*, 661–684.

McCann, I. L., & Pearlman, L. A. (1990). *Psychological trauma and the adult survivor: Theory, therapy, and transformation*. New York: Brunner/Mazel.

McGoldrick, M. (Ed.) (1998). *Re-visioning family therapy: Race, culture, and gender in clinical practice*. New York: Guilford Press.

McGoldrick, M., Pearce, J. K., & Giordano, J. (Eds.) (1982). *Ethnicity & family therapy*. New York: Guilford Press.

Meichenbaum, D. (1977). *Cognitive behavior modification*. New York: Plenum Press.

Meichenbaum, D., & Gilmore, J. B. (1984). The nature of unconscious processes: A cognitive–behavioral perspective. In K. S. Bowers & D. Meichenbaum (Eds.), *The unconscious reconsidered*. New York: John Wiley & Sons.

Mellman, T. A., Leverich, G. S., Hauser, P., & Kramlinger, K. L. (1992). Axis II pathology in panic and affective disorders: Relationship to diagnosis, course of illness, and treatment response. *Journal of Personality Disorders, 6,* 53–63.

Millon, T. (1987). *Millon Clinical Multiaxial Inventory Manual* II. Minneapolis: National Computer Systems.

Millon, T. (1992). Millon Clinical Multiaxial Inventory: I and II. *Journal of Counseling and Development, 70,* 421–426.

Millon, T. (1996). *Disorders of personality: DSM–IV and beyond*. New York: John Wiley & Sons.

Millon, T., & Everly, G. S. (1985). *Personality and its disorders*. New York: John Wiley & Sons.

Minuchin, S., & Fishman, H. C. (1981). *Family therapy techniques*. Cambridge, MA: Harvard University Press.

Mosher, D. L. (1966). The development and multitrait–multimethod matrix analysis of three measures of three aspects of guilt. *Journal of Consulting and Clinical Psychology, 30,* 25–29.

Mosher, D. L. & Tomkins, S. S. (1988). Scripting the macho man: Hypermasculine socialization and enculturation. *Journal of Sex Research, 25*(1), 60–84.

Mowrer, O. H. (1948). Learning theory and the neurotic paradox. *American Journal of Orthopsychiatry, 18,* 571–610.

Muran, J. C., & Safran, J. D. (1993). Emotional and interpersonal considerations in cognitive therapy. In K. T. Kuehlwein & H. Rosen (Eds.), *Cognitive therapies in action: Evolving innovative practice* (pp. 185–212). San Francisco: Jossey-Bass.

Muran, J. C., Samstag, L. W., Jilton, R., Batchelder, S., & Winston, A. (1992a). *Measuring patient–therapist interactions across time from a third-party perspective*. Unpublished manuscript, Beth Israel Medical Center, New York, NY.

Muran, J. C., Samstag, L. W., Jilton, R., Batchelder, S., & Winston, A. (1992b). *Relation of interpersonal behavior and transactions to alliance and outcome over time in short-term psychotherapy*. Unpublished manuscript, Beth Israel Medical Center, New York, NY.

Muran, J. C., Segal, Z. V., Wallner Samstag, L., & Crawford, C. E. (1994). Patient pretreatment interpersonal problems and therapeutic alliance in short-term cogitive therapy. *Journal of Consulting and Clinical Psychology, 62,* 185–190.

Nathanson, D. L. (1987). *The many faces of shame*. New York: Guilford Press.

Nathanson, D. L. (1992). *Shame and pride: Affect, sex, and the birth of the self*. New York: W. W. Norton.

Newberger, C. M. (1985). Parents and practitioners as developmental theorists. In E. H. Newberger & R. Bourne (Eds.), *Unhappy families* (pp. 131–144). Littleton, MA: PSB Publishing.

Nixon, C. D., & Singer, G. H. (1993). Group cognitive–behavioural treatment for excessive parental self-blame and guilt. *American Journal of Mental Retardation, 97,* 665–672.

Noshpitz, J. D., & King, R. A. (1991). *Pathways of growth: Essentials of child psychiatry. Vol. 2: Psychopathology*. New York: John Wiley & Sons.

Novaco, R. W. (1975). *Anger control: The development and evaluation of an experiential treatment*. Lexington, MA: Lexington Press.

Novaco, R. W. (1977). Stress inoculation: A cognitive therapy for anger and its application to a case of depression. *Journal of Consulting and Clinical Psychology, 45,* 600–608.

Ohlwein, A. L., Stevens, M. J., & Catanzaro, S. J. (1996). Self-efficacy, response expectancy, and temporal context: Moderators of pain tolerance and intensity. *Imagination, Cognition, and Personality, 16*(1), 3–23.

Oldham, J. M., Skodol, A. E., Kellman, H. D., & Hyler, S. E. (1995). Comorbidity of Axis I and Axis II disorders. *American Journal of Psychiatry, 152,* 571–578.

Osgood, C. E., May, W. H., & Miron, M. S. (1975). *Cross-cultural universals of affective meaning.* Urbana, IL: University of Illinois Press.

Papp, P. (1983). *The process of change.* New York: Guilford Press.

Parkes, C. M. (1972). *Bereavement: Studies of grief in adult life.* New York: International Universities Press.

Perkins, M. J., Kiesler, D. J., Anchin, J. C., Chirico, B. M., Kyle, E. M., & Federman, E. J. (1979). The Impact Message inventory: A new measure of relationship in counseling/psychotherapy and other dyads. *Journal of Counseling Psychology, 26,* 363–367.

Pfohl, B. (1983). *Structured Interview for DSM-IV Personality Disorders (SIDP).* Iowa City: University of Iowa College of Medicine.

Pine, F. (1985). *Developmental theory and clinical process.* New Haven: Yale University Press.

Plutchik, R. (1981). Group cohesion in psychoevolutionary context. In H. Kellerman (Ed.), *Group cohesion* (pp. 133–140). Baltimore: Grune & Stratton.

Plutchik, R. (1997). The circumplex as a general model of the structure of emotions and personality. In R. Plutchik & H. R. Conte (Eds.), *Circumplex models of personality and emotions* (pp. 17–46). Washington, DC: American Psychological Association Press.

Plutchik, R., & Conte, H. R. (1997). *Circumplex models of personality and emotions.* Washington, DC: American Psychological Association Press.

Pretzer, J. L., & Beck, A.T. (1986). A cognitive theory of personality disorders. In J. F. Clarkin & M. F. Lenzzenweger (Eds.), *Major theories of personality disorders* (pp. 36–105). New York: Guilford Press.

Pretzer, J., & Fleming, B. (1989). Cognitive- behavioral treatment of personality disorders. The *Behavior Therapist, 12,* 105–109.

Rice, P. L. K. (1970). The modification of interpersonal role. *Dissertation Abstracts International, 30,* 4797B.

Rind, B., Tromovitch, P., & Bauserman, R. (1998). A meta-analytic examination of assumed properties of child sexual abuse using college samples. *Psychological Bulletin, 124(1),* 22–53.

Ronningstam, E., Gunderson, J., & Lyons, M. (1995). Changes in pathological narcissism. *American Journal of Psychiatry, 152,* 253–257.

Rose, S. D. (1989). *Working with adults in groups.* San Francisco: Jossey-Bass.

Rotter, J. B. (1954). *Social learning and clinical psychology.* Englewood Cliffs, NJ: Prentice-Hall.

Rotter, J. B. (1966). Generalized expectancies for internal versus external control of reinforcement. *Psychological Monographs, 80,* whole no. 609.

Rotter, J. B. (1978). Generalized expectancies for problem solving and psychotherapy. *Cognitive psychotherapy, 2,* 1–10.

Rotter, J. B., Chance, J. E., & Phares, E. J. (1972). *Applications of a social learning theory of personality.* New York: Holt, Rinehart and Winston.

Rotter, J. B., & Hochreich, D. J. (1975). *Personality.* Glenview, IL: Scott, Foresman.

Rovee-Collier, C. K., Sullivan, M. W., Enright, M., Lucas, D., & Fagan, J. W. (1980). Reactivism of infant memory. *Science 208,* 1159–1161.

Roy, A., Virkkunen, M., & Linnoila, M. (1990). Serotonin in suicide, violence and alcoholism. In E. F. Coccaro & D. L. Murphy (Eds.), *Serotonin in major psychiatric disorders* (pp. 187–208). Washington, DC: American Psychiatric Press.

Rush, A. J., & Hollon, S. D. (1991). Depression. In B. D. Beitman & G. L. Klerman (Eds.), *Integrating pharmacotherapy and psychotherapy* (pp. 121–142). Washington, DC: American Psychiatric Press.

Sack, A., Sperling, M. B., Fagen, G., & Foelsch, P. (1996). Attachment style, history, and behavioral contrasts for a borderline and normal sample. *Journal of Personality Disorders, 10,* 88–102.

Safran, J. D. (1998). *Widening the scope of cognitive therapy: The therapeutic relationship, emotion, and the process of change.* Northvale, NJ: Jason Aronson.

Safran, J. D., Crocker, P., McMain, S., & Murray, P. (1990). Therapeutic alliance rupture as a therapy event for empirical investigation. *Psychotherapy, 27,* 154–165.

Safran, J. D., & Muran, J. C. (1995). Resolving therapeutic alliance ruptures: Diversity and integration. *In Session: Psychotherapy in Practice, 1,* 81–92.

Safran, J. D., & Muran, J. C. (Eds.) (1998). *The therapeutic alliance in brief psychotherapy.* Washington, DC: American Psychological Association.

Safran, J. D., & Segal, Z. V. (1990). *Interpersonal process in cognitive therapy.* New York: Basic Books.

Scheiner, S. B. (1969). Differential perception of personality characteristics in cross-cultural interaction. *Dissertation Abstracts International, 30,* 477B.

Schwartz, R. M. (1986). The internal dialogue: On the assymetry between positive and negative coping thoughts. *Cognitive Therapy and Research, 10,* 591–605.

Seligman, M. E. P. (1975). *Helplessness: On depression, development, and death.* San Francisco: Freeman.

Shea, M. T., Pilkonis, P. A., Beckham, E., Collins, J. F., Elkin, I., Sotsky, S. M., & Docherty, J. P. (1990). Personality disorders and treatment outcome in the NIMH treatment of depression collaborative research program. *American Journal of Psychiatry, 147,* 711–718.

Shear, M. K. (1991). Panic disorder. In B. D. Beitman & G. L. Klerman (Eds.), *Integrating pharmacotherapy and psychotherapy* (pp. 143–164). Washington, DC: American Psychiatric Press.

Shouldice, A. E., & Stevenson-Hinde, J. (1992). Coping with security distress: The Separation Anxiety Test and attachment classification at 4.5 years. *Journal of Child Psychology and Psychiatry and Allied Disciplines, 33,* 331–348.

Showalter, E. (1997). *Hystories: Hysterical epidemics and modern media.* New York: Columbia University Press.

Simeon, D., Stanley, B., Francis, A., Mann, J. J., Winchel, J., & Stanley, M. (1992). Self-mutilation in personality disorders: Psychological and biological correlates. *American Journal of Psychiatry, 149,* 221–226.

Simpson, J. A. (1990). Influence of attachment on romantic relationships. *Journal of Personality and Social Psychology, 59,* 971–980.

Soloff, P. H. (1990). What's new in personality disorders? An update on pharmacologic treatment. *Journal of Personality Disorders, 4,* 233–243.

Soloff, P. H. (1998). Algorithms for pharmacological treatment of personality dimensions: Symptom-specific treatments for cognitive–perceptual, affective, and impulsive–behavioral dysregulation. *Bulletin of the Menninger Clinic, 62,* 195–214.

Solomon, R. L., & Corbit, J. D. (1974). An opponent-process theory of motivation: I. Temporal dynamics of affect. *Psychological Review, 81,* 119–145.

Sonne, S., Rubey, R., Brady, K., Malcolm, R., & Morris, T. (1996). Naltrexone treatment of self-injurious thoughts and behaviors. *Journal of Nervous & Mental Disease, 184,* 192–195.

Spitzer, R. L., & Forman, J. B. W. (1979). DSM–III field trials: Initial interrater diagnostic relaibility. *American Journal of Psychiatry, 136,* 815–817.

Sroufe, L. A. (1983). Infant–caregiver attachment and patterns of adaptation in preschool: The roots of maladaptation and competence. In M. Perlmutter (Ed.), *Minnesota Symposium in Child Psychology,* Vol. 16 (pp. 41–81). Hillsdale, NJ: Erlbaum.

Stampfl, T. G., & Levis, D. J. (1967). Essentials of implosive therapy: A learning theory-based psychodynamic behavioral therapy. *Journal of Abnormal Psychology, 72,* 496–503.

Stern, D. N. (1985). *The interpersonal world of the infant: A view from psychoanalysis and developmental psychology.* New York: Basic Books.

Stern, J. (1996). A cognitive appraisal approach to parent training with affect-driven parents. *Psychotherapy, 33,* 77–84.

Stern, J. (2000). The parenting group. In A. Freeman & J. White (Eds.), *Cognitive–behavioral group therapy for special problems and populations* (pp. 131–160). Washington, DC: American Psychological Association Books.

Steuer, J. L., & Hammen, C. L. (1983). Cognitive–behavioral group therapy for the depressed elderly: Issues and adaptations. *Cognitive Therapy and Research, 7*(4), 285–296.

Stuart, S., Pilkonis, P., Heape, C., Smith, K., & Fisher, B. (1992, June). *The patient–therapist match in psychotherapy: Effects of security of attachment and personality style.* Paper presented at the annual meeting of the Society for Psychotherapy Research, Denver, CO.

Sullivan, H. S. (1953). *The interpersonal theory of psychiatry.* New York: W. W. Norton.

Sullivan, H. S. (1956). *Clinical studies in psychiatry.* New York: W. W. Norton.

Taffel, R. (1991). *Parenting by heart: How to be in charge, stay connected, and instill your values, when it feels like you've only got 15 minutes a day.* Reading, MA: Addison-Wesley.

Taffel, R. (1999). *Nurturing good children now: 10 basic skills to protect and strengthen your child's core self.* New York: Golden Books.

Tangney, J. P. (1992). Situational determinants of shame and guilt in young adulthood. *Personality and Social Psychology Bulletin, 18,* 199–206.

Tangney, J. P. (1994). The mixed legacy of the super-ego: Adaptive and maladaptive aspects of shame and guilt. In J. M. Masling & R. F. Bornstein (Eds.), *Empirical perspectives on object relations theory* (pp. 1–28). Washington, DC: American Psychological Association.

Tangney, J. P. (1996). Functional and dysfunctional guilt. In J. Bybee & J. P. Tangney (Chairs), *Is guilt adaptive? Functions in interpersonal relationships and mental health.* Paper presented at the 1996 meeting of the American Psychological Association (August, 1996).

Tangney, J. P., Burggraf, S. A., & Wagner, P. E. (1996). Shame-proneness, guilt-proneness, and psychological symptoms. In J. P. Tangney & K. W. Fischer (Eds.), *Self-conscious emotions: Shame, guilt, embarrassment, and pride* (pp. 343–367). New York: Guilford Press.

Tangney, J. P., & Fischer, K. W. (1995). *Self-conscious emotions: Shame, guilt, embarrassment, and pride.* New York: Guilford Press.

Tangney, J. P., Miller, R., Flicker, L., & Barlow, D. H. (1996). Are shame, guilt, and embarrassment distinct emotions? *Journal of Personality and Social Psychology, 70,* 1256–1269.

Tangney, J. P., Wagner, P., Fletcher, C., & Gramzow, R. (1992). Shamed into anger? The relation of shame and guilt to anger and self-reported aggression. *Journal of Personality and Social Psychology, 62,* 669–675.

Thorpe, G. L., & Olson, S. L. (1997). *Behavior therapy: Concepts, procedures, and applications* (2nd ed.). Boston: Allyn & Bacon.

Tinbergen, N. (1951). *The study of instinct.* London, UK: Oxford University Press.

Tomkins, S. S. (1982). Affect theory. In P. Ekman (Ed.), *Emotion in the human face* (pp. 353–395). New York: Cambridge University Press.

Tronick, E. Z. (1989). Emotions and emotional communications in infants. *American Psychologist, 44,* 112–119.

van der Kolk, B. A. (1987). *Psychological trauma.* Washington, DC: American Psychiatric Press.

Weisman, M. M., & Klerman, G. L. (1991). Interpersonal psychotherapy for depression. In B. D. Beitman & G. L. Klerman (Eds.), *Integrating pharmacotherapy and psychotherapy* (pp. 379–394). Washington, DC: American Psychiatric Press.

Wessler, R. L. (1984). Alternative conceptions of rational–emotive therapy: Toward a philosophically neutral psychotherapy. In M. Reda & M. J. Mahoney (Eds.), *Cognitive psychotherapies: Recent developments in theory, research, and practice* (pp. 65–79). Cambridge, MA: Ballinger.

Wessler, R. L. (1986). Conceptualising cognitions in the cognitive–behavioural therapies. In W. Dryden & W. Golden (Eds.), *Cognitive–behavioural approaches to psychotherapy* (pp. 1–30). London, UK: Harper & Row.

Wessler, R. L. (1987). Listening to oneself: Cognitive appraisal therapy. In W. Dryden (Ed.), *Key cases in psychotherapy* (pp. 176–212). London, UK: Croom-Helm.

Wessler, R. L. (1993a). Cognitive appraisal therapy and disorders of personality. In K. T. Kuehlwein & H. Rosen (Eds.), *Cognitive therapies in action: Evolving innovative practice* (pp. 240–267). San Francisco: Jossey-Bass.

Wessler, R. L. (1993b). *Stabilizing affect with serotonergic agents in the treatment and psychotherapy of personality disorders.* Paper presented at the Beth Israel Symposium on Practical Applications for Serotonin-Linked Disorders, New York, NY.

Wessler, R. L. (1993c). Groups. In G. Stricker & J. R. Gold (Eds.), *Comprehensive handbook of psychotherapy integration* (pp. 453–464). New York: Plenum.

Wessler, R. L. (1996). Idiosyncratic definitions and unsupported hypotheses: Rational emotive behavior therapy as pseudoscience. *Journal of Rational–Emotive and Cognitive–Behavior Therapy, 10,* 30–50.

Wessler, R. L. (2001). Cognitive appraisal therapy: A treatment plan for "Silvia". *Journal of Psychotherapy Integration, 11*(2), 207–215.

Wessler, R. L., & Hankin, S. (1988). Rational–emotive and related cognitively oriented psychotherapies. In S. Long (Ed.), *Six group therapies* (pp. 159–216). New York: Plenum Press.

Wessler, R. L., & Hankin-Wessler, S. (1986). Cognitive appraisal therapy (CAT). In W. Dryden & W. L. Golden (Eds.), *Cognitive–behavioural approaches to psychotherapy* (pp. 196–223). London, UK: Harper & Row.

Wessler, R. L., & Hankin-Wessler, S. (1989). Emotion and rules of living. In R. Plutchik & H. Kellerman (Eds.), *Emotion: Theory, research, and experience* (Vol. 5, pp. 231–253). San Diego: Academic Press.

Wessler, R. L., & Hankin-Wessler, S. (1990). Emotion and rules of living. *Emotion: Theory, Research, and Experience, 5,* 231–253.

Wessler, R. L., & Hankin-Wessler, S. W. R. (1991). La terápia de valoración cognitiva. In V. E. Carballo (Ed.), *Manual de técnicas de terápia y modificación de conducta* (pp. 551–579). Madrid: Siglo XXI de España Editores.

Wessler, R. L., & Hankin-Wessler, S. (1997). Counselling and society. In S. Palmer & V. Varma (Eds.), *The future of counselling and psychotherapy* (pp. 167–190). London, UK: Sage.

Wessler, R. A., & Wessler, R. L. (1980). *The principles and practice of rational–emotive therapy.* San Francisco: Jossey-Bass.

Westen, D. (1985). *Self and society: Narcissism, collectivism, and the development of morals.* Cambridge, England: Cambridge University Press.

Westen, D. (1991). Social cognition and object relations. *Psychological Bulletin, 109*(3), 429–455.

White, R. W. (1960). Competence and the psychosexual stages of development. In M. R. Jones (Ed.), *Nebraska Symposium on Motivation* (pp. 97–140). Lincoln, NE: University of Nebraska Press.

Wiggins, J. S. (1985). Symposium: Interpersonal circumplex models: 1948–1983: Commentary. *Journal of Personality Assessment, 49,* 626–631.

Yalom, I. D. (1985). *The theory and practice of group psychotherapy.* New York: Basic Books.

AUTHOR INDEX

A

Ainsworth, M. D. S., 13, 26, 31, 73–74
Alford, B. A., 65
Andrews, J. D. W., 49, 56
Anchin, J. C., 69
Armstrong, T., 98

B

Baak, 30
Bandura, A., 5, 63
Barkley, R. A., 98
Barlow, D. H., 63
Bartholomew, K., 75
Bateson, G., 22
Baumeister, R. F., 130
Bauserman, R., 100
Beaudry, P., 228
Beck, A. T., 23, 26, 29, 40, 48–49, 50, 65,
    103, 105
Bedrosian, R. C., 26
Beitman, B. D., 191–192
Bell, S. M., 73–74
Belsky, J., 26
Benjamin, G. A. H., 191
Benoit, D., 74
Blehar, M., 13, 26, 32–33
Bowlby, J., 25–26, 29, 59, 72
Brady, K., 190
Brazelton, T. B., 308
Brehm, J. W., 22, 55
Brickman, P., 112, 136–137
Brill, N. Q., 100

Brooks, V. R., 18
Brooks, R. B., 228
Brown, G. W., 34
Burgess, A. W., 100
Burns, D. D., 29

C

Carlin, A. S., 191
Caro, I., 121–122
Carson, R. C., 69
Cashdan, S., 5, 49, 51
Cassady, J., 73
Catanzaro, S. J., 5, 104–105
Cernic, K., 26
Chengappa, K. N. R., 190
Chevron, E. S., 191
Chibucos, T. R., 26
Chiles, J. A., 190
Chirico, B. M., 69
Choca, J. D., 116
Cicirelli, V. G., 26, 31
Clark, L., 23, 305
Clark, W. M., 18
Coates, D., 112, 136–137
Cobb, C., 73
Coccaro, E., 190
Coffey, H. S., 69
Cohen, A. R., 22
Cohn, E., 112, 136–137
Cox, M. J., 26
Cramer, B. G., 309
Crittenden, P. M., 73

SUBJECT INDEX